Haunted Museum

LONGING, TRAVEL, AND THE ART-ROMANCE TRADITION

Jonah Siegel

PRINCETON UNIVERSITY PRESS

PRINCETON AND OXFORD

Copyright © 2005 by Princeton University Press
Published by Princeton University Press, 41 William Street, Princeton, New Jersey 08540
In the United Kingdom: Princeton University Press, 3 Market Place, Woodstock,
Oxfordshire OX20 1SY

An earlier version of chapter 6 appeared in the *Henry James Review* 23,
no. 3 (2003): 233–45.

Library of Congress Cataloging-in-Publication Data

Siegel, Jonah 1963–
Haunted museum : longing, travel, and the art romance tradition / Jonah Siegel.
     p.   cm.
Includes bibliographical references and index.
ISBN 0-691-12086-2 (alk. paper) — ISBN 0-691-12087-0 (pbk. : alk. paper)
1. Literature, Modern—19th century—History and criticism. 2. Romanticism. 3. Art in
literature. 4. Artists in literature. 5. Travel in literature. 6. Italy—In literature. I. Title.
PN751.S54   2005
809′.93357—dc22   2004053456

British Library Cataloging-in-Publication Data is available

This book has been composed in Galliard

Printed on acid-free paper. ∞

pup.princeton.edu

Printed in the United States of America

10 9 8 7 6 5 4 3 2 1

Haunted Museum

to Stefan Siegel and Nancy Yousef

"It is Fate that I am here," insisted George, "but you can call it Italy if it makes you less unhappy."

E. M. Forster, *A Room with a View*

Contents

Acknowledgments

WORK ON *Haunted Museum* was aided by grants from Rutgers University, as well as from the Robinson and Rollins funds of the Harvard Department of English. Significant research was carried out at the National Humanities Center in 1998–99. More recently, final completion in distractingly beautiful surroundings was made possible by a Frederick Burkhardt Fellowship from the American Council of Learned Societies and a Rome Prize Fellowship from the American Academy in Rome, 2003–4. I am grateful for the support of these institutions and funding agencies.

I am happy to have the opportunity to thank publicly Isobel Armstrong, Bob Kiely, Tricia Lootens, Elaine Scarry, Helen Vendler, and Lynn Wardley, readers whose thoughtful comments on the manuscript were indispensable for the development of this book. More recently I have had reason to be grateful for the considered responses to particular chapters of Tom Birchenough, Jonathan Culler, and Adrian Lyttleton, and to a stringent but thoughtful response to the entire project from an anonymous reader at Princeton University Press. Early work on the topic profited from conversations with Scott Karambis and Sophia Padnos, and subsequent development was aided by the responses of audiences at the Yale English Department's Eighteenth- and Nineteenth-Century Colloquium and at the American Academy in Rome. I am grateful to Susan M. Griffin for her thoughtful editing of an earlier version of chapter 6 when it appeared in the *Henry James Review.* The two who have done the most for *Haunted Museum* are James Eli Adams and Nancy Yousef, indefatigable, alert, and extremely patient readers who have always been ready to lend something of their own rigor and clarity to even the most recalcitrant material. Even as I try to express my gratitude for aid that often goes beyond practical counsel, however, it is only fair to absolve the generous souls I identify here from any blame for the failings that are bound to appear in the pages to follow.

I am glad to acknowledge an old debt to the librarians of the National Humanities Center and two more recent ones: to Silvia Fasoli at the Library of the Fondazione Primoli, and to the staff of the Photographic Archive of the American Academy in Rome, in particular the curator, Alessandra Capodiferro.

At Princeton University Press, I am grateful to Marry Murrell for her consistent support of this project and for her light yet effective touch in moving its author toward concluding. Hanne Winarsky saw the project through its very last stages with flexibility and enthusiasm, and Ellen Foos brought her characteristic frankness and ingenuity to bear on the production of the volume. Brian R. MacDonald was typically alert and painstaking in his attempt to bring order and accuracy to the manuscript he copy-edited.

I would like to register here my gratitude to my colleagues at the Department of English at Rutgers University for the warm welcome they extended when I joined them while working on this book. Particular thanks for kindnesses that have made its completion possible and more pleasant are due to John Belton, Matthew Buckley, Brent Edwards, Kate Flint, Billy Galperin, Jonathan Kramnick, George Levine, Meredith McGill, Richard Miller, Barry Qualls, Cheryl Wall, and Carolyn Williams.

The generous imaginations of friends from the National Humanities Center—Rochelle Gurstein, Jonathan Levin, Ashraf Rushdy, Elizabeth McHenry, along with Nancy Lewis and the late Dick Lewis—have been an inspiration during the completion of this project. More recently, I have had the opportunity to be grateful for the passion and vision of my companions at the American Academy in Rome. The long-standing support of Isobel Armstrong, Meredith McGill, Barry Qualls, Elaine Scarry, Helen Vendler, and Carolyn Williams has been vital at key stages in the production of this book, and I am pleased to have this opportunity to thank them yet again for their sympathy and generosity.

As this is a book about love, travel, and inspiration, it will only be appropriate to acknowledge a number of traveling companions who have done much for the conception and writing of *Haunted Museum*. Thanks are due especially to Molly Finnerty, Peter Gordon, Erich Hahn, Oliver Herring, Kamron Keshtgar, Peter Krashes, Manlio Narici, Audrey Oster, and Rachel Porter, as well as to Freddie Baveystock, Tom Birchenough, Tim Dowling, Jane Harvey, Julian Loose, Melanie Mauthner, Valentina Di Rosa, Adam Steinhouse, Kate Teltscher, and Zhang Daxing.

To arrive at an end is to recognize yet again the power of beginnings. My parents made the question of being abroad personal and urgent for me. I am often grateful to have had the chance to experience the imaginative boldness that has always taken them so far afield, and me sometimes with them. I am extremely grateful to Stefan Siegel for having been there from the beginning and being there still.

Nancy Yousef's passion for Italy and her joy while there have been at once a special help and a challenge to a project that emphasizes the force of longing and the crises liable to be provoked by satisfaction. First, last, most generous, and most demanding reader, I am happy to have the opportunity to acknowledge yet again a debt so vast that her role in the production of this book—though immeasurably large—is only a small part of it.

This book is dedicated to my dearest traveling companions, first and last.

Cambridge-Chapel Hill-Brooklyn-Rome

Preface

The Gesture Back

Haunted Museum is a book about literary form and the desire for the South. It is also an essay on the vexed relations among originality, convention, and passion. Though largely concentrating on the nineteenth century, my aim is to describe the links uniting a set of works running from the eighteenth century to our own day and constituting a tradition whose force and longevity are due in no small measure to the overdetermined nature of the desires shaping the form. The literary tradition that developed around the representation of the encounter with the South of genius is what I call the art romance.[1] It is my hope that the interest of *Haunted Museum* will reside not simply in considering the permutations of a literary form, however, but also in engaging the historical and conceptual premises that have determined its shape. To recognize the tradition of the art romance not only brings into view an important element in the history of the nineteenth-century culture of art; it also presents an opportunity to study the disturbing relationship between desire and artifice as it has been imagined by writers for whom this relationship is a central theme.

How *does* one tell a story about culture? The nineteenth century worked from various models, many of which have been lost to modern taste, although they were pervasive in their own day. Writers throughout the period of this study wove their texts out of threads found in their predecessors, so that the engagement with the place of art was always an engagement with a prior fantasy. If the more educated upper classes could draw on a modicum of classical learning or affectation to inspire their imagination of the South of culture, the middle-class reader and tourist could look back to what was nothing less than a small but consistent and extremely effective tradition, including Germaine de Staël's *Corinne* (1807), Lord Byron's *Childe Harold* (1812–18), Letitia Landon's "Improvisatrice" (1824), and Elizabeth Barrett Browning's *Aurora Leigh* (1856). This immensely popular tradition told the story of an artist, generally half English, half foreign (that is, Italian), shaped by the visual arts as well as poetry, yet doomed to emotional misery. The aspiration toward art is typically represented as a desire for the South and for its embodied avatar, a creature of mixed blood and of astonishing ability in the poetic and plastic arts. As the story of the artist is always necessarily allied to the story of the desire for prized art objects, the trajectory of that aspiration—

no matter how individualized its expression—is typically determined by prior cultural myths, justified in relation to preexistent longings.

The art romance is one manifestation of that commitment to the aesthetic that is so important for the emergence of a culturally dominant middle class in the nineteenth century.[2] The tradition's representation of treasured destinations is therefore always as modern as it is nostalgic.

Its evocation of memories of the fading aristocratic Grand Tour is given new force by the emerging practice of tourism. Similarly, while the importance of Rome as the longed-for center of art education is traceable to neoclassical sources and beyond, the significance of the eternal city was bound to be affected by technological and political developments following the Napoleonic Wars.[3]

Italy, a powerful international symbol well before it ever was a modern nation, has had an extremely rich and varied role in the European imagination, and I have endeavored to cite the extensive literature on the topic where appropriate. But this is not a study of the representation of that much-beloved country (much less does it do justice to the rich distinctions evident in the responses provoked by individual Italian cities). What is in question in *Haunted Museum* is not the voyage itself but the relation between artistic self-imagination and the fantastic encounter with what Europe stands for. Fantasies of access to the place of creative origin, the related but equally fallacious promise of the experience of unmediated reality— these are the preoccupations driving the art romance.

Although the passions at the heart of this book have been touched on in a number of studies, the tradition the project describes has always been likely to receive limited critical attention due to crucial developments in the history of art and travel, notably the emphasis on individual subjectivity as the true measure by which to understand the encounter with art and the related tendency to understand the significant effects of travel to be those that are deeply personal because fully autonomous and free or even liberated from prior expectations.[4] But, the South of culture is never visited alone. One is always accompanied by memories—one's own and those of others.[5] As will be evident to the reader of the chapters to follow, the analysis of particular works in the art-romance tradition is consistently driven to reach back to earlier texts and images. Staël takes us back to Goethe; Landon to Byron; James to Hawthorne, and so forth. But each one of these source texts also gestures back, to even earlier texts or to childhood experiences (themselves often literary or artistic) that shaped the adult passion, in that way following the drives of the tradition itself, which is ever circling back to antecedents, to emblematic places or events identified by precursors. Indeed, these gestures back come to be one of the principal ways in which the art romance indicates its own inability to arrive at an origin for which it is nevertheless never able to stop reaching.

This study is offered as an essay in continuities among texts that I identify sometimes as part of a tradition, at other times as belonging to a subgenre or to a mode. I apply these related but distinct labels more opportunistically than with systematic rigor because the scope of the project is too wide to compel conviction that any of them will precisely capture the relations among all the texts I discuss, some of which are linked by very direct influences, some by more attenuated bonds.[6] Although as a whole these works do not make up a single line of development, many of the texts addressed in *Haunted Museum* are explicitly and even ostentatiously in relationship with each other. They may also be seen to share an insistence that the experience of a desired destination will consistently provoke an imagination of antecedents.

The attempt to group together works from quite disparate fields of study necessarily risks touching on issues that are not unknown to specialists, particularly as the authors I consider are prominent figures within several national literatures and their works span a period usually divided into a number of important subdivisions. I have not shied away from material that has already had some life in critical discussion, however, because my priority is to make visible a line of connection that has been far from self-evident for contemporary readers. To use formal literary-historical terms in order to describe degrees of similarity among texts is to contend that more than individual idiosyncratic instances of influence are at stake in the interplay of works in the art romance. The extravagant confession of antecedents at moments when a much desired individual experience is finally at hand is itself one of the determinative characteristics of romance as it is understood in this project. Although the term "tradition" struck me as useful to characterize the relationship among the texts I discuss in the following pages, it is appropriate only insofar as it is understood to describe not an unavoidable destiny but a commitment to repetition. The actual origin of a tradition, it goes without saying, is generally less significant than the imagination of a relationship to origins the evocation of tradition entails. It is the gesture back inherent in the act of repetition that matters.

Haunted Museum

Giovanni Paolo Panini, *Views of Ancient Rome*, 1757, New York, Metropolitan Museum, Gwynne Andrews Fund. Photo: Metropolitan Museum.

A Haunted Form

THE MUSEUM AND THE JOURNEY

A LONELY ARCADE of ornate classical columns leads from the beautiful sky of a tranquil day to an elaborate but rationally ordered interior. In this light-filled space elegantly dressed men are surrounded by canvases showing ruined buildings or fragments from classical sites or paintings and statues also from antiquity. Among the many admired objects, the eye picks out a few at a time: the *Farnese Hercules* and the *Dying Gladiator* are visible in the left foreground, the *Laocoön* is on the right, along with a statue far more famous in Panini's day than our own—*Silenus with the Infant Bacchus*. Down the central arcade heading out, the *Apollo Belvedere* and the *Borghese Gladiator* are visible, accompanied by numerous other noted works. Near the center of the image, connoisseurs contemplate a rare example of antique painting—the "Aldobrandini Marriage"—while artists gathered near the *Dying Gladiator* look up, perhaps momentarily distracted from their studies. On the fancifully imagined walls, famous sites have been transformed into paintings—the Colosseum, the Pantheon, and various triumphal arches from the Forum among them.

Recent years have seen renewed popular affection for Giovanni Paolo Panini's 1757 *Views of Ancient Rome*, a piece, like its companion, *Views of Modern Rome*, designed to evoke in some measure nostalgia, but also pleasure at the elegant conceit of an abundance of beauty elegantly displayed.[1] At once souvenirs of a voyage and fantasies of a perfect collection of admired art, these works of Panini, of which several versions exist, all painted for foreigners, may be understood to occupy an important point of transition between the soon-to-be-outmoded culture of the Grand Tour and the emergence of a dream that was to preoccupy later eras, that of the perfect museum. For a vision of clarity and organization such as that which covers Panini's canvas to come into being, however, as much needs to be left out as invented. To experience all the admired works of ancient Rome together is an evident impossibility. Indeed, to transmute the Colosseum into a size comparable with that of the Pantheon is just one of the flamboyant and necessary falsifications required in order to gather all these admired objects into an assimilable form. We might go further and propose that the straightforward quality of Panini's work stands against what we know of museums in general: that they are not perfect, that they cannot show us all we want to see, that we do not want to see everything they hold. Even in the most well-lit gallery each component part on display as much as the ensemble those parts constitute is shadowed by ghosts of promise or of disappointment.

Unasked-for gifts, trophies of plunder, voids suggested by the presence of objects always in surfeit though never quite sufficient—*all* museums are haunted in some measure. To gather together prized material in the hope that the Muses will thereby be encouraged to manifest themselves—that is the magic or necromancy promised by the institution. But every collection, be its aim novelty or conservation, becomes immediately historic, and it is the nature of repositories of the past to intimate more than any visitor can ever realize, to evoke memories not entirely one's own, to speak at once about the endurance of things and the impermanence of individuals, about the seductions of fame along with its evanescence.

To describe Italy as a museum is to evoke the aspiration for a world like that imagined in the fanciful views of Panini, one of order, light, and clarity, of learning and pleasure coexisting in comfort, of the simulacrum of the thing successfully standing in for the thing itself. To describe Italy as a museum, however, is also to acknowledge the world in which that aspiration is born, one that is the absolute antithesis of Panini's image, one in which admired sites can never be taken in at a view, in which works known from beloved reproduction seem different when confronted in their actual existence or, worse, in which the self that longed for a thing seems disturbingly different from the self experiencing the desired object.

Each of the texts discussed in this book describes a voyage at once toward something precious and new and toward something dangerous and old—a voyage in which the route is only valuable insofar as it is felt to offer the prospect of novelty, but is only recognizable because it is to an important degree already known. Although the museum and the voyage can seem all-too-material—and, indeed, the promise of the materialization of one's desires is a vital part of their importance—both phenomena are traceable to notably conceptual drives. Whether something is displaced in order to be shown and admired or individuals make their way to centers of culture to see marvels that exist nowhere else, the aim is evidently to move from ignorance to immediate knowledge, to make actual or tangible an object of desire. As travelers never stop discovering, however, the objectification of desire entailed in journeys and collections will tend to yield—as Proust will put it—something less and something more than satisfaction.

What is Venice to London, Naples to Weimar, or even Paris to Boston? As with any object of longing, so with an important cultural center: certainty as to its importance cannot to be confused with clarity as to the sources of a passion. The new significance of the aesthetic in nineteenth-century culture, with the attendant interest in art, artists, and prized art objects still evident today, was contemporaneous with the development of a new set of relationships, practical and imaginary, between an ascendant North and a politically weak but culturally rich South. The nature of travel itself was bound to change from the eighteenth century on, and not simply due to the ever-greater practical ease brought about by technological developments or to the collapse of old political dispensations and the consolidation of new ones. The period of this study saw concepts of cultural identity that had been emergent throughout the eighteenth century meet new social arrangements in a manner that ensured ever-greater ease of arrival at longed-for destinations but that did not make arrival itself any less troubling.

Recent decades have witnessed a flowering of interest in travel writing, an important general category subsuming many forms. Promising lines of research have studied nineteenth-century literature in relation to the rise of modern tourism, scientific exploration, and the development of anthropology, and all of these cultural phenomena have been fruitfully considered in the context of imperial expansion. Analysis of the art romance benefits from work done in these areas, but the mode's particular commitment to the fantastic and to the unavoidable force of other texts, its thoroughgoing intertextuality, makes it particularly resistant to forms of analysis that want to return to a real it has never inhabited, whether experiential or political. The argument of this book depends on recognizing the unblinking artificiality of the romance as its only access to whatever of the real it is able to represent.[2] While the cultural exploitation of an economically faded southern Europe by a newly predominant North may well offer insights for the understanding of forms of exploration or more self-evident modes of dominance that came to the fore late in the century, studies attempting to make the connection will need to begin from the insight that in the art romance access to the real is not an alternative to the tradition but the most florid and most dangerous symptom of fantasy. More convincingly the literary descendant of the Grand Tour than the ancestor of imperial exploration, the mode also only goes so far with recent work on travel and wonder.[3]

This is a book about the kind of story that emerges at the confluence of two related but distinct cultural phenomena, the nineteenth century's fascination with creative genius and the same period's insatiable appetite for tales of the European South, Italy in particular. As such, *Haunted Museum* draws on two further concerns, the genius as type and cultural difference as destiny. Where is genius born? Does it have a native land, the source of a fundamental nostalgia motivating creative souls? Today such queries, like the presuppositions about temperament and national characteristics underlying them, are likely to seem not only old-fashioned but deeply misguided. Nevertheless, the nineteenth century offered bracingly clear answers to both. Southern Europe—most compellingly Greece, most accessibly Italy (and sometimes France)—was considered to be, consistently, and with real practical results, the natural home of genius. And, indeed, longing for the South as for a lost birthright or homeland of the creative soul is a recurrent element in representations of the psychic makeup of the artist in the period, a wishful naturalization of a relation to classical antiquity that was not new in European culture but that saw a notable efflorescence in the era we have come to call neoclassical.

Haunted Museum is concerned with the two-way traffic between fiction and the culture of art during a period for which poems and novels often served as conceptual and even practical guides to the experience of art. The overlap between the exigencies of fiction and the elements of art culture was capitalized on by storytellers throughout the century, usually by referencing earlier texts in the tradition. While the art romance plays an important part in the diffusion of a notably troubled yet productive relation to art characteristic of the nineteenth century, its special interest in the phenomenon of creative ambition insistently foregrounds the complex and even embarrassing relations between passion and artifice.[4] Behind the characteristically modern notion that true creativity takes no color from convention, that genius has no necessary native home, we may detect a wish to avoid recognition of the fact that important sources of creativity develop in the interplay of received idea and emotion. The works studied in *Haunted Museum*, however, are characterized by a tendency to run counter to modern wishes—indeed, to represent passion itself as running straight (back) into the arms of convention.

The special case of artists in an era committed to the idea that the sources of culture were only accessible at certain prized locations, the resting places of admired relics, is a particularly important instance of the difficulty of arrival. As artists and critics struggled to negotiate the relationship between modern creativity and admired art, the repeated productive crisis was to find representation not only in the nascent field of art history, but in works of self-conscious fantasy. That European culture has tended to trace the origins of much it admires, much that it aspires to do or to be, to the South, that Italy in particular and Greece are not only the sources of certain traditions in pictorial and literary arts but subsequently the resting places for the chief relics of those traditions—these are inescapable historical facts. That modern achievement came to find its validation in often unsatisfactory returns to these sources is no less deniable, if not quite so self-evidently necessary.[5] The period in which the art romance emerged was one in which the possibility of fulfillment of aspirations toward the encounter with admired foreign culture was running only slightly behind the desire for that encounter. New technologies and new social arrangements made the wonders of the continent ever more available.[6] And yet, the new ease of travel did not make much-longed-for arrival any less troubling for the artist. The art romance evokes the conventional frustrations of the romance form broadly understood in order to represent an overdetermined anxiety about intimacy with culture that is particularly pressing in the artistic self-imagination of the period. If romance has at its heart the inability to arrive at a prized but ever-deferred goal, Italy is an overdetermined destination for the artist, a passionately desired space combining the prospect of erotic pleasure with the hope for intimacy with the most profound sources of culture.

Starting with the fundamental influence of eighteenth-century neoclassicism, the nineteenth-century culture of art came to be marked by a tendency to validate itself in relation to privileged historical moments linked to specific locations. Rome, Florence, Athens, eventually Venice, and in its own way Paris—art always had its home elsewhere. Indeed, a related structure underlies and makes inevitable even such variations as the claims for southern France, Polynesia, Japan, Africa, and other lands championed by avant-garde art movements that have often been seen as antithetical to nineteenth-century historicism. Yet, on the other side of the power inherent in the longing for a distant center of art, authors recognized from early on a danger inherent in satisfaction itself. There is far more at stake than a romantic challenge to neoclassical values in William Hazlitt's claim in 1827 that "Rome is of all places the worst to study in, for the same reason that it is the best to lounge in," because "[t]here is no end of objects to divert and distract the mind." While art throughout the century made recourse to admired models from the past for its validation, Hazlitt's "English Students at Rome" recognizes a recurrent anxiety: "If it were nothing else, the having the works of the great masters of former times always before us is enough to discourage and defeat all ordinary attempts." In his account of the challenge to modern achievement presented by the heterogeneity that is most recognizable in Rome, the critic draws on a striking classical reference: "Modern art is indeed like the fabled Sphinx, that imposes impossible tasks on her votaries, and as she clasps them to her bosom pierces them to the heart."[7] The Sphinx is a doubly appropriate image for the challenge Hazlitt has in mind; not only does the riddle it poses contain the shape of human development, but, as Oedipus discovered, the hero's problems only worsen when he overcomes the challenge and enters the desired city.

To such high-cultural determinants as the centrality of Rome in culture and art education throughout the period of this study, we must add another, apparently more trivial source for the fascination of Italy: its temperate climate and the related tradition (not to say wishful reputation) of sensual license that from the eighteenth century forward made the South not only the native place of artistic beauty but the site of a much-desired physical liberation. As will be clear throughout this study, the distinction between physical passion and inspiration was not always clearly maintained, even in cases where it might be insisted on in theory. In Winckelmann's seminal *Reflections on the Painting and Sculpture of the Greeks* (1755), for example, the ideal beauty of classical statues is in some measure traceable to a contingent fact of no little interest to the author—that the temperate climate of Greece allowed the natives of that fortunate land to pass much of their lives nude. Forty years later, Goethe's "Now on classical soil I stand, inspired and elated," like the rest of the *Roman Elegies* (1795) to which it belongs, only more forcefully links erotic passion, creativity, and the South. The student of Winckelmann counts out hexameters on his Roman lover's back, a playfully erotic and naturalizing culmination of the yearning for culture indicated by the opening line of the poem.[8]

In the Palace of Art / The Unanswered Question

Although the kind of elation Goethe discovers on arrival in Rome is expressed by literary visitor after visitor in later years, the fantastic harmony between creativity and sexual passion suggested in his verse is far rarer. The sometimes overwhelming love for art of the past that is characteristic of the period running from the eighteenth century to our own day is, as Hazlitt noted, far more likely to result in the emergence of an apparently unavoidable and contradictory conflict between desire and fulfillment, aspiration and achievement than in simple pleasure. In the art romance the satisfaction of longing, particularly the apparent satisfaction of a longed-for return to sources, inevitably provokes a crisis. The balance of this introduction revolves around two such crises, one provoked by the fantasy of the perfect museum, the other by the fact of travel to a much-desired center of culture.

The mutual complication of art and passion at the point of satisfaction is a theme vividly developed in Tennyson's 1832 poem, "The Palace of Art," not an art romance but perhaps the most economical literary representation of the haunted museum. "I built my soul a lordly pleasure-house," declares the speaker boldly at the outset,

> Wherein at ease for aye to dwell.
> I said, "O Soul, make merry and carouse,
> Dear soul, for all is well."[9]

The speaker divides into a self and a soul at the moment of secluding himself from the rest of mankind, as if the fantasy of a perfect museum housing ideal aesthetic isolation somehow requires or provokes a doubling form of self-alienation.

Through nearly fifty stanzas the poem traces with loving attention the furnishing of the palace for the soul's enjoyment, in itself beautiful and filled with works inviting aesthetic appreciation—an ideal museum before anything close to it was available in England. But, the claim of artificial perfection is not the main burden of the poem. The fundamental split determining the opening separation of self and soul returns with force at the center of the poem as the text swerves abruptly away from ease, merriment, carousal, and even from the indifferent intellectual self-indulgence in which the soul's pleasures culminate:

> Full oft the riddle of the painful earth
>   Flashed thro' her as she sat alone,
> Yet not the less held she her solemn mirth,
>   And intellectual throne.
>
> And so she throve and prospered: so three years
>   She prospered; on the fourth she fell,
> Like Herod, when the shout was in his ears,
>   Struck through with pangs of hell.
>
> Lest she should fail and perish utterly,
>   God, before whom ever lie bare
> The abysmal deeps of personality,
>   Plagued her with sore despair.   (213–24)

At once a moralist and a psychologist, God summons an *inborn* despair to rescue the soul from selfish isolation:

> When she would think, where'er she turned her sight
>   The airy hand confusion wrought,
> Wrote, "Mene, mene," and divided quite
>   The kingdom of her thought.
>
> Deep dread and loathing of her solitude
>   Fell on her, from which mood was born
> Scorn of herself; again, from out that mood
>   Laughter at her self-scorn.   (225–32)

When the soul tries to reassure herself she traces the power of the palace not to that external, and therefore describable, beauty that had characterized it up to this point in the poem, but to its source in her earliest desires and knowledge:

> "What! is not this my place of strength," she said,
>   "My spacious mansion built for me,

> Whereof the strong foundation-stones were laid
>> Since my first memory?"   (233–36)

The question is never answered directly. Indeed, the insistent conjunctions that characterize the stanzas that follow link nothing that is logically connected; the parataxis serves rather to evoke the shock of sudden unpleasant discovery of things that were always there, decaying though hidden:

> But in dark corners of her palace stood
>> Uncertain shapes; and unawares
> On white-eyed phantasms weeping tears of blood,
>> And horrible nightmares,
>
> And hollow shades enclosing hearts of flame,
>> And, with dim fretted foreheads all,
> On corpses three-months-old at noon she came,
>> That stood against the wall.   (237–44)

The poem's cruel response to the soul's plea raises the possibility that it may well be precisely *because* the palace of art is founded on her memories that the walls of the museum contain nightmares, blood, corpses, and phantasms. Appalling figures lurching out at soul (and reader) characterize the failure of the structure to offer the shelter promised at the outset; its stately beauty is transfigured into appalling images that are hellish, immediate, and grotesquely physical.

It is little wonder that the soul is finally driven out of the palace of art and down to the valley where the rest of humanity dwells. She dedicates herself to remorse and prayer, though her ambivalence toward the structure she has escaped is in no way resolved. If the opening of the poem identifies the museum as an everlasting site of solipsistic pleasure, its concluding lines make the palace of art into a place not of permanent habitation but of return: "[P]ull not down my palace towers," the soul declares, "that are / So lightly, beautifully built: / Perchance I may return with others there / When I have purged my guilt" (293–96).

"The Palace of Art" belongs to a discourse about self-consciousness, isolation, and art that is familiar from any number of Victorian authors. Tennyson himself links the work to debates on the practical and aesthetic life traceable to the Cambridge Apostles. The poem has more recently been studied in the context of the reception of Goethe as a figure standing for a relationship to taste and erudition so dispassionate, so free from conventional human concerns, as to risk immorality.[10] And yet, the ethical claims of "The Palace of Art" are overwhelmed by the more pressing claim for representation of the crisis of satisfaction. Recent critics, like many readers since the poem was written, have been struck by what Christopher Ricks describes as a despair that is "grimly disproportionate to the soul's error of Aestheticism." The combination of gorgeous fantasy with grotesque physicality, like the conclusion of so dramatic a crisis in so thoroughgoing an ambivalence, intimates something different from the moral-aesthetic themes openly present in the poem. Herbert Tucker writes of "an extraneous moralism that invades the parable to deform its conclusion, " an idea that contributes to his identification of "a poem that is conspicuously of two minds."[11] The reading I propose emphasizes the force of the doubling Tucker identifies, but sees the undermotivated or "disproportionate" crisis less as a result of forced moralism than as an instantiation of the uncanny challenge provoked by the fantasy of satisfied desire.

The healthy response to danger, as to pain, should be avoidance of its causes, yet the soul looks forward to an eventual return to the palace. It is an inconclusive resolution that indicates the ambivalence driving the self from the outset, shaping not only the work's quick shifts between desire and regret, its sudden swerve from fantasy to nightmare, but ultimately the soul's inability to destroy this monstrous place. The poem moves from the opening claim of assured permanence, "to dwell," to the tentative assertion of uncertain transience, "perchance I may return," and that movement is closely related to the shift from a confident active voice, "I built," to the passive recognition that the structure was "built for me." Indeed, the "ease for aye" gives way to "sore despair" precisely as "I built" becomes "built for me." The crisis of the poem suggests what the conclusion helps to clarify: at stake in the palace of art is not simply the moral error of isolating oneself in beauty while the rest of the world suffers, but the realization that the museum itself is never newly constructed.

Tennyson's poem offers a number of useful points of departure for thinking about the special kind of disappointment inherent not in the postponement of the expected or desired, but in the realization that what lies ahead is nothing other than an appointment or return. The death of longing when faced with what appears to be satisfaction is all the more poignant when it becomes clear that what was sought with such effort was precisely what could not be avoided: this place had to be visited; this discovery had to be made; this passion had to be lived in this particular manner. The disappointing nature of such realizations tends toward uncanny terms of expression, such as those rotting corpses the soul discovers. The splitting of the self that opens the poem is a characteristic form of acknowledgment that one's desire is at once deeply personal and alien.

"Is not this my place of strength / built for me, / Since my first memory?"—the unanswerable question at the heart of the poem is motivated by the dismayed recognition of a schism present from the outset. The alienation of the self at the very moment its desire is satisfied is represented by the question that cannot be answered. The palace of art is revealed to be a haunted castle, a shift onto the register of the gothic that in itself provides the best response to the soul's desperate inquiry. As Freud noted in his foundational work on the topic, the fundamental source of the sensation of the uncanny is the *return* of an imperfectly forgotten original home.[12] If the palace of art offers no escape, it does provide a vivid identification of the sources of haunting; the poem's response to the unanswerable question is not clarity, but the manifestation of corpses—already in a state of putrefaction because they have been there all along.

"At Home I Dream That at Naples, at Rome": Freud on Arrival

It is typical that the Soul's crisis in "The Palace of Art" should shift the poem into the register of Gothic, that mode in literature characterized by the fruitful coexistence of the shocking and the formulaic. Each story of the encounter with art in the nineteenth century is woven through with gaudy threads borrowed from unavoidable antecedents. The shocks represented in the texts in this study are those attendant on sudden confused partial recognitions, on the collapse of resistance or self-delusion that allows the embarrassed recognition of what was known all along. The writers in this study are interesting precisely because their tales of art and artists are so vividly aware of two qualities sometimes taken to be antithetical: longing and its mediation through a *tradition* of desire. More than a set of poems or novels in a sentimental mode set in southern Europe—generally Italy—and featuring artists as characters, the texts discussed in this study are linked by shared formal qualities appropriate to their shared thematic concerns. Like other forms of nineteenth-century romance, the art romance is characterized at its outset by a ready interplay of narrative and verse. Indeed, there is so much narrative to the verse, so many intercalated stories or vignettes in the early art romances, that it is sometimes impossible to think of them as involving one master narrative and subsidiary tales. In Landon's "Improvisatrice," for example, the distinction is blurred almost to the point of incoherence, emphasizing, as such formal features always will, the essential artifice of the text in which they are contained. In the case of the novels, the flamboyant inverisimilitude running through texts apparently written in a realist vein similarly serves to emphasize the force of artifice, of the evidently fantastic, and thereby to highlight the compound of artifice and passion the genre struggles to contain.

Emerson's brief 1841 comments on travel are worth citing not only because of their skeptical candor, but because of the stark image for inescapable haunting by which the essayist expresses the inevitable limits of self-forgetfulness: "At home I dream that at Naples, at Rome, I can be intoxicated with beauty, and lose my sadness. I pack my trunk, embrace my friends, embark on the sea, and at last wake up in Naples, and there beside me is the stern Fact, the sad self, unrelenting, identical, that I fled from. . . . My giant goes with me wherever I go."[13] To travel is to place distance between oneself and one's origins, but the direction chosen, as well as the measure of the success or failure of the voyage, will be determined by pressures that come to bear well before the journey begins. In the art romance the voyage out unavoidably becomes a voyage in, toward a haunting inescapable past—to the very earliest desires and fears. The sad fact that will accompany Emerson wherever he goes is given a fanciful form that only makes it more disturbing. The figure of a looming giant evokes not the troubles of adult life so much as the anxieties and hopes of childhood, making the sadness at issue of a longer duration than the melancholy voyager may readily understand, and all the less likely to be relieved by a change of scene. Freud's work on the uncanny usefully illuminates the characteristic splitting occasioned by arrivals that feel like returns, but it will be helpful to cite a study that engages more directly with the structure of longing, anticipation, and disappointment provoked by the *traveler's* encounter with cultural sources, the analyst's extraordinary 1936 essay, "A Disturbance of Memory on the Acropolis."

In 1904 Freud found himself at a site of preeminent significance and aesthetic fame he had hoped to see since his youth. More than three decades later he wrote a description of the circumstances that took him there, mainly focusing on his incredulous response. On the Acropolis—a privileged locus of Western civilization with a cultural centrality outweighing even the wonders of Rome—Freud is fated to discover neither rest nor satisfaction, but rather a crisis reaching back to challenge what we might take to be in some measure fixed: memory itself. Not surprisingly, the analyst's account begins well before arrival. The sudden possibility of going to Athens, which arises unexpectedly during a trip to Trieste by the analyst and his brother, provokes in both men a feeling of disbelief and anxiety. Indeed, after an acquaintance proposes in the simplest and most reasonable terms that they abandon their planned trip to Corfu and instead take a boat to the site of the Parthenon, the two men are thrown into a funk characterized by "remarkably depressed spirits . . . a discontented and irresolute frame of mind."[14] They both feel that it is impossible to put this new plan into effect, but do so nevertheless. Stranger still, the sense of disbelief does not abandon Freud, even when he actually finds himself at the Acropolis. It deepens, rather, into an episode of derealization and a strange form of melancholy:

> When, finally, on the afternoon after our arrival, I stood on the Acropolis and cast my eyes around upon the landscape, a surprising thought suddenly entered my mind: "So all this really *does* exist, just as we learnt at school!" To describe the situation more accurately, the person who gave expression to the remark was

divided, far more sharply than was usually noticeable, from another person who took cognizance of the remark; and both were astonished, though not by the same thing. (240–41)

Neither side of the split individual escapes misgivings. For one part of the traveling analyst, to see the Acropolis is an event as improbable as it might be to encounter the Loch Ness monster (the analogy is Freud's). For the other part, the wonder resides in the notion that there could be any question as to the existence of the temple whose fame motivated the voyage in the first instance. That arrival at a much-desired destination should result in doubt rather than "some expression of delight or admiration" (241) is the real puzzle and surprise.

The division into two parts of the experiencing sensibility and the surprising presence of the fantastic are two formal characteristics of the art-romance tradition that are unavoidable in Freud's essay as he attempts to account for the fated relationship between personal aspirations and culture. In "Splitting of the Ego in the Process of Defence," Freud's late return to what is a long-running concern, splitting is identified as a form of derealization determined by an "intolerable real danger."[15] This important fragment closes without any resolution on the question of fear of castration by the father, but not before a telling digression on Zeus's castrating revenge on Kronos, that dangerous sire who had set out to swallow his own children. The gloom that had overwhelmed the analyst and his brother at the very suggestion that it would be easy for them to get to Athens from Trieste is not unrelated to the account of fate that occurs late in "Disturbance of Memory." It is a concern that runs through the art-romance tradition and that Freud traces to a deeply anxious relationship between personal ambition and the father. The depression at Trieste is directly linked to the puzzling response on the Acropolis, and both are attributable to the problem of achievement that the analyst identifies with those "wrecked by success" (241–42). To arrive at a place such as the Acropolis is to satisfy a wish known from childhood, yet always felt to be impossible not simply for practical reasons but because we cannot admit the possibility that we will be granted what we most desire. "Fate which we expect to treat us so badly," proposes Freud, "is a materialization of our conscience, of the severe super-ego within us, itself a residue of the punitive agency of our childhood" (243). In the interplay between individual and social development that characterizes Freud's speculations on the genesis of culture in his later works, the superego has a self-controlling, even self-punishing role acquired from the internalized father, and the sense of fate is just one of its important manifestations. But many causes contribute to the presence of the father in Freud's disturbance. Both the achievement of getting to the Acropolis and the fact of knowing enough to want to go there in the first place provoke a sense of guilt that the feeling of derealization works to avoid (247).

What Freud describes as his "passionate" schoolboy yearning to travel and see the world is, of course, more than personal (243). Indeed, passion would be a strong term for describing the wish to visit a ruined site in a foreign country, except for the fact that it is precisely in rerouting the personal passions that culturally imposed desires find their force. When he arrives at the locus of his longing, Freud discovers a "feeling of the unbelievable and the unreal in the situation at the moment" (244) that he displaces backwards. Freud feels he had always doubted the existence of the place, though he understands that that feeling is impossible. Indeed, the essay offers a rich if inconclusive attempt to describe the sensation or concept of "derealization" (*Entfremdungsgefühl*), which the analyst puts in relation to what he calls its positive counterparts, "*fausse reconnaissance*," "*déjà vu*," "*déjà raconté*, etc." (245). In the latter cases, he postulates, we attempt to accept something as already part of the ego, whereas in the former we are eager to keep that thing away. Derealization leads Freud almost immediately to the idea of "split personality" before he closes off the entire speculative discussion with an acknowledgment of its obscurity and its lack of a scientific basis. Nevertheless, the student of the art romance recognizes familiar elements. From Goethe and beyond, the sense of recognition, of having seen before, of having heard before, of recognizing the never-before-seen is precisely the experience of the encounter with the desired object of art.

The analyst presents "A Disturbance of Memory on the Acropolis" as a commemoration of current cultural achievement, a gift or tribute on the seventieth birthday of Romain Rolland, an admired novelist. A text that is addressed to genius but does not discuss it directly—how is this a tribute? The sixth chapter of this book treats the peculiar triangulation of Freud's ambition with Italy on the one hand and with the figure of Goethe on the other, but already it is worth emphasizing how strange this piece is as an homage to an *author*. The essay is a loving gesture toward Romain Rolland, certainly, but it is also the register of a deep sense of competition. Freud points out twice in the first three paragraphs of what is an extremely brief piece that the novelist is his junior by a decade, which also makes him the same age as the brother who accompanies the analyst to the Parthenon. The complex sibling rivalry that comes into play in the Oedipal scheme Freud introduces into his account of derealization is intriguing, but not as germane to this study as the more general matter of the relationship between travel and creative ambition typical of the art romance. It is the question of Freud's achievement—at issue as much in the rivalry with Rolland/the brother as with the internalized father—that is at stake in the journey to a devoutly desired cultural center.

Freud's imagination of his intellectual aspirations often shapes itself around voyages taken or not taken, particularly in relation to traveling (or conquering) role models matched or overtopped (Hannibal, Napoleon, etc.). Nevertheless, not unlike Emerson, the analyst traces the drive to wander to quite domestic sources. The psychic force of travel is paradoxically but also predictably established at the source of all desires: the home. The voyage is an antidomestic fantasy with its roots in the domestic space. "A great part of the pleasure of travel lies in the fulfillment of . . . early wishes," writes Freud, "it is rooted, that is, in dissatisfaction with home and family." Primal drives going back to the earliest childhood experiences of home motivate the emotional response Freud describes "when first one catches sight of the sea, crosses the ocean and experiences as realities cities and lands which for so long had been distant, unattainable things of desire—one feels oneself like a hero who has performed deeds of improbable greatness" (247).

Real Romance

Henry James will surround "Europe" with quotation marks when he wants to indicate its force in the imagination. As the South of culture can never be an idiosyncratic destination, the authors in this study are original not because they record new discoveries made in the course of their travels, but because of what they do with what they could not help taking with them on their trips. It has not gone unremarked that Italy is important for Goethe, or James, or Freud—or for Letitia Landon, the Brownings, Byron, Staël, Forster, Mann, or Proust for that matter. What is of interest in *Haunted Museum* is the role of a fantastic Europe in the self-imagination of these writers. Two motivating fantasies tend to be at stake in the art romance: the encounter with the ideal creator and the force of material and contingent experience. Yet, in spite of the longing toward the real that seems bound to underlie both these aspirations, texts in the tradition are characterized by repeated and flamboyant recourse to the artificial.

Byron writes of lands where Childe Harold was "doom'd to go," and certainly destiny, fate, and fatality are always at stake in the voyage to culture. Nevertheless, authors were not doomed simply to repeat the romance they inherited. While it is not possible to identify an absolute origin for the issues and images involved, *Haunted Museum* begins with Goethe in order to introduce formal strategies pioneered by the great poet of the North's love of the South, particularly the interplay of incestuous passion and displacement Goethe manipulates in the extraordinary generic mélange of *Wilhelm Meister*. The clash between the realism of that strangely influential novel and its more fantastic elements is as important in my analysis as that vitally significant and impossible creation, Mignon, the personification at once of displaced creativity and of yearning for the South.

As the real beckons in an ever-receding distance, one of the most tantalizing forms it takes is of an overdetermined origin perhaps all too identifiable as feminine. While the second chapter of this book, "The Art-Romance Tradition," sketches out something of the afterlife of Mignon and the drives that shaped her, starting from the influential work of Letitia Landon and Germaine de Staël, she is no more bound to one chapter in this book than she could be constrained within *Wilhelm Meister*. The proliferation of Mignon figures is in itself an indication of the pervasive force of a feminine influence that will not be denied. After all, modern romance is nothing if not a female form: central texts were written by women, featured women as principal characters, and addressed emotions that in the period of this study, as today, have been typically gendered female. The suggestion presents itself inevitably that the feminine sources of the tradition make themselves known even as they are denied by male practitioners who cannot acknowledge their forebears, that elements from the prior tradition testify to their presence in the guise of a haunting, uncanny, endlessly desiring feminine form.

And yet a related but possibly more-unappeasable ghost haunts these pages, that of the natural rival for *any* form of creativity. Childe Harold does not say good-bye to his mother, but Aurora Leigh cannot say good-bye to hers. Freud's account of the guilty child overwhelmed by the shadow of fate while standing on the Acropolis evokes the memory of an unnamed classical figure that in turn may stand in for the one member of the family romance absent from the analyst's description of his disturbance of memory. If, for Hazlitt, Oedipal anxieties haunt the art student in Rome, it is Orestes, tormented matricide, who sets the precedent for the anxious voyage to the Acropolis, site of unresolved guilt and impossible expiation. The recurrence of uncanny female characters in the art romance is not coincidentally related to the difficulty of arriving at long-yearned-for destinations that is central to the tradition. What is at stake in both cases is not only the unsilenceable claims of women authors, but also the more frightening call of a return to the creative source that is always at once incestuous, impossible, and closely related to death.

The most concrete museums instantly become emblematic in Henry James, sites at which to represent a crucial ever-renegotiated relationship between a self desperately aspiring for culture and a world of culture the self cannot avoid. The innocent American overwhelmed in a vast European museum, that characteristically Jamesian figure, is a moving emblem of the promise of coming into relation with knowledge, but also of the shocks entailed in entering into a relationship that, even when new, is always predetermined. The issue for the novelist is formal as much as thematic. As the deep desires and disappointments entailed in the drama of acculturation are not likely to be best represented by recourse to realism, inverisimilitude itself becomes a pressing question in his accounts of Americans abroad. And so it is that the 1909 prefaces to the New York edition in which James revisited his earliest work offer an important recalibration of the "romantic." The novelist's nuanced account of the intricate relation between romance and realism, the formal manifestation of his commitment to the play of longing and memory, makes his terms of discussion useful in illuminating not simply the fantastic place of Italy in his own work and in that of such nineteenth-century predecessors as Staël and especially Hawthorne but also in his modernist contemporaries.

James, along with Freud and a selection of authors associated with modernism, allows *Haunted Museum* to close with a set of self-conscious reflections on a literary mode that is at every point about troubled returns to origins. As the most important thinker on the forms of desire to emerge from the nineteenth century, the founder of psychoanalysis was bound to have a privileged place in this project, particularly given the inescapable force of the South of culture in his imagination. *The Interpretation of Dreams* is the topic of one chapter, but Freud inevitably recurs in this project, from his seminal account of the uncanny, to the memoir-essay on the crisis provoked by his arrival at the Parthenon discussed already, to the study of Jensen's *Gradiva*, which is treated in the afterword of this book. A new frankness about the force of physical passion comes to the fore in the twentieth century. And, yet, not only in Freud but in the narratives of Forster, Proust, and Mann discussed in the final chapter the apparent liberation of desire in modern Italy only reopens the question of longing and satisfaction running through the art romance from the outset. The existence of a tradition of desire dating back to an earlier era becomes inspiration and humiliation all at once. The longings of the body, like the passions of the mind, are woven through with the yearnings of a past that can no more be denied than it can be satisfied.

PART ONE

The Art Romance

Jacques-Louis David, *Antiochus and Stratonice*, 1774, Paris, École Nationale supérieure des Beaux-Arts. Photo: École Nationale supérieure des Beaux-Arts.

CHAPTER 1

The Song of Mignon

The Desire of the Child

> Know you the land where the lemon blossoms blow,
> And through dark leaves the golden oranges glow,
> A gentle breeze wafts from an azure sky,
> The myrtle's still, the laurel tree grows high—
> You know it, yes? Oh there, oh there
> With you, O my beloved, would I fare.
>
> Know you the house? Roof pillars over it,
> The chambers shining and the hall bright-lit,
> The marble figures gaze at me in rue:
> "You poor child, what have they done to you?"
> You know it, yes? Oh there, oh there,
> With you, O my protector, would I fare.
>
> Know you the mountain and its cloudy trails?
> The mule picks out its path through misty veils,
> The dragon's ancient brood haunts caverns here,
> The cliff drops straight, the stream above falls sheer.
> You know it, yes? Oh there, oh there
> Our path goes on! There, Father let us fare!

I DROP THIS FAMOUS poem of longing abruptly into my text in emulation of Goethe's own treatment of the song in *Wilhelm Meister*, where, when first encountered, it opens book 4 of that novel, with no indication of its source or of its audience.[1] The poem itself is far from self-explanatory, being either an odd monologue in which knowledge and desire are anxiously put into question and almost at the same instant affirmed or one side of a dialogue that does not wait for answers because it is driven by a yearning that needs to assume recognition. As it is, the poem writes into the listener's part not simply agreement but identity of feeling: "You know it, yes?" (*Kennst du es wohl?*) is its own answer to the pressing question "Know you?" (*Kennst du?*).

To introduce the poem into the novel with no explanation, to assume recognition even as one puts it into question—these are related strategies that suggest the out-of-placedness of the poem may be as much a part of its meaning as the strange alienated recognitions its speaker demands. Mysterious and evocative like Mignon herself, who is eventually revealed to be its singer, the poem's theme is dislocation, the identification of a treasured but lost site of origins. The significance of Mignon herself is forcefully emblematic; she is a personification of the longing for Italy as lost source and as land of art and natural beauty. Carlyle is convincing on the mix of passion and intellect she brings to the novel: "The history of Mignon runs like a thread of gold through the tissue of the narrative," notes the translator of *Wilhelm Meister*, "connecting with the heart much that were else addressed only to the head."[2] Mignon was in fact the focus of nineteenth-century response to the novel, particularly her song and her dance. It is no coincidence that important settings were created for her song (by Schubert and Wolf among others), or that the opera based on the novel was given *her* name (Ambroise Thomas, 1866).[3] Her desire, disappointment, and death are among the very deepest layers of the palimpsest on which the nineteenth century was to represent the encounter with past culture.

Mignon's life became emblematic of the fragility and otherworldliness of the artistic figure, while her song and her relationship to Wilhelm (its necessary audience) came to stand for the complex recognitions that motivate the relationship of modern culture to its past. In the elaboration of Wilhelm's relations to this strange creation, Goethe presents the troubling interplay of memory and desire as constitutive of the aspiration toward art. That locus classicus of longing for Italy, the song of Mignon, was all the more sincere for being written *before* its author ever saw in person the landscape and art it celebrates. Indeed, at various points in the course of his famous voyage to the land of her desire, Goethe is moved to remark to friends how right he and his character had been to long for the place whose wonders he was finally experiencing.[4] If the poem successfully expresses the yearnings that drove him south, the novel in which Goethe placed it on his return from Italy was to represent his insights as to the nature of satisfied desire. It is a commonplace of literary history that *Wilhelm Meister* is one of several projects fundamentally altered by Goethe's long stay in Italy, but it is important to be clear that what makes such a voyage momentous is never the shock of an absolutely new discovery. Goethe himself is open on this point. In the following passage from *Italian Journey*, the author promises "many things," but novelty is not among them:

> I have had occasion to ponder much about myself, others, the world and history, and, in my own way, I shall have many things to share with you, which are good, even if perhaps not new. Everything will in the end be condensed and summed up in *Wilhelm Meister*.[5]

The absence of absolute novelty in Goethe's response to Rome is traceable to his association of the place with early domestic experiences:

> All the dreams of my youth have come to life; the first engravings I remember—my father hung views of Rome in the hall—I now see in reality, and everything I have known for so long through paintings, drawings, etchings, woodcuts, plaster casts and cork models is now assembled before me. Wherever I walk, I come upon familiar objects in an unfamiliar world; everything is just as I imagined, yet everything is new. (*Italian Journey,* 116)

There is no reason to doubt that Goethe's father decorated his home with views of Rome, but the author's evocation of the specific paternal source of his early experience of art is also an acknowledgment of the fact that the relationship with art is always a matter of repetition. "Good, even if perhaps not new" is the description of what he expects to produce in response to "familiar objects in an unfamiliar world."

The unstable blend of realism and allegory with which *Wilhelm Meister* challenges the reader is particularly effective in representing the constant interplay between culture and individual development central to the novel.[6] A network of related motifs unifies a text that is at once picaresque and quite otherwise: the relations of parents and children (which includes the knowledge or acknowledgment of fatherhood), sex as pleasure and reproduction, *Bildung* as fate. The family is an important metaphor for development or inheritance in Goethe, but it is not used to evoke reassuring certainty in the domestic sphere so much as the anxieties implicit in parenthood as well as infancy. The name "Meister" suggests that Wilhelm's achievement of mastery—the goal at the end of the apprenticeship that is the subject of his novel—will be a return to the self that has always been his. His best hope is to earn title to a name he inherited at birth. To put the matter in terms drawn from the symbolic repertoire of the novel: construction of the house in which Wilhelm is raised and in which he discovers the joy of art was financed with money raised from the sale of his grandfather's art collection; if the loss of the art that is his patrimony resulted in the house that shaped his childhood, its partial recovery is a mark of his successful development as an adult.

The force of the family in shaping Wilhelm's destiny does not preclude Goethe's consistent association of passion and ignorance with the topic of fathers. In the tale of his childhood he tells his lover Mariane in the first scene of the novel, Wilhelm's earliest infatuation, for the art of puppetry, has an overdetermined parental source: the man who brings the puppets to the family home is identified obscurely enough as someone who "had helped my father considerably in the building of our house" (9). But, as noted already, the house itself was bought with money from the sale of the grandfather's art collection, the loss that determined Wilhelm's desire in the first place. As his obsession takes hold and Wilhelm searches for the puppets, the thrilling fear of seeking them out is as exciting to the young boy as the fact of their presence in the home: "Children in well-established and well-organized homes feel rather like rats and mice: They seek out cracks and crannies to find their way to forbidden dainties. The furtive and intense fear with which they indulge in this search is one of the joys of childhood" (7). Secreted in the domestic space are not only the puppets but another theatrical treasure: the collection of plays Wilhelm discovers among his grandfather's books. Evidently, the development of Wilhelm Meister is not something separate from his inheritance. Although his birthright may be salted away in hard-to-reach places, difficulty of access only increases the charm of a home-grown passion.

The typical source of the pathos in *Wilhelm Meister* derives from the loss and deferred rediscovery of precious, rare, original things, and it is the emotional significance associated with works of art and children that is most poignantly emphasized in this manner. A powerful instance combining both child and loved art object involves the painting of a bedridden prince sick with yearning for his father's young wife. Passionately admired by Wilhelm as a boy, sold by his father, and recalled to his memory by a chance encounter with the man who arranged the purchase of the collection, the piece is rediscovered by Wilhelm only when he reaches the tower that contains his past and shapes his future.[7] "[T]he picture of a sick prince consumed by passion for his father's bride" (37) is drawn from the story of Antiochus's love for Stratonice, a tale from Plutarch and other classical sources that had reached a new level of popularity in the visual arts in the seventeenth and eighteenth centuries. This fantasy of fulfilled wishes begins with Antiochus's apparently unsatisfiable longing for the wife of his father, Seleucus, the King of Syria. Plutarch's account delineates the love fever that consumes the bedridden young man, but he also highlights the stratagem whereby Erasistratus, the wise physician who has recognized the illness, diagnoses its source by taking his patient's pulse as various women enter the room. The wily doctor subsequently manipulates the father so that it becomes impossible for him not to turn over his wife in order to save his son's life.[8] I return to the painting shortly and in chapter 6, but I cite it now, as issues it suggests run through the novel.

Wilhelm is not only the child and grandchild of parents whose actions determine his desires and ambitions; he is also a father himself, and this latter role most vividly demonstrates the uncanny drives underlying the novel's representation of family influence.[9] During the course of his apprenticeship Wilhelm acquires two children, Felix, his son by Mariane, and Mignon, whom he rescues from a group of traveling performers when she is being beaten for refusing to dance. The relationship between Wilhelm and Mignon is from its first moments at once protective and passionate: "Wilhelm could not take his eyes off her; her whole appearance and the mystery that surrounded her completely absorbed his mind" (54). The relationship of this strange creature and her protector is typical of the novel's paradoxically concrete and multivalent use of sexuality as a symbol standing for pleasure, reproduction, and unplumbable mystery all at once. The following aside—which takes place prior to the parenthood of Felix being revealed—is typical of the interplay of disturbing sexuality and parenthood in the novel:

> Since we are talking about Mignon, we must also mention the embarrassment that she had been causing our friend for some time. Whenever she came or went, bade him good morning or good night, she clasped him so firmly in her arms and kissed him so passionately, that the violence of her developing nature filled him with alarm. . . . the only thing that appeared to give her peace or serenity, was being with the boy Felix. (156)

The disruptive force of parenthood on the affective life is not limited to the experiences of Wilhelm; its effects are at play throughout the novel. To cite an instance notable for its elaborate form: Wilhelm's friend Lothario is prevented from marrying when a chance discovery reveals to him that he has had an affair with the mother of his intended. The matter is only resolved by the peculiar revelation that she was mistaken about who her mother actually was (327). The crisis, error, and solution are all typical of *Wilhelm Meister.*

The novel insistently connects the longing for a sexual intimacy shading into incest with an aspiration to return to the source of art. When Mignon's constitutional malaise is diagnosed by a kindly doctor, two unsatisfiable drives are presented at once because they are inextricably connected:

> What we are concerned with is the strange personality of that dear child Mignon. It consists almost entirely of a deep sort of yearning: the longing to see her motherland [*Vaterland*] again, and a longing, my friend, for you—these, I may say, are the only earthly things about her, and both of them have an element of infinite distance about them, both goals being inaccessible to her unusual nature. (320)

The moments that threaten Mignon's life are striking evidence of her role as the emblem of a desire that is never to be satisfied because it is at its heart a longing for return that is figured as an impossible incest. The father is multiply present in her yearning—in the figure of Wilhelm as in the *Vater* (not mother, as the translator has it) *land* she longs for. Mignon's first crisis is precipitated by witnessing the consummation of the flirtation between Wilhelm and the actress Philine at the precise juncture when she herself was hoping to bring her own ambiguous relationship with Wilhelm to the very same point. Her death is the direct result of her presence at another consummation, the apparent betrothal of Wilhelm and Therese (320, 333).

The force of the emblematic figures inhabiting the book depends on their engagement of the most basic structures of desire and satisfaction: sexual pleasure and reproduction. The figure of Mignon represents the necessary fated compounding of illicit longing for art and sexual pleasure along with the power of its frustration, but the novel also offers a corresponding association of coming into relation with admired art and the act of procreation itself. Sexuality and culture both offer the possibility of immediate pleasure along with the ramifying uncontrollable effects of potential fruitfulness. Well into the novel Wilhelm learns that Mariane has given birth to a child that is probably his (the doubt is as important as the fact) and, as a result, has lost her work and been cast out of her home. It is in response to his distress and confusion on hearing this information that Mignon offers to perform the egg dance, with its risk, its blindfolded eyes, and its threat to objects, which, in such a context, can only be understood to represent at once fertility and fragility:

> Mignon had waited up for him, with a light to guide him up the stairs. When she had put down the candle, she asked his permission to give a performance for his benefit that evening. He would rather have said no, for he did not know what this might turn out to be. But he could not refuse this good-hearted creature anything. She came back into the room after a little while, carrying under one arm a carpet which she spread out on the floor. Wilhelm let her continue. She brought four lighted candles and put one at each corner of the carpet. When she next fetched a basket of eggs, her intentions became clearer. With the measured steps of an artist she paced back and forth on the carpet, distributing the eggs in definite groups. Then she called in a servant who played the violin. . . . She blindfolded herself. . . .

Mignon's generous act speaks to the dangerous comfort of art, but it is also an instance in which art stands in for a sexual desire that is otherwise impossible to consummate—hence Wilhelm's initial trepidation. The dance itself is an exhibition of danger neatly avoided, eggs risked but spared:

> Nimbly and lightly she executed the dance with rapid precision, stepping so briskly and firmly between and beside the eggs that at any moment one thought she would crush one of them or dislodge it by the swiftness of her twistings and turnings. But she never touched an egg despite the variety of her steps. . . . Wilhelm was absolutely transported by this strange spectacle; forgetting all his cares, he followed every step of the beloved creature, amazed to see how completely her character was manifested in the dance. Severe, sharp, dry and violent—all this she certainly was; and in her quieter moments there was solemnity

rather than grace. He suddenly realized what he had been feeling about her all this time. He wanted to take this abandoned creature to his bosom as his own child, caress her and by a father's love awaken her to the joys of life. (64–65)

Mignon threatens and spares the emblems of fertility in the course of a dance that is strange, but no stranger than Wilhelm's response, which is at once paternal and amorous. Even as her real father—the mad Harper who cannot recognize his own daughter—serenades the pair from outside the room, their caresses intensify, culminating in a spasm on her part that is hard to read as other than orgasmic, and in an affirmation of the fact that erotic pleasure and paternal duties are intricately allied: "my child!"— "My father! . . . You will never leave me! You will be my father!—I am your child." As the chapter ends, Wilhelm, listening to the Harper's music and "holding his child ever closer in his arms, experienced a feeling of the most perfect, indescribable bliss" (82).

The rich confusion of passion and art with which this scene concludes is the setting of the song of Mignon that follows immediately, with no clear indication of source or significance. Its abrupt emergence should not, however, disguise the fact that the song is closely related to the material that precedes it. If anything, the poem highlights the close relation between the desires of parents and of lovers that runs through the narrative. The dance, and the fervent reconciliation it provokes, are prelude to a poem that soon took on a life of its own as the characteristic expression of modern yearning for Italy. The desire of the song and the language and images in which it is framed will recur throughout the nineteenth century. The place longed for is one in which natural comfort and warmth, combine seamlessly with the artificial beauty suggested by that shining palace full of statues and the sublime mystery of cliffs, mists, and dragons. The speaker's relation to both nature and statues is one of displaced longing, though her melancholy nostalgia is transferred to the monuments, who look down at her to note the changes she has suffered from being away: "You poor child, what have they done to you?"

Who Was Your Father?

The mystery that surrounds Mignon and her mysterious attractiveness for Wilhelm are vital elements of her emblematic role in the novel, but no less significant is the relation between the enigmas she embodies and her actual origins. In the art romance, the important determining passions are all inherited, and so it is with Mignon, product of an odd and elaborate Italian incest, which (like Wilhelm's own relation to the art treasures discarded by his father) is facilitated by a foundational paternal separation. Mignon's mother, Sperata, is never acknowledged by her own father because of an unexplained embarrassment at the fact of her birth late in his life. Given that she is raised by others, and in ignorance of her true family, her ill-fated romance with her brother Augustin might appear a limited kind of transgression, except that Augustin himself has been forced to become a priest by the same capricious father. Still, the worst implications of her offense would have been lost on Sperata but for another priest, so preoccu-pied by the crime to which he is privy that he convinces Sperata that Augustin's position as a clergyman makes her sexual relations with him the moral equivalent of incest. Sperata's sense that Mignon is the product of such a crime (which Goethe goes to great lengths to make at once true and false) determines her feelings of revulsion toward the child. The tragic death of the mother is quickly followed by the madness of Augustin—who enters the novel as the mysterious, melancholy, and dan-gerous Harper.

As Carolyn Steedman points out, this incestuous family history, which is only unraveled late in the novel, was not present in the original (*Theatrical Mission*) draft; its conception follows Goethe's Italian journey.[10] Indeed, the embarrassment of old age fated to fecundity associates Sperata's father with Italy's role in European culture—fundamental source of antiquity and of fruitful creativity, ever at risk from erotic excess as from an excessive and overwhelming accumulation of history. Mignon's elaborately incestu-ous background, with its arbitrary alienations and passionate returns, yields a temperament drawn from ideas of the artistic character that were consolidated in this period. It is a sketch Isaac D'Israeli could have written: naturally talented, nervous, high-strung, oversensitive, prone to strange moods and passions, fated to dissatisfaction, and always out of place.[11] Emblem at once of the promise and the danger of an intimate engagement with a culture that may be too old, that may make too many demands on the emotions, Mignon is either silent or speaks in a medley of European languages. She is at once preternaturally young and ageless ("How old are you?" "Nobody has counted." "Who was your father?" "The big devil is dead." [54]). The only clear things about Mignon for most of the novel are her moods, her mysteries, and her strange talents. It is these last, as represented in her song and dance, that were to become her characterizing features in nineteenth-century culture—along with her tragic fate.

Evidently, the desires of so overdetermined a creation as Mignon cannot help but be emblematic. Incestuous product of the passionate South, she longs perpetually for its warmth and beauty—a favorite pastime of hers is studying maps, as though imagining a route of return. Whenever she speaks to someone embarking on a trip, she asks if the destination is warm. But Mignon does not stand alone, nor does she have her meaning in isola-tion; her presence in the novel is due to her relationship with Wilhelm. It is the necessary conceit of the novel that her song is sung in Italian and then translated by Wilhelm, so that even in what we have, the language of the original is missing, "the childlike innocence of the style was lost" (83). The interplay of poem and narrative emphasizes the importance of the song not only as an expression of Mignon's yearnings but as a challenge to recognition addressed to Wilhelm:

> She intoned each verse with a certain solemn grandeur, as if she were drawing attention to something unusual and imparting something of importance. When she reached the third line, the melody became more somber; the words "You know it, yes?" were given weightiness and mystery, the "Oh there, oh there!" was suffused with longing, and she modified the phrase "Let us fare!" each time it was repeated, so that one time it was entreating and urging, the next time pressing and full of promise. (84)

As Mignon's father, Wilhelm becomes, by a sort of back-formation, naturalized as a displaced citizen of the South. Mignon never belongs anywhere, but her dissatisfaction may be read as half-German by adoption. The account of Mignon's performance confounds Wilhelm's passions with those of the singer, her lyrical expression of desire serving as an invitation for her listener to remember his own:

> When she had finished the song a second time she paused, looked straight at Wilhelm, and asked: "Do you know that land?" "It must be Italy," Wilhelm replied. "Where did you get the song?" "Italy!" said Mignon in a meaningful tone; "if you go to Italy, take me with you. I'm freezing here." "Have you ever been there? asked Wilhelm; but the child kept silent and not one word more could be elicited from her. (84)

Mignon has been fruitfully read as a kind of objectification of Wilhelm's aspirations, a useful interpretation if some account is taken of the ways in which the object of desire in the novel is always at once familiar and alien, immediately recognizable and entirely estranged. To identify the fact of yearning in *Wilhelm Meister* is not at all the same thing as to approach contentment. And in any case, throughout the novel consummation opens the door to something more and less than pleasure.

THE EMBRACE OF THE AMAZON

In my discussion of the role of Goethe in Freud's art romance in chapter 6 of this book I return briefly to the place of children in *Wilhelm Meister*, particularly to some of the darker pleasures the analyst finds hidden in the novelist's works even as he identifies his own deepest fears in his response to the great author. For now it suffices to point out that the weight put on the passions of fathers in determining the longings of their children raises the question of the other parent. Wilhelm's grandfather and father; Hamlet's father; Mignon's grandfather and father; Wilhelm's own role as father—such a fantastic superabundance of male progenitors begs the question: where is the mother in all this masculine reproduction? One answer to the question may be to understand the proliferation of sires in the novel as a kind of defensive protection against the maternal, one related to the ultimately sexless androgyny of Mignon and the interplay with fertility and danger symbolized in her dance.

Wilhelm's childhood home is associated with the paternal insofar as it reflects the father's taste and the value of the grandfather's collection, but important maternal elements come to the fore when artistic ambition is in question. "The smell of the larder, which still clung to the puppets," notes Wilhelm as he recollects the objects that gave the most direct inspiration to his theatrical ambition, "added considerably to my delight" (10). In one of the many exchanges between boy and mother reminiscent of similar moments in Proust, she identifies the bourgeois fear of undisciplined artistic play with her husband, and a liberality always afraid of license with herself:

> "[Y]our father likes to have his own fun of an evening. Moreover, he believes that it only distracts you, and in the end I'll be blamed when he gets cross. How often have I been reproached for giving you that wretched puppet theater for Christmas twelve years ago. It gave you that taste for the theatre."
>
> "Don't blame the puppet theater, don't regret that token of your love and care for me. Those were my first happy moments in the new and empty house." (3)

By giving Wilhelm Mignon, Goethe is able to tell a story of unbridled desire and creative displacement while saving his main character from its most disturbing implications. It is a strategy of splitting that recurs in the art-romance tradition and that serves to indicate both the power of a longing that cannot be imagined as satisfied—to be an artist, to achieve intimacy with the centers of culture—and an anxiety about origins that makes the figure of the mother more than symbolic. Which is to say, the return to the feminine is an effective emblem of the drive toward culture not only because the mother is the ultimate creative source but because the drive itself may be a displacement or rewriting of a yearning for the mother. That the puppets the boy finds smell of the mother's space is part of the pleasure they bring him, suggesting that the story of attempting to recuperate what the father gave up is ultimately far simpler than the story of trying to find what the mother hid.[12] In the former case the problem is one of competition or compensation—to have more taste than the father, to thrive without giving up as much as he had to. In the latter case, what comes to the fore is the seductive quality of imagining not something that is lost (as the art collection is) but something that is tantalizingly hidden in the home.

The complex interplay of parents comes to a head toward the middle of the book in a long emblematic section in which a superabundance of threatening fathers leads to a dream of maternal peace. Felix, the boy who may or may not be his son by his first love, Mariane, is central to whom Wilhelm will discover himself to be. As the novel nears its climax, Mignon will die when she thinks Wilhelm is engaged to be married, and the acknowledgment of Felix as his son—indeed, the simple inquiry as to whether the boy is his—will be an important mark of Wilhelm's maturation. But, halfway through the book, resolution still seems far away, and the mystery that forms part of the fascination of the Harper, Mignon, and Felix is enlivened by their interplay: the affection of Mignon for Felix, her interest in the Harper, the Harper's mysterious dread of Felix. As the Harper serves as a figure for absolute monomaniacal melancholy, he is naturally intriguing to Mignon, his daughter. It is also little wonder that Felix (or "happiness") troubles him, or that ultimately his apparent role in the boy's near death leads to the Harper's belabored suicide.[13] Mignon is Wilhelm's ward, but at this stage in the novel she is also his potential lover. Economically, and with a flamboyant disregard for verisimilitude, Goethe creates a nest of incestuous ignorant fathers and their children— that is, something very close to a family, though one in which the force of mothers is made apparent largely through their absence.

The threat of incest and the erotic force of mothers, the superabundance of fathers and the misrecognition of paternity—all of these issues and more are compounded in the much anticipated production of *Hamlet*. Indeed, the theorizing and discussion that shaped it notwithstanding, the most affecting element of the performance is the mysterious appearance of the ghost of Hamlet's father. The ghost, played by no one known to the troupe, provokes a real sense of terror and confusion in Wilhelm that adds to the power of his acting. He is particularly moved by the feeling that the mysterious stranger sounds like his own dead father (195). To the mystery of the ghost is added another. After Wilhelm goes to bed following an uproarious cast party, he hears a noise he fears might be the return of the ghost of Hamlet's father (that is, potentially his own father's ghost), but which turns out to be a woman coming to his bed. On waking and finding her gone, his uncertainty as to who the partner of his night might have been is compounded by a change in Mignon's behavior, a new maturity and reserve that serves to place her in the list of candidates.

The next night, as he awaits clarification and renewed pleasure, it is neither that comes through his unlocked door. Instead Mignon rushes into the room with claims on his responsibilities: "Master! Save the building! It's on fire!" Rushing out, he is handed Felix, with the following words from one of the actresses: "Save the child. . . . We'll look after the rest." As usual, Wilhelm misunderstands his responsibilities and is misdirected in his search for origins. He hands Felix to the Harper and goes to look for the source of the fire. His hopeless attempt to control the conflagration is cut short by the return of Mignon: "Master! Save your Felix! The old man has gone mad! He's killing him!" At the bottom of the staircase he had climbed Wilhelm finds a scene worth citing at length for its details:

> Great bundles of straw and brushwood were stored there, and were now burning fiercely. Felix was lying on the ground and crying. The old man stood leaning against the wall, his head bowed. . . . Mignon picked up Felix and dragged him with difficulty into the garden, while Wilhelm tried to separate the burning wood and smother the fire but only managed to increase the power and heat of the flames. Finally he too had to retreat to the garden, his eyelashes and hair singed as he dragged the old man through the flames, who followed him reluctantly, his beard scorched in the process. . . .
>
> By now the fire had taken hold of several houses and was lighting up the whole neighborhood. Wilhelm inspected the child by the red light of the flames, but could find no wound. . . . He felt the child all over, but there was no indication of pain. Gradually he settled down to a certain delight at the flames and the orderly progression in which the beams and rafters burned and provided such splendid illumination. . . .
>
> . . . He pressed the little one with unaccustomed intensity to his breast, and would have embraced Mignon with equal affection and joy, had she not gently resisted, taking his hand and holding it firmly.
>
> "Master," she said (she had never called him that before this evening, having addressed him first as "Sir" and then as "Father"), "Master! We have escaped great danger. Your Felix was near to death."
>
> Much questioning finally elicited from her that when they reached the cellar, the Harper had taken the candle from her and set fire to the straw. He then put down Felix, laid his hands with strange gestures on the child's head and pulled out a knife, as if he were going to sacrifice him. She had rushed up and pulled the knife from his hand, screamed, and somebody from the house . . . came to her assistance, but must in the confusion have gone away again and left the old man with the child. (200–201)

Fire, children at risk, dangerous or ineffectual fathers: Wilhelm will relive several elements from this strange interlude in a dream a little later in the narrative, but already their force should be evident. The father's failure to protect provokes a passionate recognition of responsibility that is not ultimately met. A poignant sense of paternal love is evoked by a dramatic recognition of the possibility of death and failed caretaking. The absence of the mother is notable, as is the reversal of parental authority: the father is placed in bed, and his caretaking duties are taken over by a dangerous unreliable proxy.

The threat to Felix marks a vital turning point in a text that had changed both formally and thematically from the realist account of fulfilled artistic ambition that Goethe had imagined before his Italian voyage. Wilhelm's forsaking of the theater, which is so important to Goethe's new vision of the novel, follows closely on this scene (the connection is somewhat camouflaged by the interpolated "Confessions of a Beautiful Soul"). At this moment of transition Wilhelm has a carefully framed dream that recapitulates the experience of the fire while adding resonance to its elements by taking it firmly out of the realm of incident and into the character's psychic life. The returns of the dream are themselves anticipated by a number of self-reflexive repetitions. On his fateful journey from the site of his youthful theatrical endeavors to carry a message to the home of Lothario, Wilhelm remeets the wise Abbé who has counseled him before and will do so again—and who is the same man who years before sold off the grandfather's collection. In his latest manifestation he turns out to be a counselor of Lothario. The gist of their conversation, appropriately enough, is the inevitability and danger of repetition: "Everything that happens to us leaves its traces," notes the Abbé, "everything contributes imperceptibly to our development. But it is dangerous to try to draw up a balance sheet, for in doing so we become either proud and carefree, or depressed and discouraged" (257–58). The traces and the risk identified by this sage figure soon become concrete. Unpacking in his room at the castle, Wilhelm rediscovers in his bag the scarf left by the ghost of Hamlet's father, on which the words "Flee, young man, flee!" have been embroidered. Wilhelm reads the words, which belong to the moralizing plot of the novel, in a more psychological key. He understands the exhortation to escape to involve not simply a turn away from trivial pursuits but counsel to return to a lost state:

> He repeated the words to himself, then thought: "What are these mysterious words supposed to mean? What should I flee? Where to? It would have been better if the Ghost had said: "Return to yourself!" (259)

Wilhelm studies the engravings on the wall of his bedroom, but he is only interested in one that depicts a shipwreck with a father and two beautiful daughters awaiting death from the sea. In this image, suggestive at once of incest and mortality, he identifies a figure who looks like the woman who rescued him when he was attacked and wounded by robbers earlier in the novel, a mysterious character to whom Wilhelm is deeply attracted and whom he has dubbed the Amazon. He is moved to weep until he falls asleep, and in that slumber he reexperiences the threatening fire.

Dreaming that he is happily returned to a garden he had often played in as a child, Wilhelm is glad to see his usually stern father there, friendlier than usual and walking with Mariane, the mother of Felix. Several important moments from the earlier crisis recur, starting with Felix playfully pursued by Philine, the woman who came to Wilhelm's bed the night of the production of *Hamlet*, and therefore the erotic partner he had been expecting prior to the fire. As in the previous case, however, the possibility of pleasure is answered by the sudden intrusion of fear:

> At first he was laughing as he ran and Philine chased him, but suddenly he cried out in fear as the Harper pursued him with long, slow strides. He ran straight up to a pond, Wilhelm rushed after him, but too late to reach him before he had fallen into the water. Wilhelm stood rooted to the spot.

The boy is finally rescued by the Amazon, as Wilhelm himself had been:

> Meanwhile, Wilhelm had drawn nearer, the child was burning all over, and drops of fire were falling off him. Wilhelm became more and more alarmed, but the Amazon quickly took a white veil from off her head and covered the child. The fire was soon quenched. . . . He could see his father strolling with Mariane way off, in an allée with tall trees which seemed to encircle the whole garden. (260)

Again, Wilhelm cannot reach his goal. His path is mysteriously impeded and ultimately he becomes concerned for his father and Mariane. He tries to save them from an unknown danger, but he cannot. "Impulse and desire impelled him to go to their assistance, but the Amazon's hand held him back—and how gladly he let himself be held! And so, with this mixed feeling, he woke up and found his room brightly lit by the morning sun" (260–61). Why does the very figure who saves Felix obstruct Wilhelm? Why is Felix threatened twice by flames? Why is the Amazon alone able to quench those paradoxical, if suggestive, burning drops?

I want to propose that this sequence of dangers to the child represents the deferred anxiety about the mother that runs through the text. Indeed, one source for the repertoire of images on which the incident of the fire and the dream it inspires are based is the very painting of the prince sick with longing that had such a role in shaping Wilhelm's aspirations. In order to recognize the emotion shaping the image, it may be useful to cite the original source. Here is Erasistratus, the wise doctor, studying his patient, as described in Plutarch:

> [W]henever Stratonice came to see him, as she often did, either alone, or with Seleucus, lo, those tell-tale signs of which Sappho sings were all there in him,—stammering speech, fiery flushes, darkened vision, sudden sweats, irregular palpitations of the heart and finally, as his soul was taken by storm, helplessness, stupor, and pallor.[14]

The art historian Wolfgang Stechow has pointed out that the only de-tailed description Winckelmann ever made of a painting was of this very subject as depicted by Gerald de Lairesse.[15] The observation is of interest because the founder of art history was a vital influence for Goethe—as he would be for Freud a century later. The story of Antiochus and Stratonice presents in compact form most of the principal themes that run through *Wilhelm Meister*: incest as the germ of passion, the diagnosis and guidance of young desire by wise outsiders, even the role of an admirable if manipu-lative doctor. From Winckelmann's six-page account of the image—in-cluding, as always, the lovesick young lover in bed, the wise doctor, the benign father, and the stepmother about to become wife—we may cite a description highlighting the voyeuristic erotic charge at the key moment of transition: "The charming Queen . . . with slow hesitating steps, ap-proaches the bed of her new lover; but still with the countenance of a mother, or rather of a sacred vestal." The son-lover is characterized by "a timid red spreading over his sickly face."[16] It goes without saying that the tale Plutarch and Winckelmann tell is nothing if not a fantasy of satisfied Oedipal passion. The fever of the son's craving and the blindness of the father are finally both solved by an act of magnanimous love that validates even as it satisfies the son's desire, although it requires the insight and intervention of the good doctor to come about.

Wilhelm's dream personalizes issues and images running through the story and painting, material Goethe has already made more urgent and immediate in his novel by means of the elaborately staged fire. As Goethe builds on the physicality of the love that is so important to Plutarch's story, the sweat of the prince's flushed passion becomes the drops of flame falling from Felix's endangered body. Fathers are present as failed protectors, but also as feared authorities, as checks on a pleasure in which they participate more than is healthy for the son. Otherwise, what does Wilhelm fear will happen between his father and Mariane; why the repeated confusion (in the narrative and in the dream) of the presence of Philine (or sexual plea-sure) with the father (or fear); why do both Wilhelm and Felix require the ministrations of the Amazon? Still, the maternal is not simply the location for the competing erotic drives of father and son. The absence of long-ing—not competition—is the wish in the dream.

The passion of the father anticipates and preempts that of the son. But the maternal returns as a fantastic relief following overwhelming fear, a profound loss of power, a luxurious passivity. In the dream as in the paint-ing, threatening erotic energy culminates in an incapacity that is a kind of relief, a loss of control reminiscent of the story of a bedridden young man brought the object of his yearning by the love of two father figures. The paradoxical play between unavoidable threat and a relief that is a form of surrender recurs throughout the art romance, though it only becomes fully self-conscious in the works of James and especially Freud. It is little wonder that (as I discuss in chapter 6) the figure of the burning child makes a forceful return in *The Interpretation of Dreams*, alongside Freud's forceful evocation of Goethe himself as a threatening father figure.

Haunting Inheritance

Mignon will die before she can return to the place of her birth, destroyed by her constitutional inability to moderate her passion, and Wilhelm never does reach Italy in the *Apprenticeship*. Instead, his travels are given an alternative destination that serves to illuminate what Italy stands for in the novel. As the narrative progresses, its picaresque form is brought into an unlikely and exaggerated order by the introduction of a kind of Masonic fellowship that is revealed to have had its eyes on Wilhelm's development since well before he was engaged in any serious pursuit—an important if improbable plot element ultimately related to the fantasy of powerlessness at the heart of Wilhelm's dream. Important characters from early in the novel are revealed to be part of a kind of *Bildungscabal* overseeing Wilhelm's life along with the lives of many others. This fellowship comes to control not only his future, however, but also his past. It is at the tower belonging to this shadowy group that Wilhelm reencounters the absent source of his own desire: the lost collection of art that had belonged to his grandfather:

> He went into the house, and found himself in the most solemn and, for him, sacred place he had ever seen. A low-hanging lantern gave light to the stairway opposite him, which was wide and rose gradually until it divided into two arms at a landing. There were marble statues and busts standing on pedestals and in niches. Some of them seemed familiar to him. Youthful impressions never fade away entirely. He recognized a muse which had belonged to his grandfather, not by its shape or quality, but because one arm had been restored along with various sections of the drapery. He felt as though he were in a fantasy world. The child began to weigh heavy on him. (314)

"The child" is Felix, his son by Mariane, but evidently it is also the child in his memories—himself—who starts to weigh heavy as Wilhelm is restored to the art whose loss has shaped him. And, indeed, he discovers anew the very picture of the sick prince that had been his favorite, and in which we read the shape of the forbidden longing that motivates desire in the novel (316).

Wilhelm has come to the fantastic tower in which the scroll holding the events of his life is held, and he has been allowed to read it. We are near the end of his apprenticeship, but Goethe is profligate in his climaxes, lavish in his symbols. "The manuscript had made him acquainted with this house, and he now found himself reunited with his own inheritance" (318). That the lost art collection stands in relation to Wilhelm as Italy does in relation to Mignon is made quite explicit in his response to the place:

> [I]t isn't a house, it's a temple. . . . I shall remember all my life the impression I had yesterday evening when I came in here, and there in front of me were those old treasures from my youth—there once more. I remembered the sorrowing statues in Mignon's song; but these objects have no need to sorrow for me, they looked at me in solemn seriousness, linking my earliest memories to this present moment. Here I have rediscovered the family treasures, the joys of my grandfather, set between so many other noble works of art. (318)

Wilhelm's protestations of difference in similarity notwithstanding, Goethe is clear that the encounter with prized objects from his past is unable to satisfy the quality of longing Wilhelm shares with Mignon:

> When everyone else was sleeping, he was pacing up and down in the house. The presence of those old familiar paintings partly attracted and partly repelled him. He could neither accept nor reject what surrounded him, everything reminded him of something else [*alles erinnerte ihn an alles*], he could see the whole chain of his life, but at the moment it lay in pieces which would not join together again. These works of art, the ones his father had sold, seemed to him a symbol of the fact that he too was partly excluded from calm, solid possession of what was desirable, and partly deprived of this by his own fault or that of others. He became so lost in these lugubrious reflections that he sometimes seemed to himself like a ghost, and even when he was feeling and touching objects outside himself, he could hardly resist the sense of not knowing whether he was alive or not. (349–50)

Although Goethe locates the familial art collection as beginning and aim of Wilhelm's movement toward culture, he troubles the moment of return, refusing to avoid the fact that the works of art that move Wilhelm and promise him so much are also the source of a dissatisfaction characterized by perpetual deferral. Wilhelm in the museum becomes worse than a phantom, uncertain of his very existence.

Wilhelm's ghostliness is not the first spectral moment in the novel. There is a good deal of play with the topic throughout the work. The tower at which Wilhelm is challenged before he sees the collection is a carefully protected old chapel containing family secrets and featuring a talking portrait that at once naturalizes and makes strange the Gothic motifs running through the novel:

[T]here was a slight sound and the curtain above the altar opened showing an empty dark space inside a frame. A man in ordinary clothes stepped forward and greeted [Wilhelm], saying: "Don't you recognize me? Don't you, amongst all the other things you would like to know, wish to find out where your grandfather's collection of works of art now is?" (302)

The apparition reveals himself to be the very man Wilhelm met as he first set out on his voyage, the one who had reminded him then, as he does now, about the beloved painting of the sick prince. More figures from early in the novel appear in the frame, including Hamlet's father, who astonishingly identifies himself as Wilhelm's own sire, and even more remarkably declares himself satisfied: "I am your father's ghost . . . and I depart in peace, for all I wished for you has been fulfilled more than I myself could imagine" (303). At this point Wilhelm is allowed one question, and his inquiry as to whether Felix is his son is greeted as a tremendous success. It is remarkable, then, after all this wish fulfillment, all this emptying out of the fearful supernatural by filling in its mystery, that Wilhelm himself is left feeling like a ghost, that the feast of reconciliation and knowledge at the tower results in an only more uncanny uncertainty for its principal audience.

Mignon is buried in an elaborate sepulcher designed by the same man who had bought the collection belonging to Wilhelm's grandfather. Indeed, her tomb may well be the first instance of the museum-mausoleum theme that was to have such resonance for avant-garde movements of a later era. It is at Mignon's funeral in the museum that her visiting uncle, the Italian who helped assemble the collection, recognizes her and reveals the secret of her ancestry, suggesting that her identity is most compellingly manifested in a death closely related to the institution in which it is beautifully commemorated.[17] The Italian uncle evidently stands for the hospitable human pleasures of a nation for which Mignon had only been able to express the frustrated longing. Not only is he identified as having contributed to the development of the collection of art at the tower, but the novel offers a simple recuperation of Mignon's impossible desires in his good-natured invitation: "her friends must promise to visit me in her homeland, in the place where she was born and raised. They must see the columns and statues she remembered in her song" (354). For us, however, as it was generally for nineteenth-century culture, the interest of Mignon resides less in what she promises than in what she cannot deliver.

The refrain of the song of Mignon—"You know it, yes?"—is precisely the sort of self-answering demand that might summarize the climax of a search that begins with a lost ancestral collection and ends with its uncanny and only partial restoration. The successful social integration of Wilhelm Meister requires the death of the emblem of unsatisfiable yearning: hence her demise at the moment of his apparent betrothal. But it is far from being the case that her departure from the novel opens the door to satisfaction. Wilhelm himself will eventually assume a medical, not an artistic, profession, but his importance lies always in relation to Mignon; he is remembered for the passion in which he participated, not for his achievement.[18] He is always the father-lover of the passionate creature from the South, the living man made fantasmal by his encounter with an alienated inheritance. Wilhelm will leave the tower in which so much happens to him that is not new, but his haunted unsatisfied state at the moment of learning that the discovery of lost beauty is always in fact a rediscovery comes to be a typical condition in nineteenth-century tales of the encounter with art. Nevertheless, the longing toward the South of culture that forms the passionate core of Goethe's novel becomes inescapable in later narratives of art. From Germaine de Staël's Corinne, to Letitia Landon's Improvisatrice, to any number of female characters in Henry James and beyond, Mignon herself produces more offspring than her perpetual maidenhood would suggest possible.

Richard Westall, "Roman Charity," from Byron, *Childe Harold* IV. *Oeuvres* (Paris, 1822). Courtesy Fondazione Primoli, Rome.

CHAPTER 2

The Art-Romance Tradition

LANDON: THE BIRTH OF A DAUGHTER

COMMON SENSE WOULD suggest that foreign travel is necessarily fated to offer encounters with a reality different from what one is used to, even from what one is able to anticipate. It can seem only reasonable, then, to expect that texts engaged with the foreign should revolve around the shock of the real and that realistic representation should be the characteristic mode of capturing that shock. The art-romance tradition, however, is more closely engaged with tracing the circuits of desire than it is with commemorating a newly discovered or unexpected authenticity. The essentially fictional qualities of the art romance—at every point a highly literary mode, if one characterized by an important investment in approaching the real only to shear away at key moments—are demonstrated by flamboyant returns to its literary pedigree, to a small family of works from which it descends. Indeed, though its concerns and motifs are mediated by a wide and varied network of texts, three works of great Europewide influence established the principal lines on which the form developed and to which it continually returns: *Wilhelm Meister*, *Corinne*, and *Childe Harold*.

In *Wilhelm Meister*, particularly in the character of Mignon, the nineteenth century found a figure for unsatisfiable longing symbolized by what Carolyn Steedman has called "strange dislocations," manifestations of a thoroughgoing, irreconcilable, innate, yet troubling sense of out-of-placedness. Among the elements shaping Mignon, the following are inescapable in the art romance: her mysterious origins in a complex tale of incestuous family romance, her passion, her disappointment, and her death. Yet Mignon's flamboyant "dislocation" depends on the fact that she is so very much only of one place. The suggestive account of Italy contained in the song of this uncanny creature may be traced to earlier cultural phenomena, but after her it becomes definitive. For the art romance, Italy is the place where the citron blooms, a land of warmth and beauty and of the natural production of art, but also one in which longing is always alive and satisfaction and death are closely allied.[1] Also vital to the tradition— though less likely to see the sort of flamboyant citation that characterizes evocations of Mignon—is Wilhelm's story, his original aspirations toward a world of art along with his swerve away to more practical matters while still maintaining a sometimes voyeuristic and sometimes more intimate relation to that world. The ultimate significance of Wilhelm and Mignon, however, resides in the suggestive interplay between them. Wilhelm is at once and disturbingly father, protector, and lover of Mignon. She is daughter, lover, and inscrutable inspiration. Their overdetermined relationship indicates the difficulty of isolating any element in the interpenetrating amalgamation of self and culture, passion and its source, that the tradition is committed to representing. Moreover, the character and story of Mignon provide the main components of a line of inverisimilitude—at once poetic and more generally fantastic—that drives the text outside the parameters of what might be called its realism. The formal fluidity of the novel as much as its thematic concerns provides a model for the art-romance tradition.

It is Germaine de Staël, close student of cultural difference, of Italy, and of German literature, who gave the most consistent and influential literary form to the sensibility represented in Goethe's *Italian Journey* and *Wilhelm Meister*. Staël had received a copy of the novel from Goethe himself in 1797, though she could not yet read it in the original. Sixteen years later, the comments on the book in her seminal account of German culture, *De l'Allemagne* (1813), focus almost entirely on Mignon, a figure for mixed cultural sources in whom she identifies the passion of the South blending with the reserve and repression she associates with the North: "There is developed in this extraordinary creature, a singular mixture of childishness and depth of understanding, of seriousness and imagination; ardent like the women of Italy, silent and persevering like a person of reflection, speech does not seem to be her natural language."[2] Staël gave a voice to the eloquently silent figure of longing she discovered in *Wilhelm Meister*. Indeed, it is a well-known fact of literary history that the writing of *Corinne* interrupted work on *De l'Allemagne*.[3] As the author notes in the latter text, after commenting on the difficulties of pleasing readers from different cultures, "The great advantage, therefore, which may be derived from the study of German literature, is the spirit of emulation which it imparts; we should rather seek in it the means of writing well ourselves, than expect from it works already written which may be worthy of being transmitted to other nations" (77).

For generations of women, *Corinne*, the text Staël herself was inspired to write, served as a passionate travelogue, not simply to Italy but to genius itself. Indeed, a key component of Staël's contribution to the art-romance tradition is the conflation indicated by her title, *Corinne, or Italy*.[4] Mignon does not simply grow to more than adult size; her yearning expands beyond the borders of her self. A far more imposing figure of creativity, Corinne is fated to longing, disappointment, and death, but also destined for glory, and both fates are closely connected. Corinne enters European culture as the principal instance of what became a nineteenth-century paradox, the woman genius—receiving wide acclaim, yet seeking only a personal love that is forever out of her reach.

The misery of Corinne was inherited by the nineteenth century, along with a number of plot elements that in some measure domesticate the strange story Goethe had created for Mignon. It is typical that Corinne's passionate genius and out-of-placedness are located in a narrative of frustrated love and missed opportunities in which an underdetermined parental fiat makes consummation impossible, and affection is transferred from the passionate foreign brunette to the more sedate native blonde half sister. The multiple incest that was so central to Mignon's composition and fate is typically rerouted, as in *Corinne*, into a parental coercion of the passions and a suggestive play with sisters as romantic rivals.

In 1824 Letitia Landon published her phenomenally successful art romance, "The Improvisatrice," a poem that merits close attention not only for its popularity, but because its formal qualities and the strangeness of the desires and (dis)satisfactions it celebrates mark it as an exemplary instance of the tradition. Mignon was always a longing daughter fated to woe and alienation, one whom the very statues of her native land addressed as their offspring. It is a metaphoric use of the family relationship that Landon cites at the beginning of her work when she makes the Improvisatrice the daughter not of parents but of a place:

> I am a daughter of that land
> Where the poet's lip and the painter's hand
> Are most divine,—where the earth and sky,
> Are picture both and poetry—
> I am of Florence. 'Mid the chill
> Of hope and feeling, oh! I still
> Am proud to think to where I owe
> My birth though but the dawn of woe![5]

The boon of Italian birth is excessive. No real distinction is made among picture, narrative, and song throughout the text because the point is to identify a generalized locus of creativity, the proper setting for a figure of absolute genius.[6] The site of beauty and pleasure is also one of inescapable foreordained sadness, however, of the "chill / Of hope and feeling." If the joys that are her birthright are in excess, so to, from the very outset, is an inescapable sense of melancholy, even doom. Why is the birth of the Improvisatrice "but the dawn of woe"? How is the despondency that recurs with such insistence throughout the poem related to the pleasures she describes? To raise these questions is to ask two others: Is the source of the Improvisatrice's melancholy none other than Italy itself, or a certain tradition about Italy, one not unrelated to the beauty she describes? Is it possible to understand her misery as a form of pleasure? Certainly, from these opening lines we can say that her woe is presented as having the same self-evident character—and therefore as little need of explanation—as the splendor of the place or its influence on her creativity.

It is worth noting the weakness of the Improvisatrice's celebration of Italy as a land of *natural* grandeur: introduced parenthetically, "earth and sky" are returned immediately to the world of artifice as "picture both and poetry." The second stanza of the poem offers a development of the galleries remembered in Mignon's song, but these lines emphasize the artifice woven in with the lemon blossoms in that earlier song, making clear that Italy is in no way a place of simple natural beauty. The Improvisatrice's Florence is an art gallery whose contents vie with and surpass the pleasures of the natural world.

> My childhood passed 'mid radiant things,
> Glorious as Hope's imaginings;
> Statues but known from shapes of the earth,
> By being too lovely for mortal birth;
> Paintings whose colours of life were caught
> From the fairy tints in the rainbow wrought;
> Music whose sighs had a spell like those
> That float on the sea at the evening's close;
> Language so silvery, that every word
> Was like the lute's awakening chord;
> Skies half sunshine, and half starlight;
> Flowers whose lives were a breath of delight;
> Leaves whose green pomp knew no withering;
> Fountains bright as the skies of our spring;
> And songs whose wild and passionate line
> Suited a soul of romance like mine. (1)

The natural beauty of the South competes with the inspiring objects that surround the young Improvisatrice to the point that even the verisimilitude of the statues is outweighed by their more than human beauty. The blooms that had played such a part in the longing of Mignon turn to a permanent deathless green and ultimately to the man-made pleasures of fountains, themselves offering joys as rich as the firmament. The fountains, like the long sentence itself and the childhood it describes, are tributaries that flow inexorably into the romance of the Improvisatrice's soul.

The work of the poem's opening is the creation of a world of natural artifice, the appropriate setting for a natural artificer whose very soul is shaped by generic convention. The poem as a whole is flamboyantly unreal, a gallery of conventional tales of disappointed love in a most unnatural setting. In "The Venetian Bracelet" (1829) published six years after the wild success of "The Improvisatrice," Landon offers a telling reflection on the presence of Italy in her work. The poet begins with a meditation that recapitulates much of the beginning of the work that had made her reputation but that nevertheless goes even further than its predecessor in the acknowledgment of convention:

> Another tale of thine! fair Italie—
> What makes my lute, my heart, aye turn to thee?
> I do not know thy language,—that is still
> Like the mysterious music of the rill;—
> And neither have I seen thy cloudless sky,
> Where the sun hath his immortality;
> Thy cities crown'd with palaces, thy halls
> Where art's great wonders light the storied walls;
> Thy fountain's silver sweep; thy groves where dwell
> The rose and orange, summer citadel;
> Thy songs that rise at twilight on the air,
> Wedding the breath thy thousand flowers sigh there;
> Thy tales of other times; thy marble shrines,
> Lovely though fallen,—for the ivy twines
> Its graceful wreath around each ruin'd fane,
> As still in some shape beauty would remain.
> I know them not, yet, Italie, thou art
> The promised land that haunts my dreaming heart.   (199)

A description shaped around acknowledged ignorance of the real and demonstrated expertise about convention offers poetry in the stead of experience. Indeed, the charms of the unknown country are closely allied to the *conventional* passions it is understood to provoke:

> Perchance it is as well thou art unknown:
> I could not bear to lose what I have thrown
> Of magic round thee,—but to find in thee
>   What hitherto I still have found in all—
> Thou art not stamp'd with that reality
>   Which makes our being's sadness and its thrall!   (199)

An unknown land promising passion and beauty unchecked by reality—it makes perfect sense that this should be the home of escapism. And yet what Landon represents in Italy is not the achievement of pleasure but the elaborate reiterated experience of melancholy, longing, and death. Thus, after a gesture toward the convention of Italy's natural splendor— "My lute's enchanted world, fair Italie. / To me thou art a vision half divine, / Of myriad flowers lit up with summer shine"—"The Venetian Bracelet" sounds a darker note:

Of sorrows, too; for e'en on this bright soil
Grief has its shadow, and care has its coil,
But e'en amid its darkness and its crime,
Touch'd with the native beauty of such clime,
Till wonder rises with each gushing tear:—
And hath the serpent brought its curse even here?
  Such is the tale that haunts me: I would fain
Wake into pictured life the heart's worst pain;
And seek I if pale cheek and tearful eye
Answer the notes that wander sadly by.   (200)

It is vital to recognize what Landon herself clearly does—not only the centrality of artifice and convention in her use of Italy but the function of melancholy as a form of aesthetic value. The Improvisatrice remembers with pleasure ("Oh, yet my pulse throbs to recall") the joy she felt when her first painting was displayed on a gallery wall, but the picture itself, like all of her works, is a representation of sadness:

Sad were my shades; methinks they had
Almost a tone of prophecy—
I ever had, from earliest youth,
A feeling what my fate would be.   (2)

Landon's use of Italy and of the art-romance tradition offers two related challenges: the pleasure of unpleasure or dissatisfaction, and the affective force of artifice. Her 1829 preface to the volume in which "The Venetian Bracelet" was published addresses both topics, beginning with the need to stimulate the sympathies of a jaded modernity by recourse to melancholy verse: "Aware that to elevate I must first soften, and that if I wished to purify I must first touch, I have ever endeavoured to bring forward grief, disappointment, the fallen leaf, the faded flower, the broken heart, and the early grave." A measured irony is Landon's tool when the preface turns to the question of authorial identification running through "The Improvisatrice" and shaping much of the reception of her poetry: "With regard to the frequent application of my works to myself, considering that I sometimes pourtrayed love unrequited, then betrayed, and again destroyed by death—may I hint the conclusions are not quite logically drawn, as assuredly the same mind cannot have suffered such varied modes of misery."[7]

The self-consciousness on display in this preface, and especially Landon's ironic treatment of the error of mistaking her fate for that of her melancholy characters, must lend a degree of factitiousness to the Improvisatrice's claim that it is *her* self that is poured out in her song:

I poured my full and burning heart
In song, and on the canvass made
My dreams of beauty visible. (1–2)

In order to understand the play of passion and suffering in "The Improvisatrice," it is necessary to identify Landon's misery as more than simple
self-revelation. In the melancholy that is present immediately ("I ever had
from earliest youth, / A feeling what my fate would be") and in belabored
forms throughout her tales of romantic woe, it should be impossible not
to recognize that artifice and the reiteration of suffering combine into a
form of pleasure. The Improvisatrice's first painting, Petrarch alone in a
crowd gazing at Laura in self-mortifying misery, is followed by one representing Sappho, another figure for the self-destruction of genius as a result
of unsatisfied or disappointed love. Given her unrequited passion for Lorenzo, it might appear in some measure natural that such themes should
come to the mind of the Improvisatrice, that they should burden and
scald her heart. But she has yet to meet her ill-fated lover when she paints
Petrarch and Sappho. Her unsatisfiable longing for Lorenzo is best understood not as cause, but as a further manifestation of the overdetermined
yearning for dissatisfaction that runs through the poem as a whole, from
its frame narrative to its intercalated narratives and songs.

Although the emotional drives given voice in her verses cannot be traced
to any source within the singer's own experience, the poem itself evidently
finds that source in the city in which the poem is set. Immediately following Sappho's song of farewell to her lute, the frame narrative returns with
a characteristic art-romance touch: the simple, generally capitalized, one-
sentence invocation of a storied city—"FLORENCE!"[8]

FLORENCE! with what idolatry
I've lingered in thy radiant halls,
Worshipping, till my dizzie eye
Grew dim with gazing on those walls,
Where Time had spared each glorious gift
By Genius unto memory left!
And when seen by the pale moonlight,
More pure, more perfect, though less bright
What dreams of song flashed on my brain
Till each shade seemed to live again;
And then the beautiful, the grand,
The glorious of my native land,

. . . .

In every change of earth and sky,
Breathed the deep soul of poesy.

The natural environment and the artificial world of the city come together in the songs the Improvisatrice sings, and so it is that when the frame narrative returns (after two more intercalated tales of fatal unsatisfiable longing)[9] the capitalized locus of desire also returns, no longer a city, now a man:

> LORENZO!—when next morning came
> For the first time I heard thy name!
> LORENZO!

To make clear the links connecting the setting, the Improvisatrice's passion, and her creativity, Landon places the encounter with the named lover in a museum—the heart of this city of art:

> I sought the gallery: I was wont
>   To pass the noontide there, and trace
> Some statue's shape of loveliness—
>   Some saint, some nymph, or muse's face.
> There, in my rapture, I could throw
>   My pencil and its hues aside,
> And, as the vision past me, pour
>   My song of passion, joy, and pride.
> And he was there,—LORENZO there!   (15)

As this will not be the only time Lorenzo is discovered in a gallery, it will be useful to underline the associations suggested by the quick movement and elisions of the poem, the elements that come together to precipitate the lover. To move from museum to statue or painting is of course no more than normal in a gallery; the relationship between work of art and copy is also quite close in the period; that between work of plastic art and song is more unusual, but not for a poem so deeply enmeshed in the nineteenth-century culture of art.[10] What stands out is the embedding of the encounter with Lorenzo in this setting. The repetition of an initial "And" in the last lines of the passage does no work other than to insist on the affinity among three elements: the vision of the Improvisatrice, her song, and the appearance of the lover. In its speed, the poem makes clear the close relationship, even identity, between the beloved and the world of artifice in which he is found. A later encounter emphasizes the relationship (it is a fanciful contrast of statue and human form that Hawthorne will belabor in *The Marble Faun*):

> He leant beside a pedestal.
>   The glorious brow, of Parian stone,
> Of the Antinous, by his side,
>   Was not more noble than his own!
> They were alike: he had the same

> Thick-clustering curls the Roman wore—
> The fixed and melancholy eye—
>   The smile which passed like lightning o'er
> The curved lip.   (20)

No sooner is this artful lover encountered than he is loved. No sooner is he loved, however, than he must be lost.[11] The asymptotic form of the lovers' fate is indicated by their first near-kiss, which the Improvisatrice recounts in the derealized voice of a witness to events rather than an agent:

> I saw a youth beside me kneel;
> I heard my name in music steal;
> I felt my hand trembling in his;—
> Another moment, and his kiss
> Had burnt upon it; when, like thought,
>   So swift it past, my hand was thrown
> Away, as if in sudden pain.   (20–21)

Lorenzo's sudden turn anticipates a further abandonment. He departs inexplicably, leaving the Improvisatrice to pine and waste away. Longing and the impossibility of satisfaction are so crucial to this art romance that the ghost of Mignon comes to haunt or possess every character in the frame narrative as much as in the intercalated songs. When Lorenzo does return, it is with a nearly incomprehensible story of parental control and the institution of incestuous passions by parental fiat that can only be traced to the tale of Mignon's parents, Sperata and Augustin. "I was betrothed," begins "Lorenzo's History," "from earliest youth / To a fair orphan, who was left / Beneath my father's roof and care." Fated to wed the young girl with whom he was raised, and whom he loves as (what else?) a sister, Lorenzo has never been free to love the Improvisatrice (29). For reasons the poem makes no effort to clarify, poor Ianthe (whose name suggests not only the influence of Byron's *Childe Harold*, but her role as only an intended or fiancée—never wife) dies at the point of consummation. Two telling parallel verbs describing the crisis are all the explanation the text offers as to the cause for her demise:

> *I wedded.*—I could not have borne
>   To see young Ianthe blighted
> By that worst blight the spring can know—
>   Trusting affection ill requited!
> Oh, was it that she was too fair,
>   Too innocent for this damp earth;
> And that her native star above
>   Reclaimed again its gentle birth?
> *She faded. . . .*   (31; emphases added)

I wedded / She faded. The structure determining Mignon's death returns here with an added degree of perversity; the satisfaction that precipitates the demise of the figure of longing is none other than her own. Whereas Mignon's heart breaks when she believes Wilhelm is to marry Therese, Ianthe is destroyed by the consummation of her own desire. Her demise at the threshold of consummation is then recapitulated in the Improvisatrice's own passing at the return of Lorenzo, making clear that death at the point of romantic fulfillment is more than a personal matter; it is a structural inevitability. The lover comes back too late so the death of Ianthe is merely prologue for that of the Improvisatrice, itself as much a necessary escape from the danger of fulfillment as evidence of that great sentimental conceit, the irreversible damage caused by love apparently unrequited. "LORENZO! be this kiss a spell!" she declares as she expires, capturing the speed of the crisis and the impossibility of fulfillment that drives it, "My first!—my last! FAREWELL!—FAREWELL!" (32).

The demise of the Improvisatrice goes beyond the blithe indifference to verisimilitude that characterizes the poem as a whole. It is an event so outrageous, given the first-person voice of the poem, that the coherence of the text itself must break in order to accommodate it. A second first person abruptly enters the poem at its close: the necessary witness to the fate of Lorenzo after the loss of his love. Indeed, the possibility presents itself—given the narrative instability introduced in the text at this point—that the vivid first-person narrator, so closely identified with Italy as to be its daughter, has been dead all along. She is, in any case, immediately replaced by the voice of a foreigner, an outsider—a tourist:

> There is a lone and stately hall,
> Its master dwells apart from all.
> A wanderer through Italia's land,
>   One night a refuge there I found.
> The lightning flash rolled o'er the sky,
>   The torrent rain was sweeping round:
> These won me entrance.   (32–33)

This is the only introduction the reader is given to a new narrative voice, that of a wandering traveler, not a native and apparently not even a woman. Both the literary conventions around which the poem is constructed and the apparent sincerity or self-revelation of its passion are thrown into question at the end by the introduction of this second first person, the first whose passions play no part in the poem as a whole, who is spared desire by being an intrigued but otherwise unengaged witness. Yet the splitting of the narrative is itself a convention of the art romance. The speed of the collapse of the Improvisatrice is evidently related to her destiny as an artist. But it is characteristic of the form to uncomfortably divide its narrative center, to begin with the passions and dark fates of artists, but to conclude with witnesses and connoisseurs. It is a structure already folded into *Wilhelm Meister*. As we will see, it is a formal device that Byron flamboyantly exploited in *Childe Harold* and that would become a principal tool of James, early and late.

The death of the Improvisatrice leaves Lorenzo in precisely the world of beauty and art her poem had originally celebrated, but it has now become all the more clearly a place of generalized melancholy. The romance borrows its ending from the beginning of a Gothic tale, reintroducing Lorenzo as a Byronic figure of fascinating melancholy and loss, only further ensconced within a museal setting:

> . . . He was young,
> The castle's lord, but pale like age;
> His brow, as sculpture beautiful,
>   Was wan as grief's corroded page.
> He had no words, he had no smiles,
>   No hopes:—his sole employ to brood
> Silently over his sick heart
>   In sorrow and in solitude.   (33)

Lorenzo now dwells permanently in the kind of gallery space that was the scene of his first fatal encounter with the Improvisatrice. The painting of Sappho, which had been a double work of the artist—both image and song—is now revised (perhaps newly painted by Lorenzo) and witnessed from the outside, not described by its maker. From being an object in a gallery, Lorenzo becomes painter and curator of the relics of a lost love that is emblematic of the creativity and melancholy folded into the fantasy of Italy. In this new capacity he becomes an object of the traveler's sentimental attention:

> I saw the hall where, day by day,
> He mused his weary life away;
> It scarcely seemed a place for woe,
>   But rather like a genie's home.
> Around were graceful statues ranged,
>   And pictures shone around the dome.
> But there was one—a loveliest one!—
>   One picture brightest of all there!
> Oh! never did the painter's dream
>   Shape things so gloriously fair!
> . . . .
> She leant upon a harp:—one hand
>   Wandered, like snow, amid the chords;

The lips were opening with such life,
   You almost heard the silvery words.
She looked a form of light and life,
   All soul, all passion, and all fire;
A priestess of Apollo's, when
   The morning beams fall on her lyre;
A Sappho, or ere love had turned
The heart to stone where once it burned.
But by the picture's side was placed
A funeral urn on which was traced
The heart's recorded wretchedness;—
   And on a tablet hung above,
Was 'graved one tribute of sad words—
   "LORENZO TO HIS MINSTREL LOVE."   (33)

"The Improvisatrice" is a fantasy of dissatisfaction, of never arriving or of arriving too late. The proliferation of longing in the poem is such that everyone surrenders to it because it is the condition that interests the text. The wish this fantasy poem fulfills is the wish for desire not to end. Satisfaction runs one out of the picture or into the grave, ensuring that yearning or mourning remains the only permanent and vital states of being.

MELANCHOLY POETRY

Placing the work of Landon in the art-romance tradition not only allows recognition of the complex role of suffering in her work but also raises the question of gender in relation both to art and to misery. Death and unsatisfiable longing are the lot of the artist in Landon's several returns to the art romance, and their presence is sometimes even more extraordinarily unmotivated than in "The Improvisatrice"—or, rather, more self-evidently compelled by generic convention rather than by any narrative need. To take a particularly compact example, "A History of the Lyre" (1829) tells of Eulalie, "Once the delight of Rome for that fine skill / With which she woke the lute" (223), encountered by a nameless British traveler who never quite understands her melancholy. But then, how could he unless he were well read not only in *Corinne* but in the story of Mignon as well?

"My youth has been too lonely, too much left
To struggle for itself; and this world is
A northern clime, where ev'ry thing is chill'd."   (226)

Nothing happens between Eulalie and the narrator, except that he experiences her genius and she expresses her melancholy ("I am a woman:—Tell me not of fame," 226). On his return home, he marries Emily, the nurturing Englishwoman who has been tending his flowers. When he takes Emily to Italy for her health, they visit Eulalie, who is evidently dying. She shows them a funeral statue she has designed for her future grave and tells them of her impending death. The text as a whole is at once simple and essentially incomprehensible without the background of the art romance to give it emotional resonance. To tell "A History of the Lyre" is not to tell the story of a woman but the story of the instrument that stands for poetry. The title vibrates with suggestions of Sappho and Corinne and the Improvisatrice. But by the same token, it also evokes the generic pressures shaping the literary representation of suffering women.

There has been a temptation to see the representation of the death of a woman—alongside such related but not identical phenomena as her disappointed affections (never her disappointed ambition) and her romantic humiliation—as a form of resistance to the limitations culture has imposed on the sex, politically, artistically, or even phenomenologically. Yet the suffering and death of women read differently when they are understood as part of a women's tradition rather than as an ever-original individual expression of a symbolic gender politics. Consider another Landon poem on the tragically premature but fated death of an artist:

> . . . thou didst die before thy time,
>   The tenement o'erwrought,
> The heart consumed by its desire,
>   The body worn by thought;
> Thyself the victim of thy shrine,
> A glorious sacrifice was thine. (500)

This body worn by thought, the self-sacrificing creative figure whose death is here mourned, is not an alienated despised or disdained woman poet. It is Sir Walter Scott. That artists are fated to difficult lives and early deaths has been a long-lived convention, but it is an idea whose conventional nature can be difficult to recognize or acknowledge. Wordsworth's well-known generalization in "Resolution and Independence," that "Poets in our youth begin in gladness; / But thereof come in the end despondency and madness" reflects on the poet himself, on Chatterton, his immediate topic, and on the genus as a whole.[12] The period's interest in this melancholy idea is testified to throughout the nineteenth century by the numerous editions of Isaac D'Israeli's compendia of anecdotes of suffering and quarrelsome artists. The writing of women authors participates in this tradition, but in order to recognize the force of the cultural phenomenon, it will be necessary to sacrifice the idea that the representation of misery and death must be understood as necessarily staging a kind of moral resistance against social or cultural constraints. After all, that songs on the death of poets are, as Landon herself recognized, conventional, does not make them less interesting or complex.

Two notable cultural drives shape Letitia Landon's engagement of the art-romance tradition. The first is the emergent idea of the artistic personality as one particularly prone to melancholia, disappointment, and madness, a notion that makes the manifestation of such dark qualities suggest the presence of genius. The other is that important feature in the literature of sentiment: the fascination with, even pleasure in, suffering, death, and melancholy.[13] Both of these drives are featured in the Improvisatrice's painting of Petrarch yearning for Laura. Beyond its characteristic fusion of literature and poetry, the image also combines the pleasure of longing with a version of artistic genius of which suffering is always an inherent part. Landon does recognize a special role for women in the tradition she inherited from Staël, one based in part on the important historic relation between femininity and sentimentality. Her lines on the death of Felicia Hemans identify the fatal coincidence of the poetic character and the female sex:

> The fable of the Prometheus and the vulture
>   Reveals the poet's and the woman's heart.
> Unkindly are they judged—unkindly treated—
>   By careless tongues and ungenerous words.
>
> ("Felicia Hemans," 546)

The vulnerability that links poet and woman in such a passage bears placing alongside the ironic account of self-revelation Landon offers in her preface to "The Venetian Bracelet." The image of the poet as fated to a painful self-exposure akin to that of Prometheus, whose liver was attacked ever and again by the vulture as he lay chained on Mount Caucasus, needs to be considered in relation to Landon's reminder that the portrayal of misery is not necessarily or in any simple way always a manifestation of individual self-revelation. Given the flamboyant inverisimilitude of Landon's texts, their insistent expression of both sentimentality and artifice, it may be more useful to understand the self-revelation in these instances, not as confessional, but as bearing witness to the complex ever-deflected desire Landon understands to run through her own texts, as it does through those of other women authors.

Later nineteenth-century writers would attempt to move beyond the pleasures of dissatisfaction and the characteristic modes of sentimental romance in which that pleasure was typically located. Maggie Tulliver's celebrated rejection of *Corinne* the moment the blonde enters the story is often cited as a locus classicus of women's resistance to a number of masculine cultural impositions. It is also, of course, a repudiation of sentimentality, a literary mode that had come to be identified as fundamentally feminine. *The Mill on the Floss* itself presents realism as a richer aspiration. "Take back your *Corinne*," Maggie says to Philip, the use of italics allowing the reader to recognize something her interlocutor misses, that it is a text she is rejecting. "You agree with me in not liking Corinne, then?" Philip inquires, making the object of discussion a person. "I didn't finish the book," responds Maggie, keeping to her literary engagement, and leaving the question of Corinne's own merits up in the air. "As soon as I came to the blond-haired young lady reading in the park, I shut it up and determined to read no further. I foresaw that that light complexioned girl would win away all the love from Corinne and make her miserable. I'm determined to read no more books where the blond haired women carry away all the happiness."[14] Maggie rejects not Corinne, but *Corinne*, and in doing so she refuses the pleasure she is meant to take in watching the misery of the passionate brilliant woman. (Maggie does not need to read on to know what will happen.) Not for the first time, George Eliot challenges a kind of feminine pleasure and feminine cliché—though of course, romance haunts the *Mill* itself, and one does not have to search far to find pleasure in longing, dissatisfaction, and death in Eliot's own novel.[15]

While the grandeur of Corinne is self-evidently fantastic, there is a temptation to understand her failure as all too realistic. Which is to say, that criticism sometimes ignores what Maggie knows, that the story of *Corinne* was fated to take a certain kind of shape, one characterized by inverisimilitude at the level of narrative event and abjection, misery and death at the level of character. To not reject, as Maggie does, but to overlook both the formulaic nature of the story and the abnegating pleasures driving its suffering will naturally have serious effects on the interpretation of *Corinne* and related works such as "The Improvisatrice." They will tend to be understood as realist projects gone wrong, or even as accurate representations of an unfair reality. Staël for one, careful reader of *Werther* and close student of Rousseau, is clear throughout her work on the intellectual importance of sadness. "The kind of poetry most in harmony with philosophy," she notes in "On Literature Considered in Its Relationship to Social Institutions" (1800), "is melancholy poetry. Sadness lets us understand much more about the human heart and destiny than any other emotion." This may be the most shocking part of Staël's sensibility for the modern reader, the personalization of a Schillerian sense that "Man owes his greatest achievement to his aching sensation of unfulfilled destiny."[16]

The eighteenth century was rich in the identification and analysis of uncomfortable kinds of pleasure. Recent criticism has made familiar the literary manifestations of two of these in particular: the sublime and the ironic. However, while the importance of another—longing—has been impossible to ignore in thinking on romanticism, sentimentality, a related category, has typically had a more difficult time finding a sympathetic modern audience. Although it has had a distinguished place in literature since its earliest days, the pleasure of weeping—what Keats calls "a gentle luxury"—has come to be seen more recently as an immature response to suffering. The *formal* challenge of sentimentality has also presented problems; while the pleasures of the unpleasant have been explored in recent thinking on the sublime, the disgusting, and even the abject, it has proved difficult to make a place for literature that not only works by the evocation of cliché but makes claims on the emotions while doing so.[17] To ignore their commitment to unhappiness, however, is to erase the kind of intellectual and political work authors such as Staël and Landon saw themselves as doing in an era in which the generation of sympathy was recognized as a spark for social change, and in which irony had yet to acquire the character of symbolic resistance that it did with increasing force from the middle of the nineteenth century until its hypertrophy in our own day. The rote quality of the mode, however, which Landon captures so well (and Eliot too, in her way), makes it particularly difficult to assimilate to forms of reading that look for a developed narrative arc, while those emphasizing characterological identification in response to literature will be troubled at once by the unending misery of the principal narrative focus and by the strangely impersonal source of such pervasive sadness.[18]

Landon's "Improvisatrice" vividly demonstrates the formal effects of the place of (the imagination of) Italy in culture. The telescoping of causality that characterizes the text, the speed with which things happen as much as the brevity with which they are explained, all are constitutive parts of the work. There is no need to demonstrate, only to celebrate, the function of Italy as home of art, nature, beauty, and passion. Nor is there need to justify the relationship between genius and suffering. The poem's representation of misery and dissatisfaction is an element of art-romance convention and therefore part of the pleasure that shapes the form. Others also worked in the vein Landon explored. "Properzia Rossi" (1828) is just one of a number of lyrics by Felicia Hemans in which the impossibility of a woman being satisfied with fame rather than love is developed. Caroline Norton's "The Creole Girl" (1840) is not only an interesting instance of the transposition of the Mignon/half-breed figure of the passionate South to the emergent colonial space; it also features a late-arriving first-person narrator owing something to "The Improvisatrice." In its own way, however, there may be no more perfect representation of the underdetermined melancholy of the art romance than Anna Jameson's *Diary of an Ennuye* (1826). Although Jameson's travel guides eventually participated in the rise of tourism later in the century, this early volume of fiction, whose putative author spends the entirety of her travels pining for an unspecified lost love, only to finally die soon after reentering France from Italy, draws on the melancholy and underdeveloped causality typical of Staël, Landon, and Byron for its form. The death of the first-person "author" is a return to the demise of the title character of the "Improvisatrice." It is a translation of Landon into something approaching verisimilitude.[19]

BYRON: THE FADING OF THE PILGRIM

The influence of Goethe and Staël on the art romance is formative, though it is often camouflaged or so mediated that its presence may be missed. By contrast, for the nineteenth century travel and romance would always evoke Byron, particularly *Childe Harold's Pilgrimage* (1812–18), with its fantasy of the cultured voyager driven by urges at once inexplicable and unsatisfiable.[20] The influence of this work on the tradition is evident not only, and not even most powerfully, in the recurrence of Byronic characters such as Lorenzo, however, or in the theme of glorious melancholy decay. More abstract formal features that return in later texts include elaborations on *splitting* as an indication of the force of desire and of the crisis likely to be provoked by satisfaction. It is a strange double legacy the art romance inherited from Byron: not only the pilgrim of whom we learn so little beyond the vaguest references to his disappointment and exile and the Byronic narrator who, by the time the narrative reaches Italy makes himself known as the only significant consciousness of the poem, but the illustration of the crisis of arrival by the collapse of the very framework supporting the text. Lorenzo, in "The Improvisatrice," is self-evidently a Byronic figure, but there are a number of structural elements from *Childe Harold*, that Landon also deploys, and that remain vital to the art romance. Though the destruction of her title character may be the most striking Byronic trace in Landon's poem, the preoccupation with a doom or fate at once personal and more broadly cultural is perhaps more fundamental. It is the relationship between the collapse of the character and the doom of culture that drives the poem and determines its place in the art-romance tradition:

> Patience! and ye shall hear what he beheld
> In other lands, where he was doom'd to go:
> Lands that contain the monuments of Eld
> Ere Greece and Grecian arts by barbarous hands were quell'd.[21]

The pain of the Childe, which so often seems a matter of personal regret or remorse, is only tangentially related to the foreign travels it precipitates. But, what might it mean to think of his travels to antiquity as a doom, of the foreign as something he is fated to encounter? And how does the intersection of personal and cultural fate manifest itself formally in the play of narrative and character?

Italy in *Childe Harold* is a figure for tragic beauty that knows itself to be doomed. Given the social and political decline evident to any visitor, and the glaring contrast of that condition with the nations's historic function as source of Western culture, Italy takes on the intertwined characteristics of a tragic boon and a fated destruction that recur in accounts of the artist in the early nineteenth century:

> Italia! oh Italia! thou who hast
> The fatal gift of beauty, which became
> A funeral dower of present woes and past,
> On thy sweet brow is sorrow plough'd by shame,
> And annals graved in characters of flame.
> Oh God! that thou wert in thy nakedness
> Less lovely or more powerful, and could'st claim
> Thy right . . .   (4.370–77)

The artistic traveler in Italy participates in an extraordinarily overdetermined experience, as the doom of the voyager overlaps with that of the place through which he makes his way.

As might be expected, art-romance touches are particularly in evidence in canto 4, the account of the Childe in Italy published in 1818. Indeed, the most famous solecism in the poem is shaped by a characteristic confusion:

> I stood in Venice, on the Bridge of Sighs;
> A palace and a prison on each hand:
> I saw from out the wave her structures rise
> As from the stroke of the enchanter's wand:
> A thousand years their cloudy wings expand
> Around me, and a dying Glory smiles
> O'er the far time, when the many subject land
>   Look'd to the winged Lion's marble piles,
> Where Venice sate in state, thron'd on her hundred isles!   (4.1–9)

Smiles of death, prisons superimposed on palaces: Italian pleasure is confounded inextricably with pain in Byron's bold ambiguities. The prison that beckons on each hand, like the palace with which it coexists in both places, is yet another figure for the doom of the Childe's destination. The same fate awaits no matter in which direction the bridge is crossed. Byron's metaphors arrive at a kind of signifying incoherence at important points such as this one. The play with time is characteristically fantastic; it is as impossible to see a thousand years as it is for a magician to conjure up a city in an instant, but then the word used for the action of the enchanter's wand—"stroke"—is at least as often associated with a pen as with a wand, setting up a fruitful competition between the city as physical object and as imagined by the ambitious writer. The achievements of fantastic magician and contemporary author will in any case have their meaning in relation to a millennial time frame that might well trouble the imagination with thoughts of a dying glory.

To begin with Venice is to start in the middle of a trip to Italy, and to give attention to a city whose place in traditions of travel was not yet as central as it was to become (in part due to the influence of Byron himself). It is also, as Byron makes clear, to begin not with pure experience but with experience mediated through textual fantasy.[22] The "us" in the following stanza is the English *reader*, and "story" is *history*, the factual narrative of power that offers no real competition to literature:

> But unto us she hath a spell beyond
> Her name in story, and her long array
> Of mighty shadows, whose dim forms despond
> Above the dogeless city's vanish'd sway;
> Ours is a trophy which will not decay
> With the Rialto; Shylock and the Moor,
> And Pierre, can not be swept or worn away—
> The keystones of the Arch! though all were o'er
> For us repeopled were the solitary shore.   (4.28–36)

While it begins with the historical importance of Venice ("Her name in story"), the text quickly offers an alternative: a Venice invulnerable to decay because it is purely literary. The poem moves uncertainly as it tallies the relation between the power of fictive romance and the force of actual experience. Reality comes to the fore at the close of one stanza:

> Yet there are things whose strong reality
> Outshines our fairy-land; in shape and hues
> More beautiful than our fantastic sky,
> And the strange constellations which the Muse
> O'er her wild universe is skilful to diffuse.

But, at the opening of the very next stanza, "strong reality" is lost in fantasy and experience is confounded in dream. The force of the creative imagination allows no victory to "waking Reason," so much as a kind of unstable truce based not on the power of reality but on the fear of fantasy:

> I saw or dreamed of such,—but let them go—
> They came like truth, and disappeared like dreams;
> And whatsoe'er they were—are now but so:

> I could replace them if I would, still teems
> My mind with many a form which aptly seems
> Such as I sought for, and at moments found;
> Let these too go—for waking Reason deems
> Such over-weening phantasies unsound,
> And other voices speak, and other sights surround.   (4.50–63)

The native and the foreign, the real and the fantastic, experience and either imagination or memory—contradictory dyads drive the Italian canto in ways anticipated in earlier parts of the poem but given new force by the literary ambition that is so often Byron's theme. The weakness of even a "strong reality" in commanding the attention when the poet's teeming mind is also available for consideration is suggested by the elaborate and complexly involuted meditation on artistic ambition Byron includes in this long opening passage. "I twine / My hopes of being remembered in my line," the speaker declares, standing on a foreign bridge, but evidently not looking around him, "With my land's language" (4:76–78). As with Wilhelm Meister, whose wanderings culminate not in an arrival at an entirely new place but in a return to the art collection of his grandfather, so for the speaker of *Childe Harold* the arrival in Venice actually allows a return to the passions of childhood, which in his case are literary:

> I lov'd her from boyhood—she to me
> Was a fairy city of the heart,
> Rising like water-columns from the sea,
> Of joy the sojourn, and of wealth the mart;
> And Otway, Radcliffe, Schiller, Shakespeare's art,
> Had stamp'd her image in me, and even so,
> Although I found her thus, we did not part,
> Perchance even dearer in her day of woe,
> Than when she was a boast, a marvel, and a show.   (4.154–62)

To arrive in Venice is to find oneself back in the fantasy world of one's childhood. Each step into reality takes one further back into memory and fiction. This is the context in which Byron paradoxically locates his ambition for achievement in his "land's language."

As I suggested at the outset of this section, Landon's destruction of the narrator and main character of "The Improvisatrice" before the poem she narrates is complete has a precedent in the peculiar play of narrator and persona in *Childe Harold*. Indeed, the opening and close of canto 4 may be read as composing an intriguing asymmetrical pairing, the dying glory of Venice at the outset answered by the annihilation of the Childe, his absorption at the end into the scene of destruction itself. Then again, the Childe exists in a strangely tenuous relationship with the marked persona of the author, and even with the experiences described throughout the poem. In his "Preface to the First and Second Cantos," Byron introduces a poem largely descriptive of things he himself has seen, notably minimizing the role of his ostensible alter ego:

> A fictitious character is introduced for the sake of giving some connexion to the piece; which, however, makes no pretension to regularity. It has been suggested to me by friends, on whose opinions I set a high value, that in this fictitious character, "Childe Harold," I may incur the suspicion of having intended some real personage: this I beg leave, once for all, to disclaim—Harold is the child of imagination, for the purpose I have stated. In some very trivial particulars, and those merely local, there might be grounds for such a notion; but in the main points, I should hope, none whatever.[23]

At no point is Byron's engagement with the art-romance tradition more complex than in his self-conscious play with his narrative center. But, unlike Landon in this regard, he is quite clear on the volatile qualities of his notional alter ego. In the second stanza of canto 3, for instance, a first person celebrates the return to voyaging, but it is not the Childe: "Once more upon the waters! yet once more! / And the waves bound beneath me as a steed / That knows his rider" (3.10–12). The Childe, here as throughout, is evidently nothing but an instrument subject to the will of the speaker who forms the real center of the poem; hence the second stanza, where—as in Byron's preface—this hapless traveler is introduced as a fiction: "In my youth's summer I did sing of One, / The wandering outlaw of his own dark mind; / Again I seize the theme then but begun" (3.19–21). At no point is an attempt made to even suggest the illusion that the masterful writer (or rider) might be following the adventures of an independent character. Rather, it is emphasized throughout that the speaker conjures up and abandons the Childe at will.

Given that his presence is tenuous throughout, and always subject to the interventions of a more forcefully marked narrator, the question arises: why does Byron do away with the Childe in Rome? "With regard to the conduct of the last canto," Byron warns in his dedication to Hobhouse, "there will be found less of the pilgrim than in any of the preceding, and that little slightly, if at all, separated from the author speaking in his own person." Byron attributes this double disappearance—of character and of distinction from authorial self—to the unwillingness of the public to ever believe that there was a difference, "the very anxiety to preserve this difference, and disappointment at finding it unavailing, so far crushed my efforts in the composition, that I determined to abandon it altogether."[24] Ultimately, however, the poem itself, like the dedication, draws attention to the vaporous evanescence of its ostensible narrative center without offering any convincing clarification of his disappearance.

The explanation of the fate of the Childe must be sought elsewhere than in Byron's bland justifications, and the best evidence may well be found in its setting—at the climax of the description of Rome as mother of art. The immediate context for the end of the Childe is an account of the Belvedere statues at the Vatican, heart of Rome's artistic significance for Byron, as for his contemporaries. The representation of Laocoön's dignified suffering (stanza 160) is followed by three stanzas (161–63) on the *Apollo Belvedere*, a statue of a manifold fascination, whose subject and execution both inspire and trouble the narrator. Byron's lines celebrate the god of poetry, life, and light, but also the statue itself, a manifestation of ideal beauty, and of human creativity, or *poesis*:

> And if it be Prometheus stole from Heaven
> The fire which we endure, it was repaid
> By him to whom the energy was given
> Which this poetic marble hath array'd
> With an eternal glory—which, if made
> By human hands, is not of human thought;
> And Time himself hath hallowed it, nor laid
> One ringlet in the dust—nor hath it caught
> A tinge of years, but breathes the flame with which 'twas wrought.

This celebration of the enduring creation of a "poetic marble" immediately precedes the b/vanishing of the Childe. His shadowy form fades to insignificance between the fire stolen by Prometheus and the brilliant light of the sun god:

> But where is he, the Pilgrim of my song,
> The being who upheld it through the past?
> Methinks he cometh late and tarries long.
> He is no more—these breathings are his last;
> His wanderings done, his visions ebbing fast,
> And he himself as nothing:—if he was
> Aught but a phantasy, and could be class'd
> With forms which live and suffer—let that pass—
> His shadow fades away into Destruction's mass . . .

The long and elaborate dismissal of the Childe recapitulates key themes and even terms that were presented as quite personal for the speaker at the opening of the canto. As the language of "let them go" and "let these too go" returns with "let that pass," it is difficult to avoid the suggestion that real anxiety may be hiding behind a cavalier tone. Indeed, the "overweening phantasies unsound" the speaker had dismissed earlier, along with so "many a form" teeming through his mind, are now found personi-

Apollo Belvedere, Rome, Musei Vaticani. Photo: Alinari/Art Resource, New York.

fied in the Childe himself: "if he was / Aught but a phantasy, and could be class'd / With forms which live and suffer" (see 4:55–63).

At the moment of his end the Childe takes over qualities at risk of being overwhelmed by Italy from the outset. After all, "he cometh late and tarries long" describes the condition of Byron's speaker at the beginning of the canto, considering the millennial city as he lingers on the Bridge of Sighs. As the next enjambed stanza leading to the demise of the Childe develops the crepuscular theme of the preceding, the dying glory beheld over Venice at the very opening becomes ever more broadly generalized, to the point that it threatens far more than the spectral wanderer:

> Which gathers shadow, substance, life, and all
> That we inherit in its mortal shroud,
> And spreads the dim and universal pall
> Through which all things grow phantoms; and the cloud
> Between us sinks and all which ever glowed,
> Till Glory's self is twilight, and displays
> A melancholy halo scarce allowed
> To hover on the verge of darkness; rays
> Sadder than saddest night, for they distract the gaze . . .

In the context of the Promethean artistic achievement that precedes his disappearance, it is impossible not to be reminded of the literary ambition that was identified with Venice at the opening of the canto. The beautiful sunset of a thousand years absorbs the Childe, darker by several shades, as the long sentence finds its lethal close:

> And send us prying into the abyss,
> To gather what we shall be when the frame
> Shall be resolv'd to something less than this
> Its wretched essence; and to dream of fame,
> And wipe the dust from off the idle name
> We never more shall hear,—but never more,
> Oh, happier thought! can we be made the same:
> It is enough in sooth that *once* we bore
> These fardels of the heart—the heart whose sweat was gore.
>
> (4.1459–94; emphasis in the original)

Byron's stanzas on Italy's political situation come as a kind of relief from these dark imaginations of the fate of the human body and of artistic achievement in time before the last gasp of the vanishing Childe is heard:

> But I forget.—My Pilgrim's shrine is won,
> And he and I must part,— so let it be,—
> His task and mine alike are nearly done.   (4.1567–69)

If, as Patricia Parker has pointed out, the paradoxical project of romance is a "quest for, and simultaneous distancing of, an end or presence," travel is in some ways the natural habitat of the form, while arrival is its unachievable antithesis.[25] The pilgrim reaches his end, but never quite arrives. Indeed, his tenuous hold on existence is loosened once and for all by the prospect of arrival. Byron is, as always, cavalier and offhand in his treatment of the alter ego, but there is something chilling in the cheerful way he sends the Childe to his doom, for all the world like Hamlet dispatching Rosencrantz and Guildenstern to theirs, carrying the letters sealing their own execution. But at least the Prince of Denmark is saving his own life. Is Byron?

Arrival is unimaginable in the poem, and awful because it raises the specter at once of death and of an impossible return to origins, both of which in turn are characteristic features encoded into the cultural force of Rome itself. And so it is not the Hellenic glory of the *Apollo Belvedere* that sets the tone at the end of the canto, but two Roman images of far greater pathos, that of the *Dying Gladiator* and of "Roman Charity." The first, a pathetic representation of a foreigner at the end of his wanderings, visions ebbing fast as he swoons to death, is a figure far more reminiscent of the vulnerable Childe than the Apollo, with his matchless glory (see stanzas 140–42). The second, a hallucinatory image of a young woman breastfeeding her father in prison in order to save him from starvation, is not a monument at all, but a vision evoked by the narrator in the chuch of San Nicola in Carcere. Based on a scene from classical sources that was popular in painting of the period, this theme that reverses at once erotic and familial sources in an abject return to a maternal body has a surprising presence in the poem (running from stanzas 148 to 151). Hobhouse, for one, is notably preoccupied with the legend. Although Byron locates the vision in the church said to have been built over the prison where the act of charity took place, the *Historical Illustrations* features thirteen pages devoted to the antiquarian exercise of identifying the precise location of the event—the principal result of the intervention being that the image becomes ever more diffused through the city.[26]

> . . . I see them full and plain—
> An old man, and a female young and fair,
> Fresh as a nursing mother, in whose vein
> The blood is nectar:—but what doth she there,
> With her unmantled neck, and bosom white and bare?
> .   .   .   .
> . . . here youth offers to old age the food,
> The milk of his own gift:—it is her sire
> To whom she renders back the debt of blood

Born with her birth. No; he shall not expire
While in those warm and lovely veins the fire
Of health and holy feelings can provide
Great Nature's Nile . . .

   .   .   .   .

Drink, drink and live, old man! Heaven's realm holds no such tide.

(4.1328–50)

William Galperin has noted the relation of this moment to Byron's treatment of Harold's mother, someone so unforgettable that he avoids parting from her: "Childe Harold had a mother—not forgot, / Though parting from that mother he did shun " (1.82–84). There is no Mignon in *Childe Harold*, but Byron does feature two young women who shape the longing and the motion of the poem while standing outside it, Ianthe at the outset and Ada at the (re)beginning of canto 3. "Is thy face like thy mother's, my fair child! / Ada! sole daughter of my house and heart?" (3.1–2). One way or another, a young woman stands at the door of Italy, one whose role is at once erotic and sentimental, tantalizing even at apparently wholesome moments. The question asked in canto 3 might be rephrased for canto 4, "is thy *breast* like *my* mother's, my fair child?" The deep challenge of Rome is symbolized in the suggestive image of "Roman Charity," so that the arrival of the pilgrim takes place around an eroticized return to inescapable sources that shades the sentimental paternity of the earlier cantos even as it evokes a form of fundamental nourishment in the frightening dark.

As the Bridge of Sighs that leads the reader into Italy in *Childe Harold* has a palace and a prison on each hand, it is impossible to choose a crossing that does not offer both glory and the prospect of captivity—and possibly even execution. While Byron anticipates the nineteenth century's growing celebration of Venice as a locus of mysteriously tantalizing if dangerous beauty, his representation of Rome as the mother of creative achievement is quite typical of the period. Still, the glory of this capital of art is as haunted by death as Venice's is with imprisonment: "Oh Rome! my country! city of the soul! / The orphans of the heart must turn to thee, / Lone mother of dead Empires!" (4.694–96). The mother to whom the speaker could not say good-bye in canto 1 returns, but her children are dead: "The Niobe of nations! there she stands / Childless and crownless, in her voiceless woe" (4.703–4). Niobe is not barren, of course, but a mother of great fecundity whose pride leads to the destruction of her children—her sons shot to death by an angry Apollo, her daughters by Artemis—and a paralyzing stony grief. When they are associated with Niobe's metamorphosis, the pillars of Rome become emblems of an unquenchable grief and the

Dying Gladiator, Rome, Musei Capitolini. Photo: Alinari/Art Resource, New York.

destruction of apparent fertility. Home of orphans, fruitful mother of dead children, voiceless mourner: the city offers a manifold intertwining of maternity and death along with a silence that may well be read as a troubling inspiration for the poet. Byron has in mind the faded glory of Rome's empire, but, as the apostrophe ("*My* country") suggests, he is less concerned with contemporary Italian political aspirations than with the recognitions or memories of the modern traveler:

> . . . Rome is as the desart, where we steer
> Stumbling o'er recollections; now we clap
> Our hands and cry "Eureka!" it is clear—
> When but some false mirage of ruins rises near.   (4.726–29)

Wandering through the desert, "marble wilderness," or "[c]haos of ruins" of the city (4.710, 718) the poet's memories return to him as mirages. These memories are, of course, not simply personal but cultural. (It was not Wilhelm, after all, who bought the art collection that shaped him, but his grandfather.)

In the figure of the dying gladiator, hovering forever at the point of his demise, the poem offers a stand-in for the vanishing Childe and compensation for his colorless destruction. The gladiator thinks of his children and their mother as he is not simply killed, but "[b]utchered to make a Roman holiday" (4.1267). The narrator cannot help but take personally the (re)-discovery that this place of beauty is a locus of violent death. Indeed, the terms of his self-reflexive disturbance (his voice and feet becoming too noisy) indicate a trouble not simply for his moral sensibility, but for him as *poet*:

> But here, where Murder breathed her bloody stream;
>   And here, where buzzing nations choked the ways,
>
>   . . . .
> My voice sounds much . . .
>
>   . . . .
> . . . my steps seem echoes strangely loud.   (4.1270–78)

The description of the Colosseum, at once a place of death and of design perfection, links modern and classic achievement by drawing attention to the beauty created from fragments removed from the admired structure. Similarly, the account of the Pantheon that follows identifies at once an emblem of classical achievement and of the celebration of modern genius, but the famous oculus at the top of the building invites another return of the disturbing glory of the sun:

> Relic of nobler days and noblest arts!
>   Despoiled yet perfect, with thy circle spreads

A holiness appealing to all hearts—
To art a model; and to him who treads
Rome for the sake of ages, Glory sheds
Her light through thy sole aperture . . .

. . . .

And they who feel for genius may repose
Their eyes on honoured forms, whose busts around them close.

(4.1315–23)

Byron's description of the Colosseum and Pantheon, along with the attendant questions of creativity and death that these structures raise for the poet, lead directly into the vision of "Roman Charity," of a mothering daughter hidden in what would become the church of San Nicola in Carcere. The shadow of the prison (or *carcere*) that was part of the Italian experience from the opening of the canto returns at this culminating point in the experience of Rome. Yet again, the city becomes a place of uncanny mothering, one symbolized not only by a childless Niobe and a deadly Apollo, but by a mother nurturing an imprisoned father instead of her own child.

In the unsatisfiable desires written in romance narratives the nineteenth century found ways of describing the difficult relationship between longing or ambition and arrival or achievement. In the art romance every beginning is never simply personal, every arrival is fraught because it is a return to something not fully recognized, though never completely forgotten. The splitting that is characteristic of the mode makes visible the irreconcilable relationship between aspiration and achievement, even as it mollifies its effect by taking it outside of one individual. But the division of characters also serves to identify the essentially external sources of deep personal motivations. Because of the depth of the longing written into the art romance—both the force of its passion and the unreachable earliness of its presence—much in the mode also reflects the anxiety provoked by approaching parental desire. In "A Disturbance of Memory on the Acropolis" (discussed in the introduction), and in the *Interpretation of Dreams* (the topic of chapter 6) Freud identifies a number of sources for the fear generated by gratifying an urge the parent was unable to satisfy or even fully recognize: to do so weakens the parent by demonstrating the child's power to go further, but it also places the child's desire in very close relation to that of the parent, making that of the child secondary and embarrassing or that of the parent recognizably inadequate or unrealized. While the play with mothers and children may seem too self-evident to require elucidation in stories about cultural origins, the typically Oedipal or otherwise incestuous form relationships take in the art romance should be no more surprising.

Dawn, Not Sunset: The Brownings on Arrival

What would the pilgrim's uncanny moment of arrival look like if it were visible to the reader? The culmination of another Childe's pilgrimage might help us to see why Byron cannot bring his protagonist to an end. Robert Browning fills in the blank of the Childe's fate after his abandonment by the narrator who had summoned him into being and left him in a world of shadows and phantoms. As his poem begins, Childe *Roland* has learned to mistrust success and hope for failure. The ancient cripple who guides him to the culmination of his search, and whom he mistrusts from the outset, may be read as a monstrous image of the earlier poet: Byron's club foot and the lyre that stands in for his song throughout *Childe Harold* are transposed in the first lines into indications of deception and paralysis: "My first thought was, he lied in every word, / That hoary cripple, with malicious eye / Askance to watch the working of his lie."[27]

Guilt, self-disgust, uncertainty, and loathing are the feelings of Browning's Childe as his pilgrimage reaches an end; his environment is a landscape of unrelieved misery and disorientation in which death, sexual confusion, and baffled transgression are written into the very terrain he traverses. Although the gloom of the poem is so unrelieved as to make selection of a moment of crisis or change seem a fruitless enterprise, it may be worth noting one liminal instance, something that changes the "train" of the Childe's thoughts. As he fords a "sudden little river" overhung with low vegetation, Childe Roland fears putting his foot upon a dead man's cheek, or finding his spear tangled in his hair or beard. Instead, he kills something that may have been a rat but in fact sounded like a baby shrieking (109–26). While the confusion of beard and baby blurs the boundaries of age and offers a hint of the reversal that shapes "Roman Charity," the suggestively gynophobic quality of this nightmarish encounter (the fear of the entangled spear answered by a baby's cry) reminds the reader that the uncanny in Freud has its ultimate source in the sense of return afforded by the experience of the female genital organs or, more generally, in the repressed recognition that the lover's sexual core may well be a place we have been before.

Childe Roland crosses the river at the culmination of his reminiscences about the disappointments and failures of earlier knightly questers. He finds no relief on the other side, of course, but only more misery and lack of clarity: "just as far as ever from the end! / Nought in the distance but the evening, nought / To point my footstep further!" (157–59). What Byron calls "the verge of darkness" at the moment of arrival is Browning's theme throughout. In the later poem, the final recognition is humiliating and marks the end of the poem except for an action that entails not chivalric combat but the making of music. The Childe puts his horn to his lips and blows to announce arrival and therefore an end. The moment he makes music he vanishes as the narrator of his own poem, to be replaced by third-person narrator who reinforces the citational force of the poem.

"Childe Roland to the Dark Tower Came"—who speaks at the end of the poem? Not the voice that has spoken the other 203 lines. The first person disappears into the title of the poem, which is itself identified as a quotation from Shakespeare. The moment of arrival is given voice by a mysterious speaker—or, rather, the mysterious intrusion of a new voice carrying nothing other than a quotation serves to announce that the problem of arrival is a problem of sources. Browning's editors point out that the rest of the traditional ballad Edgar quotes in the passage from Lear involves the "blood of an Englishman"—suggesting that this moment of arrival needs to be taken more as an end than a beginning.[28] As in *Childe Harold* and "The Improvisatrice," the splitting of a marked central consciousness at the close is the formal indication of displaced fear at a moment that is very much like death. In one instant the Childe is not only overwhelmed by the names of the daunting predecessors he suddenly hears all around him, but he has a vision of the same men, gathered together as threatening witnesses of his failure: "There they stood, ranged along the hill-sides, met / To view the last of me, a living frame / For one more picture!" (199–201). The Childe's quest, it turns out, is to culminate in a moment of music making. But the only sound that accompanies the blowing of the trumpet is someone else's words, and he becomes a work of art ("one more picture") at the instant of his demise.

I have focused on Browning's poem as a particularly abject representation of the end of a quest, but, in considering the special case of getting to *Italy*, one might also cite Browning's 1868 "Roman murder story," *The Ring and the Book*, a narrative structured around a hellish, dangerous road that culminates in Rome as seat of judgment and death. The association of Italy with death has an even longer pedigree in English letters than the nation's association with genius, and both are at play in the art romance. The commemoration of defunct greatness that recurs throughout canto 4 of *Childe Harold* is only further underlined by notes in which Alfieri, Ariosto, Petrarch, Machiavelli, Dante, Boccaccio, Michelangelo, and Galileo all receive their due—as does Staël. A reference to Santa Croce in Florence (4.478) leads to the following homage:

> This name will recall the memory, not only of those whose tombs have raised the Santa Croce into the center of pilgrimage, the Mecca of Italy, but of her whose eloquence was poured over the illustrious ashes, and whose voice is now as mute as those she sung. CORINNA is no more. . . . Corinna has ceased to be a woman—she is only an author.[29]

Italy is at once the cradle of genius and its grave in the art-romance tradition, a combined destiny Byron captures in the figure of Niobe, bereft mother of dead children, Hazlitt in the form of a lovely but dangerous Sphinx.[30]

Given the inescapable self-reflexivity of a mode that is at its heart a fantasy of artistic achievement, that is, indeed, a literary manifestation of the fascination with genius that characterized the decades around the turn of the nineteenth century, it is little wonder that biography was an important feature in the reception of the art romance. It is impossible to separate the response to Byron's alter egos from the phenomenon of his fame and reputation, and I cited earlier Landon's response to those who read her own experiences into the heartbreaks (and deaths) of her heroines. Landon's judicious warning offered no protection against the trend, however, and her own mysterious death on the way to Africa after an unfortunate marriage only contributed to the tendency to identify her with her countless heartbroken travelers. The effect of Byron's early death abroad was particularly powerful because, like the tragic ends of Keats and Shelley, it fit into a preexistent pattern in which foreign travel, disappointment, and death formed part of the constellation in which genius was understood to appear. Indeed, Shelley's *Adonais* finds what comfort it can offer in the ties linking creativity, death, and Italy. Keats's demise in Rome is presented as profoundly appropriate; after all, the city is the "high Capital, where kingly Death / Keeps his pale court in beauty and decay." Keats's genius *and* the death that marked its end are understood to have purchased "[a] grave among the eternal." Italy's claims as home of past greatness and as land of natural beauty are brought together in a manner evocative at once of the end and of the beginning of Landon's "Improvisatrice" in Shelley's otherwise incongruous description of the "blue Italian day" as a particularly suitable place to sepulcher genius—a "fitting charnel-roof."[31] The injunction to "Die, / If thou wouldst be with that which thou dost seek!" is followed immediately by a *place* in which to carry out this morbid program: "Follow where all is fled!—Rome's azure sky" (52.464–66). Byron is the first mourner introduced into the text, conflated with the unsatisfiable figure he had designed for himself in Childe Harold, "The Pilgrim of Eternity" (30.264). As he enters the poem, this place that is Rome and death together takes on the shadowy force and peculiar transhistorical solidarity of Shelley's account of poetic power in his *Defence of Poetry*. The eternity in which poetic achievement lives for Shelley and the tragic life that so often marks the actual existence of the poet come together when Keats becomes one of "the enduring dead" (38.336)

Before concluding this chapter with a brief consideration of Elizabeth Barrett Browning's *Aurora Leigh* (1857), the century's most ambitious challenge to the art-romance tradition, it is worth noting that the biographical element that comes into play in the reception and in the self-conceptualization of both Brownings contains in itself an important revision of the mode. To put the matter simply is to highlight the symbolic play of human desire typical of the form: the Brownings do not pine; they marry. They do not long for an unseen Italy; they move there. Barrett Browning does not die outside of the possibility of consummation; she gives birth on Italian soil. I place these well-known facts about this famous marriage alongside the fictional tropes that they challenge because to do so highlights not simply an accidental difference but the manner in which the Brownings are shaped by a relationship to Italy that they inherit but do not leave unchallenged. It bears saying that much that differs in their experience of Italy is due not simply to their own will but to changes in culture that allowed their lives abroad to take the shapes they did. Nevertheless, the escape from arbitrary paternal authority instantiated in their elopement in itself rewrites the art romance, or at least takes a form from the romance and drives it toward satisfaction rather than catastrophe.

The force of the real is a constant preoccupation of Robert Browning's major poems—from the biographically inflected antiasceticism of "Fra Lipo Lippi" to the insistent and multiform materiality of *The Ring and the Book*. But Italy has a special role in the preoccupation with represented reality that motivates both authors. When Barrett Browning rewrites the art-romance form that had been so important to women's creative self-imagination, she not only turns to the difficult task of celebrating fulfillment, but she does so with a deep commitment to the physical body; sexuality, birth, and injury runs through *Aurora Leigh* in ways that would have been impossible to imagine in her predecessors. But it is in her commitment to fulfillment that Barrett Browning most directly challenges the tradition. Repeatedly in the Italian sections of the poem motifs from the tradition are incorporated and deflected. The deep importance of the art romance for Barrett Browning is demonstrated by her constant recourse to its elements, even as she emphatically deflects the outcomes that characterize the mode.

At its heart, *Aurora Leigh*'s revision of the art romance entails the return of the maternal displaced in so many fantasies of impossible arrival.[32] "I write. My mother was a Florentine." In the same line the poet evokes the tradition of Italy as the home of genius and revises it by not leaving out the mother. To say that the poem does not leave out the mother, however, is not to say that the mother lives. Indeed, the death of the mother takes place with the speed that characterizes everything important in the art romance. We barely meet her before she is gone, snatched away in the very sentence that introduces her:

> I write. My mother was a Florentine,
> Whose rare blue eyes were shut from seeing me
> When scarcely I was four years old, my life,
> A poor spark snatched up from a failing lamp
> Which went out therefore. (1.29–33)[33]

The power of the absent is paradoxically indicated by an often gruesome materiality, as the belabored presence of Aurora's dead brings to the surface the dark substrate underlying and motivating the mode she inhabits. Our poet's birth is the death of her mother, a fact that gives shape to the formative longing she cannot fail to recognize:

> The mother's rapture slew her. If her kiss
> Had left a longer weight upon my lips
> It might have steadied the uneasy breath,
> And reconciled and fraternised my soul
> With the new order. As it was, indeed,
> I felt a mother-want about the world. (1.35–40)

We may understand the opening passages of the poem to fill in the melancholy of the Improvisatrice and give it a shape. The fated sadness the earlier poet never stopped to explain is motivated in this instance by the demise of Aurora's mother, which is a double loss, her own and her father's. Indeed, the death of the mother at the moment of her rapture (it is a long moment, as she is slain at her daughter's birth but only dies four years later) allows the possibility of an eroticization of the father-daughter bond that will culminate at his own death, though it will not end there. She learns to desire from him—and his desire is addressed to a dead mother she is understood to have killed.

Browning uses Aurora's breeziest style to describe the meeting of her mother and father—or, rather, the father's transforming vision of the mother—because it is an event in every way foreordained. It is a return of the prototypical encounter of cold North and passionate South, or rather of the North's recognition of its own passion in the face of the South.

> My father was an austere Englishman,
> Who, after a dry life-time spent at home
> In college-learning, law, and parish talk,
> Was flooded with a passion unaware,
> His whole provisioned and complacent past
> Drowned out from him that moment. As he stood
> In Florence . . . (1.65–71)

The close apposition that had indicated the role of the city as source of creativity—"I write. My mother was a Florentine"—is at work here also. Florence: writing; Florence: passion. There is no need to elaborate further on such well-established links. There is something childlike in the mother when first encountered, though she is participating in a ritual at once religious and almost grotesquely suggestive, so that the father's desire is at the same time transfiguring, inescapably sensual, and closely related to the passion of Aurora herself:

> There drifted past him (scarcely marked enough
> To move his comfortable island-scorn)
> A train of priestly banners, cross and psalm,
> The white-veiled rose-crowned maidens holding up
> Tall tapers, weighty for such wrists, aslant
> To the blue luminous tremor of the air,
> And letting drop the white wax as they went
> To eat the bishop's wafer at the church;
> From which long trail of chanting priests and girls,
> A face flashed like a cymbal on his face,
> And shook with silent clangour brain and heart,
> Transfiguring him to music.   (1.78–89)

Passion, birth, and death are compacted together repeatedly in the first book of *Aurora Leigh*. A similar unelaborated causality characterizes the father's desire, the mother's death, and Aurora's birth, all of which are indicated almost as quickly as the verse will allow. That the speed of events is closely related to such inexplicable turns as the demise of Ianthe upon her marriage to Lorenzo in "The Improvisatrice" is confessed by an anxiously reiterated "thus" that is unable to indicate any causal relation, only a mode of action:

> . . . *Thus*, even *thus*,
> He too received his sacramental gift
> With eucharistic meanings; for he loved.
>
> And *thus* beloved, she died. I've heard it said
> That but to see him in the first surprise
> Of widower and father, nursing me,
> Unmothered little child of four years old,
>
> . . . .
> . . . would almost make the stones
> Cry out for pity. . . .   (1.89–101; emphases added)

The death of the mother allows for the father's illusion that Aurora's further nurturing will be carried out by nature, like that of some Greek hero transposed to the hills outside Florence. "[U]nmothered babes," he thinks in an evocation of a classical motif that is also one of the poem's earliest elaborations on the symbolic force of the breast, "had need / Of mother nature more than others use, / And Pan's white goats, with udders warm and full / Of mystic contemplations" (1.112–15). It is not a pastoral idyll Aurora finds in the country, however, but a monstrous inspiration. A baby without a mother will certainly need alternative forms of nourishment, but the brutal creativity Barrett Browning ascribes to Pan in "A Musical Instrument" (1860) suggests that lurking behind this passage is the transgressive, even disgusting, quality unavoidable in the image of a child suckled by an animal. In any case, if the pain and alienation that are the theme in the shorter poem are not developed here, what is emphasized is not plenitude, but lack—"unmothered babes" and "need."

While she learns about books and about love (as unsatisfiable longing) from her father, the lesson of a posthumously painted portrait is the absent mother's principal contribution to Aurora's *Bildung*:

> . . . I, a little child, would crouch
> For hours upon the floor with knees drawn up,
> And gaze across them, half in terror, half
> In adoration, at the picture there,—
> That swan-like supernatural white life,
> Just sailing upward from the red stiff silk
> Which seemed to have no part in it, nor power
> To keep it from quite breaking out of bounds.
> For hours I sate and stared. Asssunta's awe
> And my poor father's melancholy eyes
> Still pointed that way. That way, went my thoughts
> When wandering beyond sight. . . .   (1.135–46)

The entrancing image of a dead woman is a principal gothic motif; one might even expect it to be veiled in mystery so early in the narrative. The only mystery about the portrait in *Aurora Leigh*, however, is the reason Barrett Browning makes its associations so grotesque:

> . . . And as I grew
> In years, I mixed, confused, unconsciously,
> Whatever I last read or heard or dreamed,
> Abhorrent, admirable, beautiful,
> Pathetical, or ghastly, or grotesque,
> With still that face . . . which did not therefore change,
> But kept the mystic level of all forms
> Hates, fears, and admirations, was by turns
> Ghost, fiend, and angel, fairy, witch, and sprite,
> A dauntless Muse who eyes a dreadful Fate,
> A loving Psyche who loses sight of Love,
> A still Medusa with mild milky brows
> All curdled and all clothed upon with snakes

Whose slime falls fast as sweat will; or anon
Our Lady of the Passion, stabbed with swords
Where the Babe sucked; or Lamia in her first
Moonlighted pallor, ere she shrunk and blinked
And shuddering wriggled down to the unclean;
Or my own mother, leaving her last smile
In her last kiss upon the baby-mouth
My father pushed down on the bed for that,—
Or my dead mother, without smile or kiss,
Buried at Florence.   (1.146–68; ellipsis in the original)

"Buried at Florence" is the end of a remarkable sentence that attempts to encapsulate a range of passionate responses containing a surprising paucity of what is "admirable, beautiful," and a great deal of the abjectly "abhorrent." Blood, and sweat, snakes, and slime—all mix with the mother's milk in this image shaped by the brutal forced affection of a father pushing his young daughter's face onto the dead or dying lips he loves. "Buried at Florence," the passionate transfiguration of the father "as he stood in Florence," and "I write. My mother was a Florentine"—these are the three points of the triangle that makes up the force of the city in the art romance: passion and creativity, but also death. The Muse who eyes a dreadful fate may be the most puzzling reference in the passage, as it does not refer to any clear classical antecedent in literature. It does serve, however, to highlight not only the interplay of destiny and creativity to be found in Florence, but the disturbing force of fate itself.

Aurora's mother is buried in Santa Croce, the final resting place—as Byron and Hobhouse had reminded the world—of Germaine de Staël. In the Muse who eyes a figure for a troubling destiny—as is the case for all of the other images she identifies in the portrait—we find an identification of Aurora herself, a girl whose Muse-shaped future depends on a preponderance of early loss and dread. And so it is that the death of the mother at birth is answered by that of the father at puberty:

. . . I was just thirteen,
Still growing like the plants from unseen roots
In tongue-tied Springs,—and suddenly awoke
To full life and life's needs and agonies
With an intense, strong, struggling heart beside
A stone-dead father. Life, struck sharp on death,
Makes awful lightning. His last word was, "Love-"
"Love, my child, love, love!"—(then he had done with grief)
"Love, my child." Ere I answered he was gone,
And none was left to love in all the world.   (1.205–14)

It would be inaccurate to understand Aurora too simply here, to take this passage to mean that the love that the father encourages is made more difficult by his death. The force of the lesson is rather strengthened by the loss of its source. Indeed, the ambiguous language that has Aurora waking up beside her father suggests an intimacy greater than one might expect between a father and a girl at puberty and supports the idea that his absence may well be necessary for her to learn the poem's lesson of love.

Although the early parts of *Aurora Leigh* appear to be driven by the hypertrophy of longing that typically characterizes the art romance, the poem is remarkable for the absolute and self-conscious refusal of key elements in the tradition. While the first book of Barrett Browning's epic elaborates on images and issues familiar from Goethe to Staël and Landon, the rest of the work offers an alternative: a fantasy of satisfaction, arrival, returned affection, and life that we may read as a revision of the commitment to disappointment that runs through the art romance. Aurora is identified with the dawn, of course, and in that way, as in so many others, she makes a contrast with the long sunset that preoccupied Byron. And so it is that by the end of the epic the poet will not only be recognized for her genius; she will be allowed to win the clear commitment and presence of Romney, the man she loves. Indeed, among the simple novelties of this text in the tradition is that Aurora will be allowed to *live* past the end of the story.

Barrett Browning includes key elements of the art romance while translating their significance or shifting their aim. The poem offers a number of rivals for Romney's affections, including one, Marian Erle, who revises the nineteenth century's tale of the fallen woman simply by not being driven from the narrative on becoming pregnant out of wedlock. In the alternative therapeutic sisterhood Aurora establishes when she finds Marian, we may read a rewriting of the sisterly rivalry that runs through the art romance, but also a new relationship to the maternal and the real. Marian's motherhood is a revision not only of cliches about fallenness but of the presence of the mother that is perpetually deferred in the art romance itself. The imagination of creativity in Barrett Browning's poem is as consistently maternal as it is insistently physical. "Shall I hope / To speak my poems in mysterious tune / With man and nature," Aurora asks, before turning to an astonishingly corporeal account of what it might mean to be in tune with both:

> . . . with the lava-lymph
> That trickles from successive galaxies
> Still drop by drop adown the finger of God
> In still new worlds?—with summer-days in this,
> That scarce dare breathe they are so beautiful?

With spring's delicious trouble in the ground,
Tormented by the quickened blood of roots,
And softly pricked by golden crocus-sheaves
In token of the harvest-time of flowers?
With winters and with autumns,—and beyond,
With the human heart's large seasons,—when it hopes
And fears, joys, grieves, and loves?—with all that strain
Of sexual passion, which devours the flesh
In a sacrament of souls? with mother's breasts,
Which, round the new-made creatures hanging there,
Throb luminous and harmonious like pure spheres?—
With multitudinous life . . .   (5.1–19)

Sexual passion as a sacrament, the breast as emblem of life—these are characteristic images in a poem in which the ambition to write an epic is described as the aspiration to "catch / Upon the burning lava of a song / The full-veined, heaving, double-breasted Age." The breast is a figure not only for life but for the undeniable power of the most primal debts. The ambition Barrett Browning describes is that after ages "May touch the impress with reverent hand, and say / 'Behold,—behold the paps we all have sucked! / This bosom seems to beat still, or at least / It sets ours beating' " (5.214–21). Later in the same book, Aurora describes a sumptuous edition of Homer with an extended metaphor that turns the poet's lines into grotesque infants floating "in cream, as rich as any sucked / From Juno's breasts," while "with their spondaic prodigious mouths / They lap the lucent margins as babe-gods" (5:1250–53).

If the creative act is associated with maternity, then the appropriate response to admirable art may well be like that of a child to a mother. Italy itself shares in this maternal quality, offering its succor to infant desire rediscovered by the adult:

    And now I come, my Italy,
    My own hills! are you 'ware of me, my hills,
    How I burn toward you? do you feel to-night
    The urgency and yearning of my soul,
    As sleeping mothers feel the sucking babe
    And smile?   (5.1266–71)

As the early books made clear, however, Italy is in no way simply a place of maternal comfort, and the family is the site of a number of productive losses. Mothers are shaping figures for creativity in part because of the uncanny qualities summed up in the portrait whose dark shapes determined so much of Aurora's childhood, and Italy's relation to creativity is simlarly impossible to divorce from its function as a place of death or absence The lava on which the age will be captured has its source, after all, in volcanic violence, and indeed, the image, evocative of Felicia Hemans's "Image in Lava" of 1827, gains its poignancy from the dead, whose relics the lava preserved even as it destroyed them.

When she arrives at Genoa and is moved to declare, "I did not think, 'my Italy,' / I thought, 'my father!' O my father's house, / Without his presence!" (7.490–92), Barrett Browning's heroine is giving voice not only to her own memory and grief but to a more general recognition of the link between Italy and fruitful death:

> . . . Italy,
> . . . I have heard thee crying through my life,
> Thou piercing silence of ecstatic graves,
> Men call that name! (5.1193–96).

Such an exclamation evokes qualities recurrent in the art romance, even as Barrett Browning introduces her remarkable novelty, the fact that her heroine does not die, that the long moment in which she should fade and expire from disappointed passion never happens. Instead, her love interest actually follows her to Italy, so that together they may revise a number of sad endings.

Romney arrives a broken man, blinded like Charlotte Brontë's Rochester, before he can consummate his affection. When he humbles himself to Aurora as "My Italy of women" (8.358), he is referring to the association of that nation with convalescence, but may we not hear the later poet writing what Staël never did for Corinne (or Italy), a recognition from a lover and not just from an adoring crowd? In the course of their reconciliation in the final book, Barrett Browning evokes even as she revises the art-romance tradition so that Aurora herself becomes the orphaned girl brought into the affective ambit of a young boy and fated to become his wife; she is at once Ianthe and the Improvisatrice, Lucille as well as her sister, Corinne:

> From the day
> I had brought to England my poor searching face,
> (An orphan even of my father's grave)
> He had loved me, watched me, watched his soul in mine,
> Which in me grew and heightened into love.
> For he, a boy still, had been told the tale
> Of how a fairy bride from Italy
> With smells of oleanders in her hair,
> Was coming through the vines to touch his hand;
> Whereat the blood of boyhood on the palm
> Made sudden heats. (9.760–70)

Aurora's love is rewritten at the close as a fated resolution of a foreordained childhood romance, one driven at once by the physical passion of a hand full of blood liable to take the human heat of another's touch and by the fantastic triangulation suggested in the tale Romney had heard of a "fairy bride from Italy." And this is what Barrett Browning, audacious student of the art romance, does with a mode that has found so many routes by which to frustrate desire. She reads it closely and revises it to make satisfaction possible. Thus, in one of those Staëlian moments in her poem in which she meditates on national character, Aurora offers some thoughts on the distinctions between French and English character that conclude with the following careful calibration of her use of "us" when she speaks of the English:

> With us, I say, though I'm of Italy
> My mother's birth and grave, by father's grave
> And memory; let it be,—a poet's heart
> Can swell to a pair of nationalities,
> However ill-lodged in a woman's breast. (6.48–52)

In a few brief lines this passage brings together key claims that motivate the poem as a whole. Aurora celebrates the fruitful discomfort inherent in the intertwining roles of poet, woman, and cultural hybrid. The function of Italy as source is none the weaker for including death (one birth is followed by two graves). A pair of nationalities is not too much for the poet. Indeed, it is the combination that swells the heart—the organ that beats beneath a woman's breast—moving in productive, if difficult coexistence.

In the art romance Italy consistently stands for the possibility of connection with the sources of creativity. But the promise of the nation is perpetually deferred. Arrival comes to be associated with death not simply because longing itself is the perfect driving mechanism of the mode, but because it suggests a return to those early origins that are never quite forgotten though they are impossible to remember—the family, childhood, perhaps even the womb. *Aurora Leigh* is run through by the desire to fill with actual life, with the material physical body, the space left open by a tradition that has typically depended on longing and the reiteration of cliché. It goes without saying, however, that the power of her epic is in large measure due to the force of Barrett Browning's evocation of the darker elements of the tradition. The forceful physicality of the poem may be compared with the hand of Aurora's father pushing the child's head down to kiss her dead mother's lips. Love, fear, and a recognition of irrecoverable origins are the lessons driving Aurora in and out of the tradition.

PART TWO

James in the Art Romance

John Henry Parker, the Forum, view from the Palatine Hill in 1874. Courtesy of the Photographic Archive of the American Academy in Rome, Fototeca Unione (FU 4362).

CHAPTER 3

Henry James: Impossible Artists and the Pleasures of Patronage

> It seems to me a rash thing for a sensitive soul deliberately to cultivate its sensibilities by rambling too often among the ruins of the Palatine, or riding too often in the shadow of the aqueducts. In such recreations the chords of feeling grow tense, and after-life, to spare your intellectual nerves, must play upon them with a touch as dainty as the tread of Mignon when she danced her egg dance.
>
> Henry James, *Roderick Hudson*[1]

THE FIRST PART OF this book has touched on key components of the art romance including not only the emergent fascination with art and artists in the nineteenth century but the association of both with melancholy, not only the identification of prized locations at which to put oneself in relation to art but also of the crisis provoked by actually approaching the sources of admired creation. The celebration of great genius in narratives featuring passionate suffering or melancholy defeat made romance the natural home for the expression of the psychic pressures provoked by the love of art. Nevertheless, sentimental literature is not the only place where the mode is important. Indeed, the reach of the tradition is nowhere clearer than in those cases where it is manifested in forms that typically share neither the commitment to the melancholy passions of the romance nor its tendency toward flamboyantly unreal and derivative fantasy. For this reason, the balance of *Haunted Museum* deals with texts in which the centrality of the romance component is in some measure surprising.

James illuminates the tradition not only because he never fully escapes it, but because his critical writings offer some of the richest reflections on romance itself. The present chapter introduces the self-reflexive quality of James's writings on the foreign in his early fiction, including *Roderick Hudson*, and his late autobiographical works. The next addresses the intricate affiliation between romance and the foreign by engaging two elements in James that can appear to be quite distinct: the overwhelming force of the museum and the presence of Hawthorne in his imagination. Following these studies of the formal effect of the encounter with Europe, the third chapter on James reads *The Golden Bowl* as a bold rewriting of the art romance demonstrating the longevity of the tradition, as well as its surprising power in representing at once the complexity of the individual's relationship to culture and the affinity of that relationship with dark human passions.

Henry James's fictional engagement with the lives of artists and writers is widely recognized. Less noticed about the novelist in this regard is his *inability* ever to tell the story of an artist's life or, rather, not to tell the story about the failure of the artistic life. The prefaces James appended to his first productions in the New York edition are characterized by a combination of affection and distress, and it is both James's confession of the emotional charms these texts hold for him and of the flaws he detects that I want to consider in what follows—indeed, it is the interrelation of flaw and charm. The problems the older James sees in his youthful productions are intimately connected to the success of these works in representing a certain kind of desire—hence the special pleasure his refined sensibility allows him to take in what he insists are defective works. The confessions of artistic shortcomings James wrote into the prefaces he composed in the first decade of the twentieth century offer a suggestive analysis of the cultural ambitions of an earlier era because of the author's sympathy for the desires and limitations driving that ambition.

Attentive readers of Henry James keep discovering that he is a realist of a very peculiar sort. Although this discovery has been made with increasing frequency in recent decades, it was anticipated earliest of all by the author himself. And so it is that James's two principal criticisms of his early efforts both ultimately come back to questions of verisimilitude or realism. In brief: *Roderick Hudson*, the first novel in his collected works, moves too quickly to be believed, and *The American*, the second, is a romance masquerading as a realist novel. James's formal discussions raise at least two questions: whence the troubling speed of *Roderick Hudson*'s catastrophe, and why or in what way is *The American* a romance? To these I would add two more considerations, which are related, but which engage elements in the prefaces at once autobiographical and more broadly cultural. In remembering the genesis of *The American* James is particularly clear on its source in the idea of an affront, an unjustifiable challenge to a good man by an older culture; what is the nature of the affront of Europe? And, ultimately, what is the place of *place* in these texts as reread by their author?

THE PASSION OF THE PILGRIM

James's "international theme" is a well-rehearsed topic of criticism; what I hope to do by placing it within this project is to restore the work of the novelist to the tradition of which this theme is a part, a tradition of powerful fantastic disinheritedness. I want to demonstrate in particular that, in spite of being one of the great poets of the foreign, James is nevertheless interesting not so much because of what he says about other nations, but because of the formal pressures put upon his artistic achievement by the relationship to culture for which the foreign stands.

To consider James's very early efforts in fiction and his returns to them in the prefaces and other autobiographical works is to think about James's inheritances, a life-long concern that always involved profound questions of form. In an important passage from *Hawthorne* (1879), James's analysis of his most significant American forebear, the connection is made explicit and takes the form of a charge:

> [H]e incurs that penalty of seeming factitious and unauthoritative, which is always the result of an artist's attempt to project himself into an atmosphere in which he has not a transmitted and inherited property. An English or a German writer . . . may love Italy well enough, and know her well enough, to write delightful fictions about her; the thing has often been done. But the productions in question will, as novels, always have about them something second-rate and imperfect.[2]

With *The Marble Faun* in his sights, James is clear and straightforward not just on Hawthorne's Italian romance but on a general principle: verisimilitude requires that works of fiction be set in places in which the author has "an inherited property." The penalty otherwise is steep. Inheritance and narrative success are closely allied, and both come back to the topic of setting, specifically, the American's use of Europe. In order to understand the threat to the disinherited novelist, it will be important to spend some time on the question of artistic failure in James.

"The Madonna of the Future" (1873), written six years before *Hawthorne*, tells the tale of Theobald, an American painter living in Florence, whose passionate relationship with the great tradition of Italian painting seems full of promise. Indeed, as the title suggests, Theobald's gift is always only a matter of promise; his great masterwork is perpetually postponed, its only physical manifestation a blank canvas cracked with age. That the model on whom he had pinned his hopes has also decayed in the long span of time between the manifestation of Theobald's aspiration and its consummation is a fact the narrator blurts out, precipitating the artist's ultimate collapse and death.

That his friend and patron is the immediate cause of Theobald's demise is typical of the kind of dangerous doubling that characterizes this tale and most of James's artist stories.[3] In his final delirious speech before dying, Theobald makes an odd declaration: "I need only the hand of Raphael. I have his brain. . . . I'm the half of a genius! Where in the wide world is my other half?"[4] It is not, however, only the artist in this story who is split; the same may be said of the principal consciousness of the tale, the narrator who meets Theobald on his first trip to Italy. "It relates," he says as preface to the painter's story, "to my youth, and to Italy: two fine things!" (202). His first-person narrative is further mediated by another voice, which is itself only identified by the suggestive initial "H." As we will see, there is an intimate connection between the travels of the narrator and the death of the artist in the works of H. James.[5]

In later tales, instances of halving and doubling will recur with regularity, as will the demise of the artist. Most striking in the latter regard may be "The Author of Beltraffio" (1884), in which a mother allows her son to die rather than have him tainted by the work of her decadent artist-husband. But essentially the same outcome is present in a tale as apparently different as "The Lesson of the Master" (1888), in which a promising young author receives a lesson in art that takes the shape of the loss of his beloved to an older author—one who has already demonstrated the impossibility of combining happy married life and fruitful authorship. Such stories may be understood as not only, and perhaps not principally, concerned with the difficult family life of the true artist, but as committed to representing the artist as a type shut off from the normal patterns of human reproduction. "The Middle Years" (1893) and "The Death of the Lion" (1894) both concern the death of an author, attended by a late-arriving admirer whose presence is unmistakable evidence of artistic success, but whose very vivacity also indicates the limits of the artist's participation in life. While well-known tales of research such as "The Aspern Papers" and "The Figure in the Carpet" are characterized by a posthumous striving after the essence of an artist whose death puts both man and work beyond reach, "The Private Life" is certainly James's most audacious use of doubling in order to represent the intertwining themes of the passionate admirer and the impossible life of the artist. At an inn in Switzerland the nameless unsuccessful author who is the narrator and the actress Blanche Adney engage in an elaborate flirtation that is only a manifestation of their desire for something quite different and impossible—for intimacy with the painter Lord Mellifont and the poet Claire Vawdrey. The passions of narrator and actress are doomed to limited satisfaction, however, as it turns out that the painter vanishes when there is no public to see him, and the gifted part of Claire Vawdrey stays in the study writing in the dark while *his* public half is dull and uninspired. Each manifest individual is, as Theobald would put it, only the half of genius.

It should not be surprising in an author whose narratives so often achieve their effects by suggesting the ghosts of other possible stories that early James shows the bare bones that will be fleshed out or discovered buried near the surface in late James. In "Travelling Companions" (1870) and "A Passionate Pilgrim" (1871) we find, drawn in exaggerated contours or bare of any covering, the shape of desires that are worked through again in the 1880s and 1890s. Passion is to companionship what pilgrimage is to travel, a franker avowal of emotional investment. "Travelling Companions" is not only, as its title intimates, a notably unadorned version of a typical Jamesian story; it is the earliest to treat what came to be called the "international theme." From its very first line, the story participates in the nineteenth-century culture of art: "The most strictly impressive picture in Italy," the narrator notes in what is certainly a strange beginning to a love story, "is incontestably the Last Supper of Leonardo at Milan."[6] The second line would seem to claim an experiential warrant for the admiration expressed: "A part of its immense solemnity is doubtless due to its being one of the first of the great Italian masterworks that you encounter in coming down from the North." But the "immense solemnity" described is not in any way provoked by the unique experience of an innocent traveler; it is the response of the pilgrim (not an "I," but a "you") arriving at a holy site, a stage in a well-trodden route. The narrator of this story is a young connoisseur who has come to Italy equipped with the list of masterpieces he is to admire and with the critical tools by which he is meant to understand their merits. Like a Hazlitt writing on the decay of a beloved Rembrandt, or Walter Pater writing on unfinished work by Leonardo or Michelangelo, the narrator is moved by the absence that provokes his imagination as much as by the evidence of remarkable achievement available to his senses:

> Another secondary source of interest resides in the very completeness of its decay. The mind finds a rare delight in filling each of its vacant spaces, effacing its rank defilement, and repairing, as far as possible, its sad disorder. . . . An unquenchable elegance lingers in those vague outlines and incurable scars; enough remains to place you in sympathy with the unfathomable wisdom of the painter. (1)

Only after a first paragraph devoted to art description and travel narrative does the story proper begin, a characteristic and yet strikingly undermotivated tale of romance between travelers. The nameless narrator, an American who has been studying in Germany for years, catches sight of a woman deeply moved by the sight of Leonardo's work. He instantly and insistently identifies this sentimental tourist as a countrywoman ("A single glance had assured me that she was an American. . . . Beyond doubt she was American," 2). Accompanied by her father—himself a "perfect American" (3)—Charlotte Evans is making an art tour of the country while reading George Sand (the narrator has Stendhal in *his* pocket). The love story is a memory of the Italian leg of the middle-class tour; it begins at the *Last Supper* in Milan and is consummated at Titian's *Sacred and Profane Love* in Rome. In the interval, the innocent couple accidentally spends an unchaperoned night in Padua after visiting Giotto's chapel, and Miss Evans's father dies in the Eternal City. The art, the romance, and the death are all structural components that will return in James's stories of the encounter with Europe, though, of course, they do not originate with him.

While "Travelling Companions" is strikingly schematic in its structure and themes, "A Passionate Pilgrim" fascinates by its bizarre agglomeration of elements. The tale of a poor and dying American poetaster attempting to reclaim some part of his ancestral patrimony, his "share" of an English estate long lost to his family, it is at once a story of insistent homecoming and of deadly exaggerated rejection. The place toward which Clement Searle aspires is aptly named "Lackley," signifying something lost, missing, or (to apply a useful Anglicism) wanting. Much as "Travelling Companions" is less interested in representing unique characters in idiosyncratic situations than in limning the typical response to hallowed European art, the compelling topic in this story is not so much the preposterous personal tragedy it recounts as the relationship of America to the English culture it celebrates as source. The narrator is another traveling American, this one returning from the continent and vividly responsive to the ways in which England is always already present to the American mind. Whereas in "The Madonna of the Future" the narrator will encounter the perfect (and perfectly ruined) incarnation of the aspiration for art, in "The Passionate Pilgrim" the narrator meets the consummate representative of the desire for England.

Clement Searle is first discovered not in front of a masterpiece by Leonardo but at an inn that both he and the narrator have evidently chosen for its characteristic Englishness. This time the meeting of the two paired characters is anticipated not by art-historical truisms but by a meditation on cultural memory:

> The latent preparedness of the American mind for even the most delectable features of English life is a fact which I never fairly probed to the depths. The roots of it are so deeply buried in the virgin soil of our primary culture, that, without some great upheaval of experience, it would be hard to say exactly when and where and how it begins. It makes an American's enjoyment of England an emotion more fatal and sacred than his enjoyment, say, of Italy or Spain. I had seen the coffee-room of the Red-Lion years ago, at home,—at Saragossa, Illinois,—in books, in visions, in dreams, in Dickens, in Smollett, and Boswell.[7]

By "fatal," James means unavoidable—"fated" (the applicability of the term for Italy, here denied, will return with a vengeance in late James)— but as the story develops, and Clement Searle dies on English soil, it becomes inescapably clear that more than destiny is involved in this fatality. The narrator's "visions" and "dreams" are sites of an internalized desire different only in degree from that of Clement Searle. "There is a rare emotion," the sentimental tourist asserts,

> familiar to every intelligent traveller, in which the mind, with a great passionate throb, asserts a magical synthesis of its impressions. You feel England: you feel Italy! The sensation for the moment stirs the innermost depths of your being. I had known it from time to time in Italy, and had opened my soul to it as to the spirit of the Lord. Since my arrival in England I had been waiting for it to come. (52)

The connection with England the narrator describes abstractly Searle typically expresses in a more melodramatic and concrete way; fatality for one man means destiny, for the other something akin to illness: "[H]aven't I been all my life long sick for Europe?" (48).

In the enthusiasm of the narrator James represents the self-conscious seeking of a predetermined experience ("We greeted these things as children greet the loved pictures in a story-book, lost and mourned and found again. It was marvelous how well we knew them," 60). Clement Searle's passionate pilgrimage is a luridly exaggerated version of the kind of aspiration the narrator expresses in terms of nostalgia, even of childish innocence. And so it is that, even though Searle is consistently identified with death, the story's overlapping centers of desire broaden the significance of haunting beyond one character. Seeing some majolica on display at the ancestral home, the *narrator* sketches a loving fantasy of the Grand Touring eighteenth-century ancestor who acquired them. Almost immediately imagination is given substance; it is revealed that this fantasy ancestor did indeed exist and was none other than the namesake of Clement Searle, a man who died en route to America. The two Clements, as might be expected, are strikingly similar in appearance—a fact revealed by comparison with a painting by no less a hand than Sir Joshua Reynolds (64–65).

The inheritance of name and appearance, along with the death of his alter ego somewhere between England and America, comes to obsess Clement Searle. He goes so far as to desire to be haunted by the ghost of the woman wronged by the earlier man. Indeed, Searle's statements insist on the overdetermined nature of haunting in this story: "She's welcome to the comfort of it. What one *can* do in the case I shall be glad to do. But can a ghost haunt a ghost? I *am* a ghost" (76, emphasis in the original). "What was I born for? What have I lived for? To see a ghost!" (86). The narrator, in response to Clement's exuberant desire to be haunted, participates in the multiplication of specters: "I confess there came upon me, by contact, a great supernatural shock. I shall always feel that I, too, have seen a ghost." As if to cement the bond between the ghost and Searle as types, when the phantom does arrive it proposes *marriage*, assuming for itself Searle's own desire to be reintegrated into his birthright, specifically, his quickly formed wish to marry his cousin, the heir of Lackley, the spirit of a tired but potentially welcoming old England (86).

Clement Searle's doomed matrimonial strategy to reconnect with his lost past anticipates "The Last of the Valerii" (1874), James's first tale of marriage between an American and a foreigner and the best-known story included in his first volume of fiction, *A Passionate Pilgrim* (1875). Searle, with his courtship of a ghost, is closely related to the Roman, Count Valerio, who risks his marriage when he falls in love with a Greek statue discovered on his property. The uncanny effects of a return to culture are as pronounced in this well-known tale of the nobleman's passion as in the lesser-known stories I have discussed. The emotion of the passionate pilgrim is personal, yet it has been foreordained by cultural history, hence the need for his story to be closely paralleled by the narrator's own responses. Personal development offers metaphors for an engagement with culture even as culture itself becomes a pressure on human relations and artistic creativity.

James's own testimony as a rereader of these tales years later is clear on both the importance of *place* to their theme and on their complex connections to his own artistic ambition and achievement:

> "A Passionate Pilgrim," written in the year 1870 . . . strikes me to-day [1908], and by the same token indescribably touches me, with the two compositions that follow it, as sops instinctively thrown to the international Cerberus formidably posted where I doubtless then didn't quite make him out, yet from whose capacity to loom larger and larger with the years there must already have sprung some chilling portent.[8]

In retrospect James is moved beyond expression by what these early works reveal of his ambition and future career, but it may be just as well to pay attention to the image he proposes. Cerberus is, of course, the many-headed hound that guards the gates of Hades, and the "sops" James throws identify the author with Psyche—who placated, pacified, or perhaps simply narcotized that ferocious guardian by the administration of sops of barley bread soaked in honey wine.[9] What kind of hell did these stories allow their author into or out of? James offers some explanation: "Cerberus would have been, thus, to one's younger artistic conscience, the keeper of the international 'books'; the hovering disembodied critical spirit with a disengaged eye upon sneaking attempts to substitute the American romantic for the American real" (1204). In what is evidently a return to the intertwined topics of place, inheritance, and "factitiousness" that preoccupied him in *Hawthorne*, James identifies these early international stories as ways of sneaking into fantasy. Although the situation facing the young Henry James himself on his return from Europe is not unrelated to the danger of falling into romance faced by the disinherited author treated in that early essay, it is impossible to miss the older novelist's new sympathy with this plight.

If James's preface is meant to illuminate the origin of the "international theme" in the recent shock of loving and losing Europe, it does a remarkable job confounding that source, losing it in an ever prior encounter. What motivates the bribe of Cerberus is an encounter with a foreign space at once new and always already known, something more like the experience of the narrator of "A Passionate Pilgrim" than that of Clement Searle himself:

> I had in the spring of 1869, and again in that of 1870, spent several weeks in England, renewing and extending, with infinite zest, an acquaintance with the country that had previously been but an uneffaced little chapter of boyish, or—putting it again far enough back for the dimmest dawn of sensibility—of infantine experience; and had, perceptively and aesthetically speaking, taken the adventure of my twenty-sixth year "hard," as "A Passionate Pilgrim" quite sufficiently attests. (1204)

The testimony of his own recollection suggests that two things had been taken "hard" by the young James: the recent voyage to Europe *and* the reawakening of a half-remembered, half-known, relationship to a cultural locus (already a "chapter") that was provoked by this experience. How else to explain that the next sentence of the preface is a turn not to any memory of England but rather to an entirely different country?—"A part of that adventure had been the never-to-be-forgotten thrill of a first sight of Italy." There are too many things being remembered and recovered here for the topic to be other than precisely memory and its recovery. The adventure in question is the mental one precipitated by half-recognized expectation interacting with "uneffaced" memory.

The author's memorial to his overdetermined youthful nostalgia is written as a remarkable collection of metaphors and analogies:

> [A] return to America at the beginning of the following year was to drag with it, as a lengthening chain, the torment of losses and regrets. The repatriated victim of that unrest was, beyond doubt, acutely conscious of his case: the fifteen months just spent in Europe had absolutely determined his situation. The nostalgic poison had been distilled for him, the future presented to him but as a single intense question: was he to spend it in brooding exile, or might he somehow come into his "own"?—as I liked betimes to put it for a romantic analogy with the state of dispossessed princes and wandering heirs. (1205)

The development of James's point is odd enough to merit pausing part way in relaying it. Already he has moved with surprising haste from England to Italy; now he highlights the formative nature of the sense of loss. The effect of his recent stay in Europe is such that the future is "presented to him but as a single intense question." The theme James is developing here is not simply one of beauty found and lost, but one of a lost property recognized without being restored. Like Clement Searle (or Wilhelm Meister, for that matter), he has been allowed to see his lost estate but not to come into his "own."

As if there were not enough at play already, the nostalgia for England that joins with the longing for Italy to create a generalized sense of unsatisfied desire and exile is then revealed to have its source in an *anterior* experience altogether:

> The question was to answer itself promptly enough—yet after a delay sufficient to give me the measure of a whole previous relation to it. I had from as far back as I could remember carried in my side, buried and unextracted, the head of one of those well-directed shafts from the European quiver to which, of old, tender American flesh was more helplessly and bleedingly exposed, I think, than today: the nostalgic cup had been applied to my lips before I was conscious of it—I had been hurried off to London and to Paris immediately after my birth, and then and there, I was ever afterwards strangely to feel, that poison had entered my veins. This was so much the case that when again, in my thirteenth year, re-exposure was decreed, and was made effective and prolonged, my inward sense of it was, in the oddest way, not of my finding myself in the vague and the uncharted, but much rather restored to air already breathed and to a harmony already disclosed. (xix)

The poignancy, then, is not traceable to the experience of a treasure newly discovered only to be lost sight of, so much as to the recognition of an inheritance that can be admired but not reclaimed. In Clement Searle's question we find a version of this realization of a long-standing (perhaps poisonous) connection: "Haven't I been all my life long sick for Europe?" The early stories are discovered by the older James to have functioned as a balm to a wound that had existed all along and which his recent voyage had uncovered:

> As I read over "A Passionate Pilgrim" and "The Madonna of the Future" they become in the highest degree documentary for myself. . . . I disengage from them but one thing, their betrayal of their consolatory use. The deep beguilement of the lost vision recovered, in comparative indigence, by a certain inexpert intensity of art—the service rendered by them at need, with whatever awkwardness and difficulty—sticks out of them for me to the exclusion of everything else and consecrates them, I freely admit, to memory. (1206)

James tells us that he found consolation in the story of Clement Searle, as much as in that of the failed painter Theobald, because he filled both of them with his longing for Europe. Both stories are of course fantastic— "romantic," as James would say—but they are hardly dreams of satisfaction so much as admissions of exile or worse. Theobald lives in the much-desired Italy, but it is precisely his desire to take into account everything he admires that results in the perpetual postponement of his "Madonna of the Future." Indeed, the futurity of the Madonna resides in its execution being endlessly and fatally lengthened by Theobald's intense and loving relationship to the past.

Patrons: Roger Lawrence, Rowland Mallet

In order to tell his tales of pleasure and frustrated ambition, James typically relies on a bipartite narrative such as that in "The Passionate Pilgrim." He writes at once the story of a character who has come abroad to aspire and suffer and of one whose aim is to cultivate the feelings he has learned to anticipate from the encounter with culture. Names for these two roles in James are readily available: artist and patron. Although he arrives late, the narrator of "The Madonna of the Future" does not sleep but wanders off to have his first views of Florence: nighttime befits the fantasy space of Italy, and tardiness is the defining quality of the always belated encounter with culture. His dreamlike sighting of a giant statue is rendered less strange by the recognition that it is Michelangelo's *David*—evidently recognized from reproductions. He then turns to Cellini's nearby *Perseus*: "Glancing from one of these fine fellows to the other, I probably uttered some irrepressible commonplace of praise" (203). The phrase is a ready confession of the prescribed paths followed not only by his aesthetic response but by the very language in which he expresses his feelings.[10] The "probable" *because* "commonplace" or typical words given voice by the art lover are what in turn provokes the appearance of Theobald, the American painter who has dedicated himself to developing his own creativity by the unwise strategy of immersion in the art of the city. The narrator will become Theobald's student and protector, his patron, but it should not be missed that it is his ejaculation that precipitates the appearance of the other man, that brings him into an ambit that will prove far from salutary for the artist. As in "The Passionate Pilgrim," the narrator in "The Madonna of the Future" has a vital role in provoking the crisis of the artist/claimant's life. In the early novels more-recognizable versions of patronage take the place of the unstable split relationship so prevalent in the stories without in any way resolving the essential complex of complicity and disappointment evident from the outset in James's representations of the interplay of artistic desire and the longing for culture.

James's first novel, *Watch and Ward* (1871), a close contemporary of the stories that make up *A Passionate Pilgrim*, begins with the frustration of a much-anticipated proposal of marriage. Roger Lawrence has been awaiting the return of Isabel Morton from Europe in order to renew his suit. She, however (like a later Isabel), has become engaged while abroad. The refusal of Roger Lawrence provides the impetus for a strange plan— all the stranger in that it is precisely the content of the novel: he adopts a thirteen-year-old girl he will *form* into his perfect object of betrothal and eventual marriage. The narrator has told us of the protagonist "He had been born a marrying man, with a conscious desire for progeny."[11] The novel promises to satisfy both desires, though not in their natural order. Nora Lambert is a "little forlorn, precocious, potential woman" (13). It is her potential womanhood that calls to Roger, and a passage such as the following is not a simple expression of sympathy for the suicide of her father, which is the event that throws them together: "His own sense of recent bereavement rose powerful in his heart and seemed to respond to hers." Hoping to do well by doing good, Roger sees in the combination of need and potential a *promising* solution to his own problem: "An irresistible sense of her childish sweetness, of her tender feminine promise, stole softly into his pulses" (13). The extraordinary first chapter of the novel begins with one proposal and ends with another: "Do you think you could love me?" he asks the pubescent girl, in what is intended by James as well as Roger as a return to the desire for marriage that opens the novel and governs its development (15). Roger's fantastic plan could have many names—Pygmalionism not least among them.[12]

While the list of James's stories involving art and artists and the people who love both stands in little need of augmentation, it is worth remarking how this first effort, following quickly on the author's return from his important first solo trip through Europe (the voyage commemorated in the preface to *The Reverberator* discussed earlier) can be read as *both* a reworking of the story of Pygmalion *and* as the beginning of that important Jamesian theme, the adventure of patronage. That Nora Lambert is Roger Lawrence's masterpiece is clearly indicated by the terms used to describe her throughout the text. The apotheosis of her beauty comes on her return from Europe, when Roger is dangerously ill, and it provokes this response from the maid who helped raise her: "You must keep yourself in cotton-wool till he recovers. You're like a picture; you ought to be enclosed in a gilt frame and stand against the wall" (95). When Nora fears for Roger's life, it is because he is at once creator and perfect audience: "[H]e was her world, her strength, her fate! He had made her life; she needed him still to watch his work" (96). A vital finishing touch in the education of Nora Lambert is the trip to Rome on which Roger Lawrence sends her, much as Roderick Hudson will be taken to Rome by Rowland Mallet in James's next novel. Looking even further ahead, we can descry another Lambert, Lambert Strether, as a version of the object of patronage sent abroad for a final polish prior to marriage. For all his uprightness of character, Roger Lawrence represents an early version of a sensibility that will be more clearly recognizable later in the century as *aesthetic*. He is characterized as possessed of a remarkable fastidiousness—intriguingly identified as characteristic of bachelors—and his main form of self-expression (barring the creation of Nora) is interior design ("He had always possessed a modest taste for upholstery," 32).[13] The fever that provokes the novel's climax is caused by Roger's sleeping in a damp basement because of the paint fumes he himself has unleashed in his home in expectation of Nora's arrival.

Roderick Hudson, the first volume of the monumental yet meticulously designed New York edition, has as its frontispiece a photograph of the author in profile. He is gazing to the right, toward the onion skin paper that bears his signature. But his piercing look is directed to the title and author that rise from under the translucent sheet: "*Roderick Hudson*, by Henry James." The two pages together suggest a triangle with corners formed by eyes, signature, and title, and it is difficult to avoid the conclusion that if two of the points of the triangle are indications of the author's own self—his face, his signature—it is simple reading to take the title of the novel as another version of this same self, one over the imprimatur of the author and under his gaze. The image James placed at the entry to his monument is one of himself literally looking over his work. And, of course, the revisions to which he subjected his texts, as well as the prefaces he prepared for each volume, are remarkable instances of authorial return. The prefaces in particular offer the cagy confessions of James late in his career, along with a rich analysis of the cultural ambitions, desires, and limitations of the nineteenth-century James. By leaving *Watch and Ward* out of the selection of works he included in the New York edition, James allowed *Roderick Hudson* to stand as his emblematic first novel. A doubled source of authorial self-presentation is offered: the *Bildungsroman* of the novel itself, and the returns its author makes, which feature as much the young novelist remembered as the old novelist remembering.[14]

In this regard, *Roderick Hudson* is a particularly interesting instance of a typical structure. The prefaces—all written at the end of the novelist's career—serve at once as an intricately layered artistic memoir and as a self-conscious return to themes around which the early work was perpetually and sometimes helplessly circling. *Roderick Hudson*, *Watch and Ward*'s immediate successor, is only more committedly a novel of patronage, but, as James himself explains more than thirty years later, it is in the fact of patronage that the salvation of the novel (and young novelist) lies:

> I make out in another quarter above all what really saved me. My subject, all blissfully, in face of difficulties, had defined itself—and this in spite of the title of the book—as not directly, in the least, my young sculptor's adventure. This it had been but indirectly, being all the while in essence and in final effect another man's, his friend's and patron's, view and experience of him. (*Prefaces*, 1049)

James, searching for the merit in his early effort, discovers he has written a novel in which the focus is not the adventure of the artist in the title, but the experience of Rowland Mallet, the man who takes him to Italy.

The preface invites the reader to consider both the failure of Roderick and the compensatory success of Rowland. Like Roger Lawrence, Roderick's patron is identified as a self-conscious bachelor; and precisely because he does not initially give the appearance of fighting this fate in the same dogged fashion as his predecessor, it is all the more striking that their emotional development proves ultimately so similar. While Roger can be read as an aesthete, it is impossible to understand Rowland in any other way. In the oddly insistent denials that make up his description, Henry James provides a psychological character sketch of the connoisseur:

> He was *neither* an irresponsibly contemplative nature *nor* a sturdily practical one, and he was forever looking in vain for the uses of the things that please and the charm of the things that sustain. He was an awkward mixture of strong moral impulse and restless æsthetic curiosity, and yet he would have made a most *ineffective* reformer and a very *indifferent* artist. It seemed to him that the glow of happiness must be found either in action, of some immensely solid kind, on behalf on an idea, or in producing a masterpiece in one of the arts. Oftenest, perhaps, he wished he were a vigorous young man of genius, *without* a penny. As it was, he could only buy pictures, and *not* paint them. (*Roderick Hudson*, 176–77; emphases added)

Rowland Mallet, identified as a man of pure expectation, occupies an unsteady position between things he is not and things he has not. He is about to go to Europe for what may turn out to be simple dilettantism, but may be something far more important, the founding of a museum. He is too practical to do nothing but contemplate, but he has too little talent to create. The only option James leaves him, is practical connoisseurship:

> There was a project connected with his going abroad which it was on his tongue's end to communicate. . . . Useful though it might be, it expressed most imperfectly the young man's own personal conception of usefulness. He was extremely fond of all the arts, and he had an almost passionate enjoyment of

pictures. He had seen many, and he judged them sagaciously. It had occurred to him some time before that it would be the work of a good citizen to go abroad and with all expedition and secrecy purchase certain valuable specimens of the Dutch and Italian schools as to which he had received private proposals, and then present his treasures out of hand to an American city, not unknown to aesthetic fame, in which at that time there prevailed a good deal of fruitless aspiration toward an art-museum. He had seen himself in imagination, more than once, in some mouldy old saloon of a Florentine palace, turning toward the deep embrasure of the window some scarcely faded Ghirlandaio or Botticelli, while a host in reduced circumstances pointed out the lovely drawing of a hand. (170)[15]

James's solution to Rowland's problem, like the problem itself, has at its heart the challenge of the encounter with Europe and its effect on artistic ambition.

"'Roderick Hudson' was begun in Florence in the spring of 1874." James's bald opening to his preface (and therefore to the entire New York edition) is apparently simple and informative. But each piece of information it proffers is charged with nostalgic suggestion. He places his text in another century, another country, another city. It seems almost unnecessary to add that it was spring in Florence, the city of art. "I yield to the pleasure," James continues, "of placing these circumstances on record." The claim is for more than pleasure, however; James engages in such recollections not only to feed the nostalgia of foreign recollection, but because retracing the genesis of his work is an especially useful exercise for a writer interested in plumbing the mysteries of his art: "This revival of an all but extinct relation with an early work may often produce for an artist, I think, more kinds of interest and emotion than he shall find it easy to express, and yet will light not a little, to his eyes, that veiled face of his Muse which he is condemned for ever and all anxiously to study" (1039). As the preface develops, it becomes clear that this first effort will set a tone of particularly self-conscious "artistic" response. The lessons of James are the lessons of the artist; his is "a given artistic case" (1039). He is interested in "the continuity of an artist's endeavor" generally (1039–40), but he is also concerned with the development and motivation of one particular artist—himself. "'Roderick Hudson' was my first attempt at a novel" begins the second paragraph, not quite accurately (1040).

Although the technical issue ostensibly preoccupying James in this preface is the speed with which the narrative unfolds, it is inescapably clear that the piece is as much about place as it is about time—or, rather, it is about both together. As in James's discussion of "The Passionate Pilgrim," personal and cultural questions overlap:

One fact about it indeed outlives all others; the fact that, as the loved Italy was the scene of my fiction—so much more loved than one has ever been able, even after fifty efforts, to say!—and as having had to leave it persisted as an inward ache, so there was soreness in still contriving, after a fashion, to hang about it and in prolonging, from month to month, the illusion of the golden air. Little enough of that medium may the novel, read over to-day, seem to supply; yet half the actual interest lurks for me in the earnest, baffled intention of making it felt. (1042)

The personal motivation behind the novel is the memory of having loved and lost Italy. The writer's pleasure resides in perpetuating the memory of a place now inaccessible. James is careful to name each location at which *Roderick Hudson* was penned: Florence, the Black Forest, somewhere "near Boston," New York. But more than nostalgia is at stake; the pleasure resides not only in the celebration of something lost, but in the attempt to recapture the memory of this thing from far away. Hence his recollection, as he finished the novel in New York, of "the felt pleasure of . . . trying, on the other side of the world, still to surround with the appropriate local glow the characters that had combined, to my vision, the previous year in Florence" (1042).

The kind of nostalgia James describes is hardly new and entirely credible. Nevertheless, the preface still presents a mystery. In a novel of over 340 pages, only roughly 12 are set in Florence. There is so little of that city in the story it is tempting to ask how it *is* present—or, rather, why does James think of his longing for Italy in general as particularly represented by this tale? What is that "local glow," and what may it have to do with the other, apparently less personal, question in the preface, the speed of the collapse of the main character? "To re-read 'Roderick Hudson' was to find one remark so *promptly* and so *urgently* prescribed that I could *at once* only take it as pointing almost too stern a moral. It stared me in the face that the time-scheme of the story is quite inadequate, and positively to that degree that the fault but just fails to wreck it" (1046–47; emphases added). The immediately evident fact of the poor time scheme of the novel stands in direct contradiction of the languorous time of enjoyed memory. "Everything occurs," the author complains, "too punctually and moves too fast" (1047). What is wrong with punctuality, we might ask, except we know that it is likely to work against the mystery and tension of a novel, suggesting as it does an inevitable appointment, a foregone and predetermined event.

James has a further complaint: Roderick is a type, even at times a stereotype, of the nineteenth-century artist—moody, egotistical, irresponsibly selfish. It is in being a type that he is uninteresting to his author, and the speed of his dissipation risks making him "a morbidly special case":

The very claim of the fable is naturally that he *is* special, that his great gift makes and keeps him highly exceptional; but that is not for a moment supposed to preclude his appearing typical (of the general type) as well; for the fictive hero successfully appeals to us only as an eminent instance, as eminent as we like, of our own conscious kind. (1047; emphasis in the original)

James describes a dilemma formed on the one side by his desire to write about a special man and on the other by the wish that he may prove nevertheless not so exceptional as to defy identification. The problem with James's solution to this dilemma is that Roderick's exceptionality is actually all-too typical (and *not* of "the general type").

The "failure" of *Roderick Hudson* is illuminated by reference to what the author understands to have been the novel's success. James's chagrin at the precipitous speed of the collapse of his title character is somewhat eased by the realization that his theme was not after all the actions or moral development of Roderick so much as the adventure of Rowland's perceptions. "The centre of interest throughout 'Roderick' is in Rowland Mallet's consciousness," he explains, "which I had of course to make sufficiently acute in order to enable it, like a set and lighted scene, to hold the play" (268). Thirty years after writing the novel, James is relieved to discover in his handling of the patron some compensation for his inability to manage the artist.

ROWLAND MALLET: THE PASSIONS OF THE CONNOISSEUR

The solution by which James declares the consciousness of Rowland Mallet the center of the novel and therefore the rushed collapse of Roderick to be of less damage to his work is only partially convincing. It is all the less satisfactory given the complicity of Rowland Mallet in the haste with which Roderick acts. Hardly has he met the benighted sculptor in Northampton before he is giving him both reason, encouragement, and means to leave: "If you mean to turn sculptor, the sooner you pack your trunk the better" (188). "The sooner the better" is the lesson of Rowland, who not only identifies the need to leave but prescribes the particular destination, activity, and his own place in it all: "In three words, if you are to be a sculptor, you ought to go to Rome and study the antique. To go to Rome you need money. I'm fond of fine statues, but unfortunately I can't make them myself. I have to order them" (189).

Rowland's emotional and artistic capital—mere disposable cash at the opening of the novel—is quickly invested in Roderick, the art appreciation always blending with a more emotional, even romantic, flirtation:

"Your statuette seems to me very good," Rowland said gravely. "It has given me extreme pleasure."

"And my cousin knows what is good," said Cecilia. "He's a connoisseur."

Hudson smiled and stared. "A connoisseur?" he cried, laughing. "He's the first I've ever seen! Let me see what they look like;" and he drew Rowland nearer to the light. "Have they all such good heads as that? I should like to model yours." (181)

The balance of this early conversation is characterized by a typical set of non sequiturs: when Roderick learns that Rowland is going to Europe and responds with melancholy envy, Rowland's own response is to be struck by the sculptor's "remarkably handsome" face (181). To mark the new closeness established by Roderick's commitment to accompany Rowland to Rome, after the culmination of what may best be described as their courtship, Roderick "passe[s] his hand through Rowland's arm" (189). In doing so, he arrives at the very gesture that marks the commitment of Nora Lambert to Roger Lawrence in *Watch and Ward*: "He passed her hand through his arm and held it there against his heart" (160). We may call this the gesture of accepted patronage.[16]

Rowland Mallet's patronage is, as I have noted, motivated by all of the things he is not quite. His incomplete nature, evidently the result of an inherited longing, leads to a need for others that James associates with both aesthetic and affective aspirations. The intertwining of the cultural and the personal is quite explicit in the character's own reflections, which are made in words that evoke at once the conclusion of Pater's *Renaissance* (1873) and the outbursts of Theobald, the painter whose Madonna was always only in the future:

> True happiness, we are told, consists in getting out of one's self; but the point is not only to get out—you must stay out. . . . I want to care for something, or for some one. And I want to care with a certain ardor; even, if you can believe it, with a certain passion. . . . Do you know I sometimes think that I'm a man of genius, half finished? The genius has been left out, the faculty of expression is wanting; but the need for expression remains, and I spend my days groping for the latch of a closed door. (171)

Cecilia, the cousin who introduces Rowland to Roderick responds with what we *may* read as the essential emotional motivation behind Rowland's desire: "What an immense number of words . . . to say you want to fall in love!"

Cecilia's answer, however, is both true and only partial. Rowland Mallet is too richly elaborate a creation, too closely connected to both the artistic ambition represented by Roderick Hudson and the fatigued corruption of the old world represented by the femme fatale of the novel, Christina

Light, for us to read his desire for love as the final answer. As in so many nineteenth-century tales of artists and the encounter with culture, interpersonal passions provide such compelling metaphors for the relationship to art just because the metaphoric relation is so oddly reversible. We need only remember the rather risqué personification of art in Pater's conclusion, the way it "comes to you proposing frankly to give nothing but the highest quality to your moments as they pass, and simply for those moments' sake," as well as the skeptical despair behind this turn to momentary passions—"that thick wall of personality through which no real voice has ever pierced on its way to us," "each mind keeping as a solitary prisoner its own dream of a world"—evoked in Rowland's confession to Cecilia to see that to trace the passion for art to an emotional need is to follow only half the story.[17]

While the important connections linking Pater and James have received useful critical attention, much of the work done in this area has focused on what we might term the "moral" influence—the call to life that rings from the original conclusion of *The Renaissance* to Strether's famous speech to Little Bilham in *The Ambassadors*—or (with reference to Wilde) on the topic of James's own complex relationship to the "type" of the aesthete as it returns in *The Portrait of a Lady*, *The Tragic Muse*, and *The Golden Bowl*, as well as in such stories as "The Author of Beltraffio." At least as important for James as the aesthetic ethos or character, however, is aesthetic historicism—what he learned from Pater about ways of thinking about culture and its transmission.[18] Looked at from this angle, the topic of James and Pater does not reveal a simple story of influence and reaction but of a meeting of shared concerns. It is only fitting that James first came across Pater's *Renaissance* during a in Florence. He was, as it were, already where he needed to be. Nevertheless, there is little question that in Pater James found—at a time when his own literary career was still at a self-consciously embryonic stage—a definition of success, an example of fastidiousness of style understood as a moral question, and a sensibility exquisitely responsive to the weight of history. Although none of these elements is wholly absent from James before Pater, it is impossible to believe that it was not from the critic that the novelist acquired important components of the vocabulary with which he would express their interactions for the rest of his career.[19]

The echo of Theobald in Rowland's declaration to Cecilia of being half a man indicates that a general cultural condition rather than the simple human need for love is at stake, particularly if we take to heart the insistently emblematic elements of "The Madonna of the Future." Theobald's mistake of waiting too long is poignant not because Theobald is a man of feelings, but because he is a man of art.[20] The explanation of Roderick's situation as an aspiring artist is run through with the language of Pater, culminating in an inescapably Paterian conclusion; he needs criticism, which means he needs Rowland and Rome: "The flame is smoldering, but it is never fanned by the breath of criticism" (185). Paterian influences are evident not only in the language used to make the claim for the artist's need of criticism, however, but also in the shape of the relationship of mentor and student running through the novel. It is a relationship in which love is never out of the question, but in which, nevertheless, the older man (as, say Ficino to Pico, Abelard to Heloise) represents not only affection but culture:

> Roderick was acutely sensitive, and Rowland's tranquil commendation had stilled his restless pulses. He was ruminating the full-flavored verdict of culture. Rowland felt an irresistible kindness for him, a mingled sense of his personal charm and his artistic capacity. He had an indefinable attraction—the something divine of unspotted, exuberant, confident youth. (186)

It is evident enough that Rowland Mallet is a connoisseur of people and things, but it is easy to miss how much his role in the too-speedy collapse of Roderick is not accidentally related to this essential quality. The danger of the connoisseur for the artist is most flamboyantly represented in the shape of Roderick's formal nemesis, and the only character other than Rowland whom James takes some pleasure in remembering when he comes to write the preface, Christina Light, the novel's most exquisite sensibility. James is well aware that the future Princess Casamassima *should* be the focus of the dangerous love interest that destroys Roderick. As I have begun to suggest, however, she has some competition in loving and, I think, in being dangerous. James himself is emphatic on Christina's role as nemesis, and on her failure in this regard—due to that much-lamented speed of dissolution. The absence of sufficient tension leading up to the collapse of Roderick Hudson means that the effectiveness of the ostensible cause of his dissolution is necessarily reduced:

> One feels indeed, in the light of this challenge, on how much too scantly projected and suggested a field poor Roderick and his large capacity for ruin are made to turn round. It has all begun too soon, as I say, and too simply, and the determinant function attributed to Christina Light, the character of well-nigh sole agent of his catastrophe that this unfortunate young woman has forced upon her, fails to commend itself to our sense of truth and proportion. (1047–48)

Rowland and Christina share a good deal, not simply as the proximate and direct cause of Roderick's precipitous downfall, but also as the two facilitators of his passion. If, in his preface, the author expresses full satisfaction about only two elements in the novel, Rowland Mallet and Christina Light, it is because it is their adventure that is really of interest. The story of those Northamptonians—Roderick, his mother, even his fiancée Mary Garland—is poor stuff in comparison to the tale of these two sensibilities and the weight of history on their souls. No wonder James bemoans the failure of Roderick to convince. His protagonist's inability to put up a real struggle before succumbing weakens the impact Christina Light can have in the novel. He falls before James has the opportunity to put his creation through her paces.

The kinship of Christina Light and Rowland Mallet runs back to the entanglement of America and Europe in each character's family roots. Roderick is typically wrong when he first sees her: "No, she's not an American, I'll lay a wager on that. She's a daughter of this elder world" (230). She is, in fact, exactly half-American and a child of art by way of the landscape painter who was her maternal grandfather. Her father is not the absent Mr. Light but the Cavaliere who now lives beside her in worshipful degradation. The mystery, the degradation, and the mixed blood that make up the background of Christina Light are not unexpected in a figure that draws on the nineteenth-century conventions found in Goethe's Mignon and Hawthorne's Miriam, Staël's Corinne and Elizabeth Barrett Browning's Aurora Leigh.[21] Christina's role is to stand as a human equivalent to Rome and all it entails for foreigners, and this requires her to be of mixed descent.[22] Perhaps more surprisingly, James also makes Rowland a hybrid figure. His mother's father (whose surname he bears as his given name) was a sea captain who found his Dutch wife abroad (173). The story of his grandfather's courtship is strangely elaborate and surrounded with a mystery that hints at secret transatlantic passions: "Why he had gone forth so suddenly across the seas to marry her, what had happened between them before, and whether . . . he would not have had a heavy weight on his conscience if he had remained an irresponsible bachelor; these questions and many others, . . . were much propounded but scantily answered." The exotic grandmother herself is characterized by the beauty of her figure and her "air of apathetic homesickness" (173), so that in both sides of this maternal source James anticipates Rowland's aesthetic passion and longing to be abroad.[23]

While Rowland Mallet shares Christina Light's quality of mixed blood and an exotic genealogy, as a born connoisseur, she also impinges on *his* essential nature. Christina is revealed as nothing less than a connoisseur of connoisseurs—in this sense a kind of self-conscious emblem of Italy, one who can look back critically at those who look at her. "I like looking at people's things. . . . It helps you to find out their characters," she comments to him. But Rowland's case challenges her skills and confuses her instincts because it is characterized by surfeit: "I am rather muddled; you have too many things; one seems to contradict another. You are very artistic and yet you are very prosaic; you have what is called a 'catholic' taste and yet you are full of obstinate little prejudices and habits of thought, which, if I knew you, I should find very tiresome" (275).[24]

Writing about Rome, James proposes the word "historic" as carrying the sense of "being weighted with a crushing past," a description that could as well describe the woman as the city. Christina's birth and upbringing make her preternaturally old ("I am not young; I have never been young!" 347), a quality she shares with Mignon, that daughter of a superannuated father, but also with the city in which she encounters Roderick and Rowland. Rowland is a connoisseur and patron because knowledge is combined in his character with the ability to make discriminations. Christina is a figure for a Rome incapacitating because of the wealth of knowledge it includes: "There's nothing I cannot imagine! That is my trouble" (351). Such a city is especially dangerous for artists, but not for people like Rowland and Christina, as it is the very environment for which they are born.

James worries about the possibility that his artist fails not because of some interesting problem in his character, but simply because of his fated participation in the most clichéd version of the story of the artistic life. Indeed, both Roderick's crisis and its hackneyed quality are anticipated early in the novel, in a conversation between Cecilia and Rowland in which she evokes precisely the stereotype James resists, but to which both he and Roderick ultimately surrender: "Perhaps you believe in the necessary turbulence of genius, and you intend to enjoin upon your protégé the importance of cultivating his passions." Rowland dismisses the idea out of hand: "On the contrary, I believe that a man of genius owes as much deference to his passions as any other man, but not a particle more, and I confess I have a strong conviction that the artist is better for leading a quiet life. That is what I shall preach to my protégé, as you call him" (199). Nevertheless, less than a hundred pages later, in the midst of Roderick's collapse, Rowland is thrown back on the hoary theme he here dismisses: "He wondered gloomily, at any rate, whether for men of his companion's large, easy power, there was not a larger moral law than for narrow mediocrities like himself" (289). Near the end of the novel there is no longer any question; the character sketch imagined by Rowland musing on Roderick could be straight out of D'Israeli:

> . . . his strength and his weakness, his picturesque personal attractiveness and his urgent egoism, his exalted ardor and his puerile petulance. . . . Suddenly he felt an irresistible compassion for his companion; it seemed to him that his beautiful faculty of production was a double-edged instrument, susceptible of being dealt in back-handed blows at its possessor. Genius was priceless, inspired, divine; but it was also, at its hours, capricious, sinister, cruel; and men of genius,

accordingly, were alternately very enviable and very helpless. It was not the first time he had had a sense of Roderick's standing helpless in the grasp of his temperament. (309–10)

This kind of analysis comes to dominate Rowland's thoughts to the point that he essentially retracts his position on genius in a letter to Cecilia from Rome: "He is the most extraordinary being, the strangest mixture of qualities. I don't understand so much force going with so much weakness—such a brilliant gift being subject to such lapses. The poor fellow is incomplete, and it is not really his own fault" (358). Incompleteness, Theobald's self-diagnosis, returns, along with a plaintive question: "Are they all like that, all the men of genius?" (359).

What James reads as his own authorial dereliction in failing to modulate the speed of Roderick's failure is the almost inevitable result of the challenge he sets himself of writing a tale in which the destination is entirely what is to be expected but the route is meant to be altogether richer and more interesting. After his initial success in Rome, Roderick falls into a life of dissipation including gambling, drinking, and womanizing, a moral collapse that predates his passion for Christina Light. But this is a kind of breakdown suitable to the pedestrian imagination of Woollet, the New England town that James will have misunderstand the sins of Chad Newsome in Paris thirty years later. Roderick is the victim of a stock moral laxity, when it is his overwhelmed response to Europe and the culture it holds that should be his real undoing.

As usual, James borrows the form of his crisis from the reserves of lurid literature—melodrama and the Gothic. Throughout the novel Roderick is fascinated by tales of individuals being buried alive; it is a motif that reaches its climax just prior to his death. It is no accident (in several senses) that Roderick dies in the mountains of Switzerland, at the St. Gotthard Pass, traditional point of entrance and egress from Italy for Grand Tourists and artists alike. By the time of Roderick's collapse his language reflects a mental state not far from that of Theobald or Clement Searle. As Rowland and Roderick approach the Pass, James develops a striking and self-conscious contrast between the beauty of the scene and the hysterical anguish of the artist: "[B]ury me alive," is the protégé's challenge to his mentor, "Take me back to Northampton" (465). But as the novel reaches its climax, it becomes clear that that metaphoric condition is not reserved for the provincial small towns of the United States:

> "Look at this lovely world, and think what it must be to be dead to it?"
> "Dead?" said Rowland.
> "Dead, dead; dead and buried! Buried in an open grave, where you lie staring up at the sailing clouds, smelling the waving flowers, and hearing all nature live and grow above you! That's the way I feel!" (470)

"I am glad to hear it," is Rowland's response, incorrigible Paterian. "Death of that sort is very near to resurrection." Both characters are wrong in their diagnosis. Roderick is not to be resurrected, and what he has to fear is not being buried alive in America but in Italy. As his death nears, James makes sure to evoke the clichéd romance of Italy to which it is closely related:

> It all was confoundingly picturesque; it was the Italy that we know from the steel engravings in old keepsakes and annuals, from the vignettes on music-sheets and the drop-curtains at theatres; an Italy that we can never confess to ourselves in spite of our own changes and of Italy's—that we have ceased to believe in. (469–70)

James offers a cruel and powerful lesson here—one E. M. Forster would take to heart. It is to this beautiful Italy, fake though it may be, and mediated though it may be through stereotyped fantasy, that Roderick cannot help responding. "This suits me" he declares just before the outburst on his death-in-life quoted above. When he asks Rowland to recognize, in speaking of him afterward, the brutality of the circumstance in which his patron has placed him, the artist's language could come from a Poe story of premature burial:

> Say that he trembled in every nerve with a sense of the beauty and sweetness of life; that he rebelled and protested and shrieked; that he was buried alive, with his eyes open, and his heart beating to madness; that he clung to every blade of grass and every way-side thorn as he passed; that it was the most horrible spectacle you ever witnessed; that it was an outrage, a murder, a massacre! (471)

Rowland does not in fact say this, but it is precisely what James *does*. In a gorge in the Italian Alps they find his character "Roderick's face stared upward, open-eyed, at the sky" (509). Roderick Hudson is destroyed with eyes open and staring—much as they had been since he came to Europe.

In Rowland Mallet James creates a character who cannot limit his connoisseurship to its usual objects, a character about whom James notes in the preface, "what happened to him was above all to feel certain things happening to others" (1050). Later in his career, James might have made Rowland more clearly morally suspect, something of a villain—after all, it is undeniable that he is the original facilitator of Roderick Hudson's collapse, merely aided at the close by his alter ego, Christina Light. The final moment, in which Rowland's exasperation drives Roderick to his death by foolhardiness or suicide, is only the ultimate demonstration of complicity. "Take me at least out of this terrible Italy, . . . where everything mocks and reproaches and torments and eludes me!" The very passivity written into Roderick's plea acknowledges Rowland's role in his situation, "Take me out of this land of impossible beauty" (467).

That the novel locates its center in Rowland's passions is evident in the turn to Mary Garland. As the story of the artist becomes more conventional, the desires of the connoisseur come to the fore. The princess will drop from sight until she returns to contribute to the destruction of another aspiring lower-class artist in her own novel, a text in which once again death and the experience of European cultural achievement are near allied. Rowland Mallet proceeds with the wooing of the dead man's fiancée. It is as patron and connoisseur, in a spirit not unlike that of Roger Lawrence toward Nora Lambert, that Rowland had approached Roderick's Mary early on. When they all travel from Rome to Florence, the story of her education in taste takes over from that of the artistic education of Roderick. "To be young and elastic, and yet old enough and wise enough to discriminate and reflect, and to come to Italy for the first time," he tells her, "that is one of the greatest pleasures that life offers us" (380). In discrimination and reflection, we recognize the work of the critic. "I don't want to seem patronizing," he will warn, the word having both its standard meaning and a more original one in this novel, "but I suspect that your mind is susceptible of a great development" (385). She is a splendid student, in part because her education is, for both of them, a way of maintaining a relationship with Roderick, the principal object of their affections.[25]

"Rowland took an immense satisfaction in observing that she never mistook the second-best for the best, and that when she was in the presence of a masterpiece, she recognized the occasion as a mighty one" (390). Among the many clues to Mary's potential is her ready responsiveness to the treasures of Rome—even identifying her rival Christina Light as one of the beautiful things of the city (388). Another aspect of her promise is her sense of the seriousness and even potential menace of culture: "It seems to me very frightful to develop" is her response to Rowland's flattering invitation (385). As Mary's aesthetic education nevertheless proceeds, she takes on the historic characteristics of Pater's Mona Lisa that had earlier been reserved for Christina. Standing on the Palatine, amid "the disinterred bones of the past" whose influence on sensitive souls Cecilia had warned about so early in the novel, Mary recognizes the historic melancholy of Rome and comes to manifest it physically: "She had begun by saying that it was coming over her, after all, that Rome was a ponderously sad place. . . . she was tired, she looked a little pale" (395). Her sadness is expressed in language evocative of that with which Pater had personified it in the Mona Lisa: "expressive of what in the ways of a thousand years men had come to desire. Hers is the head upon which all 'the ends of the world are come,' and the eyelids are a little weary."[26]

An extraordinarily subtle reading of *Wilhelm Meister* underpins the passage cited at the head of this chapter in which Rowland's cousin Cecilia evokes the careful tread of Mignon in her egg dance as an image for the appropriate response to the challenge presented by too-close an encounter with Italy's historical remains. And yet, if the dance of the uncanny child who stands for the longing for Italy is a vivid figure for risk, it is also a moment of great pleasure in Goethe's novel. The performance—with its fragile emblems of creation put in danger but spared—is a gift to comfort Wilhelm at a dark moment. While James finds some compensation for the failings of his title character by focusing on Rowland and Christina, it is nevertheless true that failure itself is a recurrent part of James's account of the encounter with Europe. Indeed, the faults he identifies are marks of precisely the kind of uncontainable grandeur reflected as much in the nostalgia of the prefaces as in the melancholy of Mary Garland. The evident pleasure James discovers in contemplating his shortcomings as a neophyte writer indicate that he reads his early imperfections as so many souvenirs of love. James's presentation of failure as evidence of an inescapable admiration demonstrates that it is not just for his characters that the challenge of place is manifested in the overwhelming power of an admired past. As will become clearer in the next chapter, the force of the international theme in James's works is indicated not simply by the subjects he chooses—those cultural pilgrims and traveling artists—but also by the structural warping the novelist discovered when he came to reread his early responses to Europe. The power of Italy to overwhelm results in both the centrality of connoisseurs and patrons—the only ones who could even begin to take in the richness with which they are confronted—and the twin failure of the artists: of James as of Roderick.

Giuseppe Castiglione: *The Salon Carré in 1865*, Paris, Louvre. Photo: Réunion des Musées Nationaux/Art Resource, New York.

CHAPTER 4

The Museum in the Romance:
James with Hawthorne

> He said to himself crudely and artlessly "It's Jacobean"—
> which it wasn't, even though he had thought but of the later
> James. The intensity of the inference and the charm of the
> mistake had marked withal his good faith; the memory of
> which was to remind him later on of how everything still to
> come was then latent in that plot of space, and of how
> everything that *had*, was accorded and attested by it.
>
> Henry James, *The Sense of the Past*[1]

THE AFFRONT OF EUROPE: CHRISTOPHER NEWMAN IN THE MUSEUM

AS IS CLEAR FROM James's treatment in the prefaces of faults he discovered
in *Roderick Hudson* and other works, "the charm of the mistake" is a characteristic and important theme in the novelist's returns to his early fictions. While *The Sense of the Past*, James's unfinishable last novel on the
pressures of history, is the topic at the close of this chapter, I anticipate
that discussion with the preceding quotation as a reminder of the personal
and long-lasting nature of James's concern with the relationship between
plotting and failure, particularly when it comes to the novelist's attempt
to trace the encounter with admired culture, to identify the plot implied
in a much-desired space. The haunted English house bequeathed to the
American Ralph Pendrel early in *The Sense of the Past* is no more Jacobean
than his error is crude or artless. "Late" or "latent," the key terms shaping
this strange digression on Ralph's uncharacteristic mistake in dating, are
related descriptors. Given the destinies of characters from Clement Searle
to Roderick Hudson, we may identify in the first term a good summary
of the situation of James's *characters* as they come into relation with a
continent fraught with associations before they ever reach it. The second
term reflects a more formal matter: the pressures that may be at work to
shape a *story* before it is even written, that which is "latent" in a "*plot* of
space." The sinuous serpentining style characteristic of "the later James"
allows the novelist's prose to turn back on itself, to reflect the pressures
shaping his very earliest efforts, the inheritance that forms the destiny of
his writing.

After *Roderick Hudson*'s representation of the miserable fate of the artist in Europe, it seems only simple justice that the novel that followed should be so entirely—from earliest conception to execution and later reconsideration—about the revenge of an American on a family representing the highest development of European culture. It is also little wonder that James is more successful in expressing the affront than in enjoying the revenge. Three things are striking about James's treatment of *The American* when he came to review it for the New York edition: his fondness for the story; his sense of its utter and inescapable implausibility, or *romance*; and the importance of its opening setting in a museum. To think about the relation of romance to place is, for James, to think about precedents— about the stories that precede him as he arrives at a "plot of space." Indeed, important elements at play in *The American* are clarified in *Hawthorne* (1879), a text with which the novel is contemporary and which could as easily have borne the same title. James famously traces the romantic tendency of Hawthorne's work to a provincialism that is not his alone but typical of a nation characterized by what it lacks: "No sovereign, no court, no personal loyalty, no aristocracy, no church, no clergy, no army, no diplomatic service, no country gentlemen, no palaces, no castles . . . no literature, no novels, no museums, no pictures, no political society . . ." It is not only in this passage that James identifies the quality of absence as the keynote of Hawthorne's America. The topic returns throughout the book, notably in an account of the pleasures that Margaret Fuller took in the meager traces of European art available to her in Boston. This passion, which is associated with her lack of access to actual Italian treasures, leads to a telling comparison:

> [T]here are pages of her letters and diaries which narrate her visits to the Boston Athenaeum and the emotions aroused in her mind by turning over portfolios of engravings. These emotions were ardent and passionate—could hardly have been more so had she been prostrate with contemplation in the Sistine Chapel or in one of the chambers of the Pitti Palace. The only analogy I can recall to this earnestness of interest in great works of art at a distance from them, is furnished by the great Goethe's elaborate study of plaster-casts and pencil-drawings at Weimar.

James cites Fuller, an "apostle of culture, of intellectual curiosity" precisely because she is a model for the touching, even pathetic aspirations of the American mind in the cultural vacuum he identifies in the first half of the nineteenth century: "I mention Margaret Fuller here," writes James, "because a glimpse of her state of mind—her vivacity of desire and poverty of knowledge—helps to define the situation."[2] The snobbishness that is one component strand of James's sensibility should not blind us to his evocation of—and participation in—a powerful tradition of longing, one running from Goethe to Fuller and Hawthorne and characterized by a poignant combination: "vivacity of desire and poverty of knowledge." Analysis of James's lifelong responsiveness to Hawthorne's art romance, *The Marble Faun*, will allow this chapter to address the formal pressures of what we might call the American situation on the narratives of the later author. Before reaching that point, however, it will be important to consider some of James's elaborate figures for the shock of vivacious desire encountering overpowering knowledge.

The American opens with Christopher Newman sprawling on a sofa in the Salon Carré of the Louvre in 1868. Guidebook and opera glass discarded at his side, the American is overwhelmed by the museum:

> [H]e was heated with walking, and he repeatedly passed his handkerchief over his forehead, with a somewhat wearied gesture. And he was evidently not a man to whom fatigue was familiar; long, lean and muscular, he suggested the sort of vigor that is commonly known as "toughness." But his exertions on this particular day had been of an unwonted sort, and he had often performed great physical feats which left him less jaded than his tranquil stroll through the Louvre. He had looked out all the pictures to which an asterisk was affixed in those formidable pages of fine print in his Bädeker; his attention had been strained and his eyes dazzled and he had sat down with an æsthetic headache. He had looked, moreover, not only at all the pictures, but at all the copies that were going forward around them, in the hands of those innumerable young women in irreproachable toilets who devote themselves, in France, to the propagation of masterpieces; and if the truth must be told, he had often admired the copy much more than the original.[3]

Following the example of James's own rough handling of Christopher Newman, I will leave him sitting where he is, stunned from unwonted effort at the very outset of his Tour. My warrant for this treatment lies in James's preface and in the novel itself, but in order to justify this procedure, I will also cite James's account, in *A Small Boy and Others* (1913), of his own youthful experience of the Louvre:

> [T]he house of life and the palace of art became so mixed and interchangeable . . . that an excursion to look at pictures would have but half expressed my afternoon. I had looked at pictures, looked and looked again, at the vast Veronese, at Murillo's moonborne Madonna, at Leonardo's almost unholy dame with the folded hands, treasures of the Salon Carré as that display was then composed; but I had also looked at France and looked at Europe, looked even at America as Europe itself might be conceived so to look.[4]

I quote this late text not only as another memorial to a space that was always emblematic to James, or because it focuses on the same Murillo that draws the attention of the tired Christopher Newman, but because of its insistence that the experience of the museum is entirely of a piece with the experience of Europe.

The novel identifies its focus of interest as not an individual so much as the representative of a nation: "An observer with anything of an eye for national types would have had no difficulty in determining the local origin of this undeveloped connoisseur . . . [and would feel] a certain humorous relish of the almost ideal completeness with which he filled out the national mould" (515–16). The affront of Europe that is the novel's burden is anticipated by its opening. Christopher Newman's Grand Tour and his search for a perfect cultured wife are twin manifestations of the desire that brought him to the Louvre and left him there stunned, by an uncharacteristic exhaustion. He seeks out a certifiable *morceau de museé* in Claire de Cintré, in much the same way as he is driven to build an art collection composed of copies of items in the museum.[5] The close links between his travel and his courtship are demonstrated when Mrs. Tristram recommends the Grand Tour as a substitute for seeing Madame de Cintré: "When Newman related to Mrs Tristram his fruitless visit to Madame de Cintré, she urged him not to be discouraged, but to carry out his plan of 'seeing Europe'" (573). The consolatory voyage, like the collection he assembles, is insistently conventional. "The regular round," he calls his tour (655), a trip whose shape is bound within the margins of the guide-books. "You want to know everything that has happened to me these three months," he writes Mrs. Tristram,

> The best way to tell you, I think, would be to send you my half dozen guide-books, with my pencil-marks in the margin. Wherever you find a scratch, or a cross, or a "Beautiful!" or a "So true!" or a "Too thin!" you may know that I have had a sensation of some sort or other. That has been about my history, ever since I left you. Belgium, Holland, Switzerland, Germany, Italy, I have been through the whole list. (585)

As was the case with Christina Light in *Roderick Hudson,* the desired woman in *The American* is a figure for European culture, this time half-French and half-English. If Christopher Newman's role as a cultural stereotype is to be the insistently American new man, Madame de Cintré is characterized by her intimate, familial relations with the past. She

> gave Newman the sense of an elaborate education, of her having passed through mysterious ceremonies and processes of culture in her youth, of her having been fashioned and made flexible to certain exalted social needs. All this, as I have affirmed, made her seem rare and precious—a very expensive article, as he would have said. (628)

Claire's attraction for Newman resides in her absolute innate culture. When she asks about herself as his ideal image, "Pray, how did she come to such perfection?" Newman's reply is complex in its emphasis, "She was never anything else" (718). Which is to say, her charms derive from the past to which she is heir. "Old races have odd secrets," he is warned by Claire's brother, but it is a needless caution: "Very good . . . that's the sort of thing I came to Europe for. You come into my programme" (626).

In revisiting the composition of *The American* in his preface, James insists on his happiness with the novel's premise in spite of what he identifies as the absurd romanticism of its development. Indeed, it is hard to miss the pleasure in James's response to his theme, or the speed of a necessary near-Archimedean discovery: "I recall sharply the felicity of the first glimpse, though I forget the accident of thought that produced it." James's pleasure, however, is taken in a situation of a notably *un*pleasant kind:

> [T]he situation, in another country and an aristocratic society, of some robust but insidiously beguiled and betrayed, some cruelly wronged, compatriot: the point being in especial that he should suffer at the hands of persons pretending to represent the highest possible civilisation and to be of an order in every way superior to his own. What would he "do" in that predicament, how would he right himself, or how, failing a remedy, would he conduct himself under his wrong?[6]

Behind the story, then, is the desire to describe an affront to a "compatriot." The germ of the tale is a wrong inflicted by a superior civilization, but the premise remains undeveloped until James finds a location: "It was all charmingly simple, this conception, and the current must have gushed, full and clear, to my imagination, from the moment Christopher Newman rose before me, on a perfect day of the divine Paris spring, in the great gilded Salon Carré of the Louvre" (1056). The novel develops, then, from a general premise but within a specific setting. As we shall see, that space distorts the narrative even as it sets it in motion and allows the offense to take *place*. The very pressure of the conceit that drives the story warps or derails its movement: "I had dug in my path, alas, a hole into which I was destined to fall. I was so possessed of my idea that Newman should be ill-used" (1065).

James's self-criticism in the preface comes down to one word: *romance*, to the serious authorial failure of producing a romance when he thought he was engaged in writing a realist novel. "I had been plotting arch-romance" he notes, "without knowing it" (1057), and it is as much the unconscious character of his fantastic creation as the actual text he produced that he finds touching. If *The American* now strikes its author as an unselfconscious and nearly vulgar romance he had mistaken for something else, however, he is now ready to reconsider what it is that romance itself has to offer, as well as the pressures that might drive one willy-nilly in its direction: "I value, in my retrospect, nothing so much as the lively light on the romantic property of my subject that I had not expected to encounter" (1061). The connection between the romance James discovers in his novel and the story the novel tells of an American in Europe first encountered at a museum will evidently only be revealed by careful consideration of what James understands by "romance"—a term that fascinates him with its links at once to wish fulfillment and to fear.

Why does James find such enjoyment in the very quality in his work he identifies as the source of its fatal weakness? And what does the professed inability to escape romance have to do with the two other elements James identifies as the determining factors of the text, the affront of Europe and Christopher Newman finding himself stretched out in the Louvre? To appreciate the uncompromising complexity of James's well-known account of the relationship between the real and romance, it is necessary to cite at length:

> The real represents to my perception the things we cannot possibly *not* know, sooner or later, in one way or another; it being but one of the accidents of our hampered state, and one of the incidents of their quantity and number, that particular instances have not yet come our way. The romantic stands, on the other hand, for the things that, with all the facilities in the world, all the wealth and all the courage and all the wit and all the adventure, we never *can* directly know; the things that can reach us only through the beautiful circuit and subterfuge of our thought and our desire. (1062–63, emphases in the original)

James has put in italics a pair of important words, but he might well have chosen to emphasize "directly." A key distinction between the real and the romantic is that the experience of romance has to be routed through desire. Romance, as a matter of fantasy and wish fulfillment is *always* and necessarily separate from the real of our experience, as that separation is an essential quality.[7] One explanation for the pleasure to be found in Christopher Newman's discomfiture is suggested when James turns to the way danger may be an element of desire:

> There have been, I gather, many definitions of romance, as a matter indispensably of boats, or of caravans, or of tigers, or of "historical characters," or of ghosts, or of forgers, or of detectives, or of beautiful wicked women, or of pistols and knives, but they appear for the most part reducible to the idea of the facing of danger, the acceptance of great risks for the fascination, the very love, of their uncertainty, the joy of success if possible and of battle in any case. This would be a fine formula if it bore examination; but it strikes me as weak and

inadequate, as by no means covering the true ground and yet as landing us in strange confusions.

The panting pursuit of danger is the pursuit of life itself, in which danger awaits us possibly at every step and faces us at every turn; so that the dream of an intenser experience easily becomes rather some vision of a sublime security like that enjoyed on the flowery plains of heaven. (1063)

James describes at least two kinds of romance. both of which are suggested to him by the inverisimilitude of *The American*: the first is quite a broad category, common in the popular understanding, which the novelist identifies by a list of exotic attributes (for convenience, I will label it r_1), but which he understands to involve some sense of threat (a mode I will label, r_1J, because it is the standard form of romance given a Jamesian interpretation). R_1J turns out ultimately to be far from a simple pattern for romance because the element of threat it contains links it to the dangers of the real ("life itself"). The second form of romance described in the passage (r_2), what we might call the Jamesian romantic, is starkly different from either the popular understanding or its Jamesian interpretation; it represents a *peace* that is the exact opposite of danger, the aspiration to encounter nothing at all. Milly Theale, dying in Venice, offers a gloss on the second meaning that is worth citing:

"Oh the impossible romance—!" The romance for her, yet once more, would be to sit there for ever, through all her time, as in a fortress; and the idea became an image of never going down, of remaining aloft in the divine dustless air, where she would hear but the plash of the water against stone.[8]

What is paradoxical in James's account of *The American* is that he evidently discovers himself to have written a novel that is an instance of *both* sorts of romance. Indeed, it is by being at once a romance of danger and a romance of safety that the novel demonstrates the complex sorts of dangers James has in view and the strange kinds of safety.

The two kinds of romance James describes meet at the topic of power. Indeed, the power of the wicked, James notes in a passage in which a triple negative is only another sign of the involuted complexity of the issue, is one of the few sure indications of romance:

It is as difficult . . . to trace the dividing-line between the real and the romantic as to plant a milestone between north and south; but I am not sure an infallible sign of the latter is not this rank vegetation of the "power" of bad people that good get into, or *vice versa*. It is so rarely, alas, into *our* power that any one gets! (1067; emphasis in the original)

In his Freudian treatment of the "seemingly perverse" pleasure in being held captive that runs through Gothic literature, David Richter suggests that even the most difficult scenarios may become pleasurable insofar as they return the individual to a kind of childlike powerlessness. As Richter puts it, in terms that usefully include the narrative instability of romance in his Freudian account of the Gothic, "Neither the moral nor the pragmatic vision of the focal characters is trustworthy; like children they tend to exaggerate enormously the power of their opponents."[9] That the fantastic subjection to an irresistible power is a dark compensation for one's essential powerlessness is suggested by the wistful tone of the novelist's observation that "[i]t is so rarely, alas, into *our* power that any one gets!" James's account of romance's unstable negotiation between peace and danger may be fruitfully compared with Freud's similarly intricate account of the paradoxical compulsion to repeat a traumatic experience in his discussion of the pleasure principle.

In the power of his enemies, as much as in the power he acquires over them that he ultimately renounces, Christopher Newman is evidently inhabiting the realm of the first kind of romance (r_1J). And yet, it is difficult to avoid the conclusion that James is proposing the paradoxical notion that his power *and* his powerlessness both may provoke visions of the kind of peace described in r_2. Freud's formulations in *Beyond the Pleasure Principle* similarly begin from the analyst's well-known observation of his grandson's reenactment in play of the loss and return of the mother, only to culminate in the postulation of an impulse beyond the possibility of desire or loss. "The dominating tendency of mental life, and perhaps of nervous life in general," he writes in a sweeping formulation, "is the effort to reduce, to keep constant or to remove internal tension due to stimuli . . . a tendency which finds expression in the pleasure principle; and our recognition of that fact is one of our strongest reasons for believing in the existence of the death instinct." Freud's account of masochism develops the relationship among Nirvana, pleasure, and death and offers a characteristic return to the analyst's career-long conflation of a tendency toward entropy at the level of the organism with a longing for unpleasure and ultimately death at the level of the individual.[10] The power of the wicked is "real" in being a threat, but it can become romantic (r_2) when it reaches a kind of certainty, even if that entails a loss of agency. Not the fear it inspires, but the presence of power it suggests may make a threat romantic—hence, the trajectory of *The American* from satisfaction to frustration. The first part of the novel is a fantasy of undermotivated wish fulfillment: American financier, having decided that he needs culture in the shape of a trip to Europe and a wife from the same place, crosses the Atlantic, finds a kind and beautiful woman from a family of great antiquity; she agrees to marry him. The second part of the novel is a chronicle of equally unlikely frustration: after appearing to accept his suit, her family takes the woman away from him; she runs away to a convent; he discovers a dark secret but, in the end, decides not to use it against the family in what is either an act of moral revulsion or a result of the family's manipulation.

Signs of inverisimilitude include not only the occurence of events that we believe are not likely to happen in life (coincidences, unlikely changes of heart, etc.), but also the unmissable presence of earlier fictions. Indeed, much in the story of Christopher Newman in the later part of the novel (the part generally identified as most factitious) is evocative of the tempestuous romance of Lord Nelvil in France before his father died and before he met Corinne. I am proposing not a direct line of literary influence, however, but rather that the ultimate source of this similarity is to be found in the nature of the encounter with admired art in the period. Throughout *The American*, and most emphatically and improbably toward its end, the text is littered with references to its own inverisimilitude: "It is like something in a play" (590); "It was a chapter for a novel" (618); "the most artistic of romancers could not have been more effective. Newman made a movement as if he were turning over the page of a novel" (813); "It was too strange and too mocking to be real; it was like a page torn out of a romance, with no context in his own experience" (831). Still, these notable confessions of inverisimilitude notwithstanding, the factitious core of the romance in this novel is most fully manifested by the force of the power of the wicked.

The story of the American in Europe becomes a romance of irresistible evil because the alternative might be to acknowledge the fact of a more overwhelming real. If the disturbing speed of *Roderick Hudson* is tied to the unavoidable challenge the old continent presents to the artist, the romance of *The American* is shaped by the threat Europe poses simply by being the seat of admired culture. In giving Europe the maleficent form of the wicked Bellegardes, James writes a tale of malevolent power and heroic resignation that, years later, he finds touching in its fantasy. We may cite the terms with which James describes his youthful visit to Paris in *A Small Boy and Others*: a "romantic or roundabout or nobly-dangerous journey" (*Autobiography*, 193). I take the condition in which we find Christopher Newman at the opening of the novel to represent more closely what there is to fear in Europe than the evildoings of aristocrats (travelers, after all, spend far more time in museums than wooing foreign beauties). Christopher Newman's failure, like that of the novel he inhabits, is closely tied to the analysis James offers of the romantic doom of the disinherited American in Europe. To think about the birthright of the American author is to think about a disturbing romance compounded of fantasy and loss of control. To think about James's relation to the great American romancer who preoccupied him throughout his career is to consider in particular the place in James's work of *The Marble Faun*, ineffable fantasy of Italy, artists, and mysterious subjection to power.

THE EMPTINESS OF PICTURE GALLERIES / SUBTERRANEAN
REMINISCENCES

In order to answer what I take to be a fundamental question raised by the
preface to *The American*, the relationship between the novel's inverisimilitude and the presence of Europe in the work, it is useful to consider both
novel and preface alongside a work from the art-romance tradition that
clearly stands behind both, Hawthorne's *The Marble Faun*.[11] James's ideas
on the necessary association between romance and Europe come back always to his great predecessor. In an important passage from *Hawthorne*
cited in chapter 3 James identified the "penalty of seeming factitious and
unauthoritative" as the necessary "result of an artist's attempt to project
himself into an atmosphere in which he has not a transmitted and inherited property" (445). To seem "factitious" is not to seem real; in literature,
it is to be unmistakably artificial. The risk for a novel dealing with foreign
places arises precisely from this threatening quality of "factitiousness." It
is the risk, in short, of being doomed to romance.

If James is strange and elaborate in his discovery that he himself wrote
romance, no one could accuse the earlier novelist of the same confusion.
Indeed, Hawthorne invites observation of the relation James appears to
find so damning. Not only does the subtitle to his Italian tale blazon its
genre—*The Marble Faun; or, The Romance of Monte Beni*—but the self-
described romancer, speaking of himself in the third person in his own
preface, identifies a necessary a link between Europe and form:

> Italy, as the site of his Romance, was chiefly valuable to him as affording a sort
> of poetic or fairy precinct, where actualities would not be so terribly insisted
> upon as they are, and must needs be, in America. No author, without a trial,
> can conceive of the difficulty of writing a Romance about a country where there
> is no shadow, no antiquity, no mystery.[12]

Not only is it the case that James criticizes Hawthorne for doing precisely
what the earlier author knows full well that he is doing, but Hawthorne's
meditation on the inextricable links connecting the fantastic and the real
in the "Postscript" to *The Marble Faun* is clearly one of the models for
the later novelist's own treatment of place, romance, and realism. "Romance and poetry, like ivy, lichens, and wall-flowers, need Ruin to make
them grow," notes Hawthorne before turning to the (unlikely) claim that
in the process of revision he was surprised to discover the inescapable presence of picturesque Italy in his novel:

> In re-writing these volumes, the Author was somewhat surprised to see the ex-
> tent to which he had introduced descriptions of various Italian objects, antique,
> pictorial, and statuesque. Yet these things fill the mind, everywhere in Italy, and

especially in Rome, and cannot easily be kept from flowing out upon the page, when one writes freely, and with self-enjoyment. And, again, while reproducing the book, on the broad and dreary sands of Redcar, with the gray German Ocean tumbling in upon me, and the northern blast always howling in my ears, the complete change of scene made these Italian reminiscences shine out so vividly, that I could not find in my heart to cancel them. (3)

Reading *The American* through *The Marble Faun* offers one answer to the simple question of why James begins in a museum his novel of desire rebuffed. Hawthorne was already standing at the intersection of place and aspiration—of museum, affront, and romance—that James only discovered on rereading his own novel. Critics have tended to focus on the relation between Hawthorne's novel and *Roderick Hudson* because of the evident parallels in setting: Rome and the American artist community living there.[13] However, the presence of *The Marble Faun* in *The American* is no less important for being largely subterranean, emerging most often not in the plot of the later novel, but in the force of its premise and, of course, in its romance. Like its own predecessor, *Corinne*, Hawthorne's novel was adopted early on as a tourist manual in which further sentimental associations were added to the experience of well-known sites. "Four individuals, in whose fortunes we should be glad to interest our reader, happened to be standing in one of the saloons of the sculpture-gallery, in the Capitol, at Rome" (5). The narrator's typically disingenuous claim notwithstanding, the setting of this simple opening is evidently far from accidental. The novelist makes sure to indicate that the room in which we find his protagonists houses not only the *Marble Faun*, but the *Dying Gladiator*, the *Antinous*, the *Juno*, and other "famous productions of antique sculpture" (5). While in James's Louvre it is Christopher Newman who sinks into a reclining position at the center of the Salon Carré, in the Capitoline Museum a notable marble has that role: "It was that room (the first, after ascending the staircase) in the center of which reclines the noble and most pathetic figure of the Dying Gladiator, just sinking into his death swoon" (5).

It is not only in setting and description that the openings of the two novels are related. Both works from the outset seek to establish the relationship to Europe for which the museum stands. We meet Christopher Newman while he is suffering from an "aesthetic headache" brought on by the wealth available to his sight. Hawthorne is even more blunt on his authorial aim at the opening of his text. It is "the hope of putting the reader into that state of feeling which is experienced oftenest at Rome. It is a vague sense of ponderous remembrances; a perception of such weight and density in a by-gone life, of which this spot was the center, that the present moment is pressed down or crowded out" (6). The texts share a fantastic or romantic quality traceable to the attempt to represent the

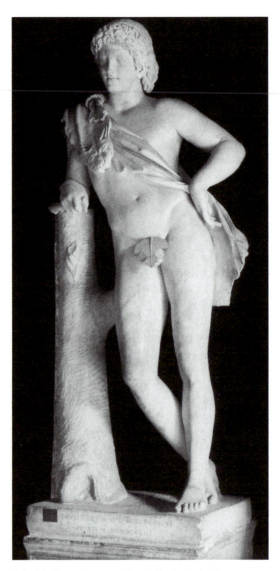

Marble Faun, Rome, Musei Capitolini. Photo:
Alinari/Art Resource, New York.

psychological effects of an overwhelmingly museal Europe. The opening of *The American* is a return with a difference to the museum setting that begins *The Marble Faun* because neither novel ever really leaves the museum. Both texts extend the boundaries of the institution so that it takes in an entire continent.

James disapproved of the American title of Hawthorne's novel, which was published as *Transformation* in England. It is misleading, he argued, to present the statue of Praxiteles as the center of the novel, when it is a flesh-and-blood faun that is at issue: "Hawthorne's choice of this appellation is, by the way, rather singular, for it completely fails to characterise the story, the subject of which is the living faun, the faun of flesh and blood, the unfortunate Donatello. His marble counterpart is mentioned only in the opening chapter" (*Hawthorne*, 444). Much as Christopher Newman fleshes out the *Dying Gladiator*, we may take James's own creation of Madame de Cintré and her family as the more "real" version of what Hawthorne aims at with Donatello and Miriam. Still, both authors are driven to romance in order to tell their tales of American intimacy with beautiful art objects and passionate involvement with Europeans. While the confused Christopher Newman turns to the pretty copyist Noémie and her reproduction as a relief from the headache that has overwhelmed him, at the opening of Hawthorne's novel the concern of his artists is to compare their faunlike friend, Donatello, to the Praxitelean original at the Capitoline museum. While Hawthorne's apparently more fanciful narrative suggests that in Donatello the American artists have direct access to an instance of the original European beauty memorialized in Greek art, James creates a fiancée for Christopher Newman whose charms are precisely the antiquity of her family, her innate affinity with culture. Rather than complain about Hawthorne's chosen title, as James does, it will be more useful to ask why it is that the romancer creates this human version of a classical statue whose crime, redemption, and marriage constitute the primary narrative content of the novel.

The Marble Faun is inescapably a romance about the encounter with Europe in one of its most fraught manifestations, the play of study, evaluation, emulation, synthesis, assimilation, and rejection that takes place when contemporary artists respond to the art of the past. The novel's setting in the expatriate American art community that flourished in Rome in the nineteenth century is not accidentally related to the tale of persecution, crime, guilt, and redemption that Hawthorne tells. The account of artists coming to Rome for inspiration but being persecuted from pillar to post by models, antique statues, and originals so great as to make them into mere copyists is familiar enough from texts such as Hazlitt's "English Students in Rome" of thirty years before. Hawthorne explores the troubled relationship of artists to the center of the culture they have been trained to admire by dwelling on the effect of the art of the city on his characters. Aesthetic judgments become manifestations of the moral qualities that shape the stories of individuals. Hilda, the pure and chaste copyist, spends her time faithfully reproducing the work of the Old Masters; otherwise, she lives in a tower where her main task is to tend a lamp devoted to the Virgin. The purity and limits of her practice have everything to do with her response to the city:

> Hilda, in her native land, had early shown what was pronounced by connoisseurs a decided genius for the pictorial art. . . . Had Hilda remained in her own country, it is not improbable that she might have produced original works, worthy to hang in that gallery of native art, which, we hope, is destined to extend its rich length through many future centuries. (55)

The novel is clear on the link between Hilda's worship of the art around her and her loss of individual creative power:

> Certain it is, that, since her arrival in the pictorial land, Hilda seemed to have entirely lost the impulse of original design, which brought her thither. No doubt, the girl's early dreams had been, of sending forms and hues of beauty into the visible world out of her own mind; of compelling scenes of poetry and history to live before men's eyes, through conceptions and by methods individual to herself. But, more and more, as she grew familiar with the miracles of art that enrich so many galleries in Rome, Hilda had ceased to consider herself an original artist. (56)

Hawthorne returns repeatedly to the paradoxically debilitating effect of Rome on artists whose ambitions had led them to the city. "So Hilda became a copyist" is the uninflected presentation of an actual loss (57). The challenge of the place is as evident in the surrender of Hilda to mere copying as in the other extreme, the creation of a kind of pastiche work that attempts to take all prior achievement into account: "How terrible should be the thought," declares Miriam, "that the nude woman whom the modern artist patches together, bit by bit, from a dozen heterogeneous models, meaning nothing by her, shall last as long as the Venus of the Capitol!" (136).

That Donatello is at once and unstably a man of flesh and blood and the *Marble Faun* of Praxiteles, the very feature that so troubled James, is—as the title that distressed him suggests—key to the meaning of this murky novel. More than simply an admired statue, the faun stands for the tradition of depending on the antique for creative inspiration. That the crime of the faun is the murder of a mysterious character known only as "the Model," no less than the fact that the act is committed at the unspoken behest of an artist, should only contribute to our sense that it is as a story of *artistic* conflict that this Gothic romance finds its meaning. The

Marble Faun is a memorial of a past of which Donatello is a *living* version—beautiful, yet dangerous because of his intimate relation to the darkest and most primitive parts of the desire of the artist. Needless to say, Donatello is dangerous for precisely the reasons he is attractive.

Unlike Hilda, her polar opposite, Miriam, the tempestuous European with mixed blood and a secret, cannot keep herself pure. Her work is not slavish reproduction but rather imitation skewed by the force of passion. Nevertheless, she is all the more clear on the ways in which her existence depends on emulation. At a crucial juncture in the novel, it is her *literary* forebears Miriam acknowledges. "I have often intended to visit this fountain by moonlight," she declares at the Trevi Fountain, "because it was here that the interview took place between Corinne and Lord Nelvil, after their separation and temporary estrangement. Pray come behind me, one of you, and let me try whether the face can be recognized in the water" (146). The simplicity of Miriam's "because" is indicative of the textual nature of the Europe she inhabits; it reminds the reader of how much the novel owes to Staël—including the antithesis of the pure blond creature of the North and the history-burdened and (therefore) doomed dark woman inescapably tainted with the unspeakable passions of the South. That Miriam is a figure belonging to the family of Mignon, Corinne, or even Aurora Leigh is evident from the elements that make up her history: the mysterious European childhood; the mixed blood (in Miriam's case, an English mother combining with Jewish and Italian nobility); the transgressive mystery in her background; and, most strikingly, perhaps, the hint of incest behind her transgression—a specter raised by the repeated references to Beatrice Cenci running through Hawthorne's description (429–31).

The novel repeatedly underlines Miriam's literary sources, as in the instance at the Trevi Fountain, which combines those two typical period tropes, not only the tour of Rome by moonlight but also the mediation of prized locations by earlier texts:

> The moonshine fell directly behind Miriam, illuminating the palace-front and the whole scene of statues and rocks, and filling the basin, as it were, with tremulous and palpable light. Corinne, it will be remembered, knew Lord Nelvil by the reflection of his face in the water. In Miriam's case, however, . . . no reflected image appeared; nor . . . would it have been possible for the recognition between Corinne and her lover to take place. The moon, indeed, flung Miriam's shadow at the bottom of the basin, as well as two more shadows of persons who had followed her, on either side. (146–47)

Instead of the floating reflection of her lover on the surface of the water, Miriam sees something darker, her own silhouette accompanied by two others cast to the very bottom of the fountain. The shades that surround her belong to Donatello and the hated Model.

Although the adventure of Rome is textually inspired, Hawthorne's artist, unlike Staël's, is accompanied not by a noble English lord but by two kinds of models. If Miriam is a version of Corinne or even Mignon—passionate, longing creatures of uncertain genesis—Donatello is not only a revival or continuation of the line of fauns, he is also the kind of prince Letitia Landon's Improvisatrice dies for. The similarities between Donatello in his ancestral home of Monte Beni, bemoaning his fate after his separation from Miriam, and Lorenzo, the statuesque lover of the Improvisatrice who lives on in mourning after her death, serve to further underline Miriam's pedigree.

Miriam inhabits a villa composed of antique fragments emblematic of the promise and challenge of Rome's accumulated greatness. A description of this space and its decor takes up the first two pages of the chapter entitled "Miriam's Studio," not merely to set the scene, but to describe her situation as artist in a world of unassimilable spolia. Her nemesis, the Model, is first encountered in the underground depths the novel repeatedly identifies not only with death but with the weight of Roman history that also surrounds Miriam. He appears mysteriously between the chapter entitled "Subterranean Reminiscences," in which her friends lose Miriam underground, and the one that follows it, "The Spectre of the Catacomb," in which they find her accompanied by a mysterious figure. Specter, catacomb, subterranean reminiscence: these elements compound together to precipitate the figure with whom Miriam has an unspeakable relationship, all the more troubling for being unexplained. The account of Miriam's mysterious background is in turn sandwiched between manifestations of the Model, suggesting the depth of their connection, the impossibility of encountering one without the other:

> Miriam's model has so important a connection with our story, that it is essential to describe the singular mode of his first appearance, and how he subsequently became a self appointed follower of the young female artist. In the first place, however, we must devote a page or two to certain peculiarities in the position of Miriam herself.

The murder of the Model by Donatello is one of the two dark centers around which the novel moves, and like the other—Hilda's disappearance—it is shrouded in a manifold indeterminacy. The Model, a figure for the transgressive, perhaps incestuous past that shadows Miriam's life, is a more maleficent version of the Harper in *Wilhelm Meister*. The absence of any identification aside from his role in the studio—"the Model"—underlines his association with the theme of art in particular, as does the place from which he challenges Miriam immediately prior to his death: "In the basement-wall of the palace, shaded from the moon, there was a deep, empty niche, that had probably once contained a statue; not empty, neither; for a figure now came forth from it, and approached Miriam" (170–71). It would be unrewarding to attempt to parse out every component part of the allegorical suggestions and symbolic displacements of a novel that tantalizes with such an excess of apparent significance. Still, the practice of art is evidently at stake in the crises at the heart of *The Marble Faun*, so that a wish-fulfillment fantasy is identifiable in the novel's transposition of the order of things: the artist is loved by a beautiful living antiquity (instead of obsessively pursuing a dead past); she is implacably pursued by the modern model (rather than depending on his services in order to realize her visions). We may think of the concern expressed by the statues of Italy in the song of Mignon ("The marble figures gaze at me in rue: / 'You poor child, what have they done to you?'"). Needless to say, in both cases the passion really runs the other way; the desire is all on the side of the artist or art lover. Antiquity is indifferent to our needs, and the modern model is the necessary requirement for the production of new art.

The crime itself is never shown, only its effect on those who witnessed or participated in it, so that Hilda is as affected by what she *sees* as Miriam and Donatello by their actions. Indeed, the novel goes to great lengths to validate the way in which Hilda's sensibility transforms seeing into complicity, particularly as the crime itself takes place in a play of glances: "Miriam seemed dreamily to remember falling on her knees; but, in her whole recollection of that wild moment, she beheld herself as in a dim show, and could not well distinguish what was done and suffered; no, not even whether she were really an actor and sufferer in the scene" (171). Not surprisingly, when she asks Donatello, "What have you done?" his answer is at once about passionate intimacy and about *looking*: "I did what your eyes bade me do, when I asked them with mine, as I held the wretch over the precipice!" Her response only emphasizes the specific faculty identified in his claim: "'And my eyes bade you do it!' repeated she" (172–73). Hilda's own account of the crime returns to the visual:

"A look passed from your eyes to Donatello's—a look—"

"Yes, Hilda, yes!" exclaimed Miriam, with intense eagerness. "Do not pause now! That look? . . . Ah, Donatello was right, then! . . . My eyes bade him do it! . . ."

"It all passed so quickly—all like a glare of lightning!" said Hilda. "And yet it seemed to me that Donatello had paused while one might draw a breath. But that look!—Ah, Miriam, spare me! Need I tell more?" (210)

Appropriately enough, the murder, with its muffled yet suggestively erotic description, is also evidently the moment at which Miriam and Donatello consummate their love. In this passionate crime caused and shared by looking, in which victim and perpetrator are model and statue, and in which artist and antique inspiration are linked in an unspeakable passion, Hawthorne offers a rich figure for the challenge of Rome.

I have mentioned that *The Marble Faun* has a second mystery, one less dramatic than the murder of the Model but more ineffable: the disappearance of Hilda. Ultimately it is in the romantic modulation of separation and intimacy that *The Marble Faun* is most indebted to *Corinne*, and that both indicate their affinity to *The American*. The separation and desire that characterize Staël's novel are unmissable, but they are perhaps most vividly represented in the scene at the Sistine Chapel in which Nelvil suddenly catches sight of Corinne but she is completely out of his reach:

> While Oswald was absorbed in the thoughts aroused by all the objects around him, he saw Corinne enter the women's gallery behind the grill which separates them from the men. He had not hoped to see her yet; she was dressed in black, pale from fasting, and trembling so much at the sight of Oswald that she had to lean on the railing to keep walking. At that moment, the *miserere* began.
>
> Perfectly trained in this pure, ancient music, the voices emanate from a gallery where the vault begins to curve. The singers are invisible.[14]

A related but more complete religious captivity becomes important at the end of *The Marble Faun* as it will become in *The American*. In Hawthorne's novel, however, the Gothic frustrations of the lovers are inextricably linked to the challenge of art.

"The Emptiness of Picture Galleries" is the evocative title of the chapter devoted to Hilda's malaise after witnessing the crime of Miriam and Donatello, to her new inability to take pleasure in the art objects that had become the center of her life. In spite of having been warned to escape the insalubrious atmosphere of the city during the summer months, which is described, in a phrase that captures the claustrophobic antiquity of the place, as "air has been breathed too often," Hilda stays through the summer to copy. Her answer to the warning is an important anticipation of her future captivity: "The Old Masters will not set me free!" (333–34). Like Christopher Newman years later, Hilda is overpowered by the claims of art in the museum to the point that even admiration is no longer possible:

> So the melancholy girl wandered through those long galleries. . . . She grew sadly critical and condemned everything that she was wont to admire. . . .
>
> And as for these galleries of Roman palaces, they were to Hilda—though she still trod them with the forlorn hope of getting back her sympathies—they were drearier than the white-washed walls of a prison corridor. (341)

Hilda's story moves surprisingly in parallel to Donatello's. Like him, she has to be subjected to a dark vision of the world before she can fully participate in a redemptive love. Like him also, she must go through a process of purging through incarceration in order to be redeemed from the tainting power of the knowledge she had to take on. These are characteristic themes in Hawthorne, but it is also clear that in this novel the crime and Hilda's response are intimately connected to her role as artist, otherwise, why would she feel guilty at witnessing the statue kill the model at the bidding of her passionate alter ego? It would be a strange development for *her* relations with the Old Masters to have changed, unless her desires were in some measure also represented in the crime. Though her spirits are lifted when—in a scene particularly admired and eventually emulated by James—she goes to confession and shares her burden with a priest, the narrator notes that "[i]t is questionable whether she was ever so perfect a copyist thenceforth" (375).

When Hilda abruptly vanishes soon after her confession, the novel moves beyond the allegorical matrix it has established toward a fantasy that is ever more flamboyantly strange and uncomfortable. Rather than offering any account of her whereabouts, the narrative focuses on her lover, the sculptor Kenyon, and the bewildered loss he feels at her disappearance on the very day he intended to propose marriage. Kenyon's fearful speculations tend toward the kind of melodramatic events characteristic of crisis in the romance:

> Hilda was most likely a prisoner in one of the religious establishments that are so numerous in Rome. The idea, according to the aspect in which it was viewed, brought now a degree of comfort, and now an additional perplexity. On the one hand, Hilda was safe from any but spiritual assaults; on the other, where was the possibility of breaking through all those barred portals, and searching a thousand convent-cells, to set her free. (416)

The influence of the frustrated Oswald and his perpetual circlings around Corinne are readily evident in this strange inexplicable separation with its roots in the Radcliffean Gothic. The frustration of the desirous man arbitrarily bereft of his lover will also shape the affront of Europe Christopher Newman has to feel, hence Madame de Cintré's loss to a harsh convent in which he can only hear her voice mingled indistinguishably with many others. The subtitle of *Corinne—or Italy*—advertises the analogy between the beautiful and endlessly fascinating central character and the cultural object of desire. Although they differ in important details, a similar relationship exists in both *The American* and *The Marble Faun*, novels in which travel to centers of culture stands in for courtship, and in which the encounter with admired achievement (or "Europe") is represented by narratives run through with inverisimilitude. That Hawthorne never reveals where Hilda has been taken, much as James cannot identify the real necessity for the frustration of Christopher Newman, suggests that the distance and longing both texts represent have a source that is extraliterary (which is not, in these cases, all that different from being *extra* literary).

Before he can think how to recover his beloved, Kenyon is tempted by another mystery evidently connected to that of Hilda's fate. As the novel nears its end, he is summoned to a spot on the Campagna, where he finds a newly happy Donatello and Miriam waiting for him, as well as an antique statue of Venus that they have apparently dug up. Subterranean memories of past achievement are brought to light at this moment, not as uncanny model but as emblem of inexplicable love. His friends tell him that Hilda is safe and will soon be returned to him, but it is clear that on the day this happens they themselves will lose their own happiness. He encounters Donatello and Miriam again in the frenzy of the Carnival, at which point they make their farewells, and he rediscovers Hilda. The bafflement and frustration that characterize the end of the novel come to include the reader, as the narrator is flamboyant in his obfuscation as to where she has been:

> Whence she had come, or where she had been hidden, during this mysterious interval, we can but imperfectly surmise, and do not mean, at present, to make it a matter of formal explanation with the reader. It is better, perhaps, to fancy that she had been snatched away to a Land of Picture; that she had been straying with Claude in the golden light which he used to shed over his landscapes, but which he could never have beheld with his waking eyes. . . . We will imagine that, for the sake of the true simplicity with which she loved them, Hilda had been permitted, for a season, to converse with the great, departed Masters of the pencil, and behold the diviner works which they have painted in heavenly colours. (452)

The explanation—insofar as this is one—returns the story to the museum, now become a beautiful overwhelming prison. Hilda's captivity shades into a fantasy of intimacy with a pantheon of admired artists of the sort the nineteenth century loved to produce—for all the word as though she had entered Delaroche's Hemicycle at the École des Beaux Arts in Paris, the frieze at the foot of the Albert Memorial, or even the transhistorical universe of poets described in Shelley's *Defense of Poetry* or Barrett Browning's *A Vision of Poets*.[15] It is clear in any case that Hilda's captivity is in some measure a further manifestation or exaggeration of her love of the Old Masters.

Each solution of the mysteries offered in *The Marble Faun* results in further mystification—the proliferation of choices itself undermining the possibility of clarification. Hilda's imprisonment, the narrator suggests, is due to either "the stratagems of a religious body, or the secret acts of a despotic government" (456). Adding these two coercive forces to the earlier proposal that Hilda has been snatched away "to converse with the great departed Masters," it becomes possible to propose that her unlikely disappearance is not so strange to the novel as it at first appears. James's intimation of the link between romance and irresistible power in the preface to *The American* is helpful at this juncture. After all, Hawthorne may not be attempting to obscure by excess so much as to locate by triangulation the force that has held Hilda in thrall, not only for the sixty pages during which she is lost sight of, but for the duration of the novel. The coercive power that has made it impossible for Hilda to undertake original creative work in Rome is given its most exaggerated presentation in the novel's last and most baffling conceit. Somewhere between stratagem and power, between religion and despotism, Hilda's location when she is lost sight of may be just where Hawthorne suggests: among the Old Masters, in the museum.

Be it the subterranean reminiscences of Miriam, or the emptiness of picture galleries experienced by Hilda, the novel presents a consistently challenging view of the relationship between art and artist. The literary repetitions informing the romance of the plot only add to the sense of Rome as a space at once inviting the admiration of beauty and disabling original creation. The negotiation among pleasure, abundance, and control typical of the experience of the museum is precisely the difficult task of the artist in this novel. So it is that the elaborate though never clarified scene in which Hilda is released into the Carnival is a moment of creative frenzy and pleasure (particularly for Donatello and Miriam) identified by Kenyon as difficult to reconcile with the "despotic" political and religious authorities in charge of the city. The pleasure of the artist is a moment of license in what is otherwise a condition of subjection.

Immediately on publication frustrated readers demanded clarification of the mysteries of the novel. The "Postscript" Hawthorne obligingly provided clears up little, but it does demonstrate the debt *The American* owes this novel. The author (over) explains where Hilda was kept (precisely in the kind of location in which Madame de Cintré will find her own relief), "a prisoner in the Convent of the Sacré Coeur, in the Trinità de' Monti" (466). He also returns to the topic of Miriam's guilt, noting with a repetition that only highlights prior statements that "her crime lay merely in a glance" (467). As is the case with Hilda, trapped by her admiration for the Old Masters, the organ of Miriam's strange crime is the eye. Hawthorne not only proposes solutions to some of the mysteries of the novel in this "Postscript" but also offers what amounts to a methodological justification of the status of the faun. Instead of clarifying whether Donatello really was a kind of mythical being or simply an entirely human member of an ancient family, the author explains that he "had hoped to mystify this anomalous creature between the Real and the Fantastic" (463). If James learns on rereading *The American* that he too has located his narrative in an indeterminate space "between the Real and the Fantastic," it is because both authors are driven to romance when attempting to account for the power of the encounter with culture.

The Monster in the Gallery and the Reflective Challenge of the Museum

I have tried to suggest ways in which the romance that James could not help writing in *The American* is shaped (even *mis*shaped) by a tradition of narratives structured around art, desire, and distance. James's preface confesses not simply that he wrote romance but that he apparently could no more stop himself from doing so than he could recognize what he was up to at the time. We may understand the distortion of James's tale as having its source in the need to mold his story around shapes that had become unavoidable for the tradition in which he was participating, a tradition that gave James the language to deal with institutions that for him were always charged with the promise and fear of culture.

That so dynamic a character as Christopher Newman begins his adventure in a museum and never really leaves it is emblematic of the power of the institution in James. I have cited the novelist's first memoir, *A Small Boy and Others,* on the ways in which the Louvre served as a sort of window on Europe during his youthful stay in Paris. But windows can be understood as metaphors for escape, and escape *from* the museum is not, ultimately, what James offers. James's first visit to the Louvre took place in 1857, and it is marked in his memoirs as a moment of beautiful, but not for that less frightening, initiation:

> [T]here was alarm in it somehow as well as bliss. The bliss in fact I think scarce disengaged itself at all, but only the sense of a freedom of contact and appreciation really too big for one, and leaving such a mark on the very place, the pictures, the frames themselves, the figures within them, . . . the smell of the massively enclosed air, that I have never since renewed the old exposure without renewing again the old emotion and taking up the small scared consciousness. *That* . . . is the charm—to feel afresh the beginning of so much that was to be. (*Autobiography,* 198; emphasis in the original)

The expansive quality of the museum for the young James is unmissable: "The great premises" are "the house of life" or the very "image of the world" (198). His focus at the collection was, like that of Christopher Newman, on the paintings in the Salon Carré. But the impact of the experience is attributable to something larger than one image or one collection—to what the museum stands for as an introduction to self-conscious culture.

A well-known passage from the same memoir records a dream of escape not from but *inside* the museum. A moment of subterranean reminiscence, of the emptiness of picture galleries, it is also a vivid demonstration of the human pathos involved in the circulation of experience through desire that characterizes romance for the novelist. In James's dream, the museum becomes a home, a place of ghosts, site of an unforgettable affront and of an act of brave pursuit that leads one back to where one began. While serving as a vivid representation of the forces motivating James's imagination of the encounter with Europe from Clement Searle to Christopher Newman to his very last works, this constellation of elements is anticipated as far back as Wilhelm Meister's unsettled response to the restitution of his grandfather's art collection.

Speaking of himself and his brother, James opens with a reminiscence of that nineteenth-century trope he memorably recreated in Christopher Newman's aesthetic headache, the overwhelming effect of accumulated art:

> We were not yet aware of style, though on the way to become so, but were aware of mystery, which indeed was one of its forms—while we saw all the others, without exception, exhibited at the Louvre, where at first they simply overwhelmed and bewildered me.
>
> It was as if they had gathered there into a vast deafening chorus; I shall never forget how—speaking, that is, for my own sense—they filled those vast halls with the influence rather of some complicated sound, diffused and reverberant, than of such visibilities as one could directly deal with. To distinguish among these, in the charged and coloured and confounding air, was difficult—it discouraged and defied; which was doubtless why my impression originally best entertained was that of those magnificent parts of the great gallery simply not inviting us to distinguish. (195)

The museum serves at once as invitation and challenge (James writes later in the autobiographies of "the great insolence of the Louvre" (274). But the notion that the institution stands for Europe as a whole serves to justify and explain the bewilderment provoked by the encounter with so much accumulated culture:

> They only arched over us in the wonder of their endless golden riot and relief, figured and flourished in perpetual revolution, breaking into great high-hung circles and symmetries of squandered picture, opening into deep outward embrasures that threw off the rest of monumental Paris somehow as a told story, a sort of wrought effect or bold ambiguity for a vista, and yet held it there, at every point, as a vast bright gage, even at moments a felt adventure, of experience. This comes to saying that in those beginnings I felt myself most happily cross that bridge over to Style constituted by the wondrous Galerie d'Apollon, drawn out for me as a long but assured initiation and seeming to form with its supreme

covered ceiling and inordinately shining parquet a prodigious tube or tunnel through which I inhaled little by little, that is again and again, a general sense of *glory*. The glory meant ever so many things at once, not only beauty and art and supreme design, but history and fame and power, the world in fine raised to the richest and noblest expression. . . . But who shall count the sources at which an intense young fancy (when a young fancy *is* intense) capriciously, absurdly drinks?—so that the effect is, in twenty connections, that of a love-philtre or fear-philtre which fixes for the senses their supreme symbol of the fair or the strange. (195–96; emphases in the original)

In this confused potion, which blends love and fear in an undefinable amalgamation of contraries, of the attractive or the repulsive or both at once, we may hear a description of what Christopher Newman had to find in Europe: love and fear emerging from the museum. The fantastic drink is, of course, related to that poison unconsciously drunk out of "the nostalgic cup" described in the preface to "A Passionate Pilgrim" (*Prefaces*, 1205) discussed previously. But the love and fear that he drinks in, the attraction and repulsion represented by the gallery, is given even more vivid shape in the dream return of the older James to this setting:

The Galerie d'Apollon became for years what I can only term a splendid scene of things, even of the quite irrelevant or, as might be, almost unworthy; and I recall to this hour, with the last vividness, what a precious part it played for me, and exactly by that continuity of honour, on my awaking, in a summer dawn many years later, to the fortunate, the instantaneous recovery and capture of the most appalling yet most admirable nightmare of my life. The climax of this extraordinary experience—which stands alone for me as a dream-adventure founded in the deepest, quickest, clearest act of cogitation and comparison, act indeed of life-saving energy, as well as in unutterable fear—was the sudden pursuit, through an open door, along a huge high saloon, of a just dimly-descried figure that retreated in terror before my rush and dash (a glare of inspired reaction from irresistible but shameful dread,) out of the room I had a moment before been desperately, and all the more abjectly, defending by the push of my shoulder against hard pressure on lock and bar from the other side. The lucidity, not to say the sublimity, of the crisis had consisted of the great thought that I, in my appalled state, was probably still more appalling than the awful agent, creature or presence, whatever he was, whom I had guessed, in the suddenest wild start from sleep, the sleep within my sleep, to be making for my place of rest. The triumph of my impulse, perceived in a flash as I acted on it by myself at a bound, forcing the door outward, was the grand thing, but the great point of the whole was the wonder of my final recognition. Routed, dismayed, the tables turned upon him by my so surpassing him for straight aggression and dire intention, my visitant was already but a diminished spot in the long perspective, the tremendous, glorious hall, as I say, over the far-gleaming floor of which, cleared for the occasion of its great line of priceless vitrines down the middle, he sped for *his* life, while a great storm of thunder and lightning played through the deep embrasures of high windows at the right. The lightning that revealed the retreat revealed also the wondrous place and, by the same amazing play, my young imaginative life in it of long before, the sense of which, deep within me, had kept it whole, preserved it to this thrilling use; for what in the world were the deep embrasures and the so polished floor but those of the Galerie d'Apollon of my childhood? The "scene of something" I had vaguely then felt it? Well I might, since it was to be the scene of that immense hallucination. (196-97)

James is profligate in his metaphors, as in most of his attempts to account for the Europe in his psyche. It is nevertheless evident that the combined pleasure and revulsion of this nightmare are as characteristic of his reminiscences of encounters with Europe as of his account of *The American* in his preface. The quality in question is well summarized in James's paradoxical description of his nightmare, "the most appalling yet most admirable." This passage contains three mysteries: the source of the pleasure, the nature of the fear, and the character of James's so memorable and triumphant resistance. Following as it does the author's reminiscence of a real visit to the Louvre, the pleasure of this dream may be seen to consist in his overcoming of the original confusion that characterized his response to the museum: hence the reflective, even ratiocinative verbs that are used to describe the climax of "a dream-adventure founded in the deepest, quickest, clearest act of *cogitation* and *comparison*." Calm terms not generally appropriate for heroic struggles, cogitation and comparison are in fact the very faculties of analysis that the original experience of the museum had entirely incapacitated: "[T]hey simply overwhelmed and bewildered me. . . . To distinguish among these, in the charged and coloured and confounding air, was difficult—it discouraged and defied; which was doubtless why my impression originally best entertained was that of those magnificent parts of the great gallery simply not inviting us to distinguish."

The threat and the self-defense of the dream nevertheless present a strange paradox. Insofar as James describes his fearful act, he is clear on the fact that he is resisting a pressure from the outside ("defending by the push of my shoulder against hard pressure on lock and bar from the other side"). It is striking, then, that at the moment ("the lucidity, not to say the sublimity of the crisis") when he realizes the almost symmetrical relationship in which he stands to the object of his fear (expressed in language itself richly symmetrical—"I, in my appalled state, was probably still more appalling"), he is instantaneously able to push through the door he had been defending with such difficulty. This door that swings two ways is a pure creation of James's dream logic, but it also suggests, taken along with the symmetries of language describing the dreamer and his nemesis, another piece of furniture: a mirror. The rush that takes James through his threatened liminal space is too precisely the same as the force that opposes him not to be understood as virtually identical with it. The insistent speed of the dream is the speed of self-recognition.[16]

Doors and hallways proliferate in James's imagination of important relationships—to Europe and to the past principal among them. "To knock at the door of the past," he notes at the outset of the *A Small Boy and Others*, "was in a word to see it open to me quite wide" (3). In England, later, he finds "the mild forces making for our conscious relief, pushing the door to Europe definitely open" (129). The attempt to write a story capturing the peculiar notion of a man pursuing his own ghost goes back in James's oeuvre at least to Clement Searle in "The Passionate Pilgrim," but it reaches its apotheosis in "The Jolly Corner," a tale in which it is abundantly clear that the apparition is an uncanny vision of the self. In this well-known story of 1906 in which James rewrites his dream of self-persecution in the Louvre, Spencer Brydon spends his nights wandering the halls of his childhood home in New York City, tracking the ghost of who he would have been had he not left the country for Europe.[17] As rich in autobiographical elements, as in narrative complexity, this story of a return to the site of youthful experience leads to an improbable ballet in which Brydon quite literally seems to be turning and re-turning in order to catch a glimpse of himself: "[H]is only recourse then was in abrupt turns, rapid recoveries of ground. He wheeled about, retracing his steps, as if he might so catch in his face at the least the stirred air of some other quick revolution" (714). The story's dense complexity serves as the narrative indication of the impossible project of return James seeks to represent. As in James's Louvre dream, the unstable point at the core of the matter is the reversal of the standard relationship between haunter and haunted; in both accounts, the living person is himself an object of fear to his ghost: "People enough, first and last, had been in terror of apparitions, but who had ever before so turned the tables and become himself, in the apparitional world, an incalculable terror?" (712). Indeed, when the two figures (Brydon past and present) meet, the living man is dismayed to realize that he cannot be faced by the specter of the man he might have been.[18]

Spencer Brydon is intemperate on the pleasure that is to be found in the attempt to reclaim one's past self, "a thrill that represented sudden dismay . . . but also represented, and with the selfsame throb, the strangest, the most joyous, possibly the next minute almost the proudest, duplication of consciousness" (715). The sensations of fear and pleasure that James identifies with his dream of the Louvre, are also to be found at the climax of his character's encounter with his "duplicated consciousness." Spencer Brydon identifies his actions as he stalks his past as "an image almost worthy of an age of greater romance," but he soon corrects himself, "since what age of romance, after all, could have matched either the state of his mind, or . . . the wonder of his situation" (716). If the adventure of the hunt is reminiscent of romance, Brydon's ghost-self is himself a figure drawn from the registers of melodrama or romance, a tortured mustachioed millionaire dandy (with the added color of two fingers lost from his hand, "as if accidentally shot away," 725). The description is clear: the sought-after stranger Brydon discovers haunting his home is "evil, odious, blatant, vulgar," and—in a further reversal—irresistibly pushing toward him at the very moment he loses consciousness and falls into a dead faint (725).

The sudden turns that characterize the story and the dream are traceable in both cases to the impossible action of self-recuperation both narratives strive to represent. In Brydon's pursuit through the house, culminating in the surging forward of his other self at the end of the tale, as in James's pursuit of his own persecutor through the corridors of the Louvre, we have a representation of two qualities James discovered to be central to his early works when he reread them: speed and romance. Lightning flashes in the dream as James chases his alter ego; Brydon encounters himself as an unpleasant plutocrat who is not only "evil, odious," but—two words as suitable for a story as for a person—"blatant, vulgar." "Ghosts," it is worth noting, and "historical characters" are two of the elements James mentions in his preface to *The American* as incorrectly understood to be indispensable for romance. In that account, an action such as that undertaken by Brydon or by James in his dream, "the panting pursuit of danger," is identified as "the pursuit of life itself, in which danger awaits us possibly at every step and faces us at every turn." The dream and the story include the panting pursuit of life, along with characteristics that can be mistaken for nothing other than romance, which "stands, on the other hand, for the things that, with all the facilities in the world, all the wealth and all the courage and all the wit and all the adventure, we never *can* directly know; the things that can reach us only through the beautiful circuit and subterfuge of our thought and our desire" (*Prefaces*, 1063).

Although texts such as the dream of the Louvre and "The Jolly Corner" seem to call for autobiographical reading, the confessional impulse in James only has its full meaning within the broader cultural complex giving it form. Like Wilhelm Meister when he finds himself again before his grandfather's collection, James recognizes the moving quality of the return along with an uncanny sense—both fearful and pleasant to the novelist—that he himself may be becoming something like a ghost. The margins of the museum are so wide that it is as if the very door of James's bedroom opened on to its corridors, or as if he slept in the Salon Carré. The return to the Louvre by means of a Gothic tale of monsters, haunted palaces, and wild pursuits amid flashes of lightning is an emphatic demonstration of the romantic drives that shape James's stories of the self's encounter with Europe. The speed of *Roderick Hudson*, the romance of *The American*—James finds pleasure in his inability to modulate these, because in his failures he identifies traces of the place Europe held in his youthful imagination. In rereading himself he revisits at once a museum, the world, "and the house of life":

> *That*, with so many of the conditions repeated, is the charm—to feel afresh the beginning of so much that was to be. . . . one's stretched, one's even strained, perceptions, one's discoveries and extensions piece by piece, come back, on the great premises, almost as so many explorations of the house of life, so many circlings and hoverings round the image of the world. (*A Small Boy and Others*, 198, emphasis in the original)

If the magical quality of passing through the mirror suggests the challenge of self-recognition, the contiguity of bedroom and museum confounds the domestic with the fantastic, the near and familiar with the unreachable. The initial double surge toward the door of the dream recalls Dorian Gray lunging at the portrait of the real self he has hidden in his childhood school room, a climactic moment resulting in an inversion closely related to that in James's dream. As the fantastic ageless image of Dorian attacks the hideous likeness of his real self, his weapon is immediately turned against himself. The preface of Wilde's novel, it is worth noting, also anticipates the unstable dialectical interplay of romantic and real of the preface to *The American*. The best known of the mirror aphorisms of Wilde's polemic—"The nineteenth century dislike of Realism is the rage of Caliban seeing his own face in a glass. The nineteenth century dislike of Romanticism is the rage of Caliban not seeing his own face in a glass"—return in another, more threatening shape in James. "All art is at once surface and symbol. Those who go beneath the surface do so at their peril. Those who read the symbol do so at their peril."[19] Wilde describes an oscillation between surface and depth that is only likely to be overcome in the wish fulfillment of the dream or fantasy.

As pleasure is apparently at stake no matter who has the upper hand—whether James is pursued or he is pursuing—it is difficult to avoid the suggestion that what is being enacted in James's "most appalling yet most admirable" dream is a structure of desire consistent with that described in the preface to *The American*, in which simplified power relations are among the surest signs of romance: "I am not sure an infallible sign of the latter [the romantic] is not this rank vegetation of the 'power' of bad people that good get into, or *vice versa*. It is so rarely, alas, into *our* power that any one gets!" (1067). James is more interested in where his terms meet than in where they separate. The difference between romantic and real that he describes is a thin line—as thin as the quicksilver on a sheet of glass that makes a mirror. The novelist's fastidious differentiations indicate the difficulty of separating his categories rather than any success in sorting them out—hence his admission in a passage from the preface to *The American* cited earlier: "It is as difficult . . . to trace the dividing-line between the real and the romantic as to plant a milestone between north and south" (1067). On the one hand James proposes the real as what cannot *not* be met, on the other the romantic as what our desire wishes us to encounter. He raises the specter of danger not only in the elements of the romantic that he dismisses in the preface, but also in the fantasies of encounter and return in the narratives I have discussed. The nightmare pursuit and counterpursuit of the terrifying figure in the Louvre are romantic (r_1) in their conventional details (the stormy night in a haunted castle) and in their representation of danger (r_1J). But the context in which James presents the dream, along with the pleasure he takes in retelling it, also suggests a stranger reading: that the dream of threat may be a *relief* from the overwhelming proliferation of the Louvre—that, for all its agitation, it may well be a paradoxical version of the romance of peace (r_2). If the treatment of the Louvre in James's biographical writings and in *The American* makes the continent into a museum, in the unforgettable dream the museum is itself reduced to a hallway, and the experience of this prized space into an essentially simplified structure of pursuit, counterpursuit, and fantastic partial recognition.

THE SENSE OF THE PAST

That romance bears witness to its literary antecedents is not simply a formal matter. In its endless iterations of suffering and relief, the mode allows authors to intimate ways in which a restless insatiability may be the other side of a desire to be at rest. James's own formulations are useful not because they amount to a careful morphology of romance or a set of precise distinctions. On the contrary, what stands out is the starkly different elements he identifies as closely connected—the real and the romantic, the hoped for and the feared. The next chapter demonstrates the force of romance in the museum world James imagined in his last great novel, *The Golden Bowl*. But the terms he developed are notably useful in addressing authors whose careers are more fully associated with the twentieth century, such as Freud, Forster, Mann, and Proust—writers whose engagements with the art romance are addressed in the final chapters of this book. Before turning to the manifestations of the art romance in a set of highly wrought modernist works, however it will be useful to touch on one of James's most important failures and its nineteenth-century sources.

As Richard Brodhead has demonstrated, James could never escape the force of Hawthorne in his imagination. Indeed, the place of the romancer is still at issue in *The Sense of the Past*, the longest of the unfinished fragments on which James was working before his death, and a text that brings the longings of the early nineteenth century to the threshold of an era that often gives the appearance of being so committed to satisfaction as to have left the commemoration of desire far behind.[20] In the discussion of *The Marble Faun* in his earliest book, the young James found not simply romance but a troubling failure in negotiating between the claims of the fantastic and the real. "The fault of *Transformation*," he asserts, using the English title he always preferred because of his discomfort with the character of the Faun that gave the American edition its title, "is that the element of the unreal is pushed too far, and that the book is neither positively of one category nor of another" (*Hawthorne*, 447). As we will see, James closes on a markedly negative note, but he is as clear on the sources of pleasure in the novel as he is on his complaints. At the heart of his admiration is Hilda's turn to the confessional to unburden herself of a guilt acquired in spite of herself:

> The character of Hilda has always struck me as an admirable invention—one of those things that mark the man of genius. It needed a man of genius and of Hawthorne's imaginative delicacy, to feel the propriety of such a figure as Hilda's and to perceive the relief it would both give and borrow. (446)

Genius, relief given, relief borrowed—James is prolific but unclear in his praise. "If I have called the whole idea of the presence and effect of Hilda in the story a trait of genius, the purest touch of inspiration is the episode in which the poor girl deposits her burden" (446) In his praise of Hilda for her role in confessing her burden, James markedly ignores her participation in the very kind of inverisimilitude for which he faults the novel, particularly her vanishing at the doorway of the Palazzo Cenci, not to be seen again for sixty pages. Or, rather, such material is present only as it is described in quite uncomplimentary terms at the close of James's account:

> And since I am speaking critically, I may go on to say that the art of narration, in *Transformation*, seems to me more at fault than in the author's other novels. The story straggles and wanders, is dropped and taken up again, and towards the close lapses into an almost fatal vagueness. (447)

Much in this material—the genius of the confession as much as the fatal vagueness and the dropped story—returns in *The Sense of the Past*, an improbable recapitulation of the attempt to represent the desire for culture that drove James's early work, from *Hawthorne* to "The Passionate Pilgrim" to *Roderick Hudson* and *The American*. Given that "transmitted and inherited property" was the prescription for avoiding factitiousness offered in *Hawthorne*, Ralph Pendrel, the history-loving American author, who is the protagonist of the novel might seem very safe in this regard. After all, he learns at the beginning of the book that he has been left a home in England by an admirer of his work—a member of the alienated British side of his family who has read Ralph's one book: *The Sense of the Past*. And yet, Ralph's acquisition of property does not usher him into a deeper reality. Instead, he finds himself in the first instance haunting the house in the attempt to satisfy an impossible wish typical of James: to catch a glimpse of the face in a portrait from the first quarter of the eighteenth century representing a man turned away from the viewer. Rather than ever-less factitious, Ralph becomes quite fantastic, a new version of Spencer Brydon or Clement Searle, tantalized restless searchers for contact with the representatives of a lost age. Ralph soon discovers the vision he is pursuing to be none other than an image of *himself* in the past, a realization made all the more uncanny by the discovery that the figure from the past has been as eager in pursuit of him in the future as he has been of himself in the past. "To look back at all," explains James in *A Small Boy and Others*, "is to meet the apparitional and to find in its ghostly face the silent stare of an appeal" (54). *The Sense of the Past* is an attempt to give a new life and impossible agency to the ghostly face looking back at the anxious retrospective sensibility.

The encounter with the ancestral self from 1820 might have been the climax of one of the late short stories, but it only concludes the opening stages of the novel. In the next part of the work, Ralph finds himself living the life of the Ralph from the past, while the Ralph from the past is living his life in the future (though this is never described). "The sense of the past," Ralph had been told by the woman he loves as she refused his proposal of marriage at the opening of the novel, "*is* your sense" (33; emphasis in the original). All Ralph has ever wanted, marriage to Aurora Coyne aside, is to put himself in the closest possible relation to bygone eras. Like Hilda, lost to vision after stepping through a doorway and perhaps finding herself in her beloved land of painting, Ralph disappears into the very place he had sought for so long, gone from the real world into an impossible vision.

One scene acts as the hinge between Ralph's pursuit of the past and Ralph's taking up his abode there, that is, the elaborately described visit to the American ambassador—a moment the narrator compares to the visit to the confessional by Hilda that James had so admired forty years before:

> The upshot of the state in which he found himself . . . was a sudden decision to call on the Ambassador. . . . He recalled the chapter in Hawthorne's fine novel in which the young woman from New England kneels . . . to the old priest at

St. Peter's, and felt that he sounded as never before the depth of that passage. *His* case in truth was worse than Hilda's and his burden much greater, for she had been but a spectator of what weighed upon her, whereas he had been a close participant. It mattered little enough that his sense was not the sense of crime; it was the sense, in an extraordinary degree, of something done in passion, and of an experience far stranger than a mere glimpse, or than, if it came to that, a positive perpetration of murder. (87–88; emphasis in the original)

The novel invites the reader to see Ralph's stay in the past as comparable with Hilda's disappearance, which so closely follows her confession (indeed, Hawthorne suggests that one may have provoked the other). Disappearance from the world is marked in both cases by the simple transition of going through a door. Ralph in the past becomes a complicated recalibration of the American engaging Europe—a revision of Christopher Newman as much as of Hilda. Here then is one fantastic solution to the *Hawthorne* problem, namely the unavoidable provincialism of America and Americans in the first half of the nineteenth century: Send a *modern* back in time. Ralph, finding himself in the very period James described in *Hawthorne* as characterized by the lack of all cultural amenities is in fact able to operate with consumate ease. As a modern sophisticate, he can bring more culture to bear than the distinguished English family of the wife he is courting in the past:

[H]e soon ceased to care that he was after all apparently not able to pass for a barbarian—his connection with the secure world, that of manners and of every sort of cross-reference, that of the right tone and the clear tradition, had been settled at every point at which equivocation would otherwise have waited. (146)

And yet, in spite of Ralph's inherited ownership of his home and the exquisite culture he demonstrates whenever he is face-to-face with Europe, at the moment he comes to confess his situation to the ambassador to Britain (surely an inflation of Hawthorne's position as American consul in Liverpool) that august individual sees nothing real in what his compatriot describes. "[T]here would have been a failure of verisimilitude," James writes in one of the many self-reflexive moments in this strange novel, "if his host hadn't visibly wondered" (98). But then, Ralph himself insists on the unreal nature of the relationship in which he has found himself:

"Is the fact of your situation that you've seen a ghost?" . . .
"He was much better than any ghost." . . .
" 'Better?' "
"Well, much more contrary to nature." (100)

Ralph's enthusiasm aside, his adventure, like the novel itself, is a manifold fiasco. At first Ralph's time in the past, where he relives the life of the self now in the future, proves strangely easy. James uses a metaphor typical of successful rebuffs of the challenge of culture: "It's as if there were a few doors that don't yield to my push," he tells his intrigued but puzzled interlocutors in 1820, his language possibly about his negotiation of a foreign culture, but really about managing his uncanny return, "though we've seen most of them fly open, haven't we? Those I mean have to be opened from within, as you've also seen" (208). In spite of all the doors that fly open before this time-traveling adventurer, however, *A Sense of the Past* is the record of two failures, of Ralph to quite fit in in the past, and of Henry James to finish his work. The story breaks off, and in its posthumously published version it is completed only by an extensive set of notes James dictated—plans that demonstrate at every point the impossibility of seeing the project through. James apparently envisioned some very dark turns, especially in his treatment of the uncanny nature of Ralph's presence in the past. "[H]e fits in above all because he pleases," explains the author, "pleases at the same time that he creates malaise, by not being *like* them all" (290; emphasis in the original).

The narrative of Ralph in the past is most interesting, as James himself observes, in its representation of the character's double consciousness, the drama of his discovery that in spite of the fact that he is from the future, he has been supplied with a knowledge of the past that he does not quite know he possesses. "[T]he very beauty of the subject," the author suggests, is in Ralph's self alienation, "in the fact of his at the same time watching himself, watching his success, criticising his failure, being both the other man and not the other man, being just sufficiently the other, his prior, his own, self, not to be able to help living in that a bit too" (294). This unstable situation cannot last, however, and the alienation proves to be too strong for those with whom he is in contact. Indeed, it is the "malaise" he provokes that steadily drives Ralph back to his original (modern) self: "[H]e begins to live more, to live most, and most uneasily, in what I refer to as his own, his prior self, and less, uneasily less, in his borrowed, his adventurous, that of his tremendous speculation" (295).

As Ralph shows signs of failing in his inescapable mission of recapitulating the past, the man whose place he has taken comes back to haunt him. It is an almost indescribable paradox James outlines, one not liable to easy narrative representability—the past returning from the future to police the future in the past:

> He is liable then say to glimpses of vision of the other man, . . . to recurrences of a sense of that presence—which thus, instead of being off in the boundless vast of the modern, that is of the Future, as he has described its being to the Ambassador, *does* seem to him at times to hover and to menace. (305; emphasis in the original)

The story becomes confused to the point that it is impossible to imagine a resolution to the play of overlapping temporalities. Indeed, James himself becomes flustered on what has to be one of the key issues informing the story—whether or not his future person (the original Ralph) repeats the actions of the man in the portrait. "Just now," James confesses in the course of the dictation, "a page or two back, I lost my presence of mind, I let myself be scared, by a momentarily-confused appearance or assumption that he doesn't repeat it" (334). James's insistence that everything really hangs together, in spite of his own doubts, is a wonderful confession of the unrealizable nature of the project he has undertaken:

> The whole effect of my story is exactly his disconcerted and practically defeated face-to-faceness with the way in which they do take it—a matter, a fact, an appearance, that gives me all I want for accounting for his deflection. Thus is our having, his having, everything *en double* regulated and exhibited: he is doing over what the other fellow has done (though it acts for the other persons in it as if it were the first time—this quite all right, though not looking so at first)—and that accordingly hangs together and stands firm. Therefore accordingly my start, a little above, at being what I there for a moment called disconcerted and defeated was groundless: I was going on perfectly straight and right—and am now doing so again. (334-35)

"The story struggles and wanders, is dropped and taken up again, and towards the close lapses into an almost fatal vagueness"—this was James's description of the final chapters of *The Marble Faun*. What I am trying to suggest as I conclude this discussion at once of place, romance, and James's great and productive ambivalence toward a vital forebear, is that danger—the risk of defeat—is closely related to the inescapability of repetition ("doing over what the other fellow has done") that is the very promise and threat of the past. James's beloved Hilda was a copyist, we might remember. Old James revises young James on the formal pressures of writing while alienated from admired culture. Not only does the alienation become more general in the later work, but arrival itself is found to present challenges that fantasies of inheritance will not solve and that simple realism will never be able to express. And so it is that Ralph experiences an ever-greater mystification as he gets closer to satisfying the sense of the past that is his author's passion as much as his own. It is appropriate, after all, that Ralph is never rescued in the pages James managed to write—that the novel leaves him forever in 1820, in midthought, for all the world like Byron's Childe Harold abandoned in the shadows.

The notes, on the other hand, are quite clear on Ralph's fate. They end as they begin, with that ambassador who is a return to the figure of the patron surviving after the principal desiring character is lost, but also a stand-in—as all of James's patrons are—for the author, and so at once for James and (*en double*) for Hawthorne. The ambassador becomes the narrator of the destiny of Ralph and Aurora—who was apparently intended to reenter the picture and ultimately requite Ralph's affection. The final lines of the book ring with the happiness in James's voice as temporality and place merge together into the desire we may recognize as constitutive of romance: "He has only to give us in advance all that the duo must and will consist of in order to leave us just where, or at least just *as*, we want!" Pleasure shapes the concluding passage, but a deep constraint is unmissably present in James's "must and will," as is bound to be the case for a story that is given in advance (the way we are left is "just as we want"). The confusion of place, desire, and self in these closing words is characteristic of both the promise and the peril of an encounter with Europe understood to be always at once an experience of personal yearning satisfied and of the filling in of an inherited form.

The British Museum at the end of the nineteenth century. Photo: *The Queen's London: A Pictorial and Descriptive Record* (New York: Cassell Publishing, 1896).

CHAPTER 5

Speed, Desire, and the Museum: *The Golden Bowl* as Art Romance

SPEED, DESIRE, AND ROMANCE: *THE GOLDEN BOWL*

"YOU AMERICANS ARE almost incredibly romantic," observes the prince in an early conversation with Maggie Verver, his fiancée. She entirely agrees, proposing her father as a particularly egregious example:

> "His relation to the things he cares for . . . is absolutely romantic. So is his whole life over here—it's the most romantic thing I know."
>
> "You mean his idea for his native place?"
>
> "Yes—the collection, the Museum with which he wishes to endow it, and of which he thinks more, as you know, than of anything in the world. It's the work of his life and the motive of everything he does." . . .
>
> "Has it been his motive in letting me have you?"
>
> "Yes, my dear, positively—or in a manner. . . . You're at any rate a part of his collection . . . one of the things that can only be got over here. You're a rarity, an object of beauty, an object of price. . . . you belong to a class about which everything is known. You're what they call a *morceau de musée*.[1]

The prince's words encapsulate in a phrase much of what is at stake in this novel—Americans, romance, and what is or is not credible. *The Golden Bowl* (1904) provides a double lesson in romance, instructing both characters and readers. The question is why this lesson needs to be taught from inside the museum.[2] Maggie's father, Adam, aspires to build what is described, in a phrase of telling redundancy, as "a museum of museums." What is at stake is not simply a great inflation of Rowland Mallet's ambition for an American institution that will belong among the very greatest museums of the world. Adam Verver aims to construct a museum composed of museums, of what is already accredited as museum-worthy. In this sense, the prince is a museum piece in a number of ways, not least among them the fact that he is quite openly part of the collection the Ververs are assembling in their time in Europe. And so it is that when Maggie has concerns about her husband, she comforts herself with a visit to the British Museum archives, which house a room dedicated to Amerigo's family. When she calls him a *morceau de musée* in the preceding exchange, Maggie is identifying not only where the prince is going but where he comes from. But this does not clarify why and in what sense Adam Verver's museum is so grandly *romantic*, or how it is characteristic of a kind of national romance.

As we have seen, James availed himself readily of the fruitful interchange the nineteenth century had discovered between terms describing the individual's relation to art and the elements with which fiction typically represents human relations. The force and longevity of the art romance are amply demonstrated in James's last completed novel, a text of the early twentieth century deeply engaged with the nineteenth-century culture of art. Richard Brodhead has indicated the importance of James's concern with romance at the time he wrote *The Golden Bowl*.[3] Composed with the self-conscious artifice and the insistent symmetries of James's late period, the novel is not merely contemporary with the preface to *The American*, however; it is a flamboyant return with a difference to the themes of the earlier fiction itself. Christopher Newman's returning Columbus is answered by Prince Amerigo, a Vespucci who never left; Christopher's status as new man is trumped by *Adam* Verver—at once the newest and oldest man. What gives these smaller echoes their significance, however, is a twofold, structural similarity—both stories take place in a museum they cannot escape, and both are instances of the Jamesian romantic.

ROMANCE

The prince's comments to Maggie on the "almost incredibly romantic" nature of her compatriots comes at one of the several moments when he tries to find his bearings in relation to the bewildering family into which he has married. Her enthusiastic response suggests that the meaning of his words is clear, and yet nothing is more striking in the preface of *The American* James wrote so soon after this novel than the complicated reformulation of what may be meant by romance. As we saw in chapter 4, James insists that it is wrong to think we can recognize the truly romantic by reference to a set of standard narrative motifs expressive of great personal risk, "the idea of the facing of danger, the acceptance of great risks for the fascination, the very love, or their uncertainty, the joy of success if possible and of battle in any case." In James, danger is all too real. What identifies romance at its most powerful is a fantasy of *safety*, "some vision of a sublime security like that enjoyed on the flowery plains of heaven." *The Golden Bowl* rewards reading as a complex lesson in the seductive dangers and terrifying safety James identifies in the romance in the preface to *The American* and in his late work generally.

The topic is anticipated as the Assinghams discuss the relationship between the prince and Charlotte, his erstwhile lover, prior to the action of the novel. In the attempt to find the correct term to describe their motivation for having broken off a passionate affair, the supersubtle Fanny is as usual misguided in her response to her vulgar-minded husband's query. "[W]here was their romance?" he inquires. "Why, in their frustration, in their having the courage to look the facts in the face," is her paradoxical reply (53). James is committed to exploring the relationship between romance and looking and facts, but Fanny is only half right. The danger which the lovers posed for each other may be "romantic" in several common senses of the word (r_1 and r_1J), but it would fall under the category of the "real" in James's analysis. On the other hand, their escape from danger is romantic in James's sense; their romance, as will be more successfully the case for the Ververs, resides in their break for safety (r_2). The colonel is right to be puzzled; he could be responding to the preface to *The American* when he asks: "And their reason is what you call their romance?" (53).

Maggie evokes the association of romance with fantasies of adventure (r_1) early in the novel when she describes her activities with her father, "We've been like a pair of pirates—positively stage pirates, the sort who wink at each other and say 'Ha-ha!' " (11). When her father is about to propose to Charlotte, a similar register of images is evoked, and clearly identified as romantic:

> He liked, in this preliminary stage, to feel that he should be able to "speak" and that he would; the word itself being romantic, pressing for him the spring of association with stories and plays where handsome and ardent young men, in uniforms, tights, cloaks, high-boots, had it, in soliloquies, ever on their lips. (155)

That this kind of image or language will not aid the Ververs when they confront the infidelity of their spouses is indicated by Maggie's response to the crisis, which includes the language of romance only to demonstrate its inadequacy more fully. The precipitous swerve of an eastern caravan is fit metaphor for the failure of at least one kind of romance. The range of feelings of terror and disgust to which she refuses expression

> figured nothing nearer to experience than a wild eastern caravan, looming into view with crude colours in the sun, fierce pipes in the air, high spears against the sky, all a thrill, a natural joy to mingle with, but turning off short before it reached her and plunging into other defiles. She saw at all events why horror itself had almost failed her; the horror that, foreshadowed in advance, would, by her thought, have made everything that was unaccustomed in her cry out with pain. . . . It was the first sharp falsity she had known in her life, to touch at all, or be touched by; it had met her like some bad-faced stranger surprised

in one of the thick-carpeted corridors of a house of quiet on a Sunday afternoon; and yet, yes, amazingly, she had been able to look at terror and disgust only to know that she must put away from her the bitter-sweet of their freshness. (470–71)

It is impossible for Maggie to respond in "any of the immediate, inevitable, assuaging ways, the ways usually open to innocence outraged and generosity betrayed" because it would threaten her real desire, which is not for self-righteous emotional release but for a peace as absolute as that "sublime security" James identified at the heart of romance (471). Maggie's romance resides in the activities designed to manage the crisis, to stop it from exploding.[4] The moment in which Maggie considers her options is a vital recalibration of what it might mean to be romantic, of the possibilities opened up and foreclosed by such a new understanding. As Maggie studies her husband, father, and stepmother playing cards at this crucial juncture, the metaphor that comes to her mind is at once dramatic and self-referentially authorial: "[T]hey might have been figures rehearsing some play of which she herself was the author" (470).

Two parts of this central moment of the novel, of its lesson in romance, are worth some pause. If the image for the *impossibility* of self-gratifying, vulgar anger is typical of James's use of melodrama (that thrilling Eastern caravan), the figure for the sense of betrayal itself is more peculiar and evocative: this "first sharp falsity she had known in her life, to touch at all, or be touched by," has a very characteristic shape and locale: "[I]t had met her like some bad-faced stranger surprised in one of the thick-carpeted corridors of a house of quiet on a Sunday afternoon." The description of the encounter with evil is close to several disturbing meetings in houses we have already considered—in the dream of the Louvre, say, or in "The Jolly Corner." In those other instances it is an encounter with an uncanny return of *oneself* that makes the meeting at once significant and disturbing. How can this moment seem at all similar to those others, unless there is something akin to self-recognition in that ugly stranger who has surprised Maggie in her home—who has touched her or whom she has touched?[5]

The related nature of moments of challenge in the home is underlined by the defensive response they provoke in James. The quality of challenge and rebuff, of fearfully rushing up to the looking glass, then pushing through with guilty trepidation and anxious pleasure—all that made the encounters in the dream of the Louvre and in "The Jolly Corner" so constantly dynamic—is also present in this instant. As Maggie surveys her family and considers her options once the vulgar ones of rage and its gratification are discounted, she encounters not an ugly-faced stranger but the challenge of Charlotte herself. Indeed, Maggie's realization of a course of action is provoked by the surging presence of her rival:

It was not at once, however, that this became quite concrete; that was the effect of her presently making out that Charlotte was in the room, launched and erect there, in the middle and looking about her. . . . So definite a quest of her . . . was an impression that fairly assailed the Princess, and to which something of attitude and aspect, of the air of arrested pursuit and purpose, in Charlotte, together with the suggestion of her next vague movements, quickly added its meaning. This meaning was that she had decided, that she had been infinitely conscious of Maggie's presence before, that she knew that she would at last find her alone. (471–72)

The pursuit strikes Maggie as "a breaking of bars," one that threatens her even as it brings out Charlotte's beauty. Both Maggie's fear and her admiration are closely related to the sensations in James's dream,

The splendid shining supple creature was out of the cage, was at large; and the question now almost grotesquely rose of whether she mightn't by some art, just where she was and before she could go further, be hemmed in and secured. It would have been for a moment, in this case, a matter of quickly closing the windows and giving the alarm. (472)

Maggie feels assailed by the approach of her stepmother and rival, but it is important that *Charlotte's* own act is itself a form of self-defense. Maggie's newfound knowledge of the affair between Amerigo and Charlotte is a threat to Charlotte. In response, she attempts to stage a confrontation that will bring the moment to a crisis and make her husband, Maggie's father, privy to Maggie's suspicions, thereby destroying the deceptive "romantic" harmony of the group. Like the ghost surging toward Brydon in response to Brydon's own action of stalking, Charlotte challenges Maggie where she lives.

Two topics illuminate the significance of this action and Maggie's response: *speed* and *desire*.

SPEED

I have already noted the surprising presence of speed in James's texts dealing with museums—as remarkable in the precipitous ruin of Roderick Hudson in Rome as in the pursuit and counterpursuit of the dream in the Louvre. It is no less surprising and as true that *The Golden Bowl*, a work that gives the impression of stately, almost hieratic development, is characterized by a remarkable amount of movement at key junctures, movement of a particular sort. The *rush toward* is a crucial structural component of this novel so full of structure. Consider the oddly dynamic opening line: "The Prince had always liked his London, when it had come to him" (3).

We meet Amerigo rushing through the town, as it in turn seems to move toward him. The narrator suggests that "the last idea that would just now have occurred to him in any connection was the idea of pursuit," but that is precisely because he believes his pursuit is over, crowned with success: "He had been pursuing for six months as never in his life before" (4). Having signed the final papers in the prenuptial agreements required to seal his bond to Maggie Verver, the prince keeps moving through the city, driven no longer by his goal but by his nervous exaltation.

The prince's energy brings him ultimately to the home of Fanny Assingham, where he learns, with the reader, that he is only half of a symmetrical pattern of motion. He has been rushing to his marriage and more recently through the city as Charlotte has been hurrying over the ocean and through London, to the Assingham home, the vertex at which their trajectories intersect. Fanny is an appropriate hostess for this meeting, as she herself serves as a foundational model for romance between the two continents, though one with no illusions as to her own originality: "Mrs Assingham knew better, knew there had been no historic hour, from that of Pocahontas down, when some young Englishman hadn't precipitately believed and some American girl hadn't, with a few more gradations, availed herself to the full of her incapacity to doubt" (27). James's remarkable capsule account of the erotic relations of old world and new expresses in its briefest form the always irrecoverable origin along with the complex symmetry of desire in his international texts.

The second clause of the novel's opening sentence puts history into play from the outset: "The Prince had always liked his London when it had come to him; he was one of the modern Romans who find by the Thames a more convincing image of the truth of the ancient state than any they have left by the Tiber" (3). The liking represented or provoked by the city "coming to" the Prince is like so much other rushing and coming and liking in the novel, to be understood as a function of reflection, of a recognized return of the past. Some modern Romans find a more real-seeming version of their ancient city in modern London, hence their "liking." More than a repeated structural pattern is at stake in the coincidence of this city, which comes to one so rapidly because it is a more compelling version of the city one has left behind, and the two lovers also rushing toward (or back to) each other as the novel opens. While it is evidently the force of longing that provokes both sides of the *rush toward*, the novel insists from the first that these moments are shaped by the constant and unavoidable interpenetration of history and desire. Cultural returns and the returns of passion do not form parallel lines running alongside each other without touching; they are the warp and woof of *The Golden Bowl*.

The speed evinced at the opening is the swiftness of the recognition of identity, which is at once a recognition of the past and of desire. The

London that comes at the prince is a more convincing image of his home and of his past—and therefore of whatever is culturally significant in his background—than anything else he may encounter. Fanny Assingham is acutely aware of what is at stake in the coming together of the prince and Charlotte, and her response is about time, which is to say, it is about the past and about speed. "How will it do, *how*?" She complains to her husband, "That anything of the past . . . should come back *now*? How will it do, how will it do?" (52; emphases in the original). Fanny's remarks are not only about timing because the prince is about to be married and this is no time for his erstwhile lover to appear. Everything about the earlier relationship between the prince and Charlotte is in itself understood in temporal terms. When Fanny assures her husband that the two were never lovers because "there wasn't time," his response is characteristically at once vulgar and to the point: "Does it take so much time?" (54).

Amerigo's reaction on seeing his erstwhile lover highlights the crisis provoked by a return of the past, or, more accurately, by the recognition of a past that has never been left behind. At their meeting James develops the fact of Charlotte's presence and its implications for the prince in temporal terms: "It showed him everything—above all her presence in the world, so closely, so irretrievably contemporaneous with his own" (35). "Irretrievably contemporaneous" is a phrase that indicates a wish to retrieve a moment when they did not share the same time, a hope as impossible as any new beginning in this novel. The immediacy of her presence speaks not to a new development but to an old one. As he considers her charms Amerigo does not find anything he has not seen before, "There was but one way certainly for *him*—to interpret them in the sense of the already known" (35).

In the prince's response to Charlotte the quality of modulated distance and closeness is emphasized:

> She made no circumstance of thus coming upon him, save so far as the intelligence in her face could at any moment make a circumstance of almost anything. If when she moved off she looked like a huntress, she looked when she came nearer like his notion, perhaps not wholly correct, of a muse. (36)

In a passage from the preface to *Roderick Hudson* already cited in chapter 3, James offers a contemporary account of another hard-to-decipher Muse faintly made out in a return of the past: "This revival of an all but extinct relation with an early work may often produce for an artist, I think, more kinds of interest and emotion than he shall find it easy to express, and yet will light not a little, to his eyes, that veiled face of his Muse which he is condemned for ever and all anxiously to study" (1039). "Interest and emotion" is, of course, just what the prince is trying to avoid in this revival of an extinct relation. "Coming upon" the prince is like the unexpected "being met" in Maggie's metaphorical encounter with the ugly-faced stranger. Amerigo is worried because the arrival of Charlotte imperils the aspirations for a new beginning he understands himself to be affirming by his marriage: "This was like beginning something over, which was the last thing he wanted. The strength, the beauty of his actual position was in its being wholly a fresh start" (71). If the novel teaches a lesson in romance, it also instructs on the nature of beginnings. Like Fanny Assingham (who will later attempt to defend herself for her part in the deception by reference to "a past that I believed, with so much on top of it, solidly buried," 425), the prince is too simple in his wish for a new inception. The past comes to him in the shape of Charlotte, huntress at a distance, possible inspiration up close, but, in either case, a figure for the impossibility of new beginnings.

Indeed, the interplay of place, memory, and desire on the outing Charlotte claims from him in order to look for a wedding gift for Maggie, and on which they find the golden bowl, is reminiscent of "A Passionate Pilgrim" because it is about the passion of the not-quite new world for the old:

> Charlotte had looked about her, with expression, from the first of their coming in, quite as if for a deep greeting, for general recognition: the day was, even in the heart of London, of a rich, low-browed, weather-washed English type. It was as if it had been waiting for her, as if she knew it, placed it, loved it, as if it were in fact a part of what she had come back for. So far as this was the case the impression of course could only be lost on a mere vague Italian; it was one of those for which you had to be, blessedly, an American. (67)

The consummation of their passion comes on a rainy day Charlotte has spent touring the sights of London—notably the British Museum. Her descent on the prince in the late afternoon is one more overdetermined return to the past. The metaphors James wields in describing the effect of her arrival on the prince unmistakably demonstrate that the desire they share is the sensual form of such a return. Their physical embrace is preceded by an equally passionate entwining of temporalities past and future in Amerigo's consciousness:

> The sense of the past revived for him nevertheless as it had not yet done: it made that other time somehow meet the future close, interlocking with it, before his watching eyes, as in a long embrace of arms and lips, and so handling and hustling the present that this poor quantity scarce retained substance enough, scarce remained sufficiently *there*, to be wounded or shocked. (218; emphasis in the original)

With the past claiming such intimacy with the present, taking such liberties, it is little wonder that Charlotte can identify his feelings along with her own: "It's the charm, at any rate . . . of trying again the old feelings.

They come back—they come back. Everything . . . comes back. Besides . . . you know for yourself" (219). By the time their bodies catch up with their minds and they embrace, the act has become a meeting of past and present with an earnest of the future. The blurring of temporal distinctions in the rekindled romance of Amerigo and Charlotte is a narrative representation of the inescapable reflexivity of passion. The *rushing toward* each other that has been their trajectory in the first third of the novel culminates in an encounter that, for all its erotic force, is inextricably bound up with the reflexivity of the language with which it is described:

> [T]heir hands instinctively found their hands. . . .
>
> . . . And so for a minute they stood together, as strongly held and as closely confronted as any hour of their easier past even had seen them. They were silent at first, only facing and faced, only grasping and grasped, only meeting and met. . . .
>
> . . . Then of a sudden, through this tightened circle, as at the issue of a narrow strait into the sea beyond, everything broke up, broke down, gave way, melted and mingled. Their lips sought their lips, their pressure their response and their response their pressure; with a violence that had sighed itself the next moment to the longest and deepest of stillness they passionately sealed their pledge. (228–29)

Some kaleidoscopes are made with colored glass; some of the most striking, however, like this novel, are constructed out of the unstable, though symmetrical, juxtaposition of untinted mirrors. James is purposefully and emphatically unclear in his pronouns, erasing the possibility of imagining a delay between proposition and recognition, between recognition and response. "Meeting and met," "grasping and grasped," "facing and faced"—any gap between agents is removed in the immediate speed of the encounter. The surging motion of *rushing toward* is indicative of the hall of mirrors that makes up the text. The kaleidoscopic mirroring, which is among his principal structural tools in the novel, allows James to rewrite the (re)encounter that characterizes the passion of Charlotte and the prince several times, most elegantly perhaps at Matcham, the estate at which their indiscretion reaches its zenith: "She came toward him in silence, while he moved to meet her; the great scale of this particular front, at Matcham, multiplied thus, in the golden morning, the stages of their meeting and the successions of their consciousness" (263). The mirroring reduplication of consciousness and encounter is itself reflected not only in the magnificent scale of the mansion at which it takes place but in its very name; in "Matcham" James invents a near palindrome with "match" at one end and (mis)match at the other. The word enacts the mirroring quality of passion in the novel, though, in both cases, the symmetry is marred by a flaw at its center.

DESIRE

If the *rush toward* of this novel is a refutation of new beginnings—the figure meeting one being always an emblem of one's past and its desires—the question remains: how is it possible for Charlotte to surge out to Maggie at the moment in which Amerigo's wife surveys her imminent domestic crisis? The answer, evidently, resides in the reflexive nature of the two women, and of desire generally in the novel. While the insistent symmetries of the text, which are as manifold as the number of characters is small, suggests mirroring, the fundamental structure reflected in the relationships of the novel is the reciprocal passion of the past for the present and the present for the past. The prehistory of the novel is twofold: the romance of Charlotte and the prince and the romance of Adam Verver (and his daughter) with art. Both pasts are present at all times in the engagement and marriage of the prince and Maggie. At the heart of these shapes of longing, however, is the primal incestuous one of Maggie and her father. The ugly stranger who meets her in her home is the shape of what she wants. Maggie and her father, looking at the other couple, may see themselves, which is precisely the problem; the ugly face of their own passion needs to be rebuffed by a direct rush. The shock of the infidelity is not that of the never seen; the mirrored figure of their own wishes is an ugly shape met suddenly in a quiet home.

It is more than a conceit of the work that Maggie proposes and facilitates the marriage of her father to Charlotte as a way to feel that she has not abandoned him. As several characters (including Charlotte herself) remark, the marriage does not replace their relationship so much as keep it together (154). James repeatedly skirts vulgarity in his insistence on the passion behind Maggie's "intense devotion to her father" (40). He is, if possible, more emphatic on Charlotte's role as someone standing in for Maggie, for the abiding passion that, until Maggie's marriage, had always been a matter of fathers and daughters. In this novel, "He might have been her father" is a phrase that speaks to more than a difference in age (162). The matter is just about open in the text, as in the following exchange between Fanny and Charlotte:

> "Ah, don't talk to me of other women!" Fanny now overtly panted. "Do you call Mr Verver's perfectly natural interest in his daughter?—"
>
> "The greatest affection of which he is capable?—. . . I do distinctly—and in spite of my having done all I could think of to make him capable of a greater." (191)

The unmissable suggestion of sexuality in Charlotte's "all I could think of," along with the odd physicality of Fanny's "overt" "panting" at the idea she herself has imagined are both typical of James's treatment of the topic.

The possibility of sophisticated emotional displacements allowing one passion to stand in for another is first represented in the novel in the flamboyant overstatement of Colonel Assingham to his wife (hyperbole that the novel repeatedly matches and overtops): "What happened . . . was that you fell violently in love with the Prince yourself, and that as you couldn't get *me* out of the way you had to take some roundabout course. *You* couldn't marry him, any more than Charlotte could—that is not to yourself. But you could to somebody else—it was always the Prince, it was always marriage" (61; emphasis in the original). We may adduce a related moment that may seem more simply self-serving than it is: Charlotte's mental self-justification as she thinks of the friend who brought them all together: "Besides, didn't Fanny at bottom half expect, absolutely at the bottom half *want*, things?" (185; emphasis in the original).

In her sense that she has made things wrong by marrying, and that her father can make them right again by also doing so, Maggie's longings are as displaced as those diagnosed in the colonel's apparent overstatement or in Charlotte's self-justification. As Maggie herself says to her father: "It was as if you couldn't be in the market when you were married to *me*. Or rather as if I kept people off, innocently, by being married to you. Now that I'm married to someone else you're, as in consequence, married to nobody" (127; emphasis in the original). Her analysis of the situation offers two reasons for Adam Verver's marriage, both having to do with the romance (in terms at once Jamesian and non-Jamesian) of their lives: "What was now clear, at all events, for the father and the daughter, was their simply knowing they wanted, for the time, to be together—at any cost, as it were" (117). What father and daughter share is a desire recognizably like that Jamesian romance of safety (r_2) described in the preface to *The American*: "The not having to take the trouble and to make the fight—that's what you've lost. The advantage, the happiness of being just as you were—because I was just as *I* was—that's what you miss." Her father's response underlines how much desire in this novel has at its core the return to a past state: "So that you think . . . that I had better get married just in order to be as I was before?" (128).

If the marriage of Charlotte and Adam is most evidently and insistently founded on a doubled incestuous desire—one that aims at satisfaction by either keeping Adam and Maggie together or giving Adam a Maggie-like replacement—Maggie's own relationship with the prince is insistently incestuous in ways that mark a return to the interplay of personal and cultural passion evident in James as far back as "A Passionate Pilgrim." If her father is Adam, the first man and original name-giver, her husband is Amerigo, the second man who is nevertheless foundational, the belated name-giver to the nation after which Adam's adopted city in turn is named. Fanny Assingham's memory of the inception of the relationship makes much of his name, and the lineage it suggests:

> It began, practically, I recollect, in our drive. Maggie happened to learn, by some other man's greeting of him, in the bright Roman way, from a streetcorner as we passed, that one of the Prince's baptismal names, the one always used for him among his relations, was Amerigo: which . . . was the name, four hundred years ago, or whenever, of the pushing man who followed, across the sea, in the wake of Columbus and succeeded, where Columbus had failed, in becoming godfather, or name-father, to the new Continent; so that the thought of any connection with him can even now thrill our artless breasts. (59)

Fanny is, of course, right in noting that nothing endears the prince to Maggie more than his pedigree. For both father and daughter (not artless, so much as unquenchably desirous of art), it is part of what makes Amerigo such a prize acquisition. Amerigo is no Columbus, however, in the style of Christopher Newman, say, precisely because he is never a new man. Indeed, his role in the novel in this context, as when he reencounters Charlotte, is to stand for the never new. Nevertheless, in Fanny Assingham's uncertainty as to the precise title by which to describe the prince's ancestor, one word remains the same whether the prefix is "god-" or "name-"—*father*. If the prince is identified with the frustrated aspiration toward the new, his wife marries with an eye to retaining the oldest intimacy she has known. As the crisis develops she finds herself thinking back to the arrangement which she had set up—"by which, so strikingly, she had been able to marry without breaking, as she liked to put it, with her past" (300).

Subterranean Memories

It is as characters begin to stand in for each other that the novel most evidently shows James playing with the romance tradition he inherited from the previous century and on which he had drawn so often in his earliest works.[6] The action of the novel takes place over an imbricated set of pasts, those of its characters, and those of the tradition to which they belong. The romantic triangle of Charlotte, Amerigo, and Maggie is the direct aftereffect of two Italian adventures, Maggie's and Charlotte's, but it is also a reformulation of shapes taken from the nineteenth-century romance of art. Charlotte—raised in Florence by parents who were themselves expatriated Americans—is a new version of the talented deracinated young woman possessed of great beauty and skill but fated to lose the object of her love. Like Mignon, she is an ageless endlessly-desiring performer removed from her fecund home, like Hawthorne's Miriam, a figure of dark secrets and the consciousness of sin. Insofar as she is the descendant of such earlier Jamesian creations as Christina Light, that other scion of expatriate America in Italy, she is also the descendant of the many admired and destroyed women who stand for Europe and the troubling encounter with its culture throughout the nineteenth century. Maggie, on the other hand, is a return of Julia—the pallid figure who wins the hand of Lord Nelvil—and of Hilda in *The Marble Faun*. She as much descends from Mary Garland (the similarity of names linking the contrasting women protagonists in *Roderick Hudson* and *The Golden Bowl* points to the relationship) as from Therese, the woman who wins the love of Wilhelm Meister and provokes Mignon's death.

Charlotte's relation to Mignon is suggested not only by her gift for tongues but by the special appeal of her mystery. We may read a hearkening back to that ancestress in the language of performer, of juggler even, that James adduces in an unlikely simile for her fluency:

> [D]ifficult indeed as it might have been to disembroil in this young person *her* race-quality. Nothing in her definitely placed her; she was a rare, a special product. . . .
>
> It wasn't a question of her strange sense for tongues, with which she juggled as a conjurer at a show juggled with balls or hoops or lighted brands—it wasn't at least entirely that. . . . The point was that in this young woman it was a beauty in itself, and almost a mystery. (41; emphasis in the original)

Like Corinne, Charlotte is characterized by her ability to improvise magnificently in public: this facility is at once her strength and her taint of vulgar weakness. From her emergence on the stairway at a society function in one famous scene to her performance as tour guide in the Ververs' museum-home in another, her gift for public performance goes from being her flaw to marking her tragedy. Her ability to maneuver around London with the same ease she had shown in Rome is thought of by the prince as a mark of her "curious world-quality" (75). Indeed, it is the prince who best recognizes the particular makeup of her qualities: "Blood. . . . You've that of every race!" (266). The prince, by nature an instinctive and unerring critic, is particularly fascinated by this aspect of Charlotte. Her profound knowledge of Italian is a mark of more than simply her birth and upbringing: "Her account of the mystery didn't suffice: her recall of her birth in Florence and Florentine childhood; her parents, from the great country, but themselves already of a corrupt generation, demoralised, falsified, polyglot well before her . . ." (42).

Like her manifold forebears, Charlotte stands for the possibility of an intimate relationship with the culture of Europe. She therefore is not only possessed of an intimate practical knowledge of world capitals; she is, more strangely, characterized as ageless, particularly, and paradoxically, in relation to Adam Verver, who in this regard stands for some complex return of the innocent American: "Oh, that isn't so," she contradicts him at his proposal: "It's I that am old. You *are* young" (161; emphasis in the original). This claim to antiquity, which she shares with Christina Light ("I am not young; I have never been young!"), and ultimately Mignon ("How old are you?" "Nobody has counted"), is borne out by other witnesses, such as Fanny Assingham: "It's Mr Verver who's really young—it's Charlotte who's really old" (288–89). Finally, when Maggie is presenting to her father the need for them to separate, for him and Charlotte finally to make the move to American City, in her admiration of his power his daughter recognizes forcefully the quality of his youth: "[W]hat stood out beyond everything was that he was always, marvelously, young—which couldn't but crown, at this juncture, his whole appeal to her imagination" (498).

I have tried to indicate some of the wealth of antecedents for Maggie and Charlotte in the nineteenth-century art romance. But it would be wrong to ignore the complex turns James gives to the tradition he inherited. Inasmuch as Charlotte's passion for the prince is a gaudy reflection of that between Maggie Verver and her father, James has clearly not made his women precise antinomies. Indeed, the shadow of incest, of a profound, unsatisfiable longing for the father, allies not Charlotte, but Maggie with Mignon. "Ah, to thrust such things on *us*, to do them here between us and with us, day after day, and in return, in return—! To do it to *him*—to him, to him!" (423; emphasis in the original). This is Maggie's outburst to Fanny at the moment of the novel's crisis, after she has discovered the secret of the bowl. It is a phrase that describes and enacts the central fact at the heart of the novel, the fundamental iteration in the kaleidoscopic mirror. What the near-incoherent play of pronoun and preposition amounts to is a cry of disgust at the fact thrust upon her of the sexual secret of her father, and of its intersection with her own private life. It might be the voice of Mignon, forced to witness the sexual acts of the father she had determined to make into her own lover.

James inherits from the nineteenth century figures for the elaborate interrelation of human and artistic passion. His achievement, however, resides in what he does with this legacy: the manner in which he plays with such figures, entwines them, collapses their distinctions. Charlotte is ultimately no more like Corinne than Maggie is like Mignon. In the constant mirroring of the story, the reference to earlier modes and models is loose and flexible, more interested in drawing out the necessary lines of passion, than in simple analogies. Maggie is the uncanny daughter who is also evidently an object of desire, whose passion and life are bound up fatally with her father's own, whose fate it is to witness, know, and be hurt by the sexual secret of her father/lover—as it was Mignon's.

The Patron / The Loneliness of Picture Galleries

Because so much of the narrative follows the emotional struggles of Maggie and Charlotte in relation to the prince, there is a tendency to neglect the centrality of Adam Verver to the tale. More than a fourth corner in the emotional quadrangle that composes the novel, he is at its center; his passion is the driving force of the novel. For the reader of James's early work, Adam Verver is a register of desire realized. He is not only the heir of James's first patron and Pygmalion, Roger Lawrence, but he realizes the fantasies of *both* Rowland Mallet and Christopher Newman. Where Rowland dreamed of starting a worthy gallery in Boston, Adam Verver, with similar taste, but with the money and drive of a Christopher Newman, is ransacking Europe in order to form a "Museum of museums" beyond the Mississippi. Where Christopher Newman was flamboyantly and extraordinarily prevented from realizing his wish to marry a representative of the highest European culture, Adam Verver returns to American City with Charlotte.[7]

Two facts stand at the heart of the novel, overwhelming such transient developments as the affair of Charlotte and the prince: Adam Verver's project of museum building and his relation with his daughter. The question for the reader is what relationship there may be between these two passions, how they work together as determinant factors in the story the novel tells. As *The Golden Bowl* is a novel about the effects of the unavoidable return of the past on our desires for the future, James emphasizes the careful modulation of time in the emergence of the institution. Dilatoriness is fundamental to Adam's project, what we might call "the museum of the future":

> [R]aw haste was forbidden him in a connection so intimate with the highest effects of patience and piety; he should belie himself by completing without a touch at least of the majesty of delay a monument to the religion he wished to propagate, the exemplary passion, the passion for perfection at any price. (107)

In developing this theme, James is driven to such peculiar extremities as declaring the snail Adam Verver's favorite animal (108). The quality of expectation that characterized Rowland Mallet's ambition for a museum is dramatically amplified in the later novel, the action of which takes place during the planning and accumulation stages of the institution:

> It hadn't merely, his plan, all the sanctions of civilisation; it was positively civilisation condensed, concrete, consummate, set down by his hands as a house on a rock—a house from whose open doors and windows, open to grateful, to thirsty millions, the higher, the highest knowledge would shine out to bless the

land. In this house, designed as a gift, primarily, to the people of his adoptive city and native State, the urgency of whose release from the bondage of ugliness he was in a position to measure—in this museum of museums, a palace of art which was to show for compact as a Greek temple was compact, a receptacle of treasures sifted to positive sanctity, his spirit to-day almost altogether lived, making up, as he would have said, for lost time and haunting the portico in anticipation of the final rites. (107)

The place described is one of those fantasies of the perfect museum that proliferated throughout the nineteenth century, an instance of what Malraux would come to describe as the *musée imaginaire* suggested by the inevitable inadequacies of any collection aiming at totality.[8] The novel's concern with what is genuine, what is "real," is framed in terms of finding worthy additions to a collection. "Sifted to positive sanctity" is the phrase used—indicating that the role of the collector is not merely acquisition but the application of an eye of absolute discrimination. The ideal form of sanctification, the novel makes clear, is to come, as Amerigo does, straight from a museum.

What James terms "living" tallies strangely with the activities it involves, "haunting" and "anticipating final rites." Adam Verver marks a return to the theme of patronage that had preoccupied James from his earliest fictions, but whereas the darker side of the passion of Rowland Mallet was not entirely clear in *Roderick Hudson*, in *The Golden Bowl* James has created an aesthete whose passions are more evidently disturbing: "It was all, at bottom, in him, the æsthetic principle, planted where it could burn with a cold, still flame; where it fed almost wholly on the material directly involved, on the idea (followed by appropriation) of plastic beauty, of the thing visibly perfect in its kind" (146). The transformation of Pater's hard gemlike flame into a cold, still flame suggests something of the pedigree of Adam Verver, and also the turn from a passion for living to a passion for having. The novel is insistent and straightforward on the fungibility of people and art objects in Adam's imagination—and the fact that his taste and his money make the confusion fruitful. The prince is one prize piece, but so is Charlotte, who is acquired in a scene elaborately presented alongside the purchase of some rare tiles. Most disturbingly, perhaps, Adam Verver's connoisseurship does not stop at his own daughter. Senses "kept sharp, year after year, by the collation of types and signs, the comparison of fine object with fine object," lead him to perceive even his beloved offspring as an objet d'art with little individual identity. Looking at her, he sees

some slight, slim draped "antique" of Vatican or Capitoline halls, late and refined, rare as a note and immortal as a link, set in motion by the miraculous infusion of a modern impulse and yet, for all the sudden freedom of folds and footsteps forsaken after centuries by their pedestal, keeping still the quality, the perfect felicity, of the statue; the *blurred, absent* eyes, the smoothed, elegant, *nameless* head, the *impersonal* flit of a creature lost in an alien age and passing as an image in worn relief round and round a precious vase. She had always had odd moments of striking him, daughter of his very own though she was, as a figure thus *simplified, "generalised,"* in its grace, a figure with which his human connection was fairly interrupted by some vague analogy of turn and attitude, something shyly mythological and nymph-like. The trick, he was not uncomplacently aware, was mainly of his own mind; it came from his caring for special vases only less than for precious daughters. (138–39; emphases added)

What is chilling in passages such as this one is not that Adam Verver's perception of his daughter is shaped by his relation to objects, but that he is represented as complacently aware of the fact. If Roger Lawrence could be described as a modern Pygmalion for wanting to shape a woman to suit his desires, Adam Verver's art sensibility makes his flesh-and-blood daughter into a statue, one vivified but nevertheless maintaining all the signs of her classical origins: blurred, absent, nameless because impersonal, simplified, generalized.

Perceptive Pursuit: The Return to the Museum

Early in the novel, in the passage quoted at the opening to this chapter, the prince and Maggie find themselves discussing what is presented as the supremely "romantic" nature of Adam Verver's aspiration to found a museum for American City. It is an all-consuming ambition, and the novel is clear that the values of Adam Verver are entirely implicated with his aesthetic sensibility and his aspiration for its practical manifestation. Nevertheless, the question presented by the exchange remains: What does the museum have to do with romance? Where does the museum come into the lesson in romance of the novel?

The museum in *The Golden Bowl* achieves such proportions as to become a world. In James's treatment of the Louvre, in his autobiographical writings as well as in *The American*, the museum stands for an entire experience of Europe. The golden bowl that gives the novel its title is not only a figure for the beautiful but flawed shape of the relationships in the novel. The plot circles around the object because it represents the dilemma of what Pater—suggesting a similar paradoxical relation linking antiquity, culture, and wealth—called "a world almost too opulent in what was old."[9] The bowl enters the novel as a potential wedding gift for Maggie, an object almost impossible to locate because she already has everything. The shopkeeper indicates the function of the bowl as a potential relief from excess when he sweeps away the first baubles he has shown Charlotte and the prince with a melancholy observation and a telling error: "'You've seen, *disgraziatamente, signora principessa*,' he sadly said, 'too much'—and it made the Prince face about" (83). The shock of the moment is a rich one. To take Charlotte for a married princess, the wife of Amerigo, is—by the mirroring terms of the novel—an instance at once of confusion and perspicacity. More than this, the shopkeeper's use of Italian charges his comment with memories of Charlotte's Florentine past, and links his sad words (and the woman he is addressing) to that nation's role as source of antiquities as well as of a potential disgrace that may be erotic but that may also be linked to seeing too much.

Maggie herself will find the bowl after her trip to the British Museum to cheer herself by inspecting the pedigree of her husband. As a further relief for her perturbed emotions, she sets off in search of a gift for her father's birthday. Her challenge is, of course, only greater than that of her fiancé and his lover, as her father is all the more possessed of things. But then, as the novel enters its climactic stage (made up, eventually, of several climaxes), the museal nature of the Ververs' home, Fawns, becomes more pronounced. Indeed, an important effect of the anticipated, never-completed, nature of Adam Verver's museum, is that the most precious and portable objects that will eventually fill it are kept in his home, making it a museum *pro tem*. In the midst of the objects they themselves assembled and in spite of their well-attested taste and sophistication, Maggie and her father nevertheless come to take on the earnest desire and the apparent innocence characteristic of tourists on the continent, such as those James presented in "Travelling Companions:"

> So it was that in the house itself, where more of his waiting treasures than ever were provisionally ranged, she sometimes only looked at him—from end to end of the great gallery, the pride of the house, for instance—as if, in one of the halls of a museum, she had been an earnest young woman with a Baedeker and he a vague gentleman to whom even Baedekers were unknown. (507)

As the familial alienation grows, the museal quality goes from being a mere feature of the stately home to something far more oppressive. Like the Louvre, Fawns boasts a great gallery; in the family's general misery it also seems to offer a Salon Carré—at least of the nightmarish type that appears in James's dream of the Louvre:

> They learned fairly to live in the perfunctory; they remained in it as many hours of the day as might be; it took on finally the likeness of some spacious central chamber in a haunted house, a great overarched and overglazed rotunda, where gaiety might reign, but the doors of which opened into sinister circular passages. Here they turned up for each other, as they said, with the blank faces that denied

any uneasiness felt in the approach; here they closed numerous doors carefully behind them—all save the door that connected the place, as by a straight tented corridor, with the outer world. (509)

This dark period of uncertainty toward the end of the work, when all concerned are aware of a fundamental but unnameable disturbance in their arrangements, finds everyone constrained within a haunted museum of museums such as that in which Adam Verver has lived for years.

The shape of Charlotte's defeat is unforgettably determined in these pages, described in terms of silent screams and silken halters; but more all-encompassing is the presence of the museum in her destiny. A Corinne trivialized, she becomes a tour guide to her own home. But the subjugation of her passionate alter ego is a painful victory for Maggie:

> There was a morning when, during the hour before luncheon and shortly after the arrival of a neighbourly contingent . . . Maggie paused on the threshold of the gallery through which she had been about to pass, faltered there for the very impression of his face as it met her from an opposite door. Charlotte, half way down the vista, held together . . . the knot of her visitors. (510)

Looking at Charlotte, and beyond her to her father, Maggie finds herself weeping and discovers she is not alone in her response: "[A]cross half the gallery . . . he struck her as confessing, with strange tears in his own eyes, to sharp identity of emotion" (5–12). Among the strangest elements of this strange novel is the rescue Maggie must effect of her double rival for the affections of her husband and father before the story can be complete. It is in a certain measure the desire to save her father that is behind her recuperation of Charlotte at the end of the novel, and in a certain measure it is the desire to save herself.

SPEED, DESIRE, ROMANCE

I have described the structure of the novel as akin to a kaleidoscope composed of mirrors; it may also be fruitfully compared to a fractal—those computer-created designs in which the overall form is determined by the repetition of the same basic arabesque in every part of the shape. The *rushing toward*, which I have identified as the shape of significant motion in the novel, has larger and smaller manifestations. The scene in which Charlotte challenges the hovering Maggie as she stands apart from her family has an important and self-conscious echo, one that demonstrates vividly the museal nature of the movement for James. The first scene in which the two women come together after Maggie witnesses her stepmother at work as tour guide and weeps for her "high coerced quaver before the cabinets in the hushed gallery" (514) is an elaborately framed pursuit openly compared with that of Charlotte many pages before:

> [T]he Princess fell to wondering if her friend wouldn't be affected quite as she herself had been, that night on the terrace, under Mrs Verver's perceptive pursuit. The relation, to-day, had turned itself round; Charlotte was seeing her come . . . quite as she had watched Charlotte menace her through the starless dark; and there was a moment, that of her waiting a little as they thus met across the distance, when the interval was bridged by a recognition not less soundless, and to all appearance not less charged with strange meanings, than that of the other occasion. The point, however, was that they had changed places. (515)

Whereas before it was Charlotte who was a huntress or stalking animal, she is now escaping before the implacable sympathy of Maggie. "The point" is precisely "that they had changed places." The reversal is the novel's latest acknowledgment of the symmetries linking the two women; it is also the moment at which Charlotte is to feel the challenge of the weaker figure she had menaced. We can read here a version of that Jamesian dream figure pushing outward on the door. As in that instance, what is important is the confusion of self and pursuer, and the sense of having suddenly become frightening to the person one has dreaded:

> The Princess kept her for a few minutes in sight, watched her long enough to feel her, by the mere betrayal of her pace and direction, driven in a kind of flight, and then understood, for herself, why the act of sitting still had become impossible to either of them. There came to her, confusedly, some echo of an ancient fable—some vision of Io goaded by the gadfly or of Ariadne roaming the lone sea-strand. It brought with it all the sense of her own intention and desire. (523)

Maggie's intention and desire are brought home to her by recognizing her own restlessness in Charlotte's. The "echo" of two myths of women abandoned in the aftermath of transgressive passion serves a broader purpose than simply identifying her adulterous stepmother; it evidently speaks to Maggie herself ("It brought with it all the sense of her own intention and desire").

To justify her improbable outing, to hide its true nature as vain escape, Charlotte has carried with her a volume of a novel loaned her by Maggie. For Maggie, it is a mark of the unbearable pathos of her rival's action that she has taken the *wrong* volume (that is, not the as-yet-unread first volume, which is still in Maggie's possession) as an excuse "fantastically, at such an hour, to cultivate romance in an arbour" (524). In another instance of the myriad reiterations in the work, Maggie takes the correct volume as her own justification for pursuit. James's play with these particular objects at this climactic moment in the novel is evidently an evocation and development of the complex shape of romance that the novel is concerned with advancing. But if the pursuit of romance is at stake at this juncture, so is the proliferating significance of the museum. The most extraordinary space in the whole fantastic novel may be the labyrinthine alley of trees toward which Charlotte is making her break. If Fawns is always presented as a combination of home and museum, tending more to the latter as the human relationships within it deteriorate, the grounds of the house at this moment become a museal labyrinth:

> It was not, fortunately, however, at last, that by persisting in pursuit one didn't arrive at regions of admirable shade: this was the asylum, presumably, that the poor wandering woman had had in view—several wide alleys, in particular, of great length, densely overarched with the climbing rose and the honeysuckle and converging, in separate green vistas, at a sort of umbrageous temple, an ancient rotunda, pillared and statued, niched and roofed, yet with its uncorrected antiquity, like that of everything else at Fawns, conscious hitherto of no violence from the present and no menace from the future. (524)

In "her frenzy, or whatever it was to be called," Charlotte reaches the heart of this most museum-like natural world and stares "all unwittingly, as Maggie stopped at the beginning of one of the perspectives" (524). Escape is limited not only by Maggie's immediate pursuit, but by the fact that the place she has sought out is only a further outpost of the museum world of Fawns, "pillared and statued, niched and roofed." It is a fantasy space nevertheless, insofar as it offers a shelter from those shocks of time which characterized the opening moments of the novel, and which are in fact inescapable.

The sanctuary Charlotte has sought out is described in terms closely related to those James will use a few years later to capture for his memory of the Louvre as he first saw it:

> [T]hose magnificent parts of the great gallery . . . only arched over us in the wonder of their endless golden riot and relief, figured and flourished in perpetual revolution, breaking into great high-hung circles and symmetries of squandered picture, opening into deep outward embrasures that threw off the rest of monumental Paris somehow as a told story, a sort of wrought effect or bold ambiguity for a vista.[10]

Like the monster in James's dream, Maggie makes her way to challenge the place of rest. The novel is emphatically clear on the fact that the stepdaughter has taken the stepmother's part at the moment of counterchallenge: "It was a repetition more than ever then of the evening on the terrace" (524). Maggie herself is aware of the similarity; though she holds to the important difference in intention, the fundamental shape of confrontation and rebuff is not only maintained but reinforced. She has sought out Charlotte in order to become herself the monster who can be chased away by a sudden rush. As always in this structure, the response is an instant of stasis followed by a reversal of direction. Like the monster in the Louvre, Maggie must be resolutely chased away down the long historic vistas of Fawns. It is this goal that Maggie accomplishes in the remarkable conversation in the park during which she forces herself to force the issue as Charlotte once threatened to do, allowing Charlotte to reclaim herself in a moment of profound fiction by assuming Maggie's own passion for her father.

We may remember here the strange formulation describing Charlotte's effect on the prince: "If when she moved off she looked like a huntress, she looked when she came nearer like his notion, perhaps not wholly correct, of a muse" (36). In this *muse*um, as Maggie herself closes the distance between them, she offers a correction of her rival's inspiration. Maggie brings the proper first volume of the romance to Charlotte, much as she also carries to her the precise content and form of the Jamesian romantic, the break for safety. Charlotte's lines in their conversation are Maggie's own: "I want, strange as it may seem to you . . . to *keep* the man I've married. And to do so, I see, I must act." Maggie's eventual response—"You want to take my father *from* me?"—is delivered in a "sharp, successful, almost primitive wail," which is at once (as the second and last adjectives suggest) true and false (529–30; emphases in the original). It is a moment of deceit, but one in which the real imminent loss of her father is embedded—along with an echo of the cry of Charlotte herself, heard so vividly under the tour guide's drone. By the close of the novel, James has returned a deep human pathos to the heart of the museum, in part by recognizing the emblematic nature of the types he inherited from the nineteenth century. The museum is no place of rest or safety. Ghosts inevitably linger in the hallways of an institution characterized by the dangerous mingling of the past and desire. Not only is it the case—as he notes from the first preface to the New York edition—that even for the author the face of the Muse is veiled, but its mystery is part of his condition *as* author; it is what he is "condemned for ever and all anxiously to study." As far back as the 1870s, in engaging Hawthorne's inescapable romances, the novelist had declared that a quality of factitiousness would be the penalty incurred by the author attempting to write of a place "in which he has not a transmitted and inherited property."[11] James's ultimate embrace of the romance of art as his own inescapable factitious inheritance allows the novelist's late works to suggest ways in which even the most inverisimilitudinous fictions may lodge passions that are often monstrous, always haunting.

PART THREE

Learned Longing: Modernism and the End of the Art Romance

Porta Romana, Siena. Photo: Arturo Jahn Rusconi, *Siena* (Bergamo: Istituto Italiano d'Arti Grafiche, 1913).

CHAPTER 6

Freud on the Road to Rome

A Constant Pilgrim

> (Fragment) . . . Somewhere in Italy. Three daughters were
> showing me some small curios, as though we were in an
> antique shop, and were sitting on my lap. I commented on
> one of the objects: "Why, you got that from me."
>
> "Asking the way," moreover, was a direct allusion to *Rome*,
> since it is well known that all roads lead there.
>
> *The interpretation of dreams is the royal road to a knowledge of*
> *the unconscious activities of the mind.*
> Freud, The Interpretation of Dreams

"YOU GOT THAT FROM ME," the father says, of an object shown to him
by the three daughters he somehow balances on his lap (one more child
than Leonardo's Saint Anne). The daughters return to their father's eyes
something they received from him in the first place, itself a fragment.
Italy as at once museum and as seat of fecund pleasure. This is typical of
the art romance, of course, as is the play with fathers and daughters as
inheritance, gift, and inspiration come together. The suggestive interplay of eros and paternity in the Italian antique shop is hard to miss. It
is a suggestiveness that has everything to do with the parallel movement
of desire and inheritance. The children can only show the father something they received from him in the first place, which is in any case not
new but already antique. The circularity of admiration identified in the
claim of the father is self-evident, but it is notable that the apparently
resolute rectilinearity in the other passages I cite at the head of this
chapter ultimately also turns the same way. The interpretation of dreams
is the royal road—or the "*Via regia*," as it is in the original—that is to
say, the Appian Way, legendary construction that really does lead back
to the very place to which all roads are said to return. Straight lines curve
back inexorably, circles demonstrating the inescapable force of origins

or sources. There is as little comfort in knowing that all roads tend back in the same direction, however, as in the realization of what amounts to the same thing: that we only discover objects to admire that we forget we have already been shown. As the children are a material result of paternal passion, we may say that their presence on the father's lap is legible as at once nurturing and erotic. They return to him something they got from him; they themselves do not leave him, but accumulate on his lap. Like a road that curves ever back to the same place (or like a daughter breastfeeding her own imprisoned father), the girls are the promise of a future that is not quite able to keep itself from going backward rather than forward.

Freud's writings have already had an important place in this study. Not only is his seminal account of the uncanny bound to be a vital reference point for the identification of the imaginative returns motivating the most fearful literary fantasies, but, as I have suggested, the analyst's postulation of a drive beyond pleasure, one with dissolution or even death as its object, also offers a useful analogue for James's concept of the most perfect form of romance. The "plains of heaven" of the preface to *The American* can seem a strikingly similar place to the "Nirvana" of *Beyond the Pleasure Principle*. Nevertheless, as his memoir-essay on the "disturbance of memory" he experienced on the Acropolis makes clear, important features of the art romance are of more than simply theoretical concern to the psychoanalyst. Indeed, that piece—with its crisis provoked by arrival and its dedication to an admired creative figure—suggests what the well-known recurrence of Italy in his writings makes clear: Freud's response to the South of culture may usefully be identified as part of the long-standing phenomenon that is the topic of *Haunted Museum*.

In Freud, as in James, sites of culture are the location of agitating frightful visions because they stand for so much that is at once yearned for and feared. Freud's Italy is always overlain with biographical elements because its representation is driven by the anxiety that accompanies and shapes his personal ambition. Indeed, the interplay of ambition, memory, and literary precedent that characterizes Italy's place in the art romance also determines its significance in *The Interpretation of Dreams*, the foundational work of psychoanalysis that is also Freud's great autobiographical epic. A recurrent point of reference, Italy takes its meaning in relation to the analyst's imagination of parents and children, on the one hand, and to Goethean ghosts, on the other—elements closely allied in his writings. In the art romance Freud finds not only a shape for his personal ambitions and anxieties, however, but forms that illuminate fundamental insights on the surprising links connecting peace, pleasure, and longing. For Freud, as for James, to think about admired cultural loci is to think about what it means to desire at all. While the close if endlessly convoluted relation of romance to the real comes to the fore in James, Freud's paradoxical concern is the real wish driving the dream. For both authors, apparent lines of separation between seeming antitheses (say, what is dreamed and what is lived, what is old and what is new, or what is wished for and what is feared) are revealed to be not signs of cleavage but superficial indications of underlying circuits of desire.

Arrival in Freud's works is marked by a number of troubling overdeterminations involving at once personal success, the trauma of birth, and anxieties about death. It raises the most uncomfortable questions about desire: not only "What do I want?" "What *did* I want?" and "Why do or did I want these things?" but "Why am I not satisfied?" As one is never anywhere of importance for the first time, every arrival is at the same time a mark of forward and of retrograde movement, a sign of mature power, perhaps, but always a tribute to childhood lessons or fantasies. I have already cited Freud's account of his disturbance of memory on reaching the Acropolis, but, for the nineteenth-century traveler (in ways that are more than simply practical) Greece is generally preceded by Italy, a country whose importance to his psychic life Freud repeatedly underlines in *The Interpretation of Dreams*. Indeed, anxious voyages to Italy form an integral part of the self-analysis in this foundational work for personal as well as professional and intellectual reasons (if the three can be separated).[2] Throughout his writings, the cultural antiquities that motivate Freud's manifest interest are understood to be analogous to the remnants of the past uncovered by analysis—hence the odd fact that the challenges of Rome receive their fullest treatment in the section on "Infantile Material as a Source of Dreams." Freud's most richly developed discussion of travel arises in the course of his discussion of his *inability* to reach the eternal city (just where all roads are tending). His account of this difficulty is introduced as evidence of the sources of adult dreams in childhood:

> In another instance it became apparent that, though the wish which instigated the dream was a present-day one, it had received a powerful reinforcement from memories that stretched far back into childhood. What I have in mind is a series of dreams which are based upon a longing to visit Rome. For a long time to come, no doubt, I shall have to continue to satisfy that longing in my dreams: for at the season of the year when it is possible for me to travel, residence in Rome must be avoided for reasons of health. (4:193–94)

The importance of this well-known instance is indicated not only by its extensive discussion in the first edition but also by the analyst's inability to let his initial claim stand. In 1909 Freud added a passage to the preceding paragraph that does not address the ostensible reasons for his avoidance of Rome, but instead makes clear that the impossibility of satisfaction, like the desire it frustrates, must be traced not to the health risks associated with the miasmal swamps of Rome but to something in the traveler himself: "I discovered long since that it only needs a little courage to fulfil wishes which till then have been regarded as unattainable." By 1925 his confidence is complete enough to add the following clause "and thereafter became a constant pilgrim to Rome." The touching simplicity of such formulations makes them testimonials not only to the powerful yearning and inhibition at stake but also to the force of analysis. Freud affirms in the same place his discovery of the inhibition and the fact of its overcoming: personal and professional triumphs come together, even as the language of wish fulfillment, which is so central to *The Interpretation of Dreams*, reveals the close link between Rome and dreams, between Rome and Freud's project as a whole.

The question for the reader is not why Freud wishes to get to Rome, but what keeps him from getting there. (The hesitation is marked in the text as well: it takes the analyst three pages to reach his ostensible point after introducing it.) Like Goethe or Byron encountering childhood memories along with passion and death in Italy, Freud identifies the force of Rome in his psyche as a matter of infantile acculturation. But the analyst's account takes shape in multiple identificatory displacements:

> It was on my last journey to Italy . . . that finally—after having seen the Tiber and sadly turned back when I was only fifty miles from Rome—I discovered the way in which my longing for the eternal city had been reinforced by impressions from my youth. I was in the act of making a plan to by-pass Rome next year and travel to Naples, when a sentence occurred to me which I must have read in one of our classical authors: "Which of the two, it may be debated, walked up and down his study with the greater impatience after he had formed his plan of going to Rome—Winckelmann, the Vice-Principal, or Hannibal, the Commander-in-Chief?" I had actually been following in Hannibal's footsteps. Like him, I had been fated not to see Rome; and he too had moved into the Campagna when everyone had expected him in Rome. But Hannibal, whom I had come to resemble in these respects, had been the favourite hero of my later school days. (4:196)

What kind of study do we imagine Hannibal frequented as he made his plans for war? The trend of Freud's self-analysis is toward identification with Hannibal, the ambitious outsider challenging what would become a powerful empire, but the passage he remembers ultimately has far more to do with Winckelmann than with the Carthaginian general. Evidently the force of the analogy is all intended to reside in the passions of the general incongruously illustrating those of the founder of modern art history. After all, Freud makes recourse throughout his career to the image of the mind as a kind of accumulation of antiquities very much like Rome itself, identifying the work of the analyst with that of the archaeologist as part of his attempt to establish the professional standing of his nascent discipline:

Dreams and neuroses seem to have preserved more mental antiquities than we could have imagined possible; so that psycho-analysis may claim a high place among the sciences which are concerned with the reconstruction of the earliest and most obscure periods of the beginnings of the human race. (5:549)

The archaeologist, we may say, is what Freud can imagine he is, the conquering general, what he would like to be.

Freud's childhood formed a perpetually displaced cosmopolite in whom an acute sense of the value of culture coexists with an anxious fear about the possibility of placing oneself in relation to its centers. Thinking of Paris, Freud is reminded that all roads lead to Rome ("führen . . . alle Wege"), but the association of the two cities also makes clear the pathos implicit in the analyst's sense that the destination—which is, after all, *all* destinations—is closed off to him. In the throes of his avoidance the Hannibal analogy comes to Freud's mind, and "the semitic general" leads directly to reflection on the inherent alienation of being a Jew, "what it meant to belong to an alien race" (4:196). The prospect of arrival raises anxieties for which the only compensation is to imagine oneself as a triumphant outsider whose hesitations are tactical elements in a bold military campaign. At the culmination of this analysis Freud turns to the well-known story of his father's youthful humiliation by a brutal antisemite who forces him into the *road*way ("den Fahrweg"). The movement of Freud's analysis enacts in its own way the structure of James's appalling yet moving dream of the Louvre, in which the fear and flight of one moment are matched by an equally forceful and effective compensatory bravery, a mirroring pursuit. The thought of the father's humiliation, his inability to control his own movements, and therefore his displacement into the road, is matched by the strategic, forceful yet measured, descent on the center of power by Hannibal/Freud. Between the weakness of his father and the revenge fantasy of Hannibal, Freud establishes an important source for the need to move, but also for the difficulty of ever arriving at Rome—to do so would be to exhibit a power unavailable to his own father, to humiliate him anew.

"Father Don't You See I'm Burning?"

"Special claims upon our attention"

Children at risk and dead fathers recur throughout *The Interpretation of Dreams*, a work Freud eventually identified as having been an important part of the self-analysis provoked by the death of his own father in 1896 (4:xxvi). But it is also true that infants are inescapably present in Freud's texts as emblems of memories and desires that do not die in adults. All of his key descriptions of psychic life involve childhood, of course, while children themselves serve as the sole—and fragile—hope for individual futurity. And so it is that in *The Interpretation of Dreams* children symbolize in two directions. They stand at once for the undying experiences and emotions of the past whose recurrences shape adult lives, and also for the possibility or fantasy of human achievement in the future, even for a form of immortality ("And after all, I reflected, was not having children our only path to immortality," 5:487). From both directions children are vital to the aspirations of the book as a whole, but it would be wrong to focus only on the naturalizing and autobiographical side of Freud's project. That the child is more than a natural symbol of individual survival is suggested by a dream that is at once one of the most troubling, peculiar, and apparently impersonal in Freud's early masterpiece.

The opening of the final chapter of *The Interpretation of Dreams* is entirely unlike any of those that precede it, all of which begin with a notably clear exposition of the argument that the dreams treated will engage, or at least with a gesture toward principal concerns. The notoriously complex and ambitious concluding chapter in which Freud sketches out the structures of the mind revealed by his analysis of dreams opens not with an argument but with a dream about a child at risk, one introduced with a surprising blend of gravity and vagueness:

> Among the dreams which have been reported to me by other people, there is one which has special claims upon our attention at this point. It was told to me by a woman patient who had herself heard it in a lecture on dreams: its actual source is still unknown to me. Its contents made an impression on the lady, however, and she proceeded to "re-dream" it, that is, to repeat some of its elements in a dream of her own, so that, by taking it over in this way, she might express her agreement with it on one particular point. (5:509)

The dream the patient brings him, which is evidently no more overcharged with meaning for her than for Freud himself, has an unusual source. Not Freud's own, nor even simply a patient's, nor yet one recorded by a known authority, this thrice-told dream has an absolutely irrecoverable provenance, so that, aside from one memorable line—all that remains of the original—Freud can only summarize it. A father, tired from watching over his sick infant over many nights and days, finally gets some sleep after the child's death, only to be woken up by the child coming to him with the following chilling words: "Father, don't you see I'm burning" (*Vater, siehst du denn nicht, dass ich verbrenne?*) On waking to a glare coming from the room in which his child is lying, he discovers that the old man hired to watch over the corpse has himself fallen asleep, and a candle has set fire to the wrappings of the body.

The dream of the burning child is introduced as having special claims "at this point in the text," but Freud does not bother to explain what point he believes he has reached, or why this dream of such mysterious provenance is so important, or even if its provenance is part of its "claim." The redreaming of the patient is matched on Freud's part by a displacement of the dream throughout the rest of the book that is particularly striking, given that Freud is unusually amenable to the interpretation offered by the patient herself, following the lecturer: the father dreams as he does in order to explain away the increased glare that might disturb his sleep. Given the several returns of the dream, this interpretation is evidently no less troubling for being satisfactory. Seven paragraphs into the chapter Freud's normal expository language returns, but only in order to indicate that the chapter in question, "The Psychology of Dream-Processes," will not be a triumphant culmination, so much as an admission of incompleteness: "It is only after we have disposed of everything that has to do with the work of interpretation that we can begin to realize the incompleteness of our psychology of dreams" (5:510–11). The dream of the burning child serves to clarify the incomprehensible core at the center of the dream, what the analyst refers to (with an important gesture toward the mark of traumatic separation from the mother) as the dream's "navel" (5:525). Freud returns to the dream of the burning child many pages later, in order to attempt to explain its place in his text (5:533), and even then, he gestures to a further deferral (to 5:570). Freud presents the dream as challenging a principal tenet of his interpretative model, the centrality of wish fulfillment (how can it be the father's wish for his child to be burning?), but he acknowledges the issue even as he finds it impossible to address. "Consider instead another one," he offers in a Prufrockian non sequitur, "for instance, the dream of Irma's injection" (5:534).

A number of factors contribute to making the dream of the burning child so memorable as to resist final interpretation. The narrative context in which it arises makes it a dream of responsibility and failure: two adults who are meant to watch over a child fall asleep. The phrase at the heart of the dream is not only moving because it is a strangely dispassionate and unforgettable expression of excruciating pain and the gravest disappointment (the failure of the parent on the verge of recognition by the child), but because it contains a number of irresolvable mysteries: In what sense does the child burn? What is the relationship between the child's pain and the father's inability to see? In Freud's account, one further question is highlighted, and another is implicitly raised—not only how this can be a dream of wish fulfillment, but also, what drives Freud's own fascination.

The "welcome opportunity of considering the difficulties with which the theory of wish-fulfillment is faced" (5:550) is only allowed to conclude with the identification of the wishes the dream of the burning child aims to satisfy. On the one hand (as his patient told him in the first place), the father keeps dreaming because it allows him to satisfy the wish to stay asleep; on the other, he does so because it keeps the child alive—better to burn than to die (5:571). And yet, if the answers were so simple, it is difficult to understand Freud's repeated insistence upon the opacity of the dream. Why *does* this dream receive such special attention from the analyst, and why is it so slowly allowed to die?[3] The answer to these questions requires not only recognition of the importance of the life of the child and of the sleep that are protected by the unknown dreamer, but also of the complex formal presence of the art romance in Freud. I hope to demonstrate in what follows that some of the pressure of the dream on Freud's thought may be traceable to its evocation of another dream, another set of burning children, both with their source in Goethe.

Children, or "another absurd dream about a dead father"

"The deepest and eternal nature of man," notes Freud, "upon whose evocation in his hearers the poet is accustomed to rely, lies in those impulses of the mind which have their roots in a childhood that has since become prehistoric." Childhood is the earliest source of literature and dreams, which in turn preserve yearnings long since banished from the conscious mind: "Suppressed and forbidden wishes from childhood break through in the dream behind the exile's unobjectionable wishes which are capable of entering consciousness" (4:247). Or, as he will put it more technically, a dream is "*a substitute for an infantile scene modified by being transferred on to a recent experience*" (5:546). Or again, with forceful simplicity, "*a wish which is represented in a dream must be an infantile one*" (5:553). Children are not only emblems of the expectation of futurity, then, but the source of the significant drives motivating adult desires. Their dual role is evident in the strange riddle about ancestors at the heart of a dream about travel that Freud presents as an instance of the absurd in dreams. The dream (inspired by a canceled trip to Italy) features a number of forms of travel (including but not limited to elaborate play on the German, *fahren*), and culminates in Freud's embarrassed memory of being unable to solve a pair of riddles whose answers are "Ancestry" and "Progeny" (5:432–34). Freud proposes a straightforward compensatory dream thought as source: "It is absurd to be proud of one's ancestry; it is better to be an ancestor oneself" (5:434).

Causal dyads have a labile tendency to run two ways in Freud: the necessity of fathers is met by the necessity of children, and both needs can serve as sources of anxiety. Such a dynamic is significant, but not particularly surprising. More unusual is the text's consistent association of children and *travel*. Freud's inability to reach Rome would be a peculiar instance to choose to illustrate the presence of "Infantile Material in Dreams," if it were not for the fact that the analysis of the dream draws on a relationship among childhood, ambition, death, and Italy well established in the analyst's mind. Thus, in a related moment in his discussion of the dream of the botanical monograph, Freud explains the presence of a word he has forgotten that he never introduced into the analysis by recourse to the same set of associations. His initial interpretation seems quite likely, but I am equally interested in its continuation: "Behind 'artichokes' lay, on the one hand, my thoughts about Italy and, on the other hand, a scene from my childhood which was the opening of what have since become my intimate relations with books" (4:283). A quotation from *Faust* is what follows.

Freud's dream thought on the relative value of descendants and ancestors comes in the midst of a crucial long sequence (running from the section on the absurd to that on intellectual activity in dreams) directly responding to the death of his father with an inextricable interweaving of ambition, antiquity, children, and Italy. The sequence has an even earlier reach, however, as it begins with the revelation that an element in the important dream about Count Thun (4:208–18) was Freud's cancellation of a trip to Italy with his brother (5:432). This insight allows the analyst to highlight the importance of the word *fahren* (to travel) in the dream as a whole, and to link it to the riddle about ancestry—*Vorfahren*, that is to say, as the translator reminds us, "go in front" or, more chillingly, "predecessors." Progeny are travelers too in this riddle, "after-comers" (*Nachkommen*). We stand between those that die before us and those that come after us. As each person is traveling the same road, every individual is a *memento mori*.

Absurdity and intellectual activities in dreams are paradoxically linked in Freud because both categories keep returning to the unspeakable intersection of the death of the father with Freud's own ambitions. Goethe and Italy recur as specters of his ambivalence because both author and nation function as symbols for the aspiration and achievement that are the sources of his guilt. Italy, mortality, fathers, and children are the principal components in a densely layered dream revolving around Freud's father on his deathbed, flushed and looking like Garibaldi. Typically, bright colors suggest at once Italy and the passing of the father in *The Interpretation of Dreams*.[4] Nevertheless, the apparently absurd thought in the dream is traced to an actual observation ("Those of us who were standing round had in fact remarked how like Garibaldi my father looked on his deathbed") before the analysis quickly veers into strange territory. It is interrupted by an ellipsis and an association leading to a passage from Goethe on the death of Schiller:

He had had a *post-mortem* rise of temperature, his cheeks had been flushed more and more deeply red. . . . As I recalled this, my thoughts involuntarily ran on:

Und hinter ihm in wesenlosem Scheine
Lag, was uns alle bändigt, das Gemeine
[behind him, a shadowy illusion, lay what holds us all in bondage—the things that are common]. (5:428; ellipsis in the original)

The dream as a whole offers a Hamlet-like play with the problem of the common ("das Gemeine") nature of death—meaning at once shared or universal and vulgar. Like the Prince of Denmark, Freud cannot help oscillating between thoughts of shameful embarrassment, such as those associated with his father's constipated bowels at the end of his life (what was truly "*hinter ihm*" at his death), and the wishful dream life that identifies him with the man who unified Italy. The conquering fantasy of Hannibal is met by a related figure associated not with destruction but with forceful unification.

Freud attempts to conclude his analysis of this material with the identification of a simple and straightforward dream wish: " 'To stand before one's children's eyes, after one's death, great and unsullied'—who would not desire this?" (5:429). But Italy is not only the site at which great human achievement is marked; it is also a place (like all sites of birth) of feces and urine, a place related to the "museum of human excrement" Freud challenged with the stream of his urine (5:469), and which in turn is associated with a traumatic childhood memory of urinating in front of his parents, in their bedroom:

In the course of his reprimand, my father let fall the words: "The boy will come to nothing." This must have been a frightful blow to my ambition, for references to this scene are still constantly recurring in my dreams and are always linked with an enumeration of my achievements and successes, as though I wanted to say: "You see, I *have* come to something." (4:216; emphasis in the original)

The entire section on absurd dreams is about problems that don't add up because they cannot be allowed to. "Here is another absurd dream about a dead father," Freud writes, as though this were such a common and ever-expanding category, that to compose a more reasoned transition for any instance would be superfluous. "Here are two or three dreams," he writes again, "which deal (by chance, as it may seem at first sight) with the dreamer's dead father" (5:426). Surely Freud could count up his instances easily enough (is it two? three?). His mathematical vagueness is a further confession of the excessive presence of fathers—in the book as in the author's mind. Although the analyst is frank about the ambivalence that runs through "dreams of dead people whom the dreamer has loved" (5:431), the limits Freud himself imposes on his interpretations are generally related to the guilt and embarrassment provoked by the competition that exists between him and his father, a competition as evident in his feelings about what it means to arrive in Athens as in his fantasy of an avenging Hannibal descending in carefully calibrated stages on Rome.

The confused computations provoked by the attempt to account for the uncountable set up the important dream in which a friend of Freud's is savaged in a review by Goethe. In the ratiocination that is part of this dream, the analyst attempts to understand two absurd things: how the attack was chronologically possible and the fact that it occurred "*in Goethe's well-known essay on 'Nature'*" (5:439; emphasis in the original). Freud's analysis ultimately leads him to discover, underlying the dream, his own anxiety about the reception of his insights about the sexual sources of psychoneuroses, particularly the role of child sexuality. But the dream and its analysis suggests that sexual anxiety is itself a stand-in for professional ambivalence in relation to Goethe, an inescapable father figure.[5] The analyst cites a story he had heard about the mentally ill brother of one of his patients who, in his frenzy, had shouted, "Nature! Nature!" His doctors trace the outburst to the young man's reading of Goethe's essay and attribute the frenzy to overwork in the study of natural philosophy. Freud, however, finds a sexual meaning in the word, an interpretation he believes is validated by the young man's subsequent mutilation of his genitals. Still, at the conclusion of his analysis he returns to "Nature," and notes that the essay had a vital role in *his own* decision to follow a life of science: "There was a very clear reminder in the dream that '*mea res agitur*,' in the allusion to Goethe's short but exquisitely written essay; for when . . . I was hesitating in my choice of a career, it was hearing that essay read aloud at a public lecture that decided me to take up the study of natural science" (5:441).[6] *Mea res agitur*—"my affairs are at issue." It would be harder to find a clearer confession of professional ambivalence than the linking of the essay he repeatedly cites as determining his own career path to a threat to the organ of reproduction.

When he returns to the dream of Goethe's review a year later Freud adds elements that, in spite of their frequent opacity, help clarify its personal meaning. In the analysis presented in *On Dreams*, the short popularization of his ideas he produced in 1901, Freud is even clearer that his own ambition is at stake. The account of "Nature" in this text is made up of an odd series of broken off non sequiturs and associations all coming back to Goethe as a competitive model:

> If we pursue the dream-thoughts further, we shall keep on finding ridicule and derision as correlates of the absurdities of the manifest dream. It is well known that it was the discovery of the split skull of a sheep on the Lido of Venice that gave Goethe the idea of the so-called "vertebral" theory of the skull. My

friend boasts that, when he was a student, he released a storm which led to the resignation of an old Professor who, though he had once been distinguished (among other things in connection precisely with the same branch of comparative anatomy) had become incapable of teaching. . . . In the hospital here I had the honor of serving for years under a chief who had long been a *fossil* and had for decades been notoriously *feeble-minded*, but who was allowed to continue carrying on his responsible duties. At this point I thought of a descriptive term based upon the discovery on the Lido. Some of my young contemporaries at the hospital concocted, in connection with this man, a version of what was then a popular song: "*Das hat kein Goethe g'schrieben, das hat kein Schiller g'dicht . . .*"[7]

"This was written by no Goethe, this was composed by no Schiller" is Strachey's translation of the fragment of a popular song that provides the final words of an analysis engaging professional hopes and fears in both literary and scientific arenas. The young man whose outburst evidently awoke an echo in the analyst mutilated himself at the same age that Freud was when he heard the essay he claims established the path of his endeavors. The rage of youth against established authority is expressed by the profusion of father figures challenged in the dream. Given his place in German culture, not simply as author, but also as scientific researcher, Goethe becomes the ultimate figure for achievement. It is the implicit competition between Freud and Goethe remembered as a student of the structure of the skull (a part of the anatomy evidently closely related to that which was Freud's particular interest) that puts the author in the category of father figure and makes the "Nature" that inspired Freud not unrelated to that which made a mad young man mutilate his genitals.

I have been attempting to describe a complex whereby fathers (and the anxieties they imply) and children (and the hopes and fears they raise) are repeatedly linked both to Italy and to Goethe in Freud's text. These two vital cultural phenomena—place and author—appear to have an emotional force akin to that of the closest and most significant family relations. Thus what may be Freud's most touching Italian dream in *The Interpretation of Dreams* follows immediately on that of Goethe's hostile review and directly engages the passions and fears of the father. The material is actually separated from the "My son the Myops" dream of which it forms part and which Freud discusses earlier in the text in order to bring forward the melancholy and strange passivity affecting the parental figure in Tuscany:

> *On account of certain events which had occurred in the city of Rome, it had become necessary to remove the children to safety, and this was done. The scene was then in front of a gateway, double doors in the ancient style (the "Porta Romana" at Siena, as I was aware during the dream itself). I was sitting on the edge of a fountain*

and was greatly depressed and almost in tears. A female figure—an attendant or nun—brought two boys out and handed them over to their father, who was not myself. The elder of the two was clearly my eldest son; I did not see the other one's face. The woman who brought out the boy asked him to kiss her good-bye. She was noticeable for having a red nose. The boy refused to kiss her. (5:441; emphasis in the original)

The manifold alienation between father and children (*"their father who was not myself"*) and between dreamer and action (*"this was done"*) is linked, in the course of analysis, to the antisemitism that played such an important part in Freud's account of his father's failure and consequently in his own compensatory fantasies. Events in Rome require the protection of children. But, as is bound to be the case when fleeing from the place where all roads lead, complete escape is not possible; the family reaches only as far as a gate itself pointing back to the dangerous city. Given Freud's consistent association of children with success, this dream engages a fundamental failure on his part. He has to give up his children in order to save them. The red nose of the nun or companion associates her at once with Italy and the dead father, but the conspicuous nose also seems an evocation of Freud's own embarrassing self exposure before his parents. The refusal to kiss her suggests an attempted rejection even as it acknowledges its own impotence as an act of renunciation. But then, the culmination of this attempted escape is a series of refusals and negations—at a gate (not safely inside the city) a father who is not Freud receives children from an attendant who is not kissed, as Freud watches in misery.

Freud tries to conclude the discussion with a rather banal expression of hopes for his children's intellectual development, but it would be difficult to overestimate the extent to which both the dream and its analysis are shaped by his anxieties about his position as a Jew. He cites Theodor Herzl's play, *Das neue Ghetto* (The New Ghetto), and the concern it had raised in his mind about training his children for ease of movement through borders—for possible escape. The flight from Egypt comes up in the course of the discussion, but most poignant is the underdeveloped reference to the Babylonian captivity evoked by the fountain where Freud sits. The analyst simply quotes and emphasizes the opening of Psalm 137—*"By the waters of Babylon we sat down and wept"* (5:442)—without developing the line's relation to the theme of Jewish vulnerability and exile. The psalm as a whole, however, is about the denial of creativity in exile, or the treasonous nature of singing a song in a land that is not one's own ("How shall we sing the Lord's song in a strange land?"). Children enter the psalm at its close, in the brutal imagination of a horrible revenge on the captors: "Happy shall he be, that taketh and dasheth thy little ones against the stones."

The dreamer's misery at the moment his children are being saved in the dream at the Porta Romana is traceable to a number of sources. From the perspective of childhood vulnerability, the protection of children is the vital duty of fathers. From the point of view of fathers, the creation and protection of children is the only guarantee of posterity and, as such, the ultimate evidence of success. Freud needs his father to be the protective figure he most painfully failed to be when confronted by the antisemite who drove him into the roadway. "It is absurd to be proud of one's ancestry; it is better to be an ancestor oneself" is a dream thought that challenges at once the antisemite (whose claim against Jews comes back to a difference in ancestry) and the weak father (Freud's own most immediate ancestor). Nevertheless, insofar as it puts the power of his own father into question, Freud's protection of his children threatens the protective figure he himself needs.

Freud with Goethe: Doctors / Burning Children

The natural response to dangerous physical pain is not a question but a cry. "Father, can't you see I'm burning?" is best understood not as a call for relief from pressing physical misery so much as a plea for recognition or a declaration of disappointment given added force by being shaped as a question. To look at the dream of the burning child in the context of the tradition of the art romance on which Freud draws allows for a double illumination—of Freud's project and of the desires and fears driving the mode. In chapter 1 I discussed a dream of a burning child in *Wilhelm Meister* that is well worth placing in relation to the one Freud could not let go.[8] Indeed, "Father, can't you see I'm burning?" is the very question at issue in the tale of Antiochus, Stratonice, and Seleucus represented in Wilhelm's beloved painting, as it is in Felix's near death in the conflagration set by the Harper (that mad father), and finally in the dangerous immersion in flames that only the Amazon can extinguish in Wilhelm's dream.

Wilhelm Meister is a story about development that understands *Bildung* as a process of recovery. The force of desire itself is most powerful as it comes into relation not with unfamiliar objects but with ones that awaken long-standing—fundamental—urges. Written out in this schematic form, and particularly given such important details as the structural centrality of incest and even the related importance of *Hamlet*, *Wilhelm Meister* can sound rather like another work, *The Interpretation of Dreams*. I propose the connection tentatively here, along with the added speculation that the strangeness of the relationship among story, image, and text in *Wilhelm Meister* itself is one reason that the novel seems so ineffable a source for Freud—Plutarch inspires a painting in the novel, which in turn contributes elements to the scene of the fire; both painting and event then feed into Wilhelm's dream. The image of the lovesick prince returns to Wilhelm in a doubled form: first as the experience of his son threatened by fire and then in the dream in which the Amazon douses the flames that are consuming the boy. At the conclusion of the dream, the Amazon—that is to say, the woman without a man—becomes a kindly mother saving two sons. Her veil puts out the drops of fire suggestive of the sweat of passion described in Plutarch, but also of other bodily fluids that must be controlled. Her embrace of Wilhelm translates his inability to act into a form of pleasure, a special kind of peace emerging from the elaborate threat of the dream: "How gladly he let himself be held!" I propose identifying the dream of the burning child in Freud with the dream of the burning child in Goethe less because there is a clear line of influence connecting one text to the other than because doing so helps to open up not only the psychological depths of the novel but also the literary determinants informing Freud's own imagination. While *Wilhelm Meister* testifies to the complex form of the family romance underlying the passion for art, those passions Freud confesses everywhere in *The Interpretation of Dreams*—personal and political though they might be—are given shape by the tradition I have been calling the art romance.

From the fourth to the seventh editions, the dream of the burning child was preceded by two chapters on dreams in literature and myth by Otto Rank, but literature is richly represented in the *Interpretation of Dreams* even before this interpellation. From the well-known discussions of Oedipus and Hamlet to myriad classical sources and repeated citations of Goethe, imaginative literature enters the book not only as a vital part of the conceptualization and exposition of the nascent field of psychoanalysis but also as a central component of Freud's psychic life. Freud's direct citations tend toward *Faust* and *Iphigeneia*, rather than Goethe's novels, and his passion tends to shape itself around the figure of the author rather than in direct analysis of his texts. Still, a ghostly afterimage of *Wilhelm Meister* may be descried in *Interpretation of Dreams* when Freud makes the following addition to his forceful proposition that in dreams kings and queens stand for parents, while princes and princesses represent the dreamer: "But the same high authority is attributed to great men as to the Emperor; and for that reason Goethe, for instance, appears as a father-symbol in some dreams" (5:354). Parental returns are never simply comforting in Freud: "Robbers, burglars and ghosts, of whom some people feel frightened before going to bed, and who sometimes pursue their victims after they are asleep, all originate from one and the same class of infantile reminiscence," he explains: parents policing children in their beds. We may think back to the Harper's pursuit of Felix during the fire in *Wilhelm Meister*, and again in Wilhelm's dream. Fathers, Freud indicates in a summary that is at once general and concrete, return as robbers, mothers as ghosts (5:403). The father as threat, as robber, has evident Oedipal sources, as does the explanation for the mother appearing as a ghost—not simply because she is the object that is always lost but because of the white gowns mothers are likely to wear when standing by the bed. The Amazon's white veil in Wilhelm's dream of a burning child is a related material, of course, one that picks up on the robes of Stratonice, perhaps. The structure of threat and pleasure underpinning the typical dream is suggested when a lover's arrival in Wilhelm's bed is preceded by the fear that it might be the ghost of his father coming to threaten him instead.

The color red evokes Italy for Freud, but also a mortal crisis, a rise in temperature after death, the flushed face of a weeper (Freud himself is almost in tears on the edge of a fountain in Siena), and burning, of course. Given the description of his own father's condition at the moment of death ("He had had a *post mortem* rise of temperature, his cheeks had been flushed more and more deeply red"), the child's words in the unforgettable dream become evocative of the great loss that drives Freud's work. Indeed, a simple inversion of the child's words becomes possible: "Father I can see *you* are burning." The father in the child's position on his deathbed is evocative of many other figures in such a position, not only of the dreamer dreaming or Antinochus sick for love, but ultimately of the patient telling his dreams to a doctor who may well take on the characteristics of a new father or lover—or a new competitor to be overcome.

The Wish in the Dream: Roundabout Paths and Real Romance

By analysis of the Italy in his dreams and of his apparent inability to reach Rome in life Freud establishes the combination of pleasure, longing, and anxiety involved in the voyage to the center of culture, along with the figurative and actual role of parents and children in the latent content and manifest form of the wish. In the process he identifies Rome as the ultimate figure for the wish (the goal of Hannibal, Winckelmann, *all roads*) and Goethe as a principal model and rival. It may not be in his use of centers of culture to symbolize his own anxious relation to personal ambition that Freud is most intriguingly engaged with the art romance, however, but in his treatment of the qualities that underlie the romance itself—not only the wish fulfillment identifiable in visions of danger and unpleasure, but also the troubling implications of a subterranean desire for peace such as that which James identifies when he locates romance in the "plains of heaven." Goethe too, allowing Wilhelm the pleasure and relief of being constrained by the fearsome yet comforting Amazon, recognizes the fulfillment of that wish to return to infant or preinfant stasis that is so important and so chilling a part of Freud's imagination.[9] In the art-romance tradition Freud finds forms not simply for the ambitions that drive him and provoke his anxiety, nor solely for the Oedipal returns that ultimately motivate this ambition and fear, but also for the recognition that behind that longing itself, and the flamboyant images of satisfaction and disappointment it provokes, lies the fantasy of a deeper—though not for that less frightening—peace.

"*Dreams are the* GUARDIANS *of sleep and not its disturbers*" Freud notes, anticipating his analysis of the dream of the burning child (5:233; emphasis in the original). But a peace deeper than sleep haunts Freud's imagination, early and late. For all the variety and detail Freud adduces, his aim is to reduce, not to proliferate meanings. He is, of course, quite clear that a limited set of erotic structures underpin most dreams, notably the Oedipal drives he identifies as fundamental to human development. However, the conclusion of his treatment of what he calls typical dreams offers an extremely long footnote on the "disguised" forms of Oedipal dreams that anticipates his later discussions of the uncanny and of déjà vu. In one of those passages in *The Interpretation of Dreams*, the significance of which is indicated by its expansion as new editions were published, Freud demonstrates not only the particular force of place, but the disturbing implications of arrival. Much as undisguised dreams of sleeping with the mother were interpreted in antiquity to presage a return to one's "mother-country," Freud argues, dreams of having been somewhere before, of being back in what is in fact an unknown place should be understood to be manifestations of a fantasy of return to the mother's genitals (5:398–99). That country is given a name in the play of words of a patient whose dream the analyst uses in an interpretation of one of his own: "I recalled the meaning which references to Italy had in the dreams of a woman patient who had never visited that lovely country: '*gen Italien* [to Italy]'—'*Genitalien* [genitals]' " (4:232).

Like James, Freud is interested in understanding at once the satisfactions offered by unpleasure (the wish behind dreams of pursuit by robbers, of one's child aflame), and the realm of desire beyond the stimulation involved in dreams of sexuality or discomfort. Both authors postulate for this reason a realm of nondesire, of fantastic peace. And so it is that for the analyst dreams of sex with one's mother, like dreams about recognizing a place where one has never been, are traceable not only to the aspiration for ambitious achievement in life, but also ultimately to a longing for the surrender of aspiration—for peace. If, as Freud suggests axiomatically,

"*The act of birth is the first experience of anxiety, and thus the source and prototype of the affect of anxiety,*" the return to the womb is a fantasy of the restoration of a peace beyond (or prior to) the anxiety of life (5:400–401). Our wish for discomfort or embarrassment is only the first mystery revealed in Freud's analysis of the wishful things he takes dreams to be. The further mystery is our greater yearning for peace, a topic that will have its fullest development in *Beyond the Pleasure Principle* but that is already clearly at stake in *Interpretation of Dreams.*

As Freud makes clear in the account of his own "disturbance of memory" at the Parthenon, travel is a powerful marker of achievement for the very reason that it is driven by desires and fears learned in the home. But then again, the force of the voyage is present at the very heart of the structures Freud discovers in his study of dreams, so that the language of movement is unavoidable to the analyst even in his most abstract accounts of the mental processes. The "circuitous paths" traveled by unconscious excitations are the fundamental substrate revealed in the attempt to understand the force and form of dreams that are frequently more disturbing than pleasant to the dreamer (5:555). "The first wishing seems to have been a hallucinatory cathecting of the memory of satisfaction," he speculates. But simple hallucination will fail to fulfill real needs. The mind, for this reason "divert[s] the excitation arising from the need along a roundabout path," which in turn makes it "possible to arrive at a real perception of the object of satisfaction" (5:599). Given this hallucination of satisfaction that must be rerouted in order to access the external world, it is hard to avoid the conclusion that illusion and divagation are fundamental elements on the path to meeting real and familiar needs.

Every voyage is a voyage back, to an earlier self, to the past that shaped the desires provoking the trip, to domestic passions that may become monstrous when they are reencountered:

> [D]reams are derived from the past in every sense. Nevertheless the ancient belief that dreams foretell the future is not wholly devoid of truth. By picturing our wishes as fulfilled, dreams are after all leading us into the future. But this future, which the dreamer pictures as the present, has been moulded by his indestructible wish into a perfect likeness of the past. (5:621)

Freud's analysis goes deeper than recognizable individual memories. In 1919 he adds a passage to his treatment of regression in dreams that gestures to a shaping past that is far more than personal:

> [D]reaming is on the whole an example of regression to the dreamer's earliest condition, a revival of his childhood. . . . Behind this childhood of the individual we are promised a picture of a phylogenetic childhood—a picture of the

development of the human race, of which the individual's development is in fact an abbreviated recapitulation influenced by the chance circumstances of life. (5:548)

In this addendum he cites Nietzsche's assertion that in dreams "some primaeval relic of humanity is at work which we can now scarcely reach any longer by a direct path." Developing this idea, Freud offers the hope that "the analysis of dreams will lead us to a knowledge of man's archaic heritage, of what is psychically innate in him" (5:549). But in the model he had constructed in the first edition of *Interpretation of Dreams*, twenty years earlier, elements in the mind themselves make a voyage, the recognition of which reveals the frightening inaccessibility of the core of individual passions. All that is really available, it turns out, is the roundabout path between known wishes and the dark core that motivates them:

> In consequence of the belated appearance of the secondary processes, the core of our being, consisting of unconscious wishful impulses, remains inaccessible to the understanding and inhibition of the preconscious; the part played by the latter is restricted once and for all to directing along the most expedient paths [*Wege*] the wishful impulses that arise from the unconscious. (5:603)

To believe that all roads lead to Rome is quite a different matter from conceiving what Rome is, or even what it might mean to arrive there. The fears and pleasures of the voyage are mere suggestions of the frightening goal that may be the culmination of our wishes. Most disturbing of all is the suspicion that our arrival may be nothing other than an unavoidable return. "You got that from me," says a father to his daughters in a dream fragment set in Italy that I quoted at the opening of this chapter. And indeed it is the unavoidable inheritance not simply of objects but of desire itself that leads to the complex forms longing takes in Freud's work. Not only is all desire triangulated, but, though what occupies each point of the triangle is liable to shift, the force of the figure supplanted is never lost: the mother becomes Rome; the father becomes Goethe; Freud himself becomes his own father at times, his own children at others. Death itself is the most horrible threat at one moment, the promise of peace at another. Freud's project intimates a trajectory from danger toward a safety that is itself frightening because of the overcoming of the father it entails on the one hand and because of the return to the womb it suggests on the other.

The wish in the dream of the burning child is to stay asleep. But, in Freud such a wish represents more than a desire for rest. It is part of a broader tendency toward stasis, toward a complete loss of agitation. Given the place of the father's last moments in the work as a whole, the sleep in the dream of the child becomes yet another expression of the two frightening fundamental aspirations that run through the book: to be in the place of the father and to arrive at a stasis that is best understood as a form of death. The child's wish to be at peace in relation to the father is driven by the longing to be relieved of the burden of sadness, fear, and guilt that is the result of having hated the beloved figure as a rival, of having feared him, of having needed him dead in order to undertake the ambitious career built on *The Interpretation of Dreams*—and therefore, ultimately, on the death of the father, which is the relief and the fear of the burning child.

Baptistery, Saint Mark's, Venice. Courtesy of the Photographic Archive of the American Academy in Rome, Library Collection.

CHAPTER 7

Speed, Romance, Desire: Forster, Proust, and Mann in Italy

SPEED (ROMANCE): FORSTER

"THEN HOW LONG HAS she been engaged?" demands Philip Herriton of Caroline Abbott, inquiring urgently about his widowed sister-in-law, who is in fact already married to Gino, the charming if shiftless Italian encountered on a trip Philip himself had recommended with the aim of distracting her from the dreaded possibility of remarriage. "A short time—quite a short time," Caroline answers, "as if the shortness of the time would reassure him."[1] But speed is not a source of comfort in *Where Angels Fear to Tread*, so much as it is evidence of the force of desire—hence Philip's loss of purpose when confronted by the sudden emergence of the town of Monteriano as he rides the train on his first rescue mission (28). In Forster, the sometimes disconcerting narrative speed characteristic of the art romance is, as usual in the mode, an indication of an inevitability at once thematic and formal. When the narrator speaks of "the brief and inevitable tragedy of Lilia's married life," we are to understand both adjectives as related (41).

The art romance did not vanish at the close of the nineteenth century, though it was bound to be affected by the acceleration of changes already well under way in earlier periods. The collapse of old empires and the rise of new ones, gradually and through global conflagration, was bound to affect the culture of travel, as was the ever-increasing ease of movement brought about by technology. To these practical developments we may add the decline of the classical world as a central locus for cultural fantasies. Nevertheless, while a number of other geographical areas and historical periods were adduced as centers of inspiration or sites of ideal longing, southern Europe, and Italy in particular, maintained a privileged hold on the imagination. In a development prepared for throughout the previous century, classical monuments were replaceable as objects of nostalgia by those that spoke of the faith and cultural coherence attributed to the Middle Ages or the passions and artistic achievement connected with the Renaissance, and eventually even groups that had been defeated by the rise of the cultures that came to be called classical—the Etruscans, say, or various

Europeans tribes—were available to play the role of an alternative space in which the fantasy of origins could itself be original.

Inevitably, a self-conscious turn inward is manifested as the mode enters the twentieth century. That the mind itself is a kind of haunted museum—made and unmade by the necessary interplay of memory and desire—is in no way a discovery of the twentieth century, but texts of the period are characterized not only by a new responsiveness to the claims of physical passion but also by two closely related developments: the renewed primacy of the first person and the centrality of artistic development as a theme. The aim of this chapter is to suggest the rich presence of the art romance in the first years of the twentieth century largely by tracing a few important variations on its themes in works by Forster, Proust, and Mann. All three engage those issues which have always preoccupied the art romance, not simply the nature of desire and its relation to fantasy, but also the force of apparent inverisimilitude, of fantasies of pleasure and danger. That the secret in these texts is always ultimately sexual is only a small part of what is noteworthy about them. After all, one element that has typically underpinned the South's role as a center of longing is the fantasy of erotic liberation that has always been a part of the tradition for imaginations formed in colder climes. What stands out in the works of these modern masters, then, is not the unmissable presence of desire, but the productive interplay of the erotic with artifice on one side and with death on the other.

The preoccupation with Venice in Proust and Mann is part of a development often associated with Byron and consolidated throughout the nineteenth century. Proust's own taste was in large measure shaped by his careful study of Ruskin (whose own original passion for the city was formed in an amalgamation of Byron and Turner), not simply the great nineteenth-century theorist of the aesthetic power of the city but among the most important polemicists on the need for a turn away from the classical as a value in art. Mann does not offer a rejection of classical antiquity, of course, but a thoroughgoing revision of its seductions. Violence and passion come to the fore in his antiquity in ways that would have been unrecognizable to the exponents of ideal beauty or classical calm of earlier periods. Nevertheless, among the distinctively modern qualities of these authors is not only the alternative cultural moments they may prize, not their interpretation of the significance of particular periods, but also their keen responsiveness to the plot effects and thematic material available in the interstitial spaces that make up so much of the experience of travel: the train, the hotel, the ferry, even the car. Forster plays with these spaces throughout his career in the course of his thoroughgoing satire of the aspiration to escape the tracks laid down by culture. The fantasy of intimacy with a people whose lives the traveler barely touches anticipates the typical twentieth-century distinction between the traveler and the tourist. But it also participates in a long-standing hope: that the foreign space should be the site of a greater reality, one that will inspire even as it challenges the attentive voyager.

While the art romance has always been a way of talking about the inescapable interweaving of personal development and fantasy, it typically draws on forms borrowed from inverisimilitudinous tales of troubled passion and family constraints in order to shape its representations of desire. The very thing that made for the art romance's investment in the gothic, the externalization of longing and fear as an acknowledgment of the inevitability of both and of their inescapable and multiform connections, works to make the alternative face of the tradition essentially comic or grotesque. It is to be expected, then, that the art romance should eventually manifest itself, as it does in Forster, as comedy. The excesses that provide most of its themes, its combination of artifice and deeply felt but misunderstood or misdirected passion, were, as James himself recognized, at once tragic and risible. In Forster, fools rush headlong into places where angels fear to tread. The modulation of speed for narrative and thematic effect is an important component in E. M. Forster's work generally, but in the title of his first novel it is quite openly identified with one place: Italy. Indeed, the rushing left out of the title is to be found all over the text: in the precipitous departure with which it begins, in the speedy criss-crossing of the continent by various characters, and in Lilia's hasty marriage and quick death, as much as in the headlong rescue missions and in the rush and crash that provides the novel's climax.[2] Indeed, the speed of the novel is made abundantly clear by the wealth of events that transpire in so brief a span—courtship, marriage, and death are quickly followed by death, marriage, and courtship in this narrative that begins at a train station and ends in a railway tunnel.

While the attempt to represent desire and the crisis of its satisfaction is central to the art romance throughout its history, the early years of the twentieth century saw the emergence of a new commitment to satisfaction, as well as that new frankness about erotic passion, that together make all of Forster's work have an element of sex comedy. It is Philip's idea that Lilia be sent away to Italy for her safety because that is the nation onto which *he* deflects all of his rebellious impulses away from the deadening routines of Sawston, their miserably conventional hometown. *Where Angels Fear to Tread* revolves not around Lilia's passion but around Philip's unrealizable desire, which is twice thrown into confusion by the actual unironic drives of women in the novel. While he is quite clear from the outset on the role of his mother and sister in crushing fantasy in his life, the real shock to Philip is the concrete passions of Lilia and Caroline—the way they refuse to recognize longing as itself a pleasure of the imagination.

Lilia's miserable marriage to Gino introduces her to the banality of living with one's object of desire, but the experience is notably abbreviated. She dies with approximately two-thirds of the novel left because the text, rather like the Herritons, is not really concerned with her. Philip is the principal protagonist of a novel in which the central emotional structure comes to be the triangulated passion linking him to Gino and Caroline. Philip's misery when he hears that the father of Lilia's new husband is a dentist is personal: "He thought of Lilia no longer. He was anxious for himself: he feared that Romance might die." But the narrator expresses confidence in the essential longevity of the mode: "Romance only dies with life. No pair of pincers will ever pull it out of us." Rather, it is "a spurious sentiment which cannot resist the unexpected and the incongruous and the grotesque" that Philip loses (26–27). And indeed, when Philip hears from Caroline that Gino is sorry for shoving him in their first encounter, the narrator is proved correct: "[R]omance had come back to Italy" (111).

Philip's misplaced fear is nevertheless a manifestation of a principal concern of the novel because Forster's account of romance, like James's, engages a quality that is not absolutely separable from life. Although, in the character of Caroline, Forster allows himself to create an unironic passionate engagement with desire, he is no D. H. Lawrence. The novel does not simply ironize the pleasures to be found at a distance and in inaction. The patron saint of Monteriano, after all, is a young woman whose holiness is marked by the refusal to do anything at all. Hence the two poles of this complexly sympathetic novel: the angels who fear to tread and the fools who rush in.

Lilia's marriage to Gino threatens to ruin Italy forever for Philip (69) not simply because Gino is vulgar but because of the vulgarity of achieving satisfaction ("being both sentimental and unrefined," the narrator notes about Lilia, she "was determined to have the man and the place together," 40). Little wonder, then, that Lilia's death coincides not just with one but with two births—that of her son and that of Philip, who learns of her demise on his own birthday (68). Indeed, the summary of Philip's life and of Italy's role in it as a place of licensed escape follows immediately on the death of Lilia in childbirth at the end of chapter 4; her end is his (re)beginning.

As so often in James, the splitting characteristic of the art romance is realized by the creation of an observer who also precipitates the action. Like Rowland Mallet in *Roderick Hudson*, Philip is the connoisseur who is everywhere responsible for the manifestation of desires in which he cannot fully participate, but which he is also the only one to fully appreciate. Not only does he send Lilia to Italy, and Monteriano in particular, coaching her on her response ("Love and understand the Italians, for the people are more marvelous than the land," 4), but Caroline dates *her* own attraction to Gino (or rather her realization of that attraction) to the moment she went to see the Italian because she thought Philip ineffectual. "You" is the pronoun that gives shape to the passion described in her confession, not "I" or "him." "I thought you weak and heedless, and went instead of you to get the baby. That began it, as far as I know the beginning. Or it may have begun when you took us to the theatre, and I saw him mixed up with music and light. But didn't understand till the morning. Then you opened the door—and I knew why I had been so happy" (182–83).

Philip immediately understands his role, but his understanding is precisely what separates him from the passion he recognizes but cannot engage. Hence the use of the definite article at the close of the following passage:

> "But through my fault . . . he is parted from the child he loves. And because my life was in danger you came and saw him and spoke to him again." For the thing was even greater than she imagined. Nobody but himself would ever see round it now. And to see round it he was standing at an immense distance. He could even be glad that she had once held the beloved in her arms. (183)

At the climax everyone veers away from the beloved—Caroline from Gino and Philip from Caroline—driven away by feeling that the object is unspeakably admirable. As the tale had begun at Charing Cross Station on a train bound for Italy, it ends at the St. Gotthard tunnel, leaving that nation via a speedy route completed little more than twenty years before the novel was published. But the language of movement runs through the treatment of passion in the text, so that as Philip thinks they are coming to the consummation of their relationship "[t]he train seemed to shake him towards her" (180). When, instead of reciprocation of his desire, he discovers that her passion, like his, ultimately is for Gino, "[o]ne of them must have moved a step or two, for when she spoke again she was already a little way apart" (181).

Forster transposes any number of Jamesian motifs to bring out their comedy without erasing their essential qualities. Hints of *Portrait of a Lady* run through the novel (Philip as Ralph, Lilia as Isabel), but also of such late work as *The Ambassadors*, among others (Mrs. Herriton as Mrs. Newsom, Harriet as Sarah Pocock). From James Forster learns two key lessons: the literary possibilities inherent in the displacement of passion and the pathos of abnegation. In the interplay of Caroline and Philip, Forster is able to suggest a recognition of desire on the part of his characters by the simple expedient of keeping satisfaction at a distance. When he is sent back to Italy by his mother to forestall Caroline's attempt to rescue Lilia's child, Philip summarizes the passions at stake and the role of Italy in particular:

Let her go to Italy! . . . Let her meddle with what she doesn't understand! Look at this letter! The man who wrote it will marry her, or murder her, or do for her somehow. He's a bounder, but he's not an English bounder. He's mysterious and terrible. He's got a country behind him that's upset people from the beginning of the world. (92)

At a moment of extreme excitement in *The American* Christopher Newman makes what surely must be one of the most unlikely emotional gestures in literature, "a movement as if he were turning over the page of a novel" (813). As he comes to recognize his love for Caroline, Philip offers a strange sweet nothing worthy of putting in the same category: "'The view from the Rocca (small gratuity) is finest at sunset,' he murmured, more to himself than to her" (112). The lines are from Philip's well-thumbed Baedeker, and they indicate the source of his passion in the recognition of a fellow lover of Italy. But Caroline refuses the romance of the travel guide because on the other side of life she finds not romance but death: "Oh, you appreciate me!" She exclaims in disgust at a moment of crisis, "I wish you didn't. You appreciate us all—see good in all of us. And all the time you are dead—dead—dead" (150).

And yet, as he suspects, Philip does indeed have a great deal in common with Caroline Abbott. It is not simply that they both veer away from their object(s) of desire, but that they are both meddling connoisseurs of passion. It is Caroline, after all, who encourages Lilia's marriage, an action that precipitates a crisis on her part related to Philip's when he fears the death of romance. In this instance, however, it is the "real" that is threatened:

[I]t's the only time I've ever gone into what my father calls "real life"—and look what I've made of it! All that winter I seemed to be waking up to beauty and splendour and I don't know what; and when the spring came, I wanted to fight against the things I hated—mediocrity and dulness and spitefulness and society.

Philip, moved by her revelation, attempts to rescue Caroline from her interpretation of the real by making it into something quite close to his romance:

Society *is* invincible—to a certain degree. But your real life is your own, and nothing can touch it. There is no power on earth that can prevent your criticizing and despising mediocrity—nothing that can stop you retreating into splendour and beauty—into the thoughtss and beliefs that make the real life—the real you.

Caroline, however, resists blurring the line as he proposes: "I have never had that experience yet. Surely I and my life must be where I live" (77–78; emphasis in the original).

The unspoken but everywhere apparent importance of rushing in the novel reaches its climax in the dark crisis of the battle for Lilia and Gino's baby. The quick and easy movements of the narrative and of individual characters, as of the emotions that drive them, is arrested in the obscure crash of carriages that drops everyone in the mud and that is apparently the cause of the real death of the baby. Forster's treatment of the conclusion is strikingly grotesque, featuring as it does the distorted and incomprehensible messenger sent by Harriet (a character worthy of "Childe Roland") and the abasement, disorientation, violence, and pain of Philip's injury and his battle with Gino. In this abject amalgamation Forster offers as much as he can of the real, an inharmonious compound of intimacy, violence, confusion, and death.

In the climax to his last novel Forster would return to both of the structures of movement present in the first. The loss of distinct identity and control that marks the central crisis in the Malabar caves in *A Passage to India* is recapitulated in a far less horrifying form at the close of the novel, as boats containing all the principal characters collide with each other and with the floating village set adrift by the Hindu faithful in the course of their ritual. Divisions are overcome in the slow and dark confusion of drift and collision, a moment that is again rewritten as the apparently more controlled coming together and swerving apart of Fielding and Aziz on horseback. Given the terms established in *Where Angels Fear to Tread*, we may read the two moments of shock and confusion in the cave and on the river as instances in which the real is manifested, though it can never be fully understood. The final joint swerve of the novel, with its crisply defined separation, may be understood as a manifestation of the romance of controlled definition.

Romance (Desire): Proust

Childe Harold, we will recall, did not stop to say good-bye to his mother before leaving on his pilgrimage. Fear of a related omission will become a principal touchstone of the narrator of *Remembrance of Things Past*, the mother's kiss and certain deeply imagined destinations serving as the two poles of longing in a novel that carefully distinguishes between the force of experience and the power of desire in relation to travel:

> Even from the simplest, the most realistic point of view, the countries for which we long occupy, at any given moment, a far larger place in our actual life than the country in which we happen to be. Doubtless, if, at that time, I had paid more attention to what was in my mind when I pronounced the words "going

to Florence, to Parma, to Pisa, to Venice," I should have realised that what I saw was in no sense a town, but something as different from anything that I knew, something as delicious, as might be, for a human race whose whole existence had passed in a series of late winter afternoons, that inconceivable marvel, a morning in spring.[3]

The pleasures of anticipation, expectation, and disappointment that are introduced with the mother's kiss at the opening of the novel, and have a reiterated presence in the various *amours* described in the narrative, are given a developed conceptualization in the course of Proust's treatment of longed-for destinations. The third part of *Swann's Way*, "Place-Names: The Name" (*Noms de pays: le nom*), is answered by "Place-Names: The Place" (*Noms de pays: le pays*) in *Within a Budding Grove*, suggesting the satisfaction of long-held desire as name gives way to place. The special beauty of Proust's representation of desire, however, is that it allows him to materialize the powerful distinction between longing and arrival, name always trumping place as the source of affective response.

> I need only, to make them reappear, pronounce the names Balbec, Venice, Florence, within whose syllables had gradually accumulated the longing inspired in me by the places for which they stood. Even in spring, to come upon the name Balbec in a book sufficed to awaken in me the desire for storms at sea and for Norman Gothic; even on a stormy day the name Florence or Venice would awaken the desire for sunshine, for lilies, for the Palace of the Doges and for Santa Maria del Fiore.
>
> But if these names thus permanently absorbed the image I had formed of these towns, it was only by transforming that image, by subordinating its reappearance in me to their own special laws; and in consequence of this they made it more beautiful, but at the same time more different from anything that the towns of Normandy or Tuscany could in reality be, and, by increasing the arbitrary delights of my imagination, aggravated the disenchantment that was in store for me when I set out upon my travels. (1:420)

With a decadent's hypertrophied commitment to romantic desire, Proust's narrator offers a retrospective critique of his own naive illusion that what he longed for was arrival:

> During this month—in which I turned over and over in my mind, like a tune of which one never tires, these visions of Florence, Venice, Pisa, of which the desire that they excited in me retained something as profoundly personal as if it had been love, love for a person—I never ceased to believe that they corresponded to a reality independent of myself, and they made me conscious of as glorious a hope as could have been cherished by a Christian in the primitive age of faith on the eve of his entry into Paradise. Thus, without my paying any heed to the contradiction that there was in my wishing to look at and to touch with

the organs of my senses what had been elaborated by the spell of my dreams and not perceived by my senses at all—though all the more tempting to them, in consequence, more different from anything that they knew—it was that which recalled to me the reality of these visions that most inflamed my desire, by seeming to offer the promise that it would be gratified. And for all that the motive force of my exaltation was a longing for aesthetic enjoyments, the guide-books ministered even more to it than books on aesthetics, and, more again than the guide-books, the railway time-tables. (1:424)

Marcel's unconscious has a subtler version of desire at its disposal than he at first realizes, one that manages to stop him before he puts his true pleasure at risk. A somatic turn hidden in the space of a dependent clause protects the longing for Italy that has run through and shaped the whole first volume of the novel, a desire at serious risk of satisfaction should a planned trip materialize:

[D]ivesting myself, as of a shell that served no purpose, of the air in my own room which surrounded me, I replaced it by an equal quantity of Venetian air, that marine atmosphere, indescribable and peculiar as the atmosphere of dreams, which my imagination had secreted in the name of Venice; I felt myself undergoing a miraculous disincarnation, which was at once accompanied by that vague desire to vomit which one feels when one has developed a very sore throat; and I had to be put to bed with a fever so persistent that the doctor declared not only that a visit now to Florence and Venice was absolutely out of the question, but that, even when I had completely recovered, I must for at least a year give up all idea of travelling and be kept from anything that was liable to excite me. (1:426–27)

The approaching realization of his wishes—the simple prospect of the materialization of the name—leads to a remarkable somatic response; the Gospel of Saint John is revised when "a miraculous disincarnation" takes place. The word cannot be made flesh; or if it is, no miraculous conception results, only nausea. (Regurgitation, it is worth noting, will be among the first marks of the imminent death of the grandmother many volumes later, the event that serves as the principal representation of the abjectly real in the novel as a whole.)

Remembrance of Things Past does not simply reflect on the impossible relationship between longing and satisfaction; it repeatedly illustrates the near phantasmagoric relationship between what is wanted and what is experienced. As the narrator notes about the long-desired and now-achieved intimacy with the Swanns, satisfaction covers over his original yearning in such a way as to quite obscure its original emotional force:

[I]n such perfect coincidences as this, when reality folds back and overlays what we have long dreamed of, it completely hides it from us, merges with it, like two equal superimposed figures which appear to be one, whereas, to give our happiness its full meaning, we would rather preserve for all those separate points of our desire, at the very moment in which we succeed in touching them—and to be quite certain that it is indeed they—the distinction of being intangible. (1:578)

Proust is the poet of disappointment because of his commitment to the romance of longing: "I had already learned the lesson . . . that, whatever it might be that I loved, it would never be attained, save at the end of a long and painful pursuit, in the course of which I should have first to sacrifice my pleasure to that paramount good instead of seeking it therein" (1:695). The loss of the imagined object in the actual experience is too high a price to pay; it erases the prior state that is always the repository of the narrator's most powerful nostalgia. A brief moment between anticipation and nostalgia, actual experience has little chance to thrive—how much more powerful is the combination of remembered longing!

When he finally arrives at Balbec, the fictional seaside town that is the first geographical locus of his desire, Marcel's response has to be a derealization akin to Freud's crisis of memory at the Parthenon:

I said to myself: "Here I am: this is the Church of Balbec. This square, which looks as though it were conscious of its glory, is the only place in the world that possesses Balbec Church. All that I have seen so far have been photographs of this church—and of these famous Apostles, this Virgin of the Porch, mere casts only. Now it is the church itself, the statue itself, they, the only ones—this is something far greater."

As was the case with Freud, the dialogue with oneself is an acknowledgment of the failure of experience to match an expectation unrecognizable before the possibility of satisfaction comes into play. Indeed, the exchange is an attempt to force a confession or reassurance from a desire become mute in the face of consummation. Marcel's claim—"this is something far greater"—is *answered* immediately with a balancing proposition that has an important presence in Proust's work:

It was also something less, perhaps. . . . my mind, which had lifted the Virgin of the Porch far above the reproductions that I had had before my eyes, invulnerable to the vicissitudes which might threaten them, intact even if they were destroyed, ideal, endowed with a universal value, was astonished to see the statue which it had carved a thousand times, reduced now to its own stone semblance, occupying, in relation to the reach of my arm, a place in which it had for rivals an election poster and the point of my stick, fettered to the Square, inseparable from the opening of the main street, powerless to hide from the gaze of the café and of the omnibus office, receiving on its face half of the ray of the setting sun and presently, in a few hours' time, of the light of the street lamp of which the savings bank received the other half, affected simultaneously with that branch office of a loan society by the smells from the pastry-cook's oven, subjected to the tyranny of the Particular to such a point that, if I had chosen to scribble my name upon that stone, it was she, the illustrious Virgin whom until then I had endowed with a general existence and an intangible beauty, the Virgin of Balbec, the unique (which meant, alas, the only one), who, on her body coated with the same soot as defiled the neighbouring houses, would have displayed—powerless to rid herself of them—to all the admiring strangers come there to gaze upon her, the marks of my piece of chalk and the letters of my name, and it was she, finally, the immortal work of art so long desired, whom I found transformed, as was the church itself, into a little old woman in stone whose height I could measure and whose wrinkles I could count.

The dialogue with himself continues, the anxious shock of the real driving Marcel to the authority of the original source of his triangulated desire for the place:

> I reminded myself of what I had read about Balbec, of Swann's saying: "It's exquisite; as beautiful as Siena." And casting the blame for my disappointment upon various accidental causes . . . I endeavoured to console myself with the thought that other towns still remained intact for me. (1:709–10)

But, of course, the cause of Marcel's disappointment is not accidental but necessary. It would be a mistake to believe his wishful attempt at consolation, to take comfort, as Marcel tries to do, in imagining that the problem is the encroachment of modern vulgarity on antique beauty. Marcel's crisis has more in common with Wordsworth's engagement of the necessary disjunction between name and place "At Rome":

> Is this, ye Gods, the Capitolian Hill?
> Yon petty Steep in truth the fearful Rock,
> Tarpeian named of yore, and keeping still
> That name, a local Phantom proud to mock
> The Traveller's expectation?—Could our Will
> Destroy the ideal Power within, 'twere done
> Through what men see and touch,—slaves wandering on,
> Impelled by thirst of all but Heaven-taught skill.
> Full oft, our wish obtained, deeply we sigh.[4]

It will be during his visit to the painter Elstir that the virtues he missed in the church—because of his difficulty in seeing beyond the clash of its name and its current situation—will be explained to Marcel. Elstir's lesson in attention culminates with two notable developments, one is a brief reflection on the melancholy sense of mortality provoked by the achievement of fame: "Men who believe that their works will last . . . form the habit of placing them in a period when they themselves will have crumbled into dust. And thus, by obliging them to reflect on their own extinction, the idea of fame saddens them because it is inseparable from the idea of death" (1:901). The other is the arrival at the painter's house of Albertine—the girl he had been so eager to know since spotting her at Balbec (1:903). Arrival and satisfaction, insofar as they are possible, are framed by the presence of death. It is not vulgarity but mortality that most troubles the consummation of desire.

The lesson of transience folded into the topic of artistic ambition is given concrete form in the elaborate presentation of the death of Bergotte, not only the chief instance of literary achievement in the novel, but a figure for the impossibility of satisfaction—the author despises society, Marcel notes in a phrase that replaces causality with temporality, "not because it was beyond his reach but as soon as he had attained it" (*The Captive*, 3:181). The section on Elstir's passing returns to the relation of death and artistic fulfillment by way of an astonishing rumination on the limits of the subjective immortality available to art when faced with the end of the world. It does not close with Apocalypse, however, but with Bergotte's own demise in an art gallery. If the mere imagination of the air of the desired place provoked a dangerous fever in the young Marcel, the greater writer is even more susceptible. As the ailing author forces himself to an exhibition in order to seek out a detail in a Vermeer that will make him recognize the limits of his own accomplishments, Proust offers a note of Italy as a counterpoint to inadequate artistic achievement: "He walked past several pictures and was struck by the aridity and pointlessness of such an artificial kind of art, which was greatly inferior to the sunshine of a windswept Venetian palazzo" (3:185). Bound at once toward beauty and death, the writer is moved to celebrate the city that forms the desiring center of the novel as a whole.

While the suddenness of Marcel's own eventual arrival in Venice in *The Fugitive* is notable, given the many volumes through which it has been the prized destination, the link between the voyage and his growing indifference for Albertine is to be expected, as his relationship with her had been repeatedly offered as a contrast to that long-standing desire (e.g.: "How far removed from me now was the desire to go to Venice! Just as, long ago at Combray, had been the desire to know Mme Guermantes when the moment came at which I longed for one thing only, to have Mamma in my room," 3:431). The Venetian sections of the novel elaborate on the structure of compensation and disappointment typical of the work as a whole, much as the arrival at Balbec had been framed by the loss of interest in Gilberte ("I had arrived at a state of almost complete indifference to Gilberte when . . . I went with my grandmother to Balbec," 2:691). The language of travel, of approach and arrival, has indifference as its object, when, with the eclipse of Albertine, the city again becomes an object of desire:

> As for the third occasion on which I remember being conscious of nearing total indifference with regard to Albertine (and this time to the extent of feeling that I had finally arrived at it), it was some little while after Andrée's last visit, in Venice.
>
> My mother had taken me to spend a few weeks there, and . . . I received there impressions analogous to those which I had felt so often in the past at Combray. (3:637)

The long comparison between the two seats of his desire, Combray and Venice, culminates in a difference: the clarity and openness of his mother's love in Italy—fully manifested at this stage because of the recognition of a weakness inextricably combining his disappointment of parental ambitions with the vague physical malaise that shapes his life:

> [M]y mother sat waiting for me, gazing at the canal with a patience which she would not have displayed in the old days at Combray, at a time when, cherishing hopes for my future which had never been realised, she was unwilling to let me see how much she loved me. Nowadays she was well aware that an apparent coldness on her part would alter nothing, and the affection she lavished upon me was like those forbidden foods which are no longer withheld from invalids when it is certain that they are past recovery. (3:638–39)

Not only the mother's views are subject to revision, however. The strange long moment that closes the Venetian interlude, when his mother is leaving and Marcel pretends to himself that he can stay without her, offers a remarkable overlap of the two apparent poles of his desire—the mother and Venice. Indeed, the troubling suggestion that they form not two poles at all but two faces of a desire for the mother is unavoidable.[5] As she is leaving, Marcel gazes over the canal in the attempt not simply to force himself to remain but to save the enchantment of the place. Yet the soul of Venice seems to depart with her. Or, as he puts it with his characteristic commitment to subjective experience, "[t]he town that I saw before me had ceased to be Venice" (3:669–67).

In *Time Regained* the interplay of death, artistic ambition, and the city returns with new force at the galvanizing moment for Marcel's imagination of his writing project. The sudden happiness that passes over him at what had been a melancholy point in his life, the feeling that revitalizes his sense of the possibilities of literature, is provoked by suddenly stepping on two uneven paving stones. A vision of Venice is triggered by the sensation, a recapturing of the past and of evanescent joy closely akin to that other notable epiphany, the taste of the tea-dipped madeleine (3:899). The sensation that moves him, a return of the experience of standing on the warped floor of the baptistery of Saint Mark's, leads to a question: "[W]hy had the images of Combray and of Venice, at these two different moments, given me a joy which was like a certainty and which sufficed, without any other proof, to make death a matter of indifference to me?" (3:900). Memory offers the perfection on the other side of longing and after the disappointment of arrival because, as Marcel will famously note in this passage, "the true paradises are the paradises we have lost" (3:903). It is not merely a hopeless but unavoidable ambition to recapture a lost past that inspires Marcel at this juncture, however, and that motivates the project of the novel, but the prospect of escaping the fear of the inevitable. By becoming what he describes as "extra-temporal," the remembering individual attenuates his fear of death (3:904). Or, in a peculiar source of comfort Marcel will describe later in the volume, anxiety about death *as a writer* overcomes the fear of mortality he had lived with throughout his life (3:1094). Death and the related but not identical sense of loss that characterizes life for Marcel become the motivations for the creative project of recuperation that is the novel.

It would be perverse to propose that a work with the scope of *Remembrance of Things Past* is best described as an art romance. Yet the fantastic imagination of Venice in the novel certainly evokes the traditions of the mode, particularly the interplay of two elements closely associated with the city: death and artistic ambition.[6] The splitting of the self at points of productive crisis is another important structure we recognize from the art romance, one with real significance for Proust's project:

> As I followed the stream of memory back towards its source, I arrived eventually at images of a single person separated from one another by an interval of time so long, preserved within me by "I's" that were so distinct and themselves (the images) fraught with meanings that were so different, that ordinarily when I surveyed (as I supposed) the whole past course of my relations with that particular person I omitted these earliest images and had even ceased to think that the person to whom they referred was the same as the one whom I had later got to know, so that I needed a fortuitous lightning-flash of attention before I could re-attach this latter day acquaintance, like a word to its etymology, to the original significance, which he or she had possessed for me. (3:1017)

The inescapable force of mortality comes to characterize Marcel's thoughts as his own ambition crystallizes: "The idea of death took up permanent residence within me" (3:1100). Imagining himself as a kind of Scheherazade (3:1101), Marcel not only invokes a magical Byzantine beauty he had associated with Venice earlier in the text, and a structure in which the inability to end is a saving virtue, but a figure for the storyteller perpetually under the threat of death. Creativity becomes at once acknowledgment and deferral of mortality.

It risks redundancy to put Marcel on a couch from which he seldom shows much sign of rising. Nevertheless, it is tempting to speculate on the drives and anxieties behind the complex epiphany that allows a moment of development in a novel in which repetition and disappointment have been the rule. Why would the memory of Venice in particular have the effect of energizing the enervated character who has drifted through the narrative up to this point? One episode that offers itself for comparison is the first voyage that set the tone for so many. After all, the baptistery is a contingent manifestation of the real, just as Balbec was. The uneven floor that comes back to Marcel suggests that he is not inspired by an ideal place of the imagination, so much as by the memory of a real particular experience. So why is the joy and inspiration he feels possible or necessary when it was not at the square at Balbec? One simple answer is that in this case, the contingency experienced evokes antiquity, not modernity (not an advertising poster but the passage of time has deformed this space). A related but more complex answer has to do with the presence of the mother in *both* instances:

> [W]e would set off for St Mark's, with all the more pleasure because, since one had to take a gondola to go there, the church represented for me not simply a monument but the terminus of a voyage on these vernal, maritime waters, with which, I felt, St Mark's formed an indivisible and living whole. My mother and I would enter the baptistery, treading underfoot the marble and glass mosaics of the paving, in front of us the wide arcades whose curved pink surfaces have been slightly warped by time. (3:660–61)

The elements that will return in the epiphany about his vocation are clear already in Marcel's account: Venice, the mother, and arrival itself. If Saint Mark's is a terminus, his mother is another.

The section includes a very important set piece that raises the specter of the experience at Balbec as it moves from general claims to deeply personal ones. Marcel begins by noting that, although he had doubted the importance of the company of a loved one for the experience of art when Albertine suggested the idea in relation to Balbec, he now realizes its truth. Both woman and city are significantly different in a passage that culminates inexorably with a recognition of the power of the mother:

> To-day I am sure that the pleasure does exist, if not of seeing, at least of having seen, a beautiful thing with a particular person. A time has now come when, remembering the baptistery of St Mark's—contemplating the waters of the Jordan in which St John immerses Christ, while the gondola awaited us at the landing-stage of the Piazzetta—it is no longer a matter of indifference to me that, beside me in that cool penumbra, there should have been a woman draped in her mourning with the respectful and enthusiastic fervour of the old woman

in Carpaccio's *St Ursula* in the Academia, and that that woman, with her red cheeks and sad eyes and in her black veils, whom nothing can ever remove from that softly lit sanctuary of St Mark's where I am always sure to find her because she has her place reserved there as immutably as a mosaic, should be my mother. (3:661)

If the experience of Venice has at its core a newly vivified intimacy with the mother, the emotional relationship is written over not simply by her recognition of her son's weakness but by *his* of her age and mortality. The black she is wearing as a sign of mourning for her own recently dead mother is distressing above all as a reminder of her vulnerability and the prospect of her own death; the tulle veil she puts on fails in its attempt to mollify the severity of her appearance for her son, for whom it is "as heart-rending in its whiteness as her hair" (3:639).

The death of the grandmother, running for about fifty pages in the English translation, forms the center of a novel in which it is the most abjectly real element. The loss of control and physical beauty of this much-admired figure is offered in gruesome detail, including not only a number of comically embarrassing moments, but such irretrievably unironic elements as an extended stay in a public toilet and the disturbing presence of vomit (we may think back to the nausea Marcel feels when the possibility of going to Venice first arises). The distressing quality of her decline is manifested in the reiterated triangular structure of the section, which so often places Marcel at one corner and then either his mother or Françoise, the maid, at the third, either not quite understanding or being protected by Marcel from knowing or seeing too much. Evidently his energy is largely compensatory, a displaced indication of his own desire not to know or see. It is his mother's death, which he never will be able to represent, that Marcel fears; himself he most wants to protect from knowledge of its possibility.[7]

Among the strategies he adopts after his grandmother's stroke and the rushed visit to the doctor at which he learns she is doomed is to wrap her head in a white lace shawl so that his mother may not notice the distortion in her face. It is only after he has put this ploy into effect that he realizes that the event is not really a shock to his mother: "[F]or many years she had been holding herself quietly in readiness for an indeterminate but inexorable day" (2:329). Nevertheless, she participates in the fiction of not knowing as she helps her mother up the stairs, after having kissed her hand "as though it were that of her God." The daughter averts her eyes in a near-biblical refusal to see the shame of the parent that Marcel's inability to account for only emphasizes:

[N]ot once did she raise her eyes and look at the sufferer's face. Perhaps this was in order that my grandmother should not be saddened by the thought that the sight of her might have alarmed her daughter. Perhaps from a fear of a grief so piercing that she dared not face it. Perhaps from respect, because she did not feel it permissible for her without impiety to notice the trace of any mental enfeeblement on those revered features. Perhaps to be better able to preserve intact in her memory the image of the true face of my grandmother, radiant with wisdom and goodness. So they went up side by side, my grandmother half-hidden in her shawl, my mother averting her eyes. (2:329–30)

The shawl that here symbolizes at once the recognition of long-anticipated mortality and the impossibility of acknowledging it returns in the tulle veil the mother wears along with her mourning at Saint Mark's because Venice is always written over by death and the mother. While the passage of time has contributed unmistakably to the beauty of the church, such is not the effect of time on the human body, of course. The old lady next to Marcel on the uneven stones is the mother who will never age in his memory, which makes her at once identical and completely unlike the Virgin at Balbec. As the novel makes quite clear at key moments, *she* is his pleasure, not the mosaic, or the city architecture, or the erotic trysts he can imagine and experience in the place.[8] Paradoxically, being located at the very center of Marcel's desire makes Venice less liable to much direct representation in the text. The city's function is to be the site at which the love of the mother is most fully realized and reciprocated. The Virgin of the Porch that is the particular locus of Marcel's disappointment with Balbec ("a little old woman in stone whose height I could measure and whose wrinkles I could count") takes on all of the physical decay that his own mother needs to be spared. *She* will age no more but be ever born again in the baptismal memory of her son.

The pleasures of Venice allow a new clarity as to the sources of the disappointment with Balbec. In his youthful confusion, Marcel had tried to convince himself that what he was experiencing was "something far greater" than the passionately loved Balbec of the mind he had experienced only in reproductions. The language in which he notes his anxious realization that "[i]t was also something less, perhaps" is also present in an important draft from 1908–9 in which Marcel attempts to explain to his mother his feelings after having finally met the Guermantes. (It is outside their home that Marcel will stumble in the final volume and experience the crucial memory of Venice.) The language of Marcel's meditation on disappointment triangulates, even at this early point, with Venice and with a complex representation of Oedipal resentment in narrative:

> They are no longer a Name: what we receive from them is inevitably less than what we imagined. Less?—and also perhaps more. It is alike with a historic building as with a person; our first impression of it is determined by a feature which the descriptions we've heard beforehand generally say nothing about. . . . so in

Venice, when we see Saint Mark's for the first time our predominant impression will be of a broad squat building with Venetian masts, like an Exhibition pavilion. . . . Do you remember how pleased you were by my artless rapturous postcards from Guermantes? You have often said to me since: "Tell me something about how you enjoyed yourself." But children don't like to let it appear that they have enjoyed themselves, for fear of jeopardizing their parents' compassion.

Neither, I assure you, do they like to let it appear that they have been unhappy, for fear their parents should feel too much pity for them. I have never told you about Guermantes. Since everything I saw, everything you felt sure would please me, proved a disappointment, how came it, you asked, that I was not disappointed in Guermantes? Well, what I went to find at Guermantes, wasn't there. But I found something else. What is beautiful at Guermantes is that dead and gone centuries try to maintain themselves in it. Time has assumed a dimension of space.[9]

Venice, the mother, the name, the passage of time—these are the elements that give shape to Marcel's desire, along with the narrative that at once tells and withholds the forms of his pleasure. "Tell me a little [of] your pleasure" is the mother's plea translated literally: "Raconte-moi un peu ton plaisir." It is not in such a simple account that Marcel's narrative pleasure can reside, however, but in ruminating on and reproducing his disappointment, in telling and not telling. The dialectic is deceptively simple: disappointment answers expectation when place replaces name; something less is the result of something more. A higher synthesis is ("perhaps") available when something less becomes something more by the surprising introduction of an unexpected idiosyncrasy.

An important surplus is left over, however: the mother, the interlocutor whom Proust himself dissatisfies. What is her role in his pleasure and unpleasure? Marcel's chivalry, his unwillingness to let his mother know the disappointment he felt with what she had expected him to enjoy is evidently disingenuous. The passage clearly suggests his pleasure in modulating her experience in his narrative. But arguably there is a touch of fear running through the gratification he discovers at Guermantes, one closely related to his experience in Venice alongside his mother. Guermantes, like Saint Mark's, offers not the simple pleasures of desires satisfied, but something unexpected, the experience of time remade into space, into an object of contemplation and representation. On the other side of time recaptured, however, is mortality.

Sickness, decay, and death are vital factors in the love that is expressed or recognized in Proust. The voyage to Venice—the highly desired yet always deferred—finally takes place under the impetus of two factors: the realization of Marcel's weakness and the death of his grandmother. Both of these, however, may best be read as symmetrical misdirections of the real anxiety running through this long moment of consummation—an anxiety that nevertheless always breaks through the surface of the text—the aging and death of the mother. Marcel's description of Balbec is closely related to his account of the experience of Guermantes, but it is also structured as an anticipation of the encounter with Saint Mark's, particularly as it builds toward the aging mournful woman at its climax. Venice is a rewriting of the experience of Balbec, or Balbec is written in order to anticipate Venice, with its sacred mother at risk in the actual, no longer as she had been in the various reproductions that had fueled Marcel's imagination, "invulnerable to the vicissitudes which might threaten them, intact even if they were destroyed."

As noted earlier, the actual statue of the Virgin of Balbec is threatened by the banal facts of the modern world surrounding it—street lamps, soot, and the like. But it is worth revisiting the part *Marcel* himself plays in putting the object at risk. His account of the crisis insists on the role of his presence in reducing the glamour—the aura, perhaps—of the statue he had admired for so long. Two factors make up the conclusion of this scene. The eventual reduction of the admired ideal object—including the church itself "into a little old woman in stone whose height I could measure and whose wrinkles I could count"—is preceded by a fantasy of vandalism. Provoked by his disappointment that the object is, as he says, "subjected to the tyranny of the Particular," Marcel's instance of its vulnerability is that "if I had chosen to scribble my name upon that stone, it was she . . . who, on her body . . . would have displayed—powerless to rid herself of them . . . the marks of my piece of chalk and the letter of my name." The name that the place has betrayed may be avenged by the author marking the helpless body of the Virgin with his own signature.

The anxiety about presence that runs through the novel is a manifestation of Marcel's only real desire, which is for the mother. To write runs the risk of violating the mother by acknowledging her place in the particular, not only as an object of erotic attraction, but bound to the process of aging and death. The return in Venice to an old woman in mourning (anticipated by the defiling black soot on the statue) allows Marcel to reinscribe his experience of the aging maternal body inside a structure that is not simply beautiful and safe from the modern world, but that is also a vision of time made into permanence, not transience (the terminus of Saint Mark's versus the omnibus office at Balbec).

The scene in Balbec is run through with temporality as though Marcel's stick were the hand of a gigantic clock or the gnomon of a sundial—"the point of my stick, fettered to the Square . . . receiving on its face half of the ray of the setting sun and presently, in a few hours' time, of the light of the street lamp." The sun, with its suggestion of the passage of time and of clarifying brightness plays a related role at critical moments in

Venice. "The sun would still be high in the sky when I went to meet my mother on the Piazzetta," remembers Marcel. The sun then reshapes the palaces they pass on the Grand Canal, making them appear "not so much private habitations and historic buildings as a chain of marble cliffs at the foot of which one goes out in the evening in a boat to watch the sunset" (3:643). The song Marcel hears as he tries to remain without his mother also participates in the maternal/temporal role of the sun. He sits overlooking the canal "to watch the sunset, while from a boat that had stopped in front of the hotel a musician sang *O sole mio*. The sun continued to sink. My mother must be nearing the station. Soon she would be gone" (3:667). Finally several pages later, as Venice is reduced to insignificance and loneliness by the imminent absence of the mother, the sun comes to a standstill: "I looked on at the slow realisation of my distress, built up artistically, without haste, note by note, by the singer as he stood beneath the astonished gaze of the sun arrested in its course beyond San Giorgio Maggiore" (3:669).

The baptistery offers a more credible version of permanence than this miraculous stopping of the sun, and a more viable escape from the fate of mortality Marcel fears:

> [R]emembering the baptistery of St Mark's—contemplating the waters of the Jordan in which St John immerses Christ, while the gondola awaited us at the landing-stage of the Piazzetta—it is no longer a matter of indifference to me that, beside me there should have been a woman draped in mourning . . . and that that woman whom nothing can ever remove from that softly lit sanctuary of St Mark's where I am always sure to find her . . . should be my mother. (3:661)

Saint John's immersion of Christ and the gondola waiting for the pair are contemporaneous events in a past in which time runs together.[10] It is worth noting that if it is quite natural for Marcel to emphasize the presence of water in this Venetian scene, it is nevertheless an overdetermined element here in the company of his mother, suggestive not simply of birth or the new birth of baptism, but of the giving of a name—of that thing which exists always on the other side of place. In the baptistery Marcel has found the site at which place and name meet. The memory of that location yields both the anxiety that inspires Marcel and the possibility of using it to arrive at a new creative birth, though one only safe *as* memory.

DESIRE (SPEED): MANN

"It is a great pleasure to write the word," writes James at the opening of "Venice," the first essay of *Italian Hours*, "but I am not sure there is not a certain impudence in pretending to add anything to it."[11] Indeed, unadorned free-standing proper nouns reoccur throughout the art-romance tradition, the names of longed-for cities (Landon's "FLORENCE!") used to evoke all the self-sufficient and necessary glamour implied in certain prized destinations. We may recognize this tendency in two nouns joined by a bland preposition indicating little more than a spatial relationship between the proper and improper: *Death in Venice*. If Proust may fairly be said to embarrass analysis by his elaborate meditations on the central themes running through his work, Thomas Mann challenges the student of the art romance by the ostentatious deployment of its elements in what is certainly the most powerfully compact instance of the mode in the twentieth century. The relationship between death and the city in his title is on the one hand obvious, and on the other it forms the mystery running through a text where so much of the causality is provided by the art-romance tradition. The restraint of the title participates in the telling modulation of speed in a text that is sometimes breathtakingly quick, often elaborately slow. The rhythm of the prose itself, of the pursuit through Venice, of the rushed departures and ambivalent returns of Aschenbach— all serve as indications of a passion that is deeply intimate and undeniable yet never fully owned by the individual experiencing it.

Among the most important variations on the art romance Mann offers is to give Aschenbach the genealogical tree of a Mignon, or perhaps to make him a combination of Mignon and Wilhelm, which is easy enough, as they are two sides of one desire. The typical stereotypes of phlegmatic North and passionate South are at work: "[S]wifter, more perceptive blood had in the generation before the poet's flowed into the stock from the mother's side, she being the daughter of a Bohemian musical conductor. It was from her he had the foreign traits that betrayed themselves in his appearance. The union of dry, conscientious officialdom and ardent, obscure impulse, produced an artist."[12] From the outset, the agitation driving Aschenbach is associated with his identity as artist; like an overgrown self-conscious Mignon, his nerves are bad and he is subject to an inexplicable longing for the South.

On a walk provoked by nerves disturbed by his *writing*, Aschenbach sees a mysterious pilgrim peering out from a Byzantine chapel in a graveyard (two, if not three, key identifiers of Venice). With no more than a glance, this stranger makes the author recognize the force of his own yearning to be gone:

> [W]hether the pilgrim air the stranger wore kindled his fantasy or whether some other physical or psychical influence came in play, he could not tell; but he felt the most surprising consciousness of a widening of inward barriers, a kind of vaulting unrest, a youthfully ardent thirst for distant scenes—a feeling so lively and so new, or at least so long ago outgrown and forgot, that he stood there rooted to the spot, his eyes on the ground and his hands clasped behind him, exploring these sentiments of his, their bearing and scope. (5)

Aschenbach's meditations touch on the key challenge to desire in the art romance, the identification of its source. New or simply forgotten, a return or a new development—the text leaves the matter without resolution, even as it acknowledges an indeterminacy much like that involved in returning to Venice or arriving for the first time (Aschenbach will not be able to distinguish between the two). As in James, Mann's engagement of the art romance involves the speed of recognition blended with the strange pleasures of fear or worse:

> True, what he felt was no more than a longing to travel; yet coming upon him with such suddenness and passion as to resemble a seizure, almost a hallucination. Desire projected itself visually: his fancy, not quite yet lulled since morning, imaged the marvels and terrors of the manifold earth. He saw. He beheld a landscape, a tropical marshland, beneath a reeking sky, steaming, monstrous, rank—a kind of primeval wilderness-world of islands, morasses, and alluvial channels. Hairy palm-trunks rose near and far out of lush brakes of fern, out of bottoms of crass vegetation, fat, swollen, thick with incredible bloom. There were trees, mis-shapen as a dream, that dropped their naked roots straight through the air into the ground or into water that was stagnant and shadowy and glassy-green, where mammoth milk-white blossoms floated, and strange high-shouldered birds with curious bills stood gazing sidewise without sound or stir. Among the knotted joints of a bamboo thicket the eyes of a crouching tiger gleamed—and he felt his heart throb with terror, yet with a longing inexplicable. (5–6)

The sudden craving to travel is the manifestation of longings active in a mind able to register urges but not to recognize them fully. Desire is marked as a return, but the abject, suggestively physical landscape instantly imagined shares much with the fantasies of danger in James's account of romance and elsewhere in the tradition, especially that quality of being at once frightening and attractive.

Not only is the fecund swamp of Aschenbach's vision akin to the place of uncanny arrival that is the setting of Childe Roland's dark tower, but the representation of recognition and misrecognition in the novella is closely related to that in Browning's poem. Which is to say, like the Childe, Aschenbach at first goes the wrong way. In both cases, however, the moment of correction or recognition is marked not by new information but by an embarrassed claim of personal confusion. As the object is always in front of the searcher, the importance of pilgrimage resides not so much in the moment of physical arrival but in the instant, at once humiliating and exhilarating, of recognition:

> He could not feel this was the place he sought; an inner impulse made him wretched, urging him on he knew not whither, he racked his brains, he looked

up boats, then all at once his goal stood plain before his eyes. But of course! When one wanted to arrive overnight at the incomparable, the fabulous, the like-nothing-else-in-the-world, where was it one went? Why, obviously; he had intended to go there, what ever was he doing here? A blunder. He made all haste to correct it, announcing his departure at once. (15–16)

The comically self-evident nature of Aschenbach's desire is suggested by the interplay of the narrative voice with the ticket seller's cliché-strewn hucksterism: "An excellent choice. . . . Ah, Venice! What a glorious city! Irresistibly attractive to the cultured man for her past history as well as her present charm" (16). When finished with Aschenbach, the same man beckons and calls out "Next," though there is no one else waiting (17), further reminder of the humiliating predictability of the desire Aschenbach had initially misunderstood. He is one in a series.

The phantasmagoric voyage is marked by further instances of grotesque paralleling, such as the vulgar old man who dresses in too young a style and accompanies a party of younger men with whom he obviously does not belong. The doublings serving to objectify the most vulgar parts of Aschenbach's vague desires are cultural as well as erotic. His arrival is described in terms meant to evoke the most generalized romantic visions of Venice:

> Is there anyone but must repress a secret thrill, on arriving in Venice for the first time—or returning tither after long absence—and stepping into a Venetian gondola? That singular conveyance, come down unchanged from ballad times, black as nothing else on earth except a coffin—what pictures it calls up of lawless, silent adventures in the plashing night; or even more, what visions of death itself, the bier and solemn rites and last soundless voyage! And has anyone remarked that the seat in such a bark, the arm-chair lacquered in coffin-black and dully black-upholstered, is the softest, most luxurious, most relaxing seat in the world? (20–21)

The answer to the question that ends this passage is "yes, of course." As Mann well knows, the dark pleasures of the gondola are a well-established literary topic, going at least as far back as Goethe: "I'd say this gondola's just like a cradle, it rocks me so gently, / And its cabin on top's like a big coffin."[13] Mann's novella is Jamesian in acknowledging the pleasures derivable from the most stereotyped forms of romance—what James called "the panting pursuit of danger"—while offering a further level of romance that is the antithesis to such a pursuit, a peace that is ultimately identifiable with death. Both forms of romance are suggested when, with an over-blown fatalism, Aschenbach puts himself in the hands of the grotesque illicit gondolier. "[E]ven if you hit me in the back with your oar and send me down to the kingdom of Hades, even then you will have rowed me well," he thinks, though nothing of the sort happens. His gondola is way-laid not by pirates but by venal troubadours singing for money (23).

Contraries meet and are not reconciled in *Death in Venice*. The desire for a peace akin to death stands on the other side of a longing characterized in the first instance by hurried travel and fantasies of the dangerous and misshapen. This dialectic is the theme at the very moment Tadzio attracts Aschenbach's considered attention:

> His love of the ocean had profound sources: the hard-worked artist's longing for rest, his yearning to seek refuge from the thronging manifold shapes of his fancy in the bosom of the simple and vast; and another yearning, opposed to his art and perhaps for that very reason a lure, for the unorganized, the immeasurable, the eternal—in short, for nothingness. He whose preoccupation is with excellence longs fervently to find rest in perfection; and is not nothingness a form of perfection? As he sat there dreaming thus, deep, deep into the void, suddenly the margin line of the shore was cut by a human form. He gathered up his gaze and withdrew it from the illimitable, and lo, it was the lovely boy who crossed his vision coming from the left along the sand. (31)

This central unreconcilable moment will be recapitulated a number of times, notably at the very close of the story, at the moment of Aschenbach's death. In the interplay of Dionysian and Apollonian that marks the conceptual underpinnings of Mann's Nietzchean novella, Tadzio is an embodiment of two much-desired and contradictory elements—of both the calm perfection or classical purity of the created object and of the passionate frenzy of the creator:

> What discipline, what precision of thought were expressed by the tense youthful perfection of this form! And yet the pure, strong will which had laboured in darkness and succeeded in bringing this godlike work of art to the light of day—was it not known and familiar to him, the artist? Was not the same force at work in himself when he strove in cold fury to liberate from the marble mass of language the slender forms of his art which he saw with the eye of his mind and would body forth to men as the mirror and image of spiritual beauty.
>
> . . . This was very frenzy—and without a scruple, nay, eagerly, the aging artist bade it come. His mind was in travail, his whole mental background in a state of flux. Memory flung up in him the primitive thoughts which are youth's inheritance, but which with him had remained latent, never leaping up into a blaze. . . .
>
> . . . And the sea, so bright with glancing sunbeams, wove in his mind a spell and summoned up a lovely picture: there was the ancient plane-tree outside the walls of Athens, a hallowed, shady spot, fragrant with willow-blossom and adorned with images and votive offerings in honour of the nymphs and Achelous. (44–45)

We may take the tree to which Aschenbach's ranging thoughts finally make recourse, this shady spot of fantasy drawn from Plato, as the antithesis to that fetid jungle that had been the form of Aschenbach's original desire. And, indeed, it is in the alternating shocks of the two kinds of longing that Aschenbach meets the only end possible for his bifurcated, uncertainly oscillating passion that at one point yearns for a sensual satisfaction that knows itself to be debased and impossible and at another for the absolute peace only reachable in death.

The huckster ticket seller and the decrepit dandy on the boat are instances of the kind of grotesque repetition the novella offers as the disturbing alternative on the other side of the peace to which it is bound from the outset. The rushing and falling back that characterizes Aschenbach's passion as he pursues Tadzio around the city is most notably developed when the author attempts to escape Venice but finds he cannot and is instead forced to retrace his steps. It is a crux reminiscent of Marcel's attempt to believe that he has enough ownership of his desire to remain in the city without his mother, and like that instance, the result is the humiliating recognition of the contrary:

> What a strange adventure indeed, this right-about face of destiny—incredible, humiliating, whimsical as any dream! To be passing again, within the hour, these scenes from which in profoundest grief he had but now taken leave forever! The little swift-moving vessel, a furrow of foam at its prow, tacking with droll agility between steamboats and gondolas, went like a shot to its goal; and he, its sole passenger, sat hiding the panic and thrills of a truant schoolboy beneath a mask of forced resignation. (39)

The hotel allows a near seamless repetition. Aschenbach returns to a room that is almost identical, and his response is characteristic: "He felt rejoiced to be back, yet displeased with his vacillating moods, his ignorance of his own real desires" (40).

The doubling that characterizes his activities is a textual indication of the returns that make up his longing: "Forgotten feelings, precious pangs of his youth, quenched long since by the stern service that had been his life and now returned so strangely metamorphosed—he recognized them with a puzzled, wondering smile" (49). The embarrassment of his attempted escape and cowardly reversal pales in comparison to the humiliation of Aschenbach's participation in that most clichéd of tales, a story about Venice as a city of passion and death. It is the humiliatingly hackneyed nature of the situation in which he finds himself that he recognizes in the response of his gondolier as they set out to pursue Tadzio on a family outing. The "man's quick, sly grasp and ready acceptance of the go-between's rôle" is disturbing to the author, but no more so than the predetermined story in which he finds himself inextricably living:

Yes, this was Venice, this the fair frailty that fawned and that betrayed, half fairy-tale, half snare; the city in whose stagnating air the art of painting once put forth so lusty a growth, and where musicians were moved to accords so weirdly lulling and lascivious. Our adventurer felt his senses wooed by this voluptuousness of sight and sound, tasted his secret knowledge that the city sickened and hid its sickness for love of gain, and bent an ever more unbridled leer on the gondola that glided on before him.

It came at last to this—that his frenzy left him capacity for nothing else but to pursue his flame; to dream of him absent, to lavish, loverlike, endearing terms on his mere shadow. He was alone, he was a foreigner, he was sunk deep in this belated bliss of his—all which enabled him to pass unblushing through experiences well-nigh unbelievable. (55–56)

Mann insists throughout the text that the death that comes for Aschenbach is something he pursues, a fate related to the "belated bliss" emblematized by his helpless, disgusted yet pleased, mirroring of the actions of the gondola just ahead of his. Thus, the fever is given a source closely related to that of the desire to travel that has driven him since the beginning of the novella:

Its source was the hot, moist swamps of the delta of the Ganges, where it bred in the mephitic air of that primeval island-jungle, among whose bamboo thickets the tiger crouches, where life of every sort flourishes in rankest abundance, and only man avoids the spot. (63)

Though they meet in Venice, Aschenbach and the disease that kills him have been moving toward each other from very early. The city is the concrete manifestation of the combination of passion, abasement, and death Aschenbach has been seeking from the outset—indeed, from *before* the outset—of the story. *Death in Venice* tells of a quest that is interminable because only one end is possible. Inspiration and erotic provocation are both suggested in the final unending pursuit that describes Aschenbach's death as a choice:

It seemed to him the pale and lovely Summoner out there smiled at him and beckoned; as though, with the hand he lifted from his hip, he pointed outward as he hovered on before into an immensity of richest expectation. And, as so often before, he rose to follow. (75)

Mann's language approaches untranslatability in this passage in which Tadzio becomes Mercury come to guide a soul to Hades ("Psychagog" is the term rendered as "Summoner" by the translator), gesturing toward a tremendous world of unreal and possibly terrifying potential ("Verheissungs-voll-Ungeheure"). The author rises to follow, "as so often before," but he leaves his body behind him, the motion of pursuit having become entirely fatal because that is what it always was.

MOTHERS AND HOTELS (A NOTE)

> He loved moreover all the labyrinth of corridors, private of-
> fices, reception-rooms, cloakrooms, larders, galleries which
> composed the hotel at Balbec. With a strain of oriental ata-
> vism he loved a seraglio, and when he went out at night might
> be seen furtively exploring its purlieus.
>
> Proust, *Cities of the Plain*

It will not have escaped notice that among the many fantastic questions
running through the art romance, the symbolic force of women is always
pressing, particularly that of the mother. As Carolyn Steedman has docu-
mented, the fantastic androgynous girl in whom Goethe located the most
affecting passions in *Wilhelm Meister* found echoes throughout the nineteenth century. These echoes evoke the feminine as a figure for origins
and for a kind of emotional responsiveness that came to be ever more
closely associated with women as the century wore on—call it sensibility
or sentiment. Mignon's character and fate intimate some of the ways in
which the force of the mother might be deflected even as it is acknowledged. James, for one, is quite clear on the associations between the maternal and sites of admired culture. Early in *A Small Boy and Others*, for
instance, he notes that his mother's first visit to Europe "had quite immediately followed my birth," as though her labor and the voyage were
closely allied. James's grandmother—whose home is the model for that in
which Isabel Archer is found prior to her own epochal voyage to Europe—
is identified not only as the source of his English blood but also of his
early experience of women's novels. Related connections are also evident
in *Notes of a Son and Brother*, in which the beloved continent comes into
play at an odd moment in the account of cherished young women who
died young; Europe, in the course of this discussion, is described as "the
irrepressible even as the *ewig Weibliche* of literary allusion."[14] As this
Goethean allusion suggests, the feminine is present in the art romance
not simply in the traumatized adventurers that follow in Mignon's wake—
the Improvisatrices and Corinnes—but in the *place* of adventure, the land
itself. In the art romance, Italy, or the South generally, is consistently gendered female. But to say this is only to raise further questions, because the
role of that femininity—lover, rival, source, ultimately, *mother*—is in no
way simple or predictable.[15]

In James's novels, mothers loom largest in their absence, from the death
of Isabel Archer's that occurs just prior to the beginning of *Portrait of a
Lady*, to the vital motivating absence of Mrs. Newsome in *The Ambassadors*, to the missing maternal presences in *The Wings of the Dove* and *The
Golden Bowl*. So it is that the maleficent impact of the mother back in

England may be counted among the Jamesian touches in *Where Angels Fear to Tread*. In Gino's care for the child after Lilia's death and in Caroline's brief representation as a Madonna, Forster gestures toward a potentially redemptive possibility of alternative parenting. But this option, like the child, is short-lived. It is hard to miss the mother in Proust, of course, although I have suggested ways in which her centrality for Marcel's passion, ambition, and fear is both flamboyantly acknowledged and, at its most disturbing, shifted onto the grandmother. Elizabeth Barrett Browning, for her part, cuts to the heart of the place of mothers in the art romance by her representation of Aurora's—uncanny, monstrous, multiply desired, and forever lost. As the poem reaches its climax, however, it is quite evident that Aurora's return to Italy is a return to the irrecoverably absent mother. While *Wilhelm Meister*'s concern with fathers is unmissable, the central motivating force of the maternal is no less powerful for being sometimes displaced or hidden. Certainly the Amazon's embrace has its source in motherly caresses, or possibly in the very earliest maternal intimacy. But from the very outset the mother drives the passion of the novel, not least in being the source of the puppet theater that inspires Wilhelm's turn to art. The puppets, whose fascinations determine the lines of Wilhelm's passion, exist in a complex relationship to house and mother, one that bears striking similarities to James's careful accounts of the pleasure and fear hidden in plain sight in the romance.

Where then, it might be asked, is the mother in *Death in Venice*? One place to point to has already been mentioned: "[S]wifter, more perceptive blood in the generation before the poet's flowed into the stock from the mother's side, she being the daughter of a Bohemian musical conductor." It is the mother who makes Aschenbach's turn to the foreign a return to sources, to the "foreign traits" his appearance betrays. Still, there is another mother in the text, one with a notably attenuated presence. The noble, gray, pearl-bedecked beauty who gave birth to Tadzio barely enters the narrative. In her near absence we may find some room to speculate on the particular force of motherhood in the kinds of anxious self-imaginations with which this project as a whole has largely been concerned. Whatever psychic structures may be traceable to mothers generally, they may well offer a particular challenge for the specific case of artists. Desires that have their very earliest sources in the home (those maternal nooks and crannies, forbidden spaces Wilhelm remembers with as much fondness as the marionette theater they contained) may find their ultimate outlet in an alternative creation, or in a model of creativity potentially in competition with the natural forms of reproduction. It would be too simple to read the passage describing Aschenbach's abjection in front of his beloved after his humiliating inability to leave Venice as a kind of passionate bad faith by which unsatisfiable erotic passion is unstably transformed into aesthetic aspiration. In its strange terms distinct kinds of acts merge—the making of a person, the creation of a work of art:

> What discipline, what precision of thought were expressed by the tense youthful perfection of this form! And yet the pure, strong will which had laboured in darkness and succeeded in bringing this godlike work of art to the light of day—was it not known and familiar to him, the artist? Was not the same force at work in himself when he strove in cold fury to liberate from the marble mass of language the slender forms of his art which he saw with the eye of his mind and would body forth to men as the mirror and image of spiritual beauty?

Whatever the craft or sullen art of writing has in common with the act of procreation, it is surely not this. Neither discipline nor purity, nor an act of will creates a beautiful human body. Absent from Aschenbach's fantasy of the coming into being of the desired object are the parents who make the child and the act of making itself. As the passage continues, and the body of a boy is transmuted into a manifestation of the ideal, both the passion of desire consummated and the labor that is its most concrete result do enter the picture, but reimagined as practices of the *artist*:

> This was very frenzy—and without a scruple, nay, eagerly, the aging artist bade it come. His mind was in travail [*Sein Geist kreißte*], his whole mental background in a state of flux. Memory flung up in him the primitive thoughts which are youth's inheritance, but which with him had remained latent, never leaping up into a blaze. (44)

"Travail" is an accurately old-fashioned translation of an archaic term for "labor" (*kreißte*), that is, the painful process of giving birth. In this crisis of memory abroad, Aschenbach's inheritance is given new life—indeed, it shows signs of moving beyond gestation to birth pangs. The text follows Aschenbach toward visions of Platonic ideals made flesh, and of Platonic seductions in a dazzling sun, but I would like to stop at this incoherent fantasy in which the object of desire becomes a work of art and the artist's mind lives through the throes of reproduction in order to suggest that the relation between artist and mother here may best be understood to be one of competition.

"Childe Harold had a mother—not forgot, / Though parting from that mother he did shun." Byron's poem presents these terms as being in contradiction, but shunning may in fact be something quite closely related to not-forgetting. We may think of Mignon's egg dance: performed to cheer Wilhelm up after he learns of Mariane's pregnancy, its play with fecundity, self-expression, and risk hardly shuns *or* forgets Wilhelm's principal concerns, even though it represents an attempt to not look at them directly. As Mignon is surprisingly like Aschenbach, might it be possible to read into both characters a displaced impossible passion for the mother, compounded at once of longing and competition? The ever-unsatisfiable desires that run through both texts—like the androgynous quality of principal characters—may best be understood as the deflection of the passions provoked by the mother. The stories of Mignon and Aschenbach, like that of the Childe who vanishes into the shadows of a mournful maternal Rome may all be read as particularly flamboyant and complex instances of the attempt to represent the hopeless desire to shun something that is absolutely unforgettable.

As my study of the fantasies of creation abroad comes to a close, I will only gesture to one of the more peculiar displacements of the maternal. I have suggested that in its later years the art romance sees an ever greater fascination with the interstitial spaces of travel taking at least some of the energy once reserved for descriptions of (responses to) prized destinations. Some of the attention earlier writers had focused on the celebration of well-known sights is turned by twentieth-century writers to the means of travel itself, to trains, boats, even cars, and especially hotels. While this development is in part attributable to the evolution of the infrastructure of modern tourism, it is nevertheless true that earlier travel narratives tell us little about what must have been the extremely interesting question of transportation, while the experience of lodging itself tends not to be a feature. The new attention to the experience of places of transition rather than to destinations will be most productively understood not as a practical matter then, but as ultimately traceable to developments in the drives that shaped the art romance in the first place.

Given the ill-hidden presence of domestic passions in all fantasies of travel, it may be useful to consider briefly the role of hotels as perfect versions of certain kinds of household arrangements. The two key functions that such lodgings suggest by their nature are predictable forms of shelter and nurture and the possibility of return. As such, they evoke the traditional childhood association—not to say source—of these elements: the mother. The pleasure of repetition is the particular lure of the Grand Hotel. Here is Marcel in the hotel elevator:

> As I rose upon the ascending column, I travelled once again through what had formerly been for me the mystery of a strange hotel. . . . This time . . . I had felt the almost too soothing pleasure of passing up through an hotel that I knew, where I felt at home, where I had performed once again that operation which we must always start afresh, longer, more difficult than the turning inside out of an eyelid, and which consists in the imposition of our own familiar soul on the terrifying soul of our surroundings. (2:791)

To say that he feels at home is for Marcel to say a great deal. For home is the place that allows the possibility of repetition that makes bearable an otherwise terrifying outside world.

While the rushing of *Where Angels Fear to Tread* takes Forster's characters over and over the same ground, returning always to the same small town and inn, the structure receives its most elegantly economical manifestation in *A Room with a View*, which begins and ends with the very location that gives the work its title. When Aschenbach checks into his hotel again after his abortive attempt to leave Venice, the preposterous redoubling form of his actions is underlined by his arrival at a new room that is nevertheless essentially identical to the one he had just attempted to leave. The inescapable sanatorium in *Magic Mountain* will be one Mannian return to the deadening pleasure to be found in repetition and powerlessness. But already it is evident in Aschenbach's responsiveness to the passive transportation of the gondola when he arrives, of the boat that takes him back and forth along "the well known route" to the train station, and of the hotel elevator and its smiling operator (37–40). As is the case with Marcel, the redundant repetitiveness of his passion and the loss of autonomy it entails are both captured by Aschenbach's surrender to the control of the operator repeating his own inevitable trajectory.

For Marcel the hotel at Balbec is the place where he and his grandmother are closest, the wall that separates them serving as a method of communication between the bed-bound hypochondriac and his worried caretaker. Even after her death, the grandmother returns to him there in passionate memory (2:783–90). In *The Wings of the Dove*, Densher's rooms in Venice are not only haunted by the desire they see satisfied by his sexual tryst with Kate Croy, but they are also presided over by the ghost of Milly Theale. There is no need to elaborate on the erotic qualities implicit in a living space that is only a bedroom far away from routine domestic duties or associations. No less self-evident is the infantilization of the guest, that object of attentive care calling for no kind of reciprocity. Whether at Balbec or Venice, at each hotel Marcel rediscovers his love for his mother even as he seeks out more titillating forms of illicit pleasure. The passionate quest—be it for Albertine in Balbec, or laundresses in Venice—is a manifestation of erotic escapism away from home. But the haunting presence of death and the mother nevertheless also suggests another form of romance, one characterized not by a frenzy like that of Aschenbach staggering around the city, but by a kind of peace that aims to escape longing altogether.

Esther Boise Van Deman, Stabian Gate, Pompeii. Courtesy of the Photographic Archive of the American Academy in Rome, Van Deman Collection (VD 1579).

James, Freud, and the End of Romance

> Much as was ever to be said for our old forms of pilgrimage—
> and I am convinced that they are far from wholly
> superseded—they left, they had to leave, dreadful gaps in our
> yearning, dreadful lapses in our knowledge, dreadful failures
> in our energy; there were always things off and beyond, goals
> of delight and dreams of desire, that dropped as a matter of
> course into the unattainable.
>
> Henry James, *Italian Hours*[1]

Dreams of Desire: James and the Romance of Intimacy

"Romance" suggests the narrator in *Where Angels Fear to Tread*, "only dies with life." And certainly the art romance has proved resilient enough to survive a number of significant cultural changes. The troubled representation of a return to sources that can neither be fully achieved nor entirely avoided does not, of course, end with the authors of the early years of the twentieth century that conclude this study. Indeed, the mode continues to have an active life, in film as well as in older narrative forms. Different pasts or nations will sometimes come to the fore, but the essential structures are readily identifiable, not only in the works of Ernest Hemingway, say, or D. H. Lawrence, or Graham Greene, but also in popular fiction, where gothic ghosts return in tales of murder, betrayal, and disturbing self-invention in warm climates: Patricia Highsmith sends Ripley to southern Europe to murder the self he will become; the promise written into the name of Thomas Harris's overcultured serial killer in *Silence of the Lambs* is kept when we find Hannibal Lecter working at a museum in Florence in the sequel that bears his name.[2]

Still, if the mode is easy to identify in contemporary culture and throughout the twentieth century, it is nevertheless true that it received its most complex analysis in the work of writers who had the example of the nineteenth century most immediately available to them. I close this study with a brief return to the two most committed modern thinkers on the art romance—Freud and James—as they reflect on what the Bay of Naples might offer the thoughtful reader by way of understanding the intertwined fates of the real and romance. To do so will mean considering the psychiatrist as a reader of literature and the novelist as a student of desire. It will also entail a brief digression on the particular significance of this geographical area for the art romance.

"The last letter I had from Harold," notes the loving narrator at the beginning of Forster's early story, "Albergo Empedocle" (1903), "was from Naples."[3] As the beautiful yet troubling entrance to the southernmost reaches of Italy, as the site of the sublime experiences provided by an active volcano and of the melancholy ones suggested by the cities (at once Roman and Greek) Vesuvius had simultaneously destroyed and preserved, Naples always had a unique place in the art romance, whether as a kind of climax or extreme boundary.[4] It is this tradition that Forster can gesture to in his tale of a young man who may or may not be mad to believe he has lived before in a Hellenic Sicily.

The importance of the area around Vesuvius is indicated by its central position in both Goethe's *Italian Journey* and Staël's *Corinne*. At once end and beginning, approached for most of its history through a miasmal swamp, Naples is an important limit that suggests many others. At the close of the first part of *Italian Journey*, Goethe makes the preparation to leave Rome for Naples sound like a rehearsal for death, a troubling abandonment of well-established aesthetic and erotic attractions:

> At any departure, one inevitably thinks of earlier journeys and of that final future one. The thought is borne in on me, more forcibly than ever, that we make far too many provisions for life. Tischbein and I, for example, are about to turn our backs on so many wonderful things, including our well-stocked private museum. We now have three Junos standing side by side for comparison, but we are leaving them behind as though we had none.[5]

His anxieties notwithstanding, it is when he embarks on this voyage that Goethe begins to realize the deepest promise of his desire. All references to the unfinished *Wilhelm Meister* begin at this point in the text, the first being a thought-provoking realization about the very longings he himself had given voice: "Mignon was quite right to yearn for this country" (182).

Nelvil and Corinne come from Rome to Naples to confess their true identities to each other on a trip Corinne designs as a beautiful culmination. Staël, however, presents the journey as an overdetermined reprisal of the most disturbing themes of the novel. Pompeii is the fated crux of the lovers:

> The ruins of Pompeii are on the same side of the bay as Vesuvius, and it was with these ruins that Corinne and Lord Nelvil began their expedition. They were both silent, for the decisive moment of their fate was drawing near, and the vague hope they had been enjoying for so long, and which so well befits the indolence and reveries inspired by the Italian climate, was to be replaced at last by an actual destiny.[6]

Goethe, leaving his well-organized Junos for a voyage he cannot avoid but cannot help fearing; Corinne and Lord Nelvil, brought to the crisis of what Staël describes as a destiny they have only avoided thus far; and even, in his small way Harold, whose last attempt at controlled communication is directed from Naples before he surrenders to what Staël might have described as his own "actual destiny"—each instance speaks to the two qualities that run through the art romance and that have an especially forceful presence in the Bay of Naples, the erotic and the fatal.

Of course, Italy as a whole had served as the location of licensed and unlicensed sexual discovery for the cultured middle class from early in the nineteenth century. Dorothea Brooke honeymoons there in the 1830s, around the same time we find Heine exasperated by the crowds of English men and women he encounters everywhere in his own journey to Italy. The irritating quality of wedding trips that had become a typical complaint of more cultured travel writers still provokes authors at the beginning of the twentieth century. In both James's culminating Italian memoir, "A Saint's Afternoon" (1901; rev. 1909) and in Freud's *Delusions and Dreams in Jensen's* Gradiva (1907), the move to Naples provokes this trope, which at once acknowledges the vulgar sexual satisfactions the place is understood to make possible and suggests that such satisfactions are distractions from the aesthetic or intellectual appreciation ostensibly motivating the trip. Irony distances the pleasure of others from our own, but in James, as in Jensen, it works to protect the disinterested nature of the activities of the traveler from being put into question by the more ordinary pleasures all around him.

In Rome, Jensen's Norbert Hanold, who is in full retreat from the consummation of his own erotic desires even as he pursues them with a passion he is unable to recognize, is baffled by the presence of the amorous couples all around him:

> He found himself among the swarm of honeymooners and was forced to notice the loving couples . . . but was quite unable to understand their goings-on. He came to the conclusion that of all the follies of mankind "getting married takes first place, as the greatest and most incomprehensible, and the senseless honeymoon trips to Italy are, in a way, the crowning touch of this idiocy."[7]

Finally, after being kept awake one night by the sounds of lovers in another room, he flees further south. Believing the couples are on their way to Capri, Norbert—characteristically—undertakes a parallel trajectory with a nearby but distinct goal. He heads toward Pompeii, "contrary to his expectation and intentions" (11), driven as usual by passions that he does not believe to be his own but that he cannot for that reason ignore.

Contempt for the recently married may be read as an anxious response to sexual satisfaction, but it is also another acknowledgment of the inescapable force of desire. Which is to say, it may seem all too clear why Norbert needs to escape the presence of these couples; his flight is the practical manifestation of his long and futile attempt to flee longings he cannot recognize in himself. Disgust of this sort may also stand in for the inexpressible aspiration to love differently, to love another man, say, which is evidently the crisis behind Harold's breakdown on an engagement trip to Italy in "Albergo Empedocle." If an anxious or contemptuous relationship toward married passion may have at its source a resistance to compulsory heterosexuality, a broader formulation of what may be at stake in such a resistance is nevertheless also available: the hopeless wish that our passion belong to us entirely, that it be free from those qualities that generalize desire. Its function in social and sexual reproduction, its participation in the vulgarity of mere pleasure, its wholehearted commitment to repetition (to what in culture we might call cliché)—these are some of the faces of passion that may need to be rebuffed.

Yet the art-romance tradition makes quite clear that *all* desire participates in a humiliatingly reiterative quality. James is not kept awake by the activities of newlyweds, but they intrude into his thoughts as he approaches Capri, the island whose presence in the Bay of Naples the author nostalgically describes as a lesson in "the grand style"—that is, in a noble mode of painting of another era. While the novelist sits on deck ruminating on such themes, his fellow travelers rush to enjoy a famous natural sight, an activity described in terms that would be appropriate for a particularly inexpert and hurried form of sex: "[A] happy brotherhood of American and German tourists, including, of course, many sisters, scrambled down into little waiting, rocking tubs and, after a few strokes, popped systematically into the small orifice of the Blue Grotto." James offers an image of a manifold vulgarity to stand for the clichéd passions—sexual and touristic—of the honeymooning couples. He gleefully imagines an endless stream of honeymooners, vanishing forever into the orifice of the Grotto, a just and pleasant revenge of good taste on the part of nature (601). But such an end is not to be, of course, and the return of the cheerful tourists is instead an affirmation of their inescapable reiterated presence:

> The trail of Germanicus in Italy to-day ramifies further and bites perhaps even deeper; a proof of which is, precisely, that his eclipse in the Blue Grotto is inexorably brief, that here he is popping out again, bobbing enthusiastically back and scrambling triumphantly back. The spirit, in truth, of his effective appropriation of Capri has a broad-faced candour against which there is no standing up, supremely expressive as it is of the well-known "love that kills," of Germanicus's fatal susceptibility. If I were to let myself, however, incline to *that* aspect of the serious case of Capri I should embark on strange depths. (601)

"Again," "back," and "back"—an absence whose brevity is "inexorable" is followed by a return that is equally hyperbolic: James's prose evokes the irritatingly repetitive actions of the crowd of tourists. Returning to where others have been ("again," "back," and "back") is the characteristic activity of the public James ironically identifies with the Roman general who took his name from the northern tribes he conquered.

James's satire aside, it is hard to miss the darker turn this passage on the crossing to Capri takes at its end. Both Norbert Hanold's attempts to escape the honeymooners and James's fantasies of their absorption by nature in the course of a great final penetration evoke a theme that Forster would make his own, the comic qualities unavoidably present in the erotic heart of the art romance. But what are we to make of the strange depths of the "love that kills" in Capri? It is a question James himself raises more than once in his descriptions of the place: "the prodigious island—beautiful, horrible and haunted" (600). "Beautiful, horrible, haunted: that is the essence of what, about itself, Capri says to you" (601).

The title of the 1909 collection of essays that closes with "A Saint's Afternoon," *Italian Hours*, suggests two key issues that are present throughout the art-romance tradition: the question of time—James offers hours: not minutes, but also not years—and, homonymically, the problem of possession.[8] How time spent in Italy may be *ours* is always at issue in a book run through with the rich sense of disinheritedness that characterizes all of James's accounts of culture. In the final essay, northern visitors stand for a desire for intimacy with the South that is no less powerful for being sometimes silly, often self-evidently destructive, and ultimately impossible to realize. James writes with admiration of "The straightness and simplicity, the classic, synthetic directness of the German passion for Italy," but he finds its signs as appalling as they are unavoidable (601). Still, it is the very quality of not entirely successful transposition, of dispossession, that gives the German model its recognizable pathos:

> [S]ome such general consciousness as this may well oppress, under any sky, at the century's end, the brooding tourist who makes himself a prey by staying anywhere, when the gong sounds, "behind." It is behind, in the track and the reaction, that he least makes out the end of it all, perceives that to visit any one's country for any one's sake is more and more to find some one quite other in possession. No one, least of all the brooder himself, is in his own. (602)

We may recall that the American protagonists of "Travelling Companions" and of "Daisy Miller" are following up their German education with trips south when they are encountered in Italy. Writing in chilly England, James thinks back to his experience at the home of Axel Munthe in Capri—a memory that allows him to reflect on three central facts of the art romance, what he calls its Nordic sources, its sexuality, and its displacedness.[9] "A Saint's Afternoon" writes into its very title both the worshipful fascination the monuments of the country always held for James and the limited, evanescent, experiential qualities he is able to recognize and celebrate with greater frankness at the close of his career. The contempt for the honeymooners and the simple predictable pleasures of their explorations, their vulgarly physical satisfactions—these are displacements in an essay in which more than ever the physical, contingent, even erotic charms of the country are allowed to come to the fore. In Capri as throughout this essay, James permits himself to discover the sensual pleasures of a homoerotic South on the one hand and of a constructed German fantasy on the other. And both pleasures are all the more moving because he knows them to have been there all along.

As it happens, for James the passion of a desiring North that cannot be dismissed as simply vulgar is personified not by a German but by a Swede. The beautiful, moving, museum-home Axel Munthe constructed on the island is no Colosseum or Ducal Palace, no noble tomb or church, no royal collection or art gallery. Lacking the cultural warrant of other admired Italian sites, however, San Michele is all the more authentic a representation of the passion that moves James:

> If what had finally, with infinite patience, passion, labour, taste, got itself done there, was like some supreme reward of an old dream of Italy, something perfect after long delays, was it not verily in *ultima Thule* that the vow would have been piously enough made and the germ tenderly enough nursed? (604)

Ends meet in Capri—*ultima Thule* and the last word of Jamesian Italophilia, insofar as such a word is possible. "A Saint's Afternoon" closes *Italian Hours* because it stands for a finality that is a return, a last word that comes back, a recognition that holds the promise of that impossible thing—a new beginning:

> It was really something, at a time when the stride of the traveller had become as long as it was easy . . . to have kept one's self so innocent of strange horizons that the Bay of Naples in June might still seem quite final. That picture struck me—a particular corner of it at least, and for many reasons—as the last word; and it is this last word that comes back to me, after a short interval, in a green, grey northern nook, and offers me again its warm, bright golden meaning before it also inevitably catches the chill. (600)

James is clear on the grateful pleasure he experiences at San Michele, the materialization of a long-lasting desire for the South he recognizes with renewed force. As unmissable is his passionate response to a contingent and ephemeral kind of joy (what he calls "the happy hazard of things"). "Love and understand the Italians," Philip had told Lilia in *Where Angels Fear to Tread*, four years before this essay, "for the people are more marvelous than the land." The saint's afternoon James memorializes is the celebration of a local holiday that occurs while he is on the island. It is easy to find in the commemoration of a patron saint an analogy for James's own project of celebrating the apotheoses of this beloved land. But it is also hard to miss the fact that his experience of the beauty of Italian people, Italian men in particular, is forcefully acknowledged as an important element in his response to the event. He is similarly moved at Munthe's home not simply by the collector's carefully constructed fantasy villa, but by the charming locals who come to perform there or to decorate the structure (611). The pleasure he takes in these people is of a piece with a moment that occurs very late in the essay as James, being driven back to Rome, passes a young gamekeeper or farmer of great beauty, "one of those human figures on which our perception of the romantic so often pounces in Italy as on the genius of the scene personified" (617).

"These things are personal memories," notes James of his paragraph-long celebration of this lovely Italian man, "however, with the logic of certain insistences of that sort often difficult to seize" (618). Personal: meaning at once not more broadly public, as a monument or site might be, but also shaped by one's own desires, ultimately difficult to share (though readers are free to think we recognize "the logic of certain insistences"). While the Mediterranean has provided the North a favored venue for fantasies of sexual liberation for a long time, James recognizes no absolute distinction between his own longings and those powerful cultural urges that also motivate the response to the South. Instead, he insists on describing the pleasures of Italy as involving the interpenetration of elements; it is "the incomparable wrought *fusion*, fusion of human history and mortal passion with the elements of earth and air, of colour, composition and form, that constitute her appeal and give it the supreme heroic grace" (616–17; emphasis in the original).[10]

As Corinne and Nelvil will reach the truth of their passions and their identities in Pompeii, the same place where Norbert's desires will finally be recognized, so the recovered city is the site at which James allows himself an insight that is no less moving for its refusal of simple satisfactions. Unexpectedly alone in a space he describes as the "haunt of *all* the cockneys of creation" (613; emphasis in the original), James inscribes himself in the lists of benighted displaced travelers, even as he, nevertheless, leaves open the possibility of a closer intimacy with the beloved space:

> [T]he particular cockney who roamed without a plan and at his ease, but with his feet on Roman slabs, his hands on Roman stones, his eyes on the Roman void, his consciousness really at last of some good to him, could open himself as never before to the fond luxurious fallacy of a close communion, a direct revelation. (613–14).

James acknowledges the beauty of an intimacy he can only imagine as fallacious: a relationship no less "good to him" for being illusionary. No simpleminded absorption in a seaside orifice for this traveler. His access to an impossible intimacy with the beloved place is only possible because he knows it to be ever incomplete and never quite true.

Delusions and Dreams: The Real in Freud and James

For Freud as for James, real runs to romance; romance runs back to real. In the writings of both, the work of the memorialist shades always into fantasy and is bound to evoke ghosts. By the same token, however, it is only in relation to the fantastic and inverisimilitudinous that one can finally recognize the real force of love. Freud's difficulties closing his account of *Gradiva* are indicated by the tentative beginning of his final paragraph: "We would seem to have reached the end" (92). But his acknowledgment of the difficulty of concluding surrenders the last word of the essay to the real, now become an adjective in the service of forgetting: "But we must stop here, or we may really forget [*sonst vergessen wir vielleicht wirklich*] that Hanold and Gradiva are only creatures of their author's mind" (93). The risk described is as good a formulation as any for what may be the ultimate seduction of the art romance: the temptation to really forget in order to fantastically remember.

Freud claims that his initial interest in Jensen's novel—his first published analysis of a work of literature outside of *Interpretation of Dreams*—lay in considering what the dreams that run through *Gradiva* might yield to psychoanalytic study. But he cannot help spending more than half of the essay on the narrative itself. The disjunction between his ostensible aim and his actual practice is acknowledged at the opening of the second part of the essay, the beginning of a slow transition into the long-deferred analysis of dreams:

> But after all, what we really intended to do originally was only to investigate two or three dreams that are to be found here and there in *Gradiva*. . . . How has it come about, then, that we have been led into dissecting the whole story and examining the mental processes in the two chief characters? (41)

Here is Freud's brief description of the tale he cannot avoid examining: "[T]he story was set in the frame of Pompeii and dealt with a young archaeologist who had surrendered his interest in life in exchange for an interest in the remains of classical antiquity and who was now brought back to real life by a roundabout path [*Umwege*] which was strange but perfectly logical" (10). The necessary roundabout path linking fantasy and reality is not simply part of what Norbert lives through; it is central to the practice of analysis. Part of the charm of the story for the analyst is the fact that unavoidable or fated paths are as vital to its development as they are to his interpretation. Inevitability is the principal mechanism shaping the roundabout roads linking the two sides of the tale, be they reality and fantasy, desire and resistance, or memory and forgetting.

I have suggested that Naples has a special place in the art romance due to the exaggerated presence of elements that are central to the tradition—in particular, the sensual force of the South in liberating passion, and the associations with fate and fatality evoked by the two dead cities of Vesuvius. Like James, Freud finds in Pompeii an appropriate setting for a tale of fated attraction that at every point also suggests that intimacy will be no less beautiful for being in some measure not quite true to life. Norbert Hanold falls in love with a woman he sees in a Roman frieze, a work of art his fantasy—informed by his archaeological training—charges with significance. Nevertheless, while this object takes on all the passion he cannot give the woman he truly loves, it is also the case that the search the frieze provokes is what ultimately returns Norbert to his lover's arms.

Norbert gives the woman in the frieze the name Gradiva, which suggests motion in Latin. The ostensible reason for this is that the German family name of the real object of desire is Bertgang (Bright-going). But the passion for the tread or movement of the object of desire has many sources. After all, Zoe Bertgang/Gradiva stands for the path Norbert can resist but cannot avoid. On (re)learning the real given name of the person he takes to be the frieze come to life, Norbert illustrates the way apparent contraries will meet in the return of passion denied. "The name suits you beautifully, but it sounds to me like a bitter mockery, for Zoe means life," he tells what he thinks is a ghost. "One must bow to the inevitable," is her reply, "and I have long grown used to being dead" (17). Later in the text Zoe identifies the trajectory she has to go through as Norbert's love object when she talks of "someone having to die so as to come alive." "No doubt that must be so for archaeologists," she notes, her response to her disturbed lover oscillating between resignation and irony, not least perhaps because she is herself the daughter of another distracted scientist (37).

Freud is moved to go much further than the promised analysis of the dreams in the novel because the text as a whole offers him an irresistibly vivid representation of the creative force of displacement. Norbert's passion for the striding woman in the frieze, which seems so fantastic on its surface, is in fact a manifestation of the real desire from which Norbert has run away. As Freud points out, his search for the truth of the gesture he has come to fetishize is wonderful testimony to the misdirection of his wishes. Indeed, the return of a denied reality experienced nevertheless as chance or fate comes to be central to what the novel offers the analyst. "Gradiva's gait was not discoverable in reality," notes Freud about Norbert's quandary early in the text, "and this filled him with regret and vexation" (12). His account of the stepping girl is immediately preceded by remarks on the logic of probability, to which it is closely related: "What we call chance in the world outside can, as is well known, be resolved into laws. So, too, what we call arbitrariness in the mind rests upon laws, which we are now only beginning dimly to suspect" (9). Later in the text, the topic of chance quickly moves Freud to the issue of fatality, which for him also takes the form of a circular path. The novelist's inverisimilitude in accounting for Norbert's unlikely reencounter with Zoe (or life) in Pompeii is justified in this way: "[I]t merely makes use of chance, which unquestionably plays a part in many human histories; and furthermore he uses it to good purpose, for this chance reflects the fatal truth that has laid it down that flight is precisely an instrument that delivers one over to what one is fleeing from" (42). The step of Gradiva is an object of fascination not only to Norbert, then, but to the analyst as well, because he finds in it—as in the trajectory described in the novel as a whole—an image for the necessary returns of what is desired.

Freud is moving on the force of the delusion motivating Norbert. He points out that when, as they are leaving Pompeii at the end of the novel, Zoe (or life) walks in emulation of the relief in answer to Norbert's unspoken plea, the novel is acknowledging the power of fantasy in shaping the real. The analyst puts the matter in terms James himself might have recognized as he haunted Pompeii: "With the triumph of love, what was beautiful and precious in the delusion found recognition as well" (40). The analyst's commemoration of the precious qualities of delusion is reminiscent of the beauty James celebrates in his account of the binding and blending of apparent contraries in Italy. The "incomparable wrought *fusion*" that adds up to the sum of Italy's grandeur returns as the force behind the beauty of the bay of Naples, of which "the grand air" is "antiquity in solution" (609). To respond to the place is, therefore, to feel "afresh the old story of the deep interfusion of the present with the past" (609). And yet, it can be no surprise that in the midst of such blended pleasures the specter of something dark emerges, or returns. James needs to quote himself as he interrogates an earlier formulation that it might seem he has left well behind:

> The beauty and the poetry, at all events, were clear enough, and the extraordinary uplifted distinction; but where, in all this, it may be asked, was the element of "horror" that I have spoken of as sensible?—what obsession that was not charming could find a place in that splendid light, out of which the long summer squeezes every secret and shadow? I'm afraid I'm driven to plead that these evils were exactly in one's imagination, a predestined victim always of the cruel, the fatal historic sense. To make so much distinction, how much history had been needed!—so that the whole air still throbbed and ached with it, as with an accumulation of ghosts to whom the very climate was pitiless. (610)

While James may have in mind the cruel imperial murders of the Roman past (he recommends a reading of Tacitus), he also notes that "it is not because the trail of Tiberius is ineffaceable that you are most uneasy" (601). It is Germanicus who troubles him. Like Norbert, struggling against the foreordained quality of his relationship with Zoe, the very fact of predestination encoded into his relationship with the beloved place provokes resistance and fear.

To the dyad life/death, Freud and James both add a second: lifelike/fantastic (otherwise: real/romantic), but the pairs are not parallel. It may well be through the fantastic that life is more likely to be reached, while death is evidently all too real. Jensen, and through him Freud, give us Gradiva's tread as a figure for the relationship with a path that is round-about but beautiful, frightening because unavoidable. If *Gradiva* essentially begins and ends with a beautiful step, "A Saint's Afternoon" opens with the ever-lengthening stride of the modern traveler. Part of the thrill James wishes to commemorate in the Bay of Naples is that which comes with the surprising possibility of novelty late in life, of a new kind of arrival at a time when travel has become ever easier. The essay, and *Italian Hours* as a whole, ends with James in a car, rushing at speed through the country-side, exhilarated, and, one senses, a little scared, the rhythms of romance challenged by the speed of the conveyance taking him back to Rome. He does not close with the car in motion, however, but with a wonderfully lyric attempt to represent—or, rather, to account for the inability to repre-sent—the simple pleasures of stopping in a café in an Italian town and feeling oneself not threatened but comforted by the past: "[W]e commu-nicated to intensity, we lay at our ease in the bosom of the past," he writes, "we practiced intimacy" (618–19).

What James describes has by this time in his career become the greatest romance of all. What might it mean to "practise" intimacy? It is an activity not unrelated to that moving "fallacy of a close communion, a direct reve-lation" the novelist had described in Pompeii. Both are characterized not only by an acknowledgment of the interplay of difficulty and pleasure, but also by an elaborate if muted suggestion of something like maternal or sexual closeness. The "luxurious fallacy" of one moment returns in the wonderfully elaborate sentence that ends but does not want to end the essay and James's Italian hours, a passage that enacts as it describes "the difficulty for the right and grateful expression of" the intimacy the author feels. It is this challenge to expression that James identifies as "mak[ing] the old, the familiar tax on the luxury of loving Italy" (619). "Luxurious fallacy" becomes "luxury of loving" by the end of the essay, a point at which even the irresolvable difficulty of expressing oneself at once cor-rectly and with sufficient feeling to be accurate has become just one more testimonial of love.

Notes

PREFACE

1. I use the capacious term "romance" to describe a narrative form that is consistently and openly inverisimilitudinous, particularly in contrast to the ostensible aspiration toward the real generally associated with the novel. Both parts of Northrop Frye's definition are useful to my project: "(1) The mythos of literature concerned primarily with an idealized world. (2) A form of prose fiction practiced by Scott, Hawthorne, William Morris, etc., distinguishable from the novel." Like Frye, in what is still a seminal account, I see one of the chief indications of romance as being its approximation to wish fulfillment, by which is also suggested the relation of the form to dreams as Freud understood them. Northrop Frye, *Anatomy of Criticism* (Princeton: Princeton University Press, 1957), 110, 186, 367. See also the useful brief treatment of the question of romance and novel in Alastair Fowler, *Kinds of Literature: An Introduction to the Theory of Genres and Modes* (Cambridge: Harvard University Press, 1982), 121–22. Whereas Frye's formulations are valuable not only in indicating the aspirations of romance but for demonstrating the tendency of criticism to place it in contrast to the novel, more recent critics have seen important continuities and negotiations between the two types of narrative. See, e.g., Ian Duncan, *Modern Romance and Transformations of the Novel: The Gothic, Scott, Dickens* (Cambridge: Cambridge University Press, 1992), and especially Michael McKeon, *The Origins of the English Novel, 1600–1740* (1987; Baltimore: Johns Hopkins University Press, 2002), esp. 9–11, 26–28, 268. With earlier theorists of the novel as well as Frye in mind, McKeon, offers a salutary caution about "the inadequacy of our theoretical distinction between 'novel' and 'romance' " (3).

2. Useful studies on the nineteenth-century culture of art include the work of Francis Haskell, especially *Rediscoveries in Art: Some Aspects of Taste, Fashion, and Collecting in England and France* (Ithaca: Cornell University Press, 1980); John Steegman's *Victorian Taste: A Study of the Arts and Architecture from 1830 to 1870* (Cambridge, Mass.: MIT Press, 1971) and *The Rule of Taste: From George I to George IV* (1936; London: National Trust of Great Britain, 1986); and Brian Allen, ed., *Towards a Modern Art World*, (New Haven: Yale University Press, 1995). See also Linda Dowling, *The Vulgarization of Art: The Victorians and Aesthetic Democracy* (Charlottesville: University Press of Virginia, 1996), and Jonah Siegel, *Desire and Excess: The Nineteenth-Century Culture of Art* (Princeton: Princeton University Press, 2000). Elizabeth Holt, *The Triumph of Art for the Public* (Garden City, N.Y.: Anchor, 1979), provides a valuable compendium of sources on the international development of public interest in art.

3. For developments in travel before and during the period of this study, see William Edward Mead, *The Grand Tour in the Eighteenth Century* (1914; New York: Benjamin Blom, 1972); Jeremy Black, *The British and the Grand Tour* (Lon-

don: Croom Helm, 1985); Christopher Hibbert, *The Grand Tour* (London: Thames Methuen, 1987), and especially James Buzard, *The Beaten Track: European Tourism, Literature and the Ways to "Culture," 1800–1918* (New York: Oxford University Press, 1993).

4. We may take as typical Barbara Korte's focus on two features of travel writing "as we understand it today": "its claim to represent the travelled world authentically and empirically" and "the degree to which travel writing is subject-orientated and reveals the personality and individual experience of the traveller." Barbara Korte, *English Travel Writing from Pilgrimages to Postcolonial Explorations,* trans. Catherine Matthias (London: Macmillan, 2000), 17. A similar realist-empirical emphasis is evident in her chapter titles: "Paths to the Self" is followed by "Paths to the Real World." And yet, Korte herself points out, as early as Addison's account of his Tour in 1705, "how mechanical the Grand Tour and its account had become. . . . Addison was well aware that he was treading worn paths. Equally striking is the lack of attention which Addison's account pays to his personal travel experience" (51).

While Korte's emphasis on nonfiction accounts by actual travelers, like James Buzard's on the rise of tourism in literature, take their arguments in different directions from mine, both authors are moved to comment on the tradition of artifice that is central to this project, and both identify many moments in which nineteenth-century travel narratives recognize their own artificiality. "Two main observations recur frequently," Buzard notes of post-Napoleonic accounts of travel to Europe; "first, that the Continental tour seemed to be surrounded and regulated by a variety of guiding texts; and second, that by writing one's own travel record one had to work within the boundaries mapped out by those prior texts or somehow to stake out new territories with one's own text" (Buzard, *Beaten Track,* 156). Maria H. Frawley's analysis of women's travel writings vividly illustrates the self-reflexivity and overdetermination evident even in ostensibly nonfiction genres in the period. See *A Wider Range: Travel Writing by Women in Victorian England* (London: Associated University Presses, 1994). On this topic, see also Karen R. Lawrence, *Penelope Voyages* (Ithaca: Cornell University Press, 1994), 19–25.

On the methodological challenges of the generic study of travel literature, see the compendious account in Adrien Pasquali, *Le Tour des horizons: Critique et récits de voyage* (Paris: Klincksieck, 1994). See also McKeon's subtle analysis of the place of travel narratives in the negotiation of claims to truth, which places the issue at the heart of the emergence of the novel in the seventeenth and eighteenth centuries (*Origins,* 101–21).

5. Marie-Madeleine Martinet has offered the most thoroughgoing account of the long and dynamic history of the interplay of travel and literature as this book understands it in *Le voyage d'Italie dans les littératures européennes* (Paris: Presses Universitaires de France, 1996). On the particular case of American travelers, see especially Malcolm Bradbury, *Dangerous Pilgrimages: Trans-Atlantic Mythologies and the Novel* (1995; London: Penguin, 1996). For earlier literary sources on the topic, see Chloe Chard, *Pleasure and Guilt on the Grand Tour: Travel Writing and Imaginative Geography, 1600–1830* (Manchester: Manchester University Press, 1999), and Felicity A. Nussbaum, *Torrid Zones: Maternity, Sexuality, and Empire in Eighteenth-Century English Narratives* (Baltimore: Johns Hopkins University

Press, 1995). See also the important catalog edited by Andrew Wilton and Ilaria Bignamin, *The Grand Tour: The Lure of Italy in the Eighteenth Century* (London: Tate, 1996), as well as the collection of essays included in Clare Hornsby, ed., *The Impact of Italy: The Grand Tour and Beyond* (Rome: British School, 2000). Dennis Porter's psychoanalytically inflected study of nonfiction travel narratives, *Haunted Journeys: Desire and Transgression in European Travel Writing* (Princeton: Princeton University Press, 1991), usefully highlights the centrality of desire in the tradition, along with the important haunting fear of belatedness.

On the interplay of Italian historical developments with the sensibilities of foreigners, see Franco Venturi's sweeping survey "L'Italia fuori d'Italia," in *Storia d'Italia*, vol. 3, *Dal primo settecento all'unità* (Turin: Einaudi, 1973), 987–1481.

6. On genre, subgenre, and mode, see Fowler, *Kinds of Literature*, esp. 56, 106–29. "To determine the features of a subgenre," Fowler notes, "is to trace a diachronic process of imitation, variation, innovation—in fact, to verge on source study" (114). On the other hand, "a mode announces itself by distinct signals, even if these are abbreviated, unobtrusive, or below the threshold of modern attention. The signals may be of a wide variety: a characteristic motif, perhaps; a formula; a rhetorical proportion or quality" (107).

David Richter's account of the place of Gothic is worth citing in relation to the art romance, its close relative: "[O]nce the Gothic had become part of literary history, it became accessible as a source, not merely of spare parts—characters, plot elements, and devices of disclosure—that could be borrowed and used at will, but also of emotional resonances that could be put to other ends." *The Progress of Romance: Literary Historiography and the Gothic Novel* (Columbus: Ohio State University Press, 1996), 125

INTRODUCTION

1. On Panini's *Views*, see the recent catalog, *Art in Rome in the Eighteenth Century*, ed. Edgar Peters Bowron and Joseph J. Rishel (Philadelphia: Philadelphia Museum of Art, 2000), 425–47. On the history of the reception of particular statues, as on the topic of the taste for classical marbles in the period of this study, see Francis Haskell and Nicholas Penny, *Taste and the Antique: The Lure of Classical Sculpture, 1500–1900* (New Haven: Yale University Press, 1981). On the context for the reception of the "Aldobrandini Marriage," see Lucilla De Lachenal, "La riscoperta della pittura antica nel XVII secolo: scavi, disegni, collezioni," in *L'idea del bello*, ed. Evelina Borea and Carlo Gasparri (Roma: De Luca, 2000), 2:625–72.

A useful resource on the role of Rome as center of travel and of art education during the period that is at the heart of this study is the catalog produced for the recent exhibition, *Maestà di Roma: Da Napoleone all'Unita d'Italia*, conceived and curated by Stefano Susinno, Sandra Pinto, et al. (Milan: Electa, 2003). Essays of particular interest include Bianca Riccio, "Omaggi inglesi," 193–97; Carlo Sisi, "L'educazione accademica," 279–81; and Barbara Cinelli, "Il ritratto dell'artista," 295–99. See also the important recent anthology, Catharine Edwards, ed., *Roman*

Presences: Receptions of Rome in European Culture, 1789–1945 (Cambridge: Cambridge University Press, 1999).

2. Cf. Frye's useful identification of the impossible desire of the quest romance: "the search of the libido or desiring self for a fulfillment that will deliver it from the anxieties of reality but will still contain that reality" (193).

3. For all its conceptual sophistication in linking world and text, the analytical tradition on which Edward Said's *Culture and Imperialism* draws requires the *realist* novel understood in a surprisingly concrete way in order to make its arguments. For this reason Said tends to emphasize "the authority of the narrator, whose discourse anchors the narrative in recognizable, and hence existentially referential, circumstances." When Said reaches the point of conflating *history* and the novel, it becomes clear that his work will have limited bearing on study of the florid inverisimilitude that characterizes the art romance: "[N]arrative fiction and history . . . are premised on the recording, ordering, observing powers of the central authorizing subject, or ego." Edward Said, *Culture and Imperialism* (New York: Knopf, 1993), 77, 79.

On wonder, see in particular Stephen Greenblatt, *Marvelous Possessions: The Wonder of the New World* (Oxford: Clarendon Press, 1991), in which that sensation is the characteristic response to "the first encounter," and in which anecdotes are identified as a register for the shocks of the hitherto unknown real, "of the singularity of the contingent" (2–3). With his characteristic gestures toward autobiographical frankness, Greenblatt admits that his project is driven by a "longing for the effect of the locally real" (3), but he also offers a salutary methodological caveat: "It is, I think, a theoretical mistake and a practical blunder to collapse the distinction between representation and reality, but at the same time we cannot keep them isolated from one another. They are locked together in an uneasy marriage in a world without ecstatic union or divorce" (7).

4. It is worth citing Pierre Bourdieu's insight that the emergence of the modern figure of the artist took place in the *interplay* of the visual artist and the writer: "If the innovations that led to the invention of the modern artist and art are only intelligible at the level of all the fields of cultural production together, this is because artists and writers were able to use the lags between the transformations occurring in the literary field and the artistic field to benefit, as in a relay race, from advances carried out at different moments by their respective avant-gardes. Thus the discoveries made possible by the specific logic of one or another of the two fields could have a cumulative effect and appear retrospectively as the complementary profiles of one and the same historic process." Pierre Bourdieu, *The Rules of Art: Genesis and Structure of the Literary Field*, trans. Susan Emanuel (Stanford: Stanford University Press, 1996), 132.

5. The force of the past is, of course, central to any discussion of the art of the period. Useful treatments of the topic include Norman Bryson, *Tradition and Desire: From David to Delacroix* (Cambridge: Cambridge University Press, 1984); Hugh Honour, *Neo-classicism* (Harmondsworth: Penguin, 1968); Ann M. Hope, *The Theory and Practice of Neoclassicism in English Painting* (New York: Garland, 1988); David Irwin, *English Neoclassical Art: Studies in Inspiration and Taste* (London: Faber, 1966); and Robert Rosenblum, *Transformations in Late Eighteenth Century Art* (Princeton: Princeton University Press, 1970). For the topic

in literature, see Walter Jackson Bate, *The Burden of the Past* (London: Chatto, 1971); Harold Bloom, *The Anxiety of Influence* (London: Oxford University Press, 1975); and Jonah Siegel, *Desire and Excess: The Nineteenth-Century Culture of Art* (Princeton: Princeton University Press, 2000). On the emergence of cultural fantasies central to the period of this study, see Harold Mah, *Enlightenment Phantasies: Cultural Identity in France and Germany, 1750–1914* (Ithaca: Cornell University Press, 2003).

6. On the emergence of tourism in the nineteenth century, see James Buzard, *The Beaten Track: European Tourism, Literature and the Ways to "Culture," 1800–1918* (New York: Oxford University Press, 1993).

7. Hazlitt, "English Students at Rome" (first published in *New Monthly Magazine*, October 1827), in *The Complete Works*, Centenary Edition, ed. P. P. Howe (London: J. M. Dent, 1930–34), 17:134, 138, 139–40.

8. See Johann Joachim Winckelmann, "On the Imitation of the Painting and Sculpture of the Greeks" (1755), trans. Henry Fuseli (London, 1765); facsimile in Winckelmann, *Essays on the Philosophy and History of Art*, ed. Curtis Bowman (Bristol: Thoemmes, 2001), 1:1–2, 4–5. For a recent account of the important if paradoxical relation between the physical and the ideal in Winckelmann, see Alex Potts, *Flesh and the Ideal: Winckelmann and the Origins of Art History* (New Haven: Yale University Press, 1994). It is notable that a recent volume of Goethe entitled *Erotic Poems* consists largely of verses responding to the poet's Italian journey, namely the *Elegies* and selections from *Venetian Epigrams*. The final remarkable text in the collection, *The Diary*, while not set in Italy specifically, depends entirely on the license of travel to tell its tale of arousal and impotence. See Goethe, *Erotic Poems*, trans. David Luke (Oxford: Oxford University Press, 1997). For a brief but rich essay on the tradition of desire manifested in travel see Ian Littlewood, *Sultry Climates: Travel and Sex* (Cambridge, Mass.: Da Capo, 2001).

9. *The Poems of Tennyson*, ed. Christopher Ricks (Berkeley: University of California Press, 1987), 1: lines 1–4. The poem was subjected to a particularly thorough revision in 1842, but none of the elements I cite ever saw substantive changes. The contents of the palace varied, rather than the basic narrative of foundation and collapse. Further references are to the Ricks edition and made by line number in the text.

10. On Goethe and Tennyson, see David J. DeLaura's important "Heroic Egotism: Goethe and the Fortunes of *Bildung* in Victorian England," in *Johann Wolfgang Von Goethe: One Hundred and Fifty Years of Continuing Vitality*, ed. Ulrich Goebel and Wolodymyr T. Zyla (Lubbock: Texas Tech Press, 1984), 41–60. The essay as a whole is a nuanced treatment of the subtly pervasive and varied presence (particularly in the 1830s and 1840s) of an author, who was, as DeLaura notes, "more significant, and more widely so and in different ways, than we have assumed" (45). See also two essays by Richard Cronin, "Goethe, the Apostles, and Tennyson's Supposed Confessions," *Philological Quarterly* 72, no. 3 (1993): 337–56; and "The Palace of Art and Tennyson's Cambridge," *Essays in Criticism* 43, no. 3 (1993): 195–210. Catherine Waltraud Proescholdt-Obermann's *Goethe and His British Critics: The Reception of Goethe's Works in British Periodicals, 1779–1855* (Frankfurt: Peter Lang, 1992), is also a useful source.

11. See Christopher Ricks, *Tennyson* (Berkeley: University of California Press, 1989), 86–88, and Herbert Tucker *Tennyson and the Doom of Romanticism* (Cambridge: Harvard University Press, 1988), 118–25.

12. It is the *heim* hidden in the German *unheimlich* that famously provokes Freud to identify the uncanny as "that class of the frightening which leads back to what is known of old and long familiar." "The Uncanny" (1919), in *The Standard Edition of the Complete Psychological Works of Sigmund Freud*, trans and ed. James Strachey in collaboration with Anna Freud (London: Hogarth Press, 1953–66), 17:220. Subsequent references to Freud are to the *Standard Edition* and made by volume and page number.

13. "Self-Reliance," in *The Essays of Ralph Waldo Emerson*, ed. Alfred R. Ferguson and Jean Ferguson Carr (Cambridge: Harvard University Press, 1987), 46.

14. "A Disturbance of Memory on the Acropolis, an Open Letter to Romain Rolland on the Occasion of His Seventieth Birthday" (1936), in Freud, *Standard Edition*, 22:240.

15. Freud, "Splitting of the Ego in the Process of Defence," in *Standard Edition*, 23:273–78. The essay, written in 1937–38, was published posthumously in 1940.

CHAPTER ONE

1. Johann Wolfgang von Goethe, *Wilhelm Meister's Apprenticeship*, trans. *Eric A. Blackall* (1795–96; Princeton: Princeton University Press, 1995), 83. Further references to this edition appear parenthetically in the text.

2. Thomas Carlyle, "Translator's Preface" (1824), in *Wilhelm Meister's Apprenticeship*, Centenary Edition (1899; New York: AMS Press, 1974), 1:10. The most important recent treatment of the figure of Mignon is Carolyn Steedman's extraordinary *Strange Dislocations: Childhood and the Idea of Human Interiority, 1780–1930* (Cambridge: Harvard University Press, 1995). As her title indicates, Steedman locates Mignon's essential quality in her out-of-placedness, her "dislocation." Steedman's discussion of Mignon as the paradigmatic figure for childhood in the nineteenth century suggests the complex and important ways in which this literary creation came to be present, even pervasive, in culture.

3. Steedman provides an exhaustive and compelling account of the metamorphoses of Mignon in the nineteenth century.

4. Goethe was in Italy from 1786 to 1788, and "*Kennst du das Land*" was written in 1782 or 1783. Book 4 of *Wilhelm Meister* was composed in 1783, but this earlier text was never published in Goethe's lifetime, and was substantially revised for *Wilhelm Meister's Apprenticeship*, which was finally brought out in 1796. See Nicholas Boyle, *Goethe: The Poet and the Age* (Oxford: Clarendon Press, 2000), 2:355–69.

5. Goethe, *Italian Journey*, trans. W. H. Auden and Elizabeth Mayer (New York: Penguin, 1970), 398.

6. Eric A. Blackall is not alone in noting that the introduction of characters such as Mignon and the Harper carry the work outside of the normal expectations of a realist novel. See his discussion of their effect on the first version of the work,

Wilhelm Meister's Theatrical Mission (1783): "A new dimension has entered the novel, the dimension of the mysterious unfathomable depths of certain temperaments, a dimension of poetry such as does not naturally belong in a realistic novel of theatrical life though it might be associated somehow with Goethe's intentions in regard to his idealistic theme." Blackall, *Goethe and the Novel* (Ithaca: Cornell University Press, 1976), 68.

7. The conversation between Wilhelm and the stranger demonstrates the ideal nature of the grandfather's collection, as well as the importance of its loss for Wilhelm's development, especially for his later passion for art:

"Aren't you a grandson of old Meister who had such a fine art collection?" the stranger asked. "Yes, I am," said Wilhelm. "But my grandfather died when I was ten, and I was very grieved to see those lovely things sold." "But your father got a great sum of money for them." "How do you know that?" "Oh I saw those treasures when they were still in your house. Your grandfather was not just a collector, he knew a great deal about art. He had been in Italy in earlier and happier times, and brought back with him treasures such as could now not be bought at any price. He possessed marvelous paintings by the best artists, and you could hardly believe your eyes when you looked through his collection of drawings. He had various priceless fragments of sculpture and an instructive array of bronzes. His coins were collected with regard to art as well as history, his precious stones, few though they were, were of the highest quality. And everything was well arranged, even though the rooms in the old house were not designed symmetrically."

"Then you can imagine what a loss we children felt when all these things were taken down and packed," said Wilhelm. "Those were the first sad days of my life. I remember how empty the rooms seemed, as we watched one thing after the other disappear, things that we had enjoyed since childhood, things which had seemed to us as permanent as the house itself or the town we lived in." (36–37)

8. Goethe would have known a number of versions of the painting, as it was a popular subject in the eighteenth century. For an exhaustive survey, see Wolfgang Stechow, " 'The Love of Antiochus with Faire Stratonica' in Art," *Art Bulletin* 27, no. 4 (1945): 221–37. On the importance of this subject, especially in revisions of *Wilhelm Meister* following Goethe's voyage to Italy, see Boyle, *Goethe*, 239.

9. The elements contributing to the sense of the uncanny in the novel as a whole are strikingly congruent with those identified in Freud's famous essay of that name, not only the homely (*heimlich*) Freud finds at the heart of the uncanny (the *unheimlich*), but also the importance of "being led back" to the already-known. "The Uncanny" (1919), in *The Standard Edition of the Complete Psychological Works of Sigmund Freud*, trans and ed. James Strachey in collaboration with Anna Freud (London: Hogarth Press, 1953–66), 17:220. For Freudian treatments of Mignon, see Steedman's chapter "Childhood and the Uncanny" (*Strange Dislocations*, 149–60).

10. Steedman, *Strange Dislocations*, 41.

11. Although it was substantially revised over the years, D'Israeli's original study of genius, *An Essay on the Literary Character*, is a close contemporary of

Wilhelm Meister (London, 1795; four more editions between 1795 and 1840). It is worth citing some analytical chapter headings from a late edition to give the flavor of the work: "Genius . . . originates in peculiar qualities of the mind. . . . Of genius, its first habits.—Its melancholy.—An unsettled impulse, querulous till it finds its true occupation. . . . The self-educated are marked by stubborn peculiarities. . . . Of the irritability of genius.—Genius in society often in a state of suffering. . . . Enthusiasts in literature and art.—Of their self-immolations. . . . Of the jealousy of genius.—Jealousy often proportioned to the degree of genius.—A perpetual fever among authors and artists.—Instances of its incredible excess among brothers and benefactors.—Of a peculiar species, where the fever consumes the sufferer, without its malignancy. . . . Matrimony said not to be well-suited to the domestic life of genius.—Of unhappy unions." Isaac D'Israeli, *The Literary Character; or, The History of Men of Genius, Drawn from Their Own Feelings and Confession*, ed. Benjamin Disraeli (London, 1859). *Calamities of Authors; Including Some Inquiries Respecting Their Moral and Literary Characters* (London: John Murray, 1812) continues the topic with more instances. On D'Israeli, see Annette Cafarelli, *Prose in the Age of Poets* (Philadelphia: University of Pennsylvania Press, 1990), 90–94; James Ogden, *Isaac D'Israeli* (Oxford: Clarendon Press, 1969); and Jonah Siegel, *Desire and Excess: The Nineteenth Century Culture of Art* (Princeton: Princeton University Press, 2000), 98–99, 123–24.

12. Goethe is as elaborate in his location of the puppets in the larder as he is clear on the mother's role in tantalizing the young desires of her son: "Few joys of anticipation matched those when my mother called me in to help her carry something and, whether by her kindness or my cunning, I managed to pick up some dried prunes. Those piles of wonderful things filled my imagination with a sense of abundance, and the marvelous smell of all the spices had such a mouth-watering effect on me that I never failed to breathe in deeply when I was nearby. One Sunday morning this special key was left in the keyhole as my mother was caught unawares by the bells ringing for the church service and the rest of the house was wrapped in Sabbath stillness. As soon as I noticed it, I crept gingerly along the wall, moved quietly to the door, opened it, and with one stride was in the midst of so many long-desired delights" (7–8).

13. Cf. the Doctor's description of the Harper and his own testimony:

Completely shut up in himself, all he looked at was his own hollow and empty self, which was a bottomless pit for him. . . . "I see nothing before me, and nothing behind me . . . but the endless night of loneliness in which I find myself. I have no feeling left, except that of my guilt, but even that is only a distant, shapeless ghost that lurks behind my back. There is no height or depth, no forwards or backwards, nothing to describe this continual sameness. . . . There is nothing more horrifying to me than friendship and love: for these evoke in me the wish that the phantoms surrounding me might be real. (267)

14. "Demetrius," in *Plutarch's Lives*, trans. Bernadotte Perrin, Loeb Classical Library (London: Heinemann, 1920), 9:93–94.

15. Stechow, "The Love of Antiochus," 230.

16. Johann Joachim Winckelmann, *Reflections on the Painting and Sculpture of the Greeks and A Letter Containing Objections against the Foregoing Reflec-*

tions, trans. Henry Fuseli (London, 1765); facsimile in Winckelmann, *Essays on the Philosophy and History of Art,* ed. Curtis Bowman (Bristol: Thoemmes, 2001), 1:109, 112.

17. My reading of Mignon is related to but ultimately quite different from that of Franco Moretti who identifies "the episode that decides her death," as "one of the most disagreeably cruel in literature." In the course of his important study of the *Bildungsroman* Moretti proposes that Mignon's fate represents the novel's repudiation of unregulated passion and ultimately demonstrates the lethal effects of not belonging to a wider community or homeland. It seems to me, however, that both parts of this interpretation depend on treating the novel as an early and strange moment in the history of realism (the immediate point of comparison is Austen), opening the door to a moral reading while closing it to the psychological one that the flamboyant symbolism of the novel as a whole seems to demand. See Franco Moretti, *The Way of the World: The* Bildungsroman *in European Culture* (London: Verso, 1987), 19, 47. See also Steedman, *Strange Dislocations,* 41–42, and especially her claim that "Mignon . . . is not—was not—about a story, unless it is the story of her dying. Mignon is only about her oddness and incompleteness" (17).

18. On Goethe's original intention to make Wilhelm's education culminate in literary mastery, see Boyle, *Goethe,* 365. There is a similar account in the important nineteenth-century English biography, George Henry Lewes, *The Life of Goethe* (1855; New York: Frederick Ungar, 1965), 398–99.

CHAPTER TWO

1. The reception of *Wilhelm Meister* is distinct from the cultural afterlife of Mignon Steedman addresses so compellingly in *Strange Dislocations: Childhood and the Idea of Human Interiority, 1780–1930* (Cambridge: Harvard University Press, 1995). The novel has been recognized as important throughout its history, but the criticism suggests some confusion as to where precisely its significance may lie. From Staël on—with the important exception of Carlyle—critics tended to see the novel as largely incoherent and compendious, though enlivened by the mysteriously effective figure of Mignon. For a thoughtful and sympathetic nineteenth-century account of the novel that highlights its "obvious want of unity," see George Henry Lewes's *Life and Works of Goethe* (1855; London: J. M. Dent, 1908), 406–16. On the complex reception of the novel in England, see Susanne Howe, *Wilhelm Meister and His English Kinsmen* (New York: Columbia University Press, 1930). See also Jean-Marie Carré, *Goethe en Angleterre* (Paris: Plon, 1920). Catherine Waltraud Proescholdt-Obermann, in *Goethe and His British Critics* (Frankfurt: Peter Lang, 1992), emphasizes the role of Germaine de Staël's *Germany* as the main source for response to late Goethe in England. See also David J. DeLaura's important, "Heroic Egotism: Goethe and the Fortunes of *Bildung* in Victorian England," in *Johann Wolfgang Von Goethe: One Hundred and Fifty Years of Continuing Vitality,* ed. Ulrich Goebel and Wolodymyr T. Zyla (Lubbock: Texas Tech Press, 1984), 41–60. For a satiric evocation of Goethe's influence, particularly on feminine Italophilia, see Heine's *Journey from Munich to Genoa*

(1829), in which a chapter with the first stanza of Mignon's song as epigraph sees the author complaining of the crowds of English travellers he encounters (a common complaint in the period) in the following terms: "[I]t is impossible to imagine an Italian lemon tree [*Zitronenbaum*] without an Englishwoman sniffing it." Heinrich Heine, *Journey to Italy*, trans. Charles G. Leland, rev. Christopher Johnson (New York: Marsilio, 1998), 103 (translation modified slightly).

2. Germaine de Staël, *Germany* (Boston: Houghton Mifflin, 1859), 2:57. Further references to this work (a revision of Murray's anonymous 1814 translation) are made in the text. Venturi helpfully emphasizes the links between Staël's work and the social analysis of Sismondi, her traveling companion in Italy, especially his *History of the Italian Republics*, which appeared the same year as *Corinne*. See "L'Italia fouri d'Italia" in *Storia d'Italia*, vol. 3, *Dal primo settecento all'unita* (Turin: Einaudi, 1973), 1173–80. The association with Sismondi underlines the social analysis that is an important part of both *Germany* and *Corinne*. Sismondi's *Literature of the South of Europe*, which was published in Paris in 1813 and in London in a translation by Thomas Roscoe in 1823, is also the principal source on the phenomenon of improvisation in Italy aside from *Corinne* itself. See J.C.L. Simonde de Sismondi, *Historical View of the Literature of the South of Europe*, trans. Thomas Roscoe (1823), 4th ed. (London, 1890), 2:83–86. On Staël's cultural project, see Harold Mah, *Enlightenment Phantasies: Cultural Identity in France and Germany, 1750–1914* (Ithaca: Cornell University Press, 2003), 143–56.

3. As Simone Balaye puts it, "La genèse de *Corinne* se fait en symbiose avec la genèse de *De l'Allemagne*." *Les carnets de voyage de Mme de Staël*, ed. Balaye (Geneva: Droz, 1971), 98. On the twinned composition of the texts, see Gretchen Rous Besser, *Germaine de Staël Revisited* (New York: Twayne, 1994), 77; and Charlotte Hogsett, *The Literary Existence of Germaine de Staël* (Carbondale: Southern Illinois University Press, 1987), 94. I owe the reference to the *Carnets* to Hogsett. It is a notable part of the complex interplay of the authors that Goethe translated one of Staël's earliest efforts, "L'essai sur les fictions," as he was about to resume work on *Wilhelm Meister* in 1795. See Jacques Voisine, "Goethe traducteur de *L'essai sur les fictions* de Madame de Staël," *Études Germaniques* 50, no. 1 (1995): 73–82. See also Eric A. Blackall, *Goethe and the Novel* (Ithaca: Cornell University Press, 1976), 94–100. Blackall points out that a principal difference between the authors is the role of chance and fate in narrative. On Goethe's response to *Delphine* and *Corinne*, see Blackall, 151.

4. Ellen Moers proposes that "The oddest thing about *Corinne* is that it is a guidebook to Italy just as much as it is a guidebook to the woman of genius." Moers, *Literary Women* (1963; London: Women's Press, 1978), 200. This overlap between character and place is more than eccentric, however, it is central to the work and to its place in culture. In *Roderick Hudson*, which is set in the 1860s, Hudson's mother and fiancée prepare for their venture to Rome by spending evenings reading *Corinne* in their Northampton home. Once in Europe they will find more sophisticated reading, but the longevity of Staël's text should not be missed. It bears emphasizing, nevertheless, that the author, whose exposure to Italy was relatively brief (limited to a voyage in the first half of 1805), was not herself relaying material acquired through unmediated personal experience. As Enrico Bruschini and Alba Amoia note, in words that could be used of every participant

in the art-romance tradition, "If we are to evaluate fairly the painstaking evocations of the Roman past that bulk so largely in the earlier chapters of *Corinne*, we must admit that the author's personal preconceptions decisively influenced her response to the Roman scene and the reflections her discoveries inspired." Bruschini and Amoia, "Rome's Monuments and Artistic Treasures in Mme de Staël's *Corinne* (1807): Then and Now," *Nineteenth Century French Studies* 22, nos. 3–4 (1994): 312. Ingrid G. Daemmrich argues against criticism that sees Staël's portrayal of ruins as lacking "originality and detail" by linking her descriptions to the representation of character, particularly in relation to the perception of fate. "The Function of the Ruins Motif in Madame de Staël's *Corinne*," *Romance Notes* 15 (1973): 255–58.

   5. *Poetical Works of Letitia Elizabeth Landon, "L.E.L.,"* facsimile, 1873 ed. with an introduction and notes by F. J. Sypher (Delmar, N.Y.: Scholars' Facsimiles & Reprints, 1990), 1. Further references in text. On the centrality of the work of Landon, see Stuart Curran, "Women Readers, Women Writers," in *The Cambridge Companion to British Romanticism*, ed. Curran (Cambridge: Cambridge University Press, 1993), 177–95. See also his "The I Altered," in *Romanticism and Feminism*, ed. Anne K. Mellor (Bloomington: Indiana University Press, 1988), 185–207. See also Marlon B. Ross's *The Contours of Masculine Desire: Romanticism and the Rise of Women's Poetry* (New York: Oxford University Press, 1989), as well as revisionary work such as Harriet K. Linkin, "Romantic Aesthetic in Mary Tighe and Letitia Landon: How Women Poets Recuperate the Gaze," *European Romantic Review* 7, no. 2 (1997): 159–88; Glennis Stephenson. "Letitia Landon and the Victorian Improvisatrice: The Construction of L.E.L.," *Victorian Poetry* 30, no. 1:1–17. 1992; and Linda Peterson, "Rewriting a History of the Lyre," in *Women's Poetry: Late Romantic to Late Victorian, Gender and Genre, 1830–1900*, ed. Isobel Armstrong and Virginia Blain (London: Macmillan, 1999), 115–27; as well as Anne K. Mellor, "The Female Poet and the Poetess: The Traditions of British Women's Poetry, 1780–1830," in *Women's Poetry in the Enlightenment: The Making of a Canon, 1730–1820*, ed. Isobel Armstrong and Virginia Blain (New York: St. Martin's, 1999), 81–98.

   6. Useful recent books on the topic of Italy in nineteenth-century English culture include James Buzard, *The Beaten Track: European Tourism, Literature and the Ways to "Culture," 1800–1918* (New York: Oxford University Press, 1993); Maura O'Connor, *The Romance of Italy and the English Political Imagination* (New York: St. Martin's, 1998); John Pemble, *The Mediterranean Passion: Victorians and Edwardians in the South* (Oxford: Clarendon Press, 1987), and Kenneth Churchill, *Italy and English Literature, 1764–1930* (Totowa, N.J.: Barnes & Noble Books, 1980). See also two recent collections: Martin McLaughlin, ed., *Britain and Italy from Romanticism to Modernism* (Oxford: Legenda, 2000), and Alison Chapman and Jane Stabler, eds., *Unfolding the South: Nineteenth-Century British Women Writers and Artists in Italy* (Manchester: Manchester University Press, 2003). An older, but still useful account is provided by C. P. Brand, *Italy and the English Romantics: The Italianate Fashion in Early-Nineteenth-Century England* (Cambridge: Cambridge University Press, 1957).

7. Landon, preface to *The Venetian Bracelet, The Lost Pleiad, A History of the Lyre, and Other Poems*, in *Letitia Elizabeth Landon: Selected Writings*, ed. Jerome McGann and Daniel Riess (Peterborough, Ont.: Broadview, 1997), 102–3.

8. As Hazlitt will say about traveling, a few years after the publication of this poem, "we visit *names* as well as places." Hazlitt, *Notes of a Journey through France and Italy* (1824–25), in *The Complete Works*, Centenary Edition, ed. P. P. Howe (London: J. M. Dent, 1930–34), 10:281 (emphasis in the original).

9. Both tales are flamboyant representation of the dangerous force of passion and the impossibility of satisfaction. "A Moorish Romance" features Leila, a covertly Christian maiden ("The cross beneath a Moorish vest") fleeing marriage to Abdalla. She dies, along with her lover, within sight of the Italian shore. Their final resting place is the land toward which they were bound. "The Charmed Cup" is the story of a woman who inadvertently poisons the man she is attempting to win back with a love philtre.

10. Landon's writing, which often takes the form of a kind of narrativizing ekphrasis appropriate to the keepsakes in which it was typically published, continually creates picture galleries. It is not simply that she frequently bases poems on works of art. The traffic goes two ways; the "Subjects for Pictures" she proposes are themselves very frequently drawn from literature: "Petrarch's Dream," "Calypso Watching the Ocean," etc.

11. Cf. Jacqueline M. Labbe on the dissatisfaction inherent in romance: "[I]t largely dispenses with 'happily ever after'; lovers meet, love, are parted, but seldom are reunited, and if they are, it is seldom to good effect." *The Romantic Paradox: Love, Violence, and the Uses of Romance, 1760–1830* (New York: St. Martin's, 2000), 3.

12. William Wordsworth, "Resolution and Independence" (1802), in *Wordsworth: Poetical Works*, ed. Thomas Hutchinson, rev. Ernest de Selincourt (Oxford: Oxford University Press, 1936), 155–7, lines 48–49.

13. In *Born under Saturn: The Character and Conduct of Artists* (New York: Norton, 1963) Rudolf and Margot Wittkower offer a historical study of the links between melancholia and creativity that demonstrates the long-standing nature of the connection. Nevertheless, the emphasis on the theme in the decades around the turn of the nineteenth century is notable, especially in women's verse. In "The I Altered" Stuart Curran identifies the "darker strains" in the work of female poets of the 1820s and 1830s: "a focus on exile and failure, a celebration of female genius frustrated, a haunting omnipresence of death—that seem to subvert the role they claimed and invite a sophisticated reconsideration of their work against the complex background of the transition between Romantic and Victorian poetic modes." "Even as both Hemans and Landon moved away from such hard-minded realism into the realms of piety and sentimentality, their heroines still regularly perished. Contrary to what one might conventionally expect, in poetry at least, the unhappy ending is the norm of woman writers of the Romantic period" (189, 203). On suffering in sentimental literature, see Philip Fisher, *Hard Facts* (Oxford: Oxford University Press, 1985), 105. See also Marianne Noble, *The Masochistic Pleasures of Sentimental Literature* (Princeton: Princeton University Press, 2000), esp. 3–25. Although its focus is American, Noble's careful analysis is a salutary contribution to the study of the complex interplay of sentiment, suffering, and

gender evident on both sides of the Atlantic. See also Cheryl Walker, "The Whip Signature: Violence, Feminism, and Women Poets," in Armstrong and Blain, *Women's Poetry: Late Romantic to Late Victorian*, 33–49. Labbe offers a useful account of the relationship between violence and eros in romance in *The Romantic Paradox*. "Landon's poetry depends on love," she notes, "but it also explodes romance, substituting a world of betrayal and loss. In this way she suggests a femininity that thrives on loss and goes down fighting" (140).

Lawrence Lipking offers a thought-provoking and ambitious account of the power of feminine disappointment in *Abandoned Women: A Poetic Tradition* (Chicago: University of Chicago Press, 1988); on Staël, see 36–37. See also Joan De-Jean's magisterial *Fictions of Sappho, 1546–1937* (Chicago: University of Chicago Press, 1989). On the aesthetic force of feminine death, see Elisabeth Bronfen, *Over Her Dead Body: Death, Femininity and the Aesthetic* (New York: Routledge, 1992). For a rich treatment of suffering as a form of complex resistance, see two works by Nina Auerbach, *Woman and the Demon* (Cambridge: Harvard University Press, 1982) and *Romantic Imprisonment* (New York: Columbia University Press, 1985). For the particular force of disappointment and death in the imagination of feminine creativity, see Yopie Prins, *Victorian Sappho* (Princeton: Princeton University Press, 1999). Nineteenth-century women poets, Prins notes, "call upon Sappho to authorize a voice that proclaims itself dead, again and again" (49). Tricia Lootens offers a related argument, that for Victorian women poets, "[c]elebration and denigration are never far apart." *Lost Saints: Silence, Gender, and Victorian Literary Canonization* (Charlottesville: University Press of Virginia, 1996), 50. But, see also her subtle account of suffering and self-fashioning in "Receiving the Legend, Rethinking the Writer: Letitia Landon and the Poetess Tradition," in *Romanticism and Women Poets: Opening the Doors of Reception*, ed. Harriet Kramer Linkin and Stephen Behrendt (Lexington: University of Kentucky Press, 1999), 242–59.

Recent critics have fruitfully engaged Staël's fascination with suicide, which is worth citing in this context. See especially Margaret R. Higonnet, "Suicide as Self-Construction"; Joan Dejean, "Portrait of the Artist as Sappho"; Gita May, "Staël and the Fascination of Suicide"; and Isabelle Hoog Naginski, "Germaine de Staël among the Romantics," all in *Germaine de Staël: Crossing the Borders*, ed. Madelyn Gutwirth, Avriel Goldberger, and Karyna Szmurlo (New Brunswick: Rutgers University Press, 1991). On the importance of masochism in art more generally, see Leo Bersani, *The Freudian Body* (New York: Columbia University Press, 1986). Freud's account of masochism is still a vital source on the interplay of the love of unpleasure at the level of the individual and the tendency of the organism toward the loss of tension or excitation, and ultimately toward death. See, e.g. "The Economic Problem of Masochism" (1924), in *The Standard Edition of the Complete Psychological Works of Sigmund Freud*, trans and ed. James Strachey in collaboration with Anna Freud (London: Hogarth Press, 1953–66), 19:157–72.

14. George Eliot, *Mill on the Floss* (1860; Harmondsworth: Penguin, 1985), 432–33. On a "cross-national literary tradition in which the influence of Madame de Staël's *Corinne* is paramount," see Gill Frith, "Playing with Shawls: George Eliot's Use of *Corinne* in *The Mill on the Floss*," in *George Eliot and Europe*, ed. John Rignall (Aldershot: Scolar, 1997), 225. On the influence and afterlife of Corinne in

the nineteenth century, see Moers, "Performing Heroism: The Myth of Corinne," in *Literary Women*, 173–210. "*Corinne* stands alone in Mme de Staël's *oeuvre*," Moers comments acerbically, "in its silliness as in its enormous influence upon literary women" (174). While Eliot's "Natural History of German Life" (1856), an important document in the history of literary realism, includes a dig at Landon, sentimentality, and the "keepsake style," her "Silly Novels by Lady Novelists," from the same year describes a typical heroine with an unmissably Staëlean pedigree: "[T]here is a general propensity in her to make speeches, and to rhapsodize at some length when she retires to her bedroom. In her recorded conversations she is amazingly eloquent, and in her unrecorded conversations, amazingly witty." *Selected Critical Writings*, ed. Rosemary Ashton (Oxford: Oxford University Press, 1992), 261, 296.

15. The force of the art romance is certainly evident at the outset of Eliot's career in fiction—notably in the Mignonesque figure of Caterina in "Mr Gilfil's Love-Story," a character whose musicality, passion, jealousy, Italian birth, and death from heartache make her as out of place in her environment as her story seems to be in the otherwise gritty realism of the rest of *Scenes of Clerical Life* (1858). G. H. Lewes was, of course, the author of a major biography of Goethe, and George Eliot herself wrote an essay on "The Morality of *Wilhelm Meister*" in 1855, the year Lewes's biography was published.

16. "On Literature Considered in Its Relationship to Social Institutions" (1800), in *An Extraordinary Woman: Selected Writings of Germaine de Staël*, ed. Vivian Folkenflick (New York: Columbia University Press, 1987), 175, 177. See Anne Amend-Söchting, "Toutes les héroïnes de Mme de Staël (et Oswald dans *Corinne*) sont mélancoliques. Quoiqu'elles se resemblent, leurs mélancolies demeurent néanmoins uniques ou, pour mieux dire, individualisées. A cela s'ajoute que la mélancolie se détache de l'oeuvre staëlienne en sa qualité de concept philosophique." "La Mélancolie dans *Corinne*," in *Madame de Staël, Corinne ou l'Italie: "L'âme se mêle à tout*," ed. José-Luis Diaz (Paris: Sedes, 1999), 101–10.

17. Some of the most ambitious students of sentimental literature have attempted in recent years to address the particular challenges these texts present for modern readers. See, e.g., Isobel Armstrong, "The Gush of the Feminine: How Can We Read Women's Poetry of the Romantic Period?" in *Romantic Women Writers: Voices and Countervoices*, ed. Paula R. Feldman and Theresa M. Kelley (Hanover, N.H.: University Press of New England, 1995), 13–32; and Jerome McGann, *The Poetics of Sensibility: A Revolution in Poetic Style* (Oxford: Clarendon Press, 1996).

18. At this point in the study of Staël's work, the moralizing-realist line of criticism typical of important early feminist recovery coexists uncomfortably with more sophisticated accounts of the formal constraints and achievements of the text. Typical of the challenging point of transition at which criticism finds itself is Karyna Szmurlo's introduction to a recent anthology, which encapsulates a number of sophisticated formal insights—"For years condemned to marginality, *Corinne* is finally valorized in and because of its provocative inadequacies. The text's massive antinovelistic discussions and descriptions seem to convey both a failure of the oral feminine tradition and the problematics of coming to writing"—while nevertheless suggesting that the failure of the protagonist's affective life to con-

clude in a happy resolution is to be read as a calamity standing in for the psychological and political constraints of the period: "In the search for an ideal partner,
Corinne ironically chooses a wrong supporter who, fearing feminine superiority,
misinterprets her art and deserts her. The central antagonism between female desire and nihilizing patriarchal law reappears on many levels of the narrative."
Karyna Szmurlo, ed., *The Novel's Seductions: Staël's* Corinne *in Critical Inquiry*
(Lewisburg: Bucknell University Press, 1999), 19. The second passage, which references irony where it might do better to engage sentiment, assumes that satisfaction is always and at every point the answer to represented female desire. *Corinne*,
however, like "The Improvisatrice" after it, is quite clear in its commitment to
dissatisfaction, longing, and regret. The introduction as a whole, and the essays in
Szmurlo's collection, are important and sophisticated. I cite these passages to indicate the difficulties attendant on an approach to the romance that treats the representation of dissatisfaction as a surprise rather than as a convention. For the importance of death and mourning in French letters in the period, see Patrick Coleman,
Reparative Realism: Mourning and Modernity in the French Novel (Geneva: Droz,
1998). Coleman asks the important question, "to what extent is Corinne's death
the condition of the story's possibility?" Unlike April Alliston, who proposes that
Corinne has "failed in her own life plot" (*"Corinne* and Female Transmission," in
Szmurlo, *The Novel's Seductions*, 201), Coleman argues that "[w]hat readers like
to think of as the 'natural' consequence of a broken heart and society's hostility
must, in the light of Staël's own reflections on literature . . . be seen as no less—
or no more—the result of an artistic decision than the death of, say, Constant's
Ellénore" (2). Cf. Also Nancy K. Miller's treatment of Corinne's playing of Juliet:
"By its intertext Corinne's gaze *as* Juliet is bound to a pleasure in death" ("Perfor-
mances of the Gaze," in Szmurlo, *The Novel's Seductions*, 88). On the glorious
melancholy of Staël, see Julia Kristeva, "Gloire, deuil et écriture," *Romantisme:
Revue du Dix-Neuvième Siècle* 62 (1988): 7–14.

19. Anna Jameson, *Diary of an Ennuyée* (Philadelphia: E. Littell, 1826). The
"author" of the *Diary*, most of which is devoted to Italy, is fully immersed in the
art-romance tradition and the nineteenth-century culture of art more broadly; she
quotes Staël on travel as "un triste plaisir," and spends some time in Venice perus-
ing Byron's annotated copy of D'Israeli's *Essays on the Literary Character*, particularly his remarks on travel and alienation. For Jameson's engagement with Staël's
work, see also her *Sketches of Art, Literature, and Character*, in *Visits and Sketches
at Home and Abroad* (London: Sanders and Otley, 1835), 1:55–59.

20. Connections among these authors are manifold and usually open. Staël cites
Goethe repeatedly (*The Italian Journey* and Mignon's song in particular) as an
authority on Italy and on the proper response to its beauty. She herself will be an
important influence on Byron. That Landon's "Improvisatrice" made a poem of
the tale of genius and disappointment told in *Corinne* was not missed by her contemporaries—she was given the task of translating the poems in the novel in its
first English edition. On Staël's influence, see Moers, *Literary Women*, 173–210.
See also Kurt Mueller-Vollmer, "Staël's *Germany* and the Beginnings of an American National Literature," in Gutwirth, Goldberger, and Szmurlo, *Germaine de
Staël: Crossing the Borders*, 141–58. For an account of romance engaging Byron
and Landon, see Labbe, *Romantic Paradox*, esp. 137–64. On Byron and Staël, see

Joanne Wilkes, *Byron and Madame de Staël: Born for Opposition* (Aldershot: Ashgate, 1999). Wilkes proposes *Childe Harold* "as an extended and sometimes critical response to the much read *Corinne*" (10). But Byron's response to the friend, whose *Corinne* and *De l'Allemagne* he knew well, is generally positive, if complex. On their relationship, see Ernest Giddey, "Byron and Madame de Staël," in *Lord Byron and His Contemporaries*, ed. Charles E. Robinson (Newark: University of Delaware Press, 1982), 166–77. Lipking traces the influence of *Corinne* on *Don Juan* in *Abandoned Women*, 36–37. Byron, it is worth noting, learned of Goethe's work through *De l'Allemagne*, and the Goethe–Staël–Byron relation is intriguingly triangulated in an instance such as the charge of plagiarism at the opening of the *Bride of Abydos* ("Know ye the land where the cypress and myrtle . . ."). When it is suggested to Byron that the source of these lines is *Wilhelm Meister*, he denies it. He proposes that it is more likely that he might have gotten the lines from Staël instead—though he denies that as well. See Rowland E. Prothero, ed., *Works of Lord Byron: Letters and Journals* (London: Murray, 1898), 2:304n. For Byron on Staël, see the Countess of Blessington, *Conversations of Lord Byron* (Philadelphia: Carey and Hart, 1836), 15–20, 145. On Byron, plagiarism, and Goethe as source, see John Galt, *Life of Lord Byron* (London: Colburn and Bentley, 1830), 179–83. See also Caroline Franklin, "The Influence of Madame de Staël's Account of Goethe's *Die Braut von Korinth* in *De l'Allemagne* on the Heroine of Byron's *Siege of Corinth*," *Notes and Queries*, n.s., 35, no. 3 (1988): 307–10. On the complex relation of the two men, see E. M. Butler, *Byron and Goethe: Analysis of a Passion* (London: Bowes and Bowes, 1956).

21. Lord Byron, *The Complete Poetical Works*, ed. Jerome J. McGann (Oxford: Oxford University Press, 2000), vol. 2, *Childe Harold's Pilgrimage*, 1.950–53. Further citations are taken from this edition, and identified in the text by canto and line number.

22. On Venice in the literary imagination, see Tony Tanner, *Venice Desired* (Cambridge: Harvard University Press, 1992). "Byron arrived in Venice in 1816 but he had visited it long before in the pages of *The Mysteries of Udolpho*. Mrs Radcliffe had herself never been to Venice but had experienced it in the writing of Mrs Piozzi. It is absolutely appropriate that the image of Venice which came to dominate the nineteenth-century imagination—Ruskin's and thus Turner's—should be at least grounded in an image (Byron's) which in turn was nourished by textually based text. Venice is always the already written as well as the already seen, the already read" (17). See also Manfred Pfister and Barbara Schaff, *Venetian Views, Venetian Blinds: English Fantasies of Venice* (Amsterdam: Rodopi, 1999).

23. Byron, *Complete Poetical Works*, 2:4.

24. Byron, *Complete Poetical Works*, 2:122. Recent critics have generally concurred on the fractured or otherwise unstable form of the poem as a whole, understanding the play between the narrator and main character in relation to this broader incoherence. For quite distinct approaches to this issue, see Stuart Curran, *Poetic Form and British Romanticism* (Oxford: Oxford University Press, 1986), 152, and Jerome Christensen, *Lord Byron's Strength: Romantic Writing and Commercial Society* (Baltimore: John Hopkins University Press, 1993), 75, 213. William Galperin identifies the end of canto 4 as the culmination of a relationship that has been unstable throughout: "[T]he speaker's union with Harold is strictly

a matter of retrospection and always antecedent to the *writing* (in all its implications) to which he is 'here' committed." *The Return of the Visible in British Romanticism* (Baltimore: John Hopkins University Press, 1993), 269. On the issue in earlier cantos, see Vincent Newey, "Authoring the Self: *Childe Harold* III and IV," in *Byron and the Limits of Fiction*, ed. Bernard Beatty and Vincent Newey (Totowa, N.J.: Barnes and Noble, 1988), 148; and Paul Elledge, "Chasms and Connections: Byron Ending (in) *Childe Harold's Pilgrimage* 1 and 2," in *Byron*, ed. Jane Stabler (London: Longman, 1998), 135.

25. Patricia A. Parker, *Inescapable Romance: Studies in the Poetics of a Mode* (Princeton: Princeton University Press, 1979), 226. On the importance of romance in the early nineteenth century, see also Curran, *Poetic Form*.

26. John Hobhouse, *Historical Illustrations of the Fourth Canto of Childe Harold* (New York: Kirk and Mercein, 1818), 187–200. It is striking, given all the famous sights the text treats that this vision is the only illustration of the entire fourth canto in the important French translation of Byron with engravings after Richard Westall. See *Oeuvres*, trans. Amédée Pichot (Paris, 1822–25). The most commonly cited source of the story is Valerius Maximus (*Facta et Dicta Memorabilia* 4.4.7), but it was a well-known motif in art, painted by Rubens among others. On the popularity of the theme, see Robert Rosenblum, "Caritas Romana after 1760: Some Romantic Lactations," in *Woman as Sex Object*, ed. Thomas Hess and Linda Nochlin (New York: Newsweek, 1972), 46–63. See also Lucia Kollner, *Die tochterliche Liebe, ein Mysteriumgeheimnis: Die sogenannte Caritas Romana* (Frankfurt: Lang, 1997). On the complex role of the mother in the poem as a whole, see Galperin, *Return of the Visible*, 262–70.

27. "Childe Roland to the Dark Tower Came," in *Men and Women* (1855), vol. 5 of *The Poetical Works of Robert Browning*, ed. Ian Jack and Robert Inglesfield (Oxford: Clarendon Press, 1995), lines 1–3. All references to the poem are from this edition and made in the text by line number.

28. "Child Rowland to the dark tower came / His word was still, 'Fie, foh, and fum / I smell the blood of a British Man.' " Browning, *Poetical Works*, 5.130.

29. Byron, *Complete Poetical Works*, 2:235.

30. The very first entry in Hobhouse's *Illustrations* is a disquisition on admiration ("Attachment of the Italians to their distinguished fellow-citizens") closely related to Hazlitt's description of Rome as incapacitating: "There is no country which can contend with Italy in the honours heaped upon the great men of past ages; and the present race accuse themselves of living upon the labours of their ancestors, and, as is the usual reproach of heirs, of finding in their transmitted wealth an inducement to inactivity." Hobhouse, *Historical Illustrations*, 11.

31. Percy Bysshe Shelley's *Adonais* (1821), in *Shelley's Poetry and Prose*, ed. Donald Reiman and Neil Fraistat, 2nd ed. (New York: Norton, 2002), 7.55–60. Further citations are made in the body of the text, by stanza and line number.

32. On Italy and femininity in the poet's imagination, see especially Sandra M. Gilbert, "From *Patria* to *Matria*: Elizabeth Barrett Browning's Risorgimento," *PMLA* 99, no. 2 (1984): 194–211.

33. Elizabeth Barrett Browning, *Aurora Leigh*, ed. Margaret Reynolds (New York: Norton, 1995), 1.29–33. Further references are made in text, by book and line number.

CHAPTER THREE

1. Henry James, *Roderick Hudson*, in *Novels, 1871–1880* (New York: Library of America, 1983), 171. *Roderick Hudson* was published serially in the *Atlantic Monthly* in 1875. It was revised several times throughout James's career until its publication as the first volume of the New York edition. All references to the novel are taken from *Novels, 1871–1880*, which reprints the first American book edition of 1875.

Among James's earliest published efforts is a remarkable 1865 review of *Wilhelm Meister* prompted by a republication of Carlyle's translation: "To read *Wilhelm Meister* for the first time is an enviable and almost a unique sensation. Few other books, to use an expression which Goethe's admirers will understand, so steadily and gradually *dawn* upon the intelligence. In few works is so profound a meaning enveloped in so common a form. The slow, irresistible action of this latent significance is an almost awful phenomenon." James, "Wilhelm Meister's Apprenticeship and Travels. From the German of Goethe. By Thomas Carlyle," *North American Review* (July 1865): 281–82. This edition was in James's library at his death; see Leon Edel and Adeline R. Tintner, *The Library of Henry James* (Ann Arbor: UMI Research Press, 1987). On the complex but important relation, see Jürgen Gauss, "Henry James and the Tradition of *Wilhelm Meister*: A Study of the *Bildungsroman* in Goethe, Thomas Mann, and Henry James" (Ph.D. diss., Ohio State University, 1991). See also David J. DeLaura's "Heroic Egotism: Goethe and the Fortunes of *Bildung* in Victorian England," in *Johann Wolfgang Von Goethe: One Hundred and Fifty Years of Continuing Vitality*, ed. Ulrich Goebel and Wolodymyr T. Zyla (Lubbock: Texas Tech Press, 1984), 41–60, for some of the earlier American background to James's response, as well as Maxine Grefe, "*Apollo in the Wilderness*": *An Analysis of Critical Reception of Goethe in America, 1806–1840* (New York: Garland, 1988), which emphasizes the mediation via Staël. More broadly, it is worth noting that throughout James's autobiographical writings Italy is placed in relation to Germany, with literary ambition forming the third point of the triangle. See, e.g., *Notes of a Son and Brother*, in *Autobiography*, ed. Frederick W. Dupee (New York: Criterion Books, 1956), 260–62.

2. *Nathaniel Hawthorne*, in *Henry James: Literary Criticism, Essays on Literature, American Writers, English Writers*, ed. Leon Edel (New York: Library of America. 1984), 445. Further references are in the body of the text.

3. Richard Brodhead has identified a similar "role of a narrator who both observes and provokes the action" in "Passionate Pilgrim," the companion to "Madonna," noting only that it is "a phenomenon strangely unexplained." Richard H. Brodhead, *The School of Hawthorne* (New York: Oxford University Press, 1986), 129. See also Sharon Cameron on the question of doubling in *Roderick Hudson* in *Thinking in Henry James* (Chicago: University of Chicago Press, 1989), 44–53. On the passions at work in the tales of artists and their admirers, see Leland S. Person, "Deploying Homo-Aesthetic Desire in the Tales of Writers and Artists," in his *Henry James and the Suspense of Masculinity* (Philadelphia: University of Pennsylvania Press, 2003), 124–48.

4. Maqbool Aziz, ed., *The Tales of Henry James*, vol. 2, *1870–1874* (Oxford: Clarendon Press, 1978), 229. Further references to the stories are from this volume, which prints the text of the first serial edition of each story.

5. On the much-studied topic of James and Italy, see Christof Wegelin, *The Image of Europe in Henry James* (Dallas: Southern Methodist University Press, 1958); Cristina Giorcelli, *Henry James e l'Italia* (Rome: Edizioni di Storie e Letteratura, 1968); Carl Maves, *Sensuous Pessimism: Italy in the Work of Henry James* (Bloomington: Indiana University Press, 1973); James W. Tuttleton and Agostino Lombardo, eds., *The Sweetest Impression of Life: The James Family and Italy* (New York: New York University Press, 1990); James Buzard, *The Beaten Track: European Tourism, Literature and the Ways to "Culture," 1800–1918* (New York: Oxford University Press, 1993); and Michael L. Ross, *Storied Cities: Literary Imaginings of Florence, Venice, and Rome* (Westport, Conn.: Greenwood Press, 1994).

While my own focus is on James as displaced cosmopolite, that characterization—as James well knew—is far from being in contradiction with a deep-seated Americanism. Recent texts that attempt to place James's travels in an American context include Malcolm Bradbury's *Dangerous Pilgrimages: Trans-Atlantic Mythologies and the Novel* (1995; London: Penguin, 1996), as well as William W. Stowe, *European Travel in Nineteenth-Century American Culture* (Princeton: Princeton University Press, 1994); Larzer Ziff, *Return Passages: Great American Travel Writing, 1780–1910* (New Haven: Yale University Press, 2000); and Leland S. Person, *Roman Holidays: American Writers and Artists in Nineteenth-Century Italy* (Iowa City: University of Iowa Press, 2002). Useful earlier books include Van Wyck Brooks, *The Dream of Arcadia: American Writers and Artists in Italy, 1760–1915* (New York: Dutton, 1958); Cushing Stout, *The American Image of the Old World* (New York: Harper and Row, 1963); and Paul R. Baker, *The Fortunate Pilgrims: Americans in Italy, 1800–1860* (Cambridge: Harvard University Press, 1964). For the particular case of England as destination, see Christopher Mulvey, *Anglo-American Landscapes: A Study of Nineteenth-Century Anglo-American Travel Literature* (Cambridge: Cambridge University Press, 1983).

Generally speaking, it is the Italian critics who are most clear on the conventionality of James's Italy; in the words of Agostino Lombardo: "One thinks . . . of the almost complete lack in his fiction of Italian characters that are not conventional, 'literary,' or indeed operatic." Lombardo, "Italy and the Artist in Henry James," in Tuttleton and Lombardo, *The Sweetest Impression of Life*, 230. There is ultimately surprisingly little difference between this observation and that of Leon Edel: "It was James . . . who brought modern Italy into American fiction, as Shakespeare and Jonson and Otway had used the Italy of the Renaissance for the drama" (Tuttleton and Lombardo, *The Sweetest Impression of Life*, 20). One can only agree with the second clause, and point out that it fatally undermines the first, unless we take *Romeo and Juliet* as an authentic representation of sixteenth-century Verona. On this topic, see also Giorcelli, *Henry James e l'Italia*, 150–52.

6. "Travelling Companions," first published in *Atlantic Monthly*, 1870, in Aziz, *The Tales of Henry James*, 1. Further references are from this edition. For James's close engagement with the nineteenth-century culture of art, see the collection of reviews published as *The Painter's Eye*, ed. John L. Sweeney (Madison: University of Wisconsin Press, 1989). The vital secondary source on the topic is Adeline R. Tintner, *The Museum World of Henry James* (Ann Arbor: UMI Research Press, 1986). Among the most subtle and interesting recent accounts of James and aestheticism are Richard Ellmann, "Henry James among the Aesthetes" (1983), reprinted in *Along the Riverrun: Selected Essays* (New York: Knopf, 1989), 132–49;

and Jonathan Freedman, *Professions of Taste: Henry James, British Aestheticism, and Commodity Culture* (Stanford: Stanford University Press, 1990).

7. "A Passionate Pilgrim," first printed in *Atlantic Monthly*, 1871, was much revised by James over the years. My citations are from the original serial text as reprinted in Aziz, *The Tales of Henry James*, 42–43. For the autobiographical elements woven into passages such as this one, cf. *A Small Boy and Others*, a text that picks up steam in Europe, as the "others" of its title give way to James's innate responsiveness to place. "It was the romance of travel, and it was the *suggested* romance, flushed with suppositions and echoes, with implications and memories, memories of one's 'reading,' save the mark!" (*Autobiography*, 160).

8. Henry James, "*The Reverberator, Madame de Mauves, A Passionate Pilgrim, The Madonna of the Future, Louisa Pallant*," in *Literary Criticism: French Writers, Other European Writers, the Prefaces to the New York Edition* (New York: Library of America, 1984), 1204. Further references from the prefaces are taken from this edition and made in the text. The two tales after "A Passionate Pilgrim" are "The Madonna of the Future" and "Louisa Pallant."

9. On Psyche's adventures, see Apuleius, *The Golden Ass*, trans. Jack Lindsay (Bloomington: Indiana University Press, 1962). James could have recalled the story from Pater's extensive retelling in *Marius* or from Apuleius's text directly; both were in his library (see Edel and Tintner, *The Library of Henry James*). The tale is also retold in William Morris's *Earthly Paradise*, which James reviewed twice in 1868, for the *North American Review* and for the *Nation*. See James, *Literary Criticism*, 1182–91.

10. We may compare James's comment on reading William Wetmore Story's remarks at the Pitti Palace: "I like to look over his shoulder, not because his judgments are rare . . . but because they are delightedly usual." *William Wetmore Story and His Friends* (1903; New York: Da Capo Press, 1969), 96–97. In these moments, we see James's self-conscious evocation of what in *Beaten Track* Buzard usefully describes as the "scripted continent."

11. Henry James, *Watch and Ward*, in *Novels, 1871–1880* (New York: Library of America, 1983), 7. Further citations are made in the text and refer to this edition. After its serial publication in the *Atlantic Monthly* (Aug.–Dec. 1871), James revised the novel for publication in one volume in 1878. He did not include it in the New York Edition, thus making *Roderick Hudson* his sanctioned novelistic debut. *Novels* reprints the text of the serial edition.

12. For James's fondness for this theme, we may compare the terms of the 1868 review of William Morris's *The Earthly Paradise* for the *Nation*: "The finest and sweetest poem in the volume, to our taste, is the tale of 'Pygmalion and the Image.' The merit of execution is perhaps not appreciably greater here than in the other pieces, but the legend is so unutterably charming that it claims precedence of its companions. As beautiful as anything in all our later poetry, we think, is the description of the growth and dominance in the poor sculptor's heart of his marvelous passion for the stony daughter of his hands" (*Literary Criticism*, 1189–90). James responds in particular to the *Bildung* of the object of desire; he confesses to being especially moved by a scene in which the sculptor *reads* to his "stony daughter." The influence of *Wilhelm Meister* is also unmissable, not only in the premise of *Watch and Ward*, but in the tone of the narrative. "She looks as if she belonged

to a circus troupe," thinks Roger, prior to deciding to adopt her (12)—a thought that does more to remind one of Mignon than to develop the plot of the novel.

13. "You describe him perfectly when you say that everything in the house here sings his praise," says his cousin and rival Hubert, in terms that wander suggestively from the practical to the aesthetic, to the tendentiously personal: "The chairs are all straight, the pictures are admirably hung, the locks are oiled, the winter fuel is stocked, the bills are paid! Look at the tidies pinned on the chairs. I'll warrant you he pinned them with his own hands. Such is Roger! . . . He ought never to marry" (97).

14. Cf. Philip Horne, *Henry James and Revision: The New York Edition* (Oxford: Clarendon Press, 1990): "Though *Roderick Hudson* is not exactly an autobiographical novel, much of its life . . . springs from its intimate relation to James's own career. At the beginnings of his career James was repeatedly preoccupied with beginnings, and with premature ends, of careers; with the idea of, and the delusions of, genius; and with artists' relations to their imagination" (102–3). Agostino Lombardo suggests a reading of the prefaces "as a *novel* on the artist and on the artistic process" (Tuttleton and Lombardo, *The Sweetest Impression of Life*, 229). See also Sharon Cameron's subtle account of the play between the claims of the prefaces and the novels in *Thinking in Henry James*, 32–82. For a recent treatment of James's self-presentation in the New York edition, see David McWhirter, ed., *Henry James's New York Edition: The Construction of Authorship* (Stanford: Stanford University Press, 1995). On Coburn's frontispieces, see especially Ira Nadel, "Visual Culture: The Photo Frontispieces to the New York Edition," in McWhirter, 90–108.

15. James demonstrates Rowland Mallet's erudite taste. Botticelli and Ghirlandaio are both masters whose reputations were in the process of formation in the 1870s—with no little help from Ruskin and Pater. The latter compares the two in *The Renaissance*, only three years prior to *Roderick Hudson*. See Walter Pater, *The Renaissance: Studies in Art and Poetry*, ed. Donald L. Hill (Berkeley: University of California Press, 1981), 41.

16. Cf. Maria Gostrey's assumption of the direction of Lambert Strether early in *The Ambassadors*: "[S]he took over the job, as she had called it, on the spot. 'Trust me!' she exclaimed; and the action of this, as they retraced their steps, was presently to make him pass his hand into her arm in the manner of a benign dependent paternal old person who wishes to be 'nice' to a younger one." Henry James, *The Ambassadors* (1903; New York: Norton, 1994), 27.

17. Pater, *The Renaissance*, 190, 187, 188.

18. On Pater's historicism, see especially Carolyn Williams, *Transfigured World: Walter Pater's Aesthetic Historicism* (Ithaca: Cornell University Press, 1989). See also Jonah Siegel, *Desire and Excess: The Nineteenth-Century Culture of Art* (Princeton: Princeton University Press, 2000).

19. For detailed accounts of James and Pater, see Adeline R. Tintner, *The Book World of Henry James: Appropriating the Classics* (Ann Arbor: UMI, 1987), 143–63. Also, Ellmann, "Henry James among the Aesthetes," 132–34 and Freedman, *Professions of Taste*, esp. 133–66. Tintner hints at what Freedman tentatively proposes, that James may have been familiar with Pater's writings from their earlier periodical appearances. This is certainly a tempting speculation, but it is hard to

imagine that a series of magazine articles that had so pervasive an effect on the novelist would have left no other trace in letters or other contemporary commentary. See Tintner, *Book World*, 144, and Freedman, *Professions of Taste*, 273–74n. Critics have remarked on James's letter responding to William James's recommendation that he should review *The Renaissance*: "I saw Pater's *Studies* just after getting your letter . . . and was inflamed to think of buying it and trying a notice. But I see it treats of several things I know nothing about." See Leon Edel, ed., *Henry James Letters*, vol. 1, *1843–75* (Cambridge: Harvard University Press, 1974), 391. While the not quite convincing dismissal of William's suggestion has provoked comment (particularly that so Paterian "inflammation"), it is worth noting that there must have been a sense on William James's part that his brother was particularly qualified to evaluate the work, or that he would have a special interest in its content. Certainly Henry's declaration that there are "several things" he knew nothing about in the volume is far from a statement of ignorance of things aesthetic (or Aesthetic for that matter). Freedman probably overstates somewhat in identifying James's phrase as a misleading or a disingenuous "assertion that he knew nothing about Italian Renaissance art" (*Professions of Taste*, 133). It seems unlikely that William James would have forgotten his brother's early reviews of works touching on artistic topics such as Taine's *Italy: Rome and Naples* (*Nation*, May 7, 1868). See *Literary Criticism*, 826–31. There is enough variety in Pater's collection of essays to make a declaration that one feels unqualified to evaluate it something other than false humility. A skim deep enough to pick up the flame of the conclusion would have shown any reader that the book includes not only discussion of central figures in Renaissance art but also some quite recondite topics in art and otherwise. Eric Savoy points out in a brief but forceful article illustrating Pater's early influence, that the correspondence contains evidence of a now lost review of *The Renaissance* from late in 1873. Savoy speculates that an anxious James himself might have suppressed publications of the piece. Eric Savoy, "*Hypocrite Lecteur*: Walter Pater, Henry James and Homotextual Politics," *Dalhousie Review* 72 (1992): 12–36. See *Letters*, 1:411.

20. If Rowland's complaint has an antecedent in Theobald, Cecilia's answer has an echo. It is what May Bartram will propose thirty years later to John Marcher as an interpretation of the great event for which he spends his life waiting: "Isn't what you describe perhaps but the expectation—or, at any rate, the sense of danger, familiar to so many people—of falling in love?" "The Beast in the Jungle" (first printed in *The Better Sort*, 1903), in Henry James, *Complete Stories, 1898–1910* (New York: Library of America, 1996), 504.

The ever-growing body of work devoted to James and sexual desire suggests the force of a theme in the novelist that had not received its due until recent years—that in some measure could not receive it before the development of modern sexual politics and the emergence of related critical approaches. It bears saying that the quantity of work in this area is also evidence of the rich deflections through which the novelist expresses his passions. In this study at least, identification of real desires is less central than the interplay of form and longing that characterizes the art romance. To identify or assume that James's own sexual desires are represented in any simple way in his texts can run the risk of evading promising difficulties present in the work, among them the relation of passion and convention, of secret wishes and flamboyant self-revelation. To argue, as Eric Haralson does, that "Roderick's fate, of course, is death, because neither James *nor* his culture could imagine a narrative of homosexual love in which he might not only live, but also survive and thrive" is in a way to give May Bartram the last word. Worse, it is to say of the work what Cecilia says to Rowland: "What an immense number of words . . . to say you want to fall in love!" (*Roderick Hudson*, 171). See Eric Haralson, *Henry James and Queer Modernity* (Cambridge: Cambridge University Press, 2003), 44.

For a subtle treatment of the displacements of desire in James—the immense number of words and the difficult expression of love—see Eve Sedgwick's groundbreaking "The Beast in the Closet: James and the Writing of Queer Panic" (1986), reprinted in *Epistemology of the Closet* (Berkeley: University of California Press, 1990), 182–212. See also Hugh Stevens, *Henry James and Sexuality* (Cambridge: Cambridge University Press, 1998), especially the first chapter, "Henry James and the Language of Sex," 1–19. Stevens, like Leland Person in *Henry James and the Suspense of Masculinity*, is commendably alive not only to the range of manifestations by which desire makes itself known in James, but also to the many functions such varied representations may serve. John Bradley's *Henry James's Permanent Adolescence* (Houndmills: Palgrave, 2000) offers a particularly measured account of the controversies that have developed in recent work in this area, and his anthology of essays is a useful resource: *Henry James and Homo-Erotic Desire* (Houndmills: Palgrave, 1998).

21. It is a sign of the widespread diffusion of their influence that the mediation of these authors was not always direct. James's *Autobiography* testifies with some embarrassment to the importance of popular women authors of the 1850s and 1860s in his development, an intriguing topic especially in the early parts of *A Small Boy and Others*. The novelists his grandmother enjoyed are, for example, an important memory (14). It is by these lights that we may read his complaint: "It was an humiliation to me at first, small boys though we were, that our instructors kept being instructresses" (11). It is also worth citing in this context the name by which the mother of Gilbert Osmond liked to be known: "The American Corinne." See *The Portrait of a Lady* (1881; New York: Norton, 1996). The force of the feminine in James's professional self-imagination has received various kinds of attention, including Frederick W. Dupee's tantalizing suggestion that James might be called "the great feminine novelist of a feminine age in letters" (Dupee, *Henry James* [New York: Dell, 1965], 97]), as well as the more developed polemical work of Alfred Habegger, *Henry James and the "Woman Business"* (Cambridge: Cambridge University Press, 1989). "James cannot be fully and rightly understood unless we confront the enormous culture of nineteenth-century literary women against which he often wrote" (4). An important source on the cultural determinants behind these kinds of claims is Ann Douglas, *The Feminization of American Culture* (London: Macmillan, 1996), esp. 62–66, 96. On James and the conventions of popular literature, see William Veeder, *Henry James: The Lessons of the Master, Popular Fiction and Personal Style in the Nineteenth Century* (Chicago: University of Chicago Press, 1975). For an attempt to link James's response to the feminine to the homoerotic themes that have dominated recent criticism, see Scott S. Derrick, *Monumental Anxieties: Homoerotic Desire and Feminine Influence in 19th-Century U.S. Literature* (New Brunswick: Rutgers University Press, 1997).

22. Michael L. Ross usefully summarizes the arguments for reading Christina Light as an embodiment of Rome. Ross, *Storied Cities*, 249–51.

23. There is a tendency, due perhaps to a desire to simplify what James meant by having Americans go to Europe, to neglect somewhat Rowland's odd ancestry. Michael L. Ross, for instance, refers to his "puritan ancestors," as though that summed up the elaborate genealogy James goes to some trouble to sketch (*Storied Cities*, 249).

24. James is clear on the fact that the space Christina is studying is typical, characteristic: "Rowland had found a convenient corner in a stately old palace not far from the Fountain of Trevi, and made himself a home to which books and pictures and prints and odds and ends of curious furniture gave an air of leisurely permanence. He had the tastes of a collector." (231).

25. "As to Miss Garland being in love with Roderick and becoming charming thereby, this was a point with which his imagination ventured to take no liberties; partly because it would have been indelicate, and partly because it would have been vain" (281–82).

26. Pater, *The Renaissance*, 98.

CHAPTER FOUR

1. Henry James, *The Sense of the Past* (1915; London: Collins, 1917), 62. Further references are taken from this edition and made in the body of the text.

2. *Hawthorne*, in Henry James, *Literary Criticism: Essays on Literature, American Writers, English Writers*, ed. Leon Edel (New York: Library of America, 1984), 315–457; 351–52 and 372. Further references are taken from this edition and made in the text.

3. *The American*, in *Novels, 1871–1880* (New York: Library of America, 1983), 515. *The American* was written in Paris 1875–76 and published in monthly installments in the *Atlantic Monthly*, 1876–77. The first edition of the novel was published in 1877 and was much revised for the New York edition in 1907. Further page references are made in the text, following *Novels*, which reprints the text from the first volume edition of 1877.

4. Henry James, *A Small Boy and Others*, in *Autobiography*, ed. Frederick W. Dupee (New York: Criterion Books, 1956), 198–99. Further references are made in the text.

5. The following exchange reveals not only the potential deceptiveness of sophisticated Europeans, but also the relation between the desired art object and its validation by its presence in a museum:

> "Bought a picture?" said Mr. Tristram, looking vaguely round at the walls. "Why, do they sell them?"
>
> "I mean a copy."
>
> "Oh, I see. These," said Mr. Tristram, nodding at the Titians and Vandykes, "these, I suppose, are originals."
>
> "I hope so," cried Newman. "I don't want a copy of a copy."
>
> "Ah," said Mr. Tristram, mysteriously, "you can never tell. They imitate, you know, so deucedly well." (528)

6. Henry James, "*The American*," in *Literary Criticism: French Writers, Other European Writers, the Prefaces to the New York Edition* (New York: Library of America, 1984), 1054. Further references to the prefaces are taken from this edition and made in the text.

7. R.W.B. Lewis describes the preface as marking "a conspicuous moment in the development from the special Jamesian mode of romance to the special Jamesian mode of realism." *The Jameses* (New York: Farrar, Straus and Giroux, 1991), 294. On the American context, see Joel Porte, *The Romance in America: Studies in Cooper, Poe, Hawthorne, Melville, and James* (Middletown, Conn.: Wesleyan University Press, 1969), 193–229. See also Elissa Greenwald, *Realism and the Romance: Nathaniel Hawthorne, Henry James, and American Fiction* (Ann Arbor: UMI Research Press, 1989).

For a recent account of the challenge of the romance, particularly in the last third of the novel, see Peter Brooks, "The Turn of *The American*," in *New Essays on* The American, ed. Martha Banta (New York: Cambridge University Press, 1987), 43–67. See also Brook's discussion of James, and this novel in particular, in *The Melodramatic Imagination: Balzac, Henry James, Melodrama, and the Mode of Excess* (New York: Columbia University Press, 1976), esp. 153–57. Brooks's interest is, of course, the *theatrical* inverisimilitude of melodrama, an important analogue to romance.

Leo Bersani's account of "The Jamesian Lie," in *A Future for Astynax: Character and Desire in Literature* (Boston: Little, Brown, 1976), is useful to cite in this context for its insistence on the *formal* pressures involved in the evasions of what James calls romance: "The greatest Jamesian and Stendhalian sophistication," Bersani argues, "is to find a kind of sensual pleasure in following the ingenious evasions and indirections with which language deflects and serves insistent desires" (129). Romance has the characteristic of the primary elements of literature described by Bersani: "Language and thought, as I've been suggesting, inevitably compromise desire, but the compromises themselves may offer us more than the meager satisfaction of seeing through them. The surfaces of our thought and our speech don't merely cover up the depths behind thought and speech. They have appeals of their own, and as we compose our sublimations we can discover pleasures distinct from those for the sake of which we perhaps 'began' to sublimate" (129). On the signifying force of James's apparently evasive figures, see also Ruth Yeazell, *Language and Knowledge in the Late Novels of Henry James* (Chicago: University of Chicago Press, 1976).

8. Henry James, *The Wings of the Dove* (1902), ed. J. Donald Crowley and Richard A. Hocks (New York: Norton, 1978), 266.

9. David Richter, *The Progress of Romance: Literary Historiography and the Gothic Novel* (Columbus: Ohio State University Press, 1996), 97, 100.

10. See Sigmund Freud, *Beyond the Pleasure Principle*, in *The Standard Edition of the Complete Psychological Works of Sigmund Freud*, trans and ed. James Strachey in collaboration with Anna Freud (London: Hogarth Press, 1953–66), 18:67. Freud quickly connects the term Nirvana—which he attributes to Barbara Low's 1920 work, *Psycho-Analysis*—to the pleasure principle in its darkest manifestation. See also Freud's "The Economic Problem of Masochism," in *Standard Edition*, 19:157–72. On masochism in James, see Hugh Stevens, *Henry James and Sexuality*

(Cambridge: Cambridge University Press, 1998), 61–89; and Leland S. Person, *Henry James and the Suspense of Masculinity* (Philadelphia: University of Pennsylvania Press, 2003), 149–74.

11. Thaddeo K. Babiiha, *The James-Hawthorne Relation* (Boston: G. K. Hall, 1980), provides a useful synoptic view of the much studied topic of James and Hawthorne up to the early 1970s. See also Richard Brodhead's magisterial treatment of the theme in *The School of Hawthorne* (New York: Oxford University Press, 1986), especially 104–200. On the relation between *The Marble Faun* and *Roderick Hudson*, see 132–33. For a rich treatment of James's return to romance near the time of the prefaces, see 186–96. Brodhead's work is especially useful for its insistence on the pervasive, insistent, nature of Hawthorne's influence: "James's fiction displays its descent from Hawthorne in peculiarly persistent and obtrusive ways. . . . the striking fact about James's involvement with Hawthorne is that it is exactly not a *passing* thing. . . . he is if anything more pervasive in late James" (Brodhead, 105; emphasis in the original).

12. Nathaniel Hawthorne, *The Marble Faun; or, The Romance of Monte Beni* (1860; Harmondsworth: Penguin, 1990), 3. Further references are in the text. That James and Hawthorne are engaging a well-known complex is suggested by an article in *Putnam's Monthly* in 1855 comparing travelers of various nations: "The American has a pleasure in foreign travel, which the man of no other nation enjoys. With a nature not less romantic than others; with desires and aspirations for the reverend and historically beautiful, forever unsatisfied at home, fed for years upon the splendid literature of all time, and the pompous history of the nations that have occupied and moulded the earth, and yet separated from those nations and that history . . . the American mind is solicited by Europe with unimagined fascination." The American voyager to Europe goes "to take possession of his dreams, and hopes, and boundless aspirations." George William Curtis, "American Travelers," *Putnam's Monthly Magazine* 5 (1855): 563–64. Quoted in Beth L. Lueck, *American Writers and the Picturesque Tour: The Search for National Identity, 1760–1860* (New York: Garland, 1997), 3.

13. One intriguing comparison of the two novels is Leland Person's "Aesthetic Headaches and European Women in *The Marble Faun* and *The American*," *Studies in American Fiction* 4, no. 1 (Spring 1976): 64–77. Person's analysis, which focuses on the shocking encounter with the "European woman," concludes with a vision of "the encounter with Europe" as entailing "a self-endangering release of the formless, irrational, sexual nightmares of the Gothic romance" (72, 77).

14. Germaine de Staël, *Corinne, or Italy*, trans. Sylvia Raphael (New York: Oxford University Press, 1998), 174.

15. On artistic pantheons, see Francis Haskell, *Rediscoveries in Art: Some Aspects of Taste, Fashion, and Collecting in England and France* (Ithaca: Cornell University Press, 1980), 8–21 and Jonah Siegel, *Desire and Excess: The Nineteenth-Century Culture of Art* (Princeton: Princeton University Press, 2000), 140–50.

16. Adeline R. Tintner argues for the formative influence of the experience in the Louvre for James's work early and late. See *The Museum World of Henry James* (Ann Arbor: UMI Research Press, 1986), 5–14. On the passage in relation to James's artistic self-imagination, see Stephen Donadio, *Nietzsche, Henry James,*

and the Artistic Will (New York: Oxford University Press, 1978), 254–58. See also Lewis, *The Jameses*, 238. Lewis is convincing in his proposal that the figure in the dream may well be identifiable as William James. After all, *A Small Boy and Others* sets out to be about the older brother, and certainly there is no contradiction in seeing versions of James's self and of his brother coming together to shape a fearful pursuit that stands for an anxious relation to achievement. Cf. the language of some of the descriptions of the older brother in the memoir: "already beforehand . . . already there an embodied demonstration of the possible— already wherever it might be that there was a question of my arriving, when arriving at all, belatedly and ruefully . . . I never for all the time of childhood and youth in the least caught up with him or overtook him. He was always round the corner and out of sight, coming back into view but at his hours of extremest ease" (7–8). "I remember how far ahead of us my brother seemed to keep . . . my vision of him in these connections is not so much of his coming toward me, or toward any of us, as of his moving rapidly away in fantastic garb and with his back turned" (145).

17. The play with doors and corridors in that story is a prolonged version of the main actions of the dream in the Louvre, but the relation between the two narratives is evident in the very description of the setting: "They were back in the hall then for departure, but from where they stood the vista was large, through an open door, into the great square main saloon, with its almost antique felicity of brave spaces between windows." "The Jolly Corner," in *Complete Stories, 1898– 1910* (New York: Library of America, 1996), 704. Further references are in the text. "The Jolly Corner" has pride of place in Tzvetan Todorov's discussion of the uncanny in *The Poetics of Prose* (Ithaca: Cornell University Press, 1977).

18. "[H]e could but gape at his other self in this other anguish, gape as a proof that *he*, standing there for the achieved, the enjoyed, the triumphant life, couldn't be faced in his triumph" (725).

19. Oscar Wilde, *The Complete Works of Oscar Wilde* (London: Collins, 1986), 17

20. James began *The Sense of the Past* in 1900, but put it aside until 1914. The resumption of work on the novel is generally explained biographically, as an attempt on the novelist's part to escape his own age at the outset of a bleak period in European history. See Leon Edel, *Henry James: The Treacherous Years, 1895– 1901* (New York: Lippincott, 1969), 334–36. Beverly Haviland addresses the complex history of the work and some of the changes James's return entailed in *Henry James's Last Romance: Making Sense of the Past and the American Scene* (Cambridge: Cambridge University Press, 1997). Susan S. Williams argues for the work as an attempt to embrace the modern and touches on the presence of Hawthorne in "The Tell-Tale Representation: James and *The Sense of the Past*," *Henry James Review* 14 (1993): 72–86. Martha Banta offers a particularly compelling reading of the text in relation to "The Jolly Corner"—a story whose premise James knew he was in some measure borrowing from his unfinished novel—and to the dream of the Louvre in *Henry James and the Occult: The Great Extension* (Bloomington: Indiana University Press, 1972), 136–53.

CHAPTER FIVE

1. Henry James, *The Golden Bowl* (1904; Oxford: Oxford University Press, 1983), 9–10. Further references to this edition are made parenthetically in the text.

2. The antivisual tendency of much modern critical thought, well described recently by Martin Jay in *Downcast Eyes: The Denigration of Vision in Twentieth-Century French Thought* (Berkeley: University of California Press, 1993), along with the long-standing and still underexamined antipathy to institutions of culture that characterized influential lines of twentieth-century criticism, has tended to result in fairly reductive moralizing accounts of the place of the museum in the novel—as though looking, owning, or displaying were always and necessarily pernicious human activities. The most commendably nuanced and historically engaged recent treatment of the museum in the novel is Stephen D. Arata, "Object Lessons: Reading the Museum in *The Golden Bowl*," in *Famous Last Words: Changes in Gender and Narrative Closure*, ed. Alison Booth (Charlottesville: University Press of Virginia, 1993), 199–229. On the emergence of the museum and antimuseal impulses, see Jonah Siegel, *Desire and Excess: The Nineteenth-Century Culture of Art* (Princeton: Princeton University Press, 2000). See also Andreas Huyssen's important essay, "Escape from Amnesia: The Museum as Mass Media," in his *Twilight Memories: Marking Time in a Culture of Amnesia* (New York: Routledge, 1995). On museums in American culture, see Steven Conn, *Museums and American Intellectual Life, 1876–1926* (Chicago: Chicago University Press, 1998), and Joel J. Orosz, *Curators and Culture: The Museum Movement in America, 1740–1870* (Tuscaloosa: University of Alabama Press, 1990). Arata's essay is also a useful source for contemporary texts on museums and secondary works on the topic. On the contingent nature of visuality for the novelist, see Susan M. Griffin, *The Historical Eye: The Texture of the Visual in Late James* (Boston: Northeastern University Press, 1991). Among the most thoughtfully polemical accounts of the visual in James is Michael Moon's influential "Sexuality and Visual Terrorism in *The Wings of the Dove*," *Criticism* 28, n. 4 (1986): 427–43.

3. Richard Brodhead, *The School of Hawthorne* (New York: Oxford University Press, 1986), 186–200.

4. We may compare the prince's disappointed sense that among the people into which he has married, one never has to "wait with the dagger, or to prepare, insidiously, the cup. These were the services that, by all romantic traditions, were consecrated to affection quite as much as to hate" (230).

5. Ruth Yeazell, in what is still among the most nuanced readings of the novel, suggests that the challenges presented by the ending and by the role and character of Maggie in particular have yielded a text of unparalleled and even distressing ambiguity: "[N]o Jamesian novel has left its readers themselves more *en l'air.*" *Language and Knowledge in the Late Novels of Henry James* (Chicago: University of Chicago Press, 1976), 100–130. In attempting to resolve the challenges of this difficult work, criticism has repeatedly returned to the tantalizing question of the moral complicity or innocence of the characters, especially of the interested or

disinterested nature of the actions of Maggie and her father, who are sometimes taken to stand in as a proxies for the author or to be emblematic of his values. The quite distinct readings of Aratra, Griffin, and Yeazell are exemplary responses to the more reductive moralizing tendencies to which even quite careful readings of the novel often fall prey—the urge to sort out villains and victims, to find points of separation that will allow the discovery of distinctions in James's tale of excruciatingly interwoven passions. Mark Seltzer usefully suggests that "love and power in *The Golden Bowl* are not finally opposed . . . love and power are in effect two ways of saying the same thing." Mark Seltzer, "James, Pleasure, Power," *Henry James Review* 5 (1984): 201. It is not necessary to entirely endorse Seltzer's concept of power—more fully developed in his *Henry James and the Art of Power* (Ithaca: Cornell University Press, 1984)—in order to benefit from the important insight that Maggie, though clearly the manipulating agent in the later part of the novel, is *herself* nevertheless not free, but subject to her situation: "Maggie's power is at last a 'power of surrender' to a more comprehensive mechanism of control—to the 'love' that logically and inevitably exposes through the organic and normalizing power of form" (202). The novel's evocation of the force of form and its illustration of the inextricable relationship between power and love ensure that Maggie Verver, as Yeazell points out, "arouses in us at once an intenser sympathy and a more profound fear" than any similar character in James.

6. Griffin is particularly interesting on the desperate quality of Maggie's attempts to forestall the returns of the past, and on the ways in which Maggie recognizes in Charlotte her own frightening power (*Historical Eye*, 72–90). My reading of the novel, like Griffin's, sees a temporal fatality at work ("Actively struggling to perceive new images of a free future, Maggie sees instead historical sights," 79), but I believe the problem starts earlier and involves *all* the principal characters.

7. Though Adam Verver is inescapably a father, he evidently has problems being a married man. Not only does his self-defining passion for art require the death of his first wife, but James indicates something of his connection to such bachelors of the early novels as Rowland and Roger in a passage that is, not coincidentally, richly Paterian: "He had learnt the lesson of the senses, to the end of his own little book, without having, for a day, raised the smallest scandal in his economy at large; being in this particular not unlike those fortunate bachelors or other gentlemen of pleasure, who so manage their entertainment of compromising company that even the austerest housekeeper, occupied and competent below-stairs, never feels obliged to give warning" (146).

8. See André Malraux, *Les voix du silence* (Paris: Galerie de la Pléiade, 1951), 11–125, translated by Stuart Gilbert as *The Voices of Silence* (London: Secker and Warburt, 1954), 13–127.

9. Walter Pater, *Marius the Epicurean* (1885; Harmondsworth: Penguin, 1985), 120

10. Henry James, *A Small Boy and Others*, in *Autobiography*, ed. Frederick W. Dupee (New York: Criterion Books, 1956), 195.

11. *Nathaniel Hawthorne*, in *Henry James: Literary Criticism, Essays on Literature, American Writers, English Writers*, ed. Leon Edel (New York: Library of America, 1984), 445.

CHAPTER SIX

1. Sigmund Freud, *The Interpretation of Dreams*, in *The Standard Edition of the Complete Psychological Works of Sigmund Freud*, trans and ed. James Strachey in collaboration with Anna Freud (London: Hogarth Press, 1953–66), 4:167, 195, 608. *Interpretation of Dreams* was published late in 1899, though its title page gives the year as 1900. The work runs through volumes 4 and 5 of the *Standard Edition*. Further references are to this edition, and made by volume and page number.

2. Among recent works illuminating the interplay of Freud's biography, his professional development, and his imagination of Italy, one must cite Carl E. Schorske's political-biographical study, "Politics and Patricide in Freud's *Interpretation of Dreams*" in his *Fin-de-siècle Vienna: Politics and Culture* (New York: Vintage, 1981), 181–207. For an exhaustive psychoanalytic study illuminating the interplay of the biography and the emergence of the field, see Didier Anzieu, *Freud's Self-Analysis*, trans. Peter Graham (Madison: International Universities Press, 1986). See also William J. McGrath, *Freud's Discovery of Psychoanalysis: The Politics of Hysteria* (Ithaca: Cornell University Press, 1986), esp. 197–275. Dennis Porter offers a suggestive analysis of Freud's work as a response to earlier travel writings in *Haunted Journey* (Princeton: Princeton University Press, 1991), 187–201. For a useful recent compendium of Freud's letters from Italy, including photographs from the analyst's collection, see Christfried Tögel, ed., *Unser Herz zeigt nach dem Süden: Reisebriefe 1895–1923* (Berlin: Aufbau-Verlag, 2002).

3. The troubling returns of this dream do not end with Freud; it has an important place in Lacan's seminar as part of his recalibration of the place of the real in the unconscious. For the later analyst, the dreamer awakes because the encounter with the child is *more* terrifyingly real than the world into which he can return on awaking. See *Four Fundamental Concepts of Psychoanalysis*, trans. Alan Sheridan (New York: Norton, 1998), 57–80, 68–69, 259. On this key moment in Lacan, see Malcolm Bowie, *Lacan* (Cambridge: Harvard University Press, 1991), 105–7, and Slavoj Zizek, *The Sublime Object of Ideology* (London: Verso, 1989), 44–49. For an ambitious and wide-ranging account of the figure in psychoanalysis and literature, see David Lee Miller, *Dreams of the Burning Child: Sacrificial Sons and the Father's Witness* (Ithaca: Cornell University Press, 2003), esp. 160–94. Preoccupied as he is by Freud's own psychic life, Anzieu does not do much with this dream, although he notes that it is one of only three dreamed by others that receive repeated discussion in the text (Anzieu, *Freud's Self-Analysis*, 550).

4. If the Kafkaesque dream of a castle by the sea in which Freud causes the death of the governor by asking questions during a mysterious period of war is revealed by analysis to have Italy at its core, the thought behind the dream has to do with Freud's anxieties about his own family in the event of his death ("*I* was the Governor who suddenly died" [5:465; emphasis in the original]). While anxiety about children is unmissably part of the motivation of such a dream, the role of offspring becomes only more central when the instance returns in the final chapter, with Freud's explanation that the colors that dominated this unusually vivid dream had their source in "those of a box of toy bricks with which, on the day before the dream, my children had put up a fine building and shown it off for my

admiration. . . . This was associated with colour impressions from my last travels in Italy" (5:547).

5. Freud's brief late reflections on winning the Goethe Prize include not only the proposal that Goethe anticipated many of the insights of psychoanalysis but also the following characteristic reflection: "Our attitude to fathers and teachers is, after all, an ambivalent one since our reverence for them regularly conceals a component of hostile rebellion. That is a psychological fatality . . . bound to extend to our relations with the great men whose life histories we wish to investigate." Freud, "The Goethe Prize," in *The Standard Edition*, 21:212. The father-Goethe analogy was to concern Freud until the end of his career, when it returns in *Moses and Monotheism* (1939). On the role of Goethe in the analyst's imagination, see Jack J. Spector's useful study, *The Aesthetics of Freud* (New York: McGraw-Hill, 1972), esp. 68–69. "Freud's failure to recognize the boundaries between Goethe and himself," notes Ludwig Marcuse "was one of the few illusions of this very illusionless scientist." See "Freud's Aesthetics," *Journal of Aesthetics and Art Criticism* 12 (1956): 16–17 (quoted in Spector, 68).

6. Goethe's essay serves as a central and determining experience in Freud's imagination of his professional and intellectual life. It returns at the conclusion of the first paragraph of his *Autobiographical Study*, as the culmination of his early development: "[I]t was hearing Goethe's beautiful essay on Nature read aloud at a popular lecture by Professor Carl Brühl just before I left school that decided me to become a medical student." *An Autobiographical Study* (1925), in *Standard Edition*, 20:8.

7. Sigmund Freud, *On Dreams*, in *Standard Edition*, 5:664–65; emphases in the original.

8. Though Freud makes reference to Goethe repeatedly in *The Interpretation of Dreams* and throughout his career, his only direct references to *Wilhelm Meister* are both quotations from the most famous song of the Harper ("Ihr führt ins leben"). He quotes these dark lines devoted to the centrality of guilt twice, in *On Dreams* (1901) and at the conclusion of his principal argument in *Civilization and Its Discontents* (1930). In both instances he profits from the ambiguity of the pronominal reference they contain—notably making the plural "You" [*Ihr*] into parents in *On Dreams*:

> You lead us into life, ordain
> That wretches pile up guilt from birth,
> And then you yield them up to pain;
> For all guilt is atoned on earth.

Johann Wolfgang von Goethe, *Wilhelm Meister's Apprenticeship*, trans Eric A. Blackall (1795; Princeton: Princeton University Press, 1995), 77. See Freud, *On Dreams*, in *Standard Edition*, 5:639, and *Civilization and Its Discontents*, in *Standard Edition*, 21:133.

9. Freud treats it as an obvious matter that in some measure it is not suffering so much as the loss of power that the masochist craves. To realize that "the masochist wants to be treated like a small and helpless child" is only to make a beginning on the deep-seated longings determining this desire. Freud, "The Economic Problem of Masochism" (1924), in *Standard Edition*, 19:162.

CHAPTER SEVEN

1. E. M. Forster , *Where Angels Fear to Tread* (1905; New York: Vintage, 1920), 23. Further citations are taken from this edition and made in the text.

2. In his classic study, Lionel Trilling identifies the prevalence of "sudden unmotivated deaths" in Forster's novels, and the "brusque casualness" that characterizes their handling. He also touches on the important Forster-James connection. See Lionel Trilling, *E. M. Forster* (1943; New York: New Directions, 1964), 58, 63. For an illuminating treatment of the history of the title of Forster's first novel, see S. P. Rosenbaum, "Toward a Literary History of *Monteriano*," *Twentieth Century Literature* 31 (1985); reprinted in *E. M. Forster: Critical Assessments*, ed. J. H. Stape, vol. 3 (East Sussex: Helm, 1997), 39–54. On the melodramatic quality of events in the novel, see Alan Wilde, "The Aesthetic View of Life: *Where Angels Fear to Tread*," *Modern Fiction Studies* 7 (1961): 3; reprinted in Stape, *E. M. Forster*, 3–12.

3. Marcel Proust, *Remembrance of Things Past*, trans. C. K. Scott Moncrieff and Terence Kilmartin (New York: Random House, 1981), 1:423–24. English quotations are taken from this widely available three-volume translation and are cited in the text by volume and page number.

4. Wordsworth, "At Rome," *Memorials of a Tour in Italy.* The author's headnote for this 1837 poem is notably Proustian: "Sight is at first a sad enemy to imagination and to those pleasures belonging to old times with which some exertions of that power will always mingle: nothing perhaps brings this truth home to the feelings more than the city of Rome; not so much in respect to the impression made at the moment when it is first seen and looked at as a whole, for then the imagination may be invigorated and the mind eye's quickened; but when particular spots or objects are sought out, disappointment is I believe invariably felt. Ability to recover from this disappointment will exist in proportion to knowledge, and the power of the mind to reconstruct out of fragments and parts, and to make details in the present subservient to more adequate comprehension of the past." *Poetical Works of Wordsworth*, ed. Paul D. Sheats (Boston: Houghton Mifflin, 1982), 748.

5. Tony Tanner offers a subtle and attentive discussion of Proust and the city in *Venice Desired* (Cambridge: Harvard University Press, 1992), 243. "Le désir de Venise,' " he notes, "is the desire that runs through the book." See also Malcolm Bowie, *Freud, Proust and Lacan: Theory as Fiction* (Cambridge: Cambridge University Press, 1987): "Venice is a place where memory and forgetfulness are inseparably woven together; it offers release from the traumatic residues of passion yet at the same time provides countless associative paths by which that passion may by accident be revived" (73). Julia Kristeva is particularly interesting on the role of Venice throughout the complex development of the novel in *Time and Sense: Proust and the Experience of Literature*, trans. Ross Guberman (New York: Columbia University Press, 1996), esp. 108–17. The most thorough account of the topic is Peter Collier, *Proust and Venice* (Cambridge: Cambridge University Press, 1989). The relationship with the mother has inevitably received a great deal of attention, and among the most sophisticated analyses are those to be found in the work of the critics just cited. See also Leo Bersani's stark formulation of the paradox that re-

sides at the heart of the novel: "In the reassurance and illusory permanence of the maternal glance, Marcel has found his most reliable source of self-recognition." *Marcel Proust: The Fictions of Life and of Art* (Oxford: Oxford University Press, 1965), 56.

6. It bears emphasizing that throughout his life Proust was closely engaged with the nineteenth-century culture of art. His careful study of Ruskin, whom he translated, was of course formative. Goethe also has an interesting presence in his critical works. See Proust, *Contre Sainte Beuve* (Paris: Gallimard, 1971), 647–50, and especially the intriguing interplay of Ruskin, Carlyle, and Goethe in Proust's 1902 review of recent work on the art critic (479–80). For a broad account of Proust and the English nineteenth century, see Robert Fraser, *Proust and the Victorians: The Lamp of Memory* (London: Macmillan, 1994).

7. On the importance of the grandmother, see Elyane Dezon-Jones, "Death of My Grandmother / Birth of a Text," in *Critical Essays on Marcel Proust*, ed. Barbara J. Bucknall (Boston: Hall, 1987), 192–204. See also Malcolm Bowie, *Proust among the Stars* (London: HarperCollins, 1998), 273–80. In a simple but thought-provoking interpretative move, Roger Shattuck, consistently runs together the mother and grandmother in *Proust's Way: A Field Guide to* In Search of Lost Time. (New York: Norton, 2000). Although Gérard Genette's argument is largely engaged with the self-betraying declarations of characters, it is worth citing his identification of the centrality of indirectness in the novel. See "Proust and Indirect Language," in Genette, *Figures of Literary Discourse*, trans. Alan Sheridan (New York: Columbia University Press, 1982), 229–95. See also the critic's account of the fundamental "inextricability" of figures and meanings in "Proust's Palimpsest" (Genette, 203–28).

8. Malcolm Bowie presents a particularly rich analysis of the triangulation of Marcel, Venice, and the mother: "At the centre of the Venetian chiasmus, the narrator's mother stands (or sits, or kneels,) as an intractable stone guest, calling him back from his erotic adventures and re-infantilising his once-defiant adult emotion" (*Freud, Proust and Lacan*, 94). Kristeva's description of "The purity of this incestuous Venice" is paradoxically not unrelated to Shattuck's description of "The passionate, enduring, and never sullied love between Marcel and his mother and grandmother." See Kristeva, *Time and Sense*, 114, and Shattuck, *Proust's Way*, 36.

9. Marcel Proust, *By Way of Sainte-Beuve*, trans. Sylvia Townsend Warner (1958; London: Hogarth Press, 1984), 181. This material is no longer included in the more recent French edition of the work, which has been stripped of most narrative material. The draft is now reprinted in *À la recherche du temps perdu*, ed. Jean-Yves Tadie et al. (Paris: Gallimard, 1988), 2:1045–48.

10. "Une heure est venue pour moi où quand je me rappelle le baptistère, devant les flots du Jourdain où saint Jean immerge le Christ tandis que la gondole nous attendait devant la Piazzetta il ne m'est pas indifférent que dans cette fraîche pénombre, à côté de moi il y eût une femme drapée dans son deuil . . . et que cette femme aux joues rouges, aux yeux tristes, dans ses voiles noirs, et que rien ne pourra plus jamais faire sortir pour moi de ce sanctuaire doucement éclairé de Saint-Marc où je suis sûr de la retrouver parce qu'elle y a sa place réservée et immuable comme une mosaïque, ce soit ma mère." Proust, *Albertine disparue*

(1925), in *À la recherche du temps perdu*, ed. Jean-Yves Tadié et al. (Paris: Galli-mard, 1989), 4:225. In his exhaustive account of this moment Peter Collier sees a kind of choice of Hercules preceding Marcel's becoming an artist, one in which "purified love for the mother is enthroned" (*Proust and Venice*, 128). Like Collier, I recognize in this scene a desire to "save" the mother, although I am less con-vinced that the love for the mother should be understood as pure, as opposed to that for Albertine. See also Bowie, *Freud, Proust and Lacan*, and Kristeva, *Time and Sense*, on the scene.

11. Henry James, *Italian Hours* (1909), in *Collected Travel Writings: The Con-tinent* (New York: Library of American, 1993), 287.

12. Thomas Mann, *Death in Venice* [*Der Tod in Venedig*] (1911), in *Death in Venice and Seven Other Stories*, trans. H. T. Lowe-Porter (New York: Vintage Books, 1963), 8. Further citations are made in the body of the text.

13. *Venetian Epigrams* (1790), no. 6, in Goethe, *Erotic Poems*, trans. David Luke (Oxford: Oxford University Press, 1997), 71.

14. See *Autobiography*, ed. Frederick W. Dupee (New York: Criterion Books, 1956), 6, 5, 518. Lyndall Gordon traces as much as is probably possible the com-plex biographical lines linking admiration, passion, and death to a number of young women who came to shape James's imagination. Lyndall Gordon, *A Private Life of Henry James* (London: Vintage, 1999). It does not in any way detract from the idea of Minny Temple as the source of Milly Theale to note that—from the mysterious paternal vice of Lionel Croy to the voyeuristic force of sexual betrayal folded into Milly's Mignonesque fate—the art-romance tradition is one source for the perverse energy of *Wings of the Dove*. Before her death, it is worth noting, Densher's mother had participated in a characteristic activity. She "copied, patient lady, famous pictures in great museums" (71).

15. On Italy and femininity in the poet's imagination, see especially Sandra M. Gilbert, "From *Patria* to *Matria*: Elizabeth Barrett Browning's Risorgimento," *PMLA* 99, no. 2 (1984): 194–211. See also Freud's treatment (discussed in chap-ter 6) of the "mother-country," and the woman patient for whom Italy and genita-lia are closely allied.

AFTERWORD

1. Henry James, *Italian Hours* (1909), in *Collected Travel Writings: The Conti-nent* (New York: Library of American, 1993), 317.

Notes to Afterword

2. Lecter, the murderous reader whose given name is that of the nemesis of Rome who so fascinated Freud, is first encountered in a hospital for the criminally insane decorated with sketches of Florence. If his initial request to Clarice Starling is for a room with a view, the climax of their relationship in the sequel is a particu-larly disturbing version of the Roman Charity theme. Thomas Harris, *Silence of the Lambs* (1988; New York: St. Martin's, 1989); *Hannibal* (1999; New York: Dell, 2000). Patricia Highsmith, *The Talented Mr. Ripley* (1955; New York: Vin-tage, 1992) . On travel writing after the period of this study, see Mark Cocker, *Loneliness and Time: The Story of British Travel Writing* (New York: Pantheon,

1992); Paul Fussell, *Abroad: British Literary Traveling between the Wars* (Oxford: Oxford University Press, 1980); and Barbara Korte, *English Travel Writing from Pilgrimages to Postcolonial Explorations*, trans. Catherine Matthias (London: Macmillan, 2000). Films worth citing for their place in the tradition include self-confident masterpieces such as Rossellini's *Viaggio in Italia*—also known as *Strangers* (1953)—as well as more unqualifiable work such as Bertolucci's *Stealing Beauty* (1996). But elements of the romance are evident in outstanding generic achievements such as Minnelli's *American in Paris* (1951), Wyler's *Roman Holiday* (1953), and Lean's *Summertime* (1955), as well as in outright commercial dross such as the Jean-Claude van Damme–Dennis Rodman vehicle *Double Team* (Hark, 1997). Literary Italy is the location of so many elaborate murders as to make Italian mysteries constitute a subgenre of their own. Roeg's 1973 *Don't Look Now* and Schrader's 1991 *The Comfort of Strangers*, films based on texts by Daphne Du Maurier (1971) and Ian McEwan (1981), respectively, participate in the tradition of erotically suggestive gothic horror the art romance draws on throughout its history.

   3. E. M. Forster, "Albergo Empedocle," in *The Life to Come and Other Short Stories* (New York: Norton, 1972), 10.

   4. An extremely useful anthology of writings on the city is Fabrizia Raimondino and Andreas Friedreich Muller's *Dadapolis: Caleidoscopio Napoletano* (Turin: Einaudi, 1992).

   5. Goethe, *Italian Journey*, trans. W. H. Auden and Elizabeth Mayer (New York: Penguin, 1970), 165.

   6. Germaine de Staël, *Corinne*, trans. Sylvia Raphael (Oxford: Oxford University Press, 1998), 198.

   7. "Delusions and Dreams in Jensen's *Gradiva*," in *The Standard Edition of the Complete Psychological Works of Sigmund Freud*, trans. and ed. James Strachey in collaboration with Anna Freud (London: Hogarth Press, 1953–66), 9:15. Further page references are made in the text.

   8. "The Saint's Afternoon" (without "others") was first published in *The May Book* in 1901. The title changed with the addition of parts 6 and 7 for *Italian Hours*. Bonney MacDonald, *Henry James's Italian Hours Revelatory and Resistant Impressions* (Ann Arbor: UMI Research Press, 1990) is a useful source on the collection, though it surprisingly does not address "A Saint's Afternoon" at all. The most interesting extended treatment of the collection as a whole is to be found in Tony Tanner, *Henry James and the Art of Nonfiction* (Athens: University of Georgia Press, 1995).

   9. Axel Munthe, the Swedish doctor who came to fame in the first half of the twentieth century for a 1929 memoir largely devoted to his life in Italy and in particular to the villa he built in Capri, ascribes the inspiration to write his own book to James. The festival James describes is the topic of one chapter of Munthe's work. See *The Story of San Michele* (New York: Dutton, 1929), ix–x, 466–73. On Munthe, see Gustaf Munthe and Gudrun Uexküll, *The Story of Axel Munthe*, trans. Malcolm Munthe and Lord Sudley (New York: Dutton, 1953). See also Leon Edel, *Henry James, a Life* (New York: Harper and Row, 1985), 493–94. San Michele is only one of the countless and varied instances of northerners materializing their fantasies of an authentic Italian past. Other homes comparable with Munthe's in-

clude two in Ravello, the Villa Cimbrone, almost in its entirety a twentieth-century invention of Ernest William Beckett, and the Villa Rufolo, a ruined ancient estate acquired by the Scotsman, Sir Francis Nevil Reid, in 1851 and remade into the vision that eventually inspired Wagner in his writing of *Parsifal*. Certainly the urge of foreigners to invent a past in Italy by means of the restoration of old buildings is more common today than ever, but it is part of a tradition that includes Munthe, Beckett, and Reid and in which more than material reconstruction is always at stake. In this context we may cite, at the turn of the twentieth century, the photographer Wilhelm von Gloeden's homoerotic recreation of poor Sicilian youths into visions of a lost Arcadian sensuality, as well as Iris Origo's attempt, a few decades later, not simply to recreate a Renaissance garden but to introduce into a Tuscan valley a benign form of feudal farming. See the recent catalog by Charles-Henry Favrod, Monica Maffioli, et al., *Von Gloeden, Fotografie: Capolavorie dalle Collezione Alinari* (Florence: Alinari, 2000). On Iris Origo, see her autobiography, *Images and Shadows* (1970; London: Butler & Tanner, 1972), esp. 199–255.

   10. On "fusion" as a term, see Tanner, *Art of Nonfiction* 13

Index

Note: Page numbers in italic indicate illustrations.